Natsume's
BOOK of FRIENDS

Shojo Beat

Natsume's BOOK of FRIENDS

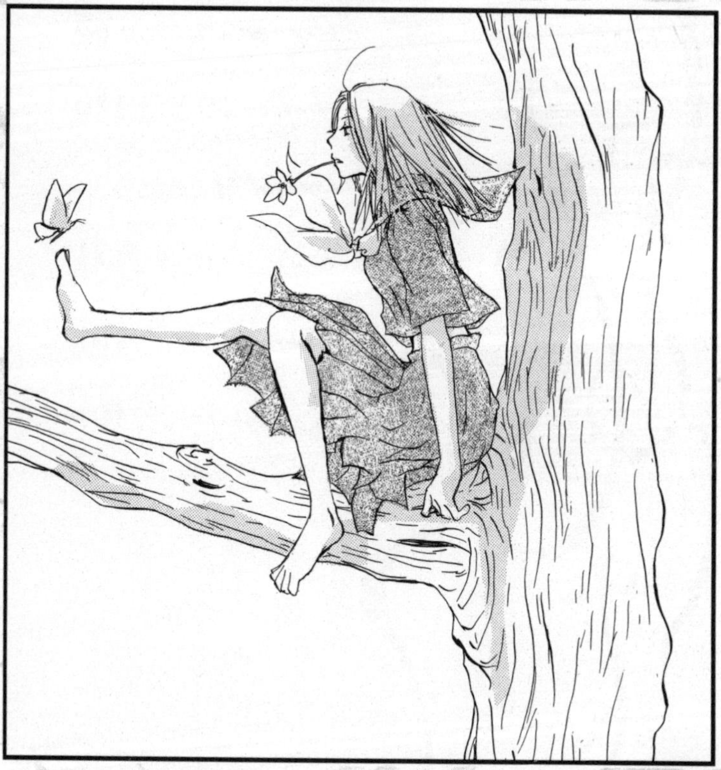

STORY and ART by
Yuki Midorikawa

VOLUME 5

Natsume's
BOOK of FRIENDS
VOLUME 5 CONTENTS

Natsume's BOOK of FRIENDS
CHARACTER GUIDE

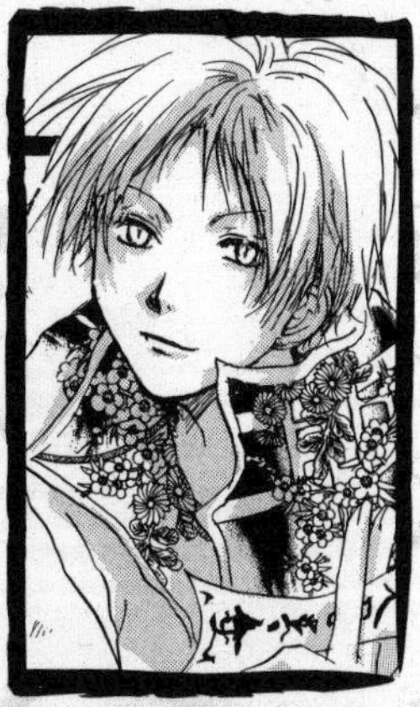

Takashi Natsume

A lonely orphan with the ability to see the supernatural. He inherited the *Book of Friends* from his grandmother and currently lives with the Fujiwaras, to whom he is distantly related. His powers enable him to fend off yokai with his bare hands, just like his grandmother.

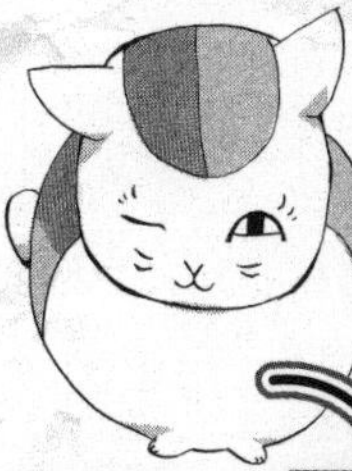

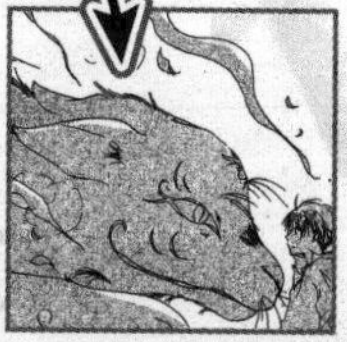

(TRUE FORM)

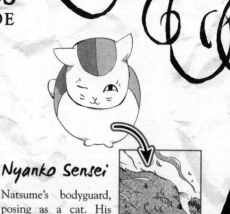

Nyanko Sensei

Natsume's bodyguard, posing as a cat. His yokai name is Madara. He saves Natsume when danger strikes, but he has a noninterference policy and is thus usually out drinking.

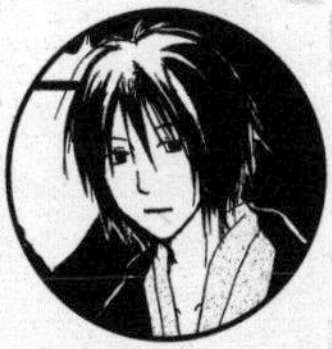

Kaname Tanuma

The son of the priest of Yatsuhara and Natsume's friend. More sensitive to yokai presence than normal people.

THE STORY

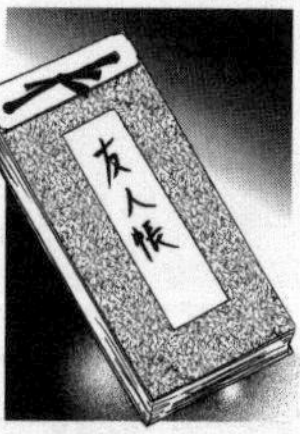

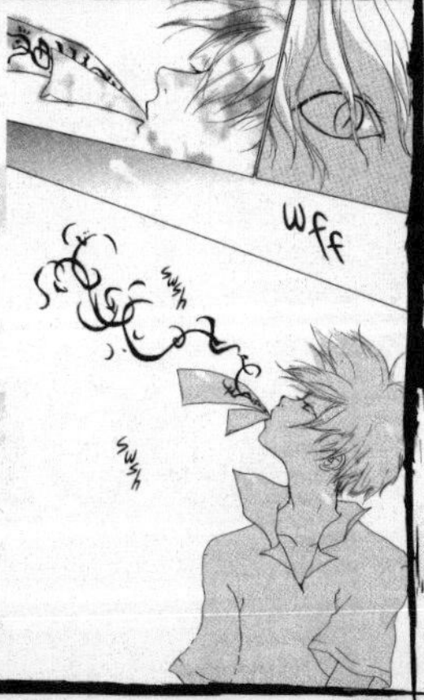
Wff

Takashi Natsume has a secret sixth sense—he can see supernatural creatures called yokai. And ever since he inherited the *Book of Friends* from his grandmother, the local yokai have been coming after him. Takashi frees Nyanko Sensei from imprisonment and promises he will get the *Book* when Takashi dies. With his new bodyguard, Takashi leads a busy life returning names to yokai.

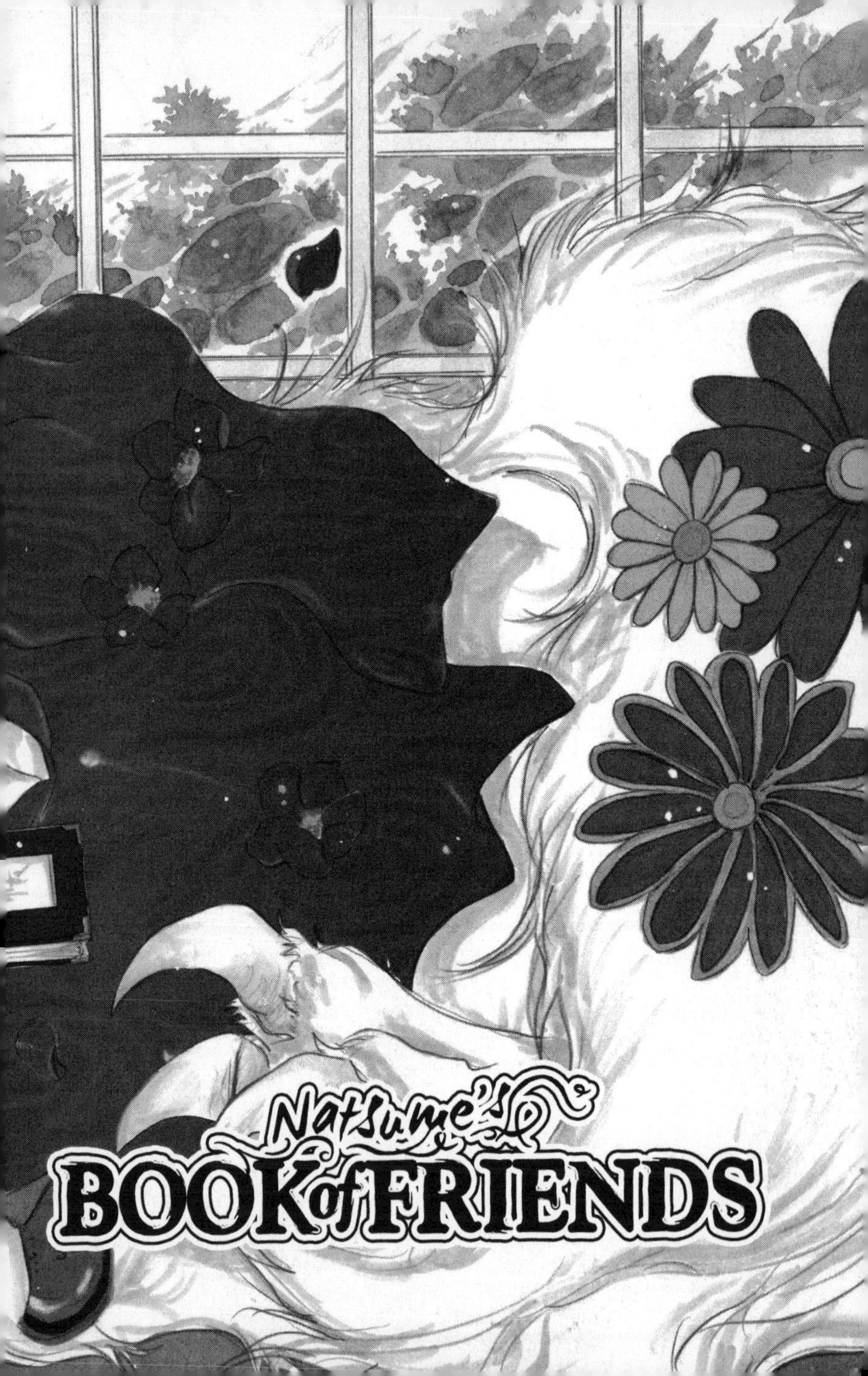
Natsume's
BOOK of FRIENDS

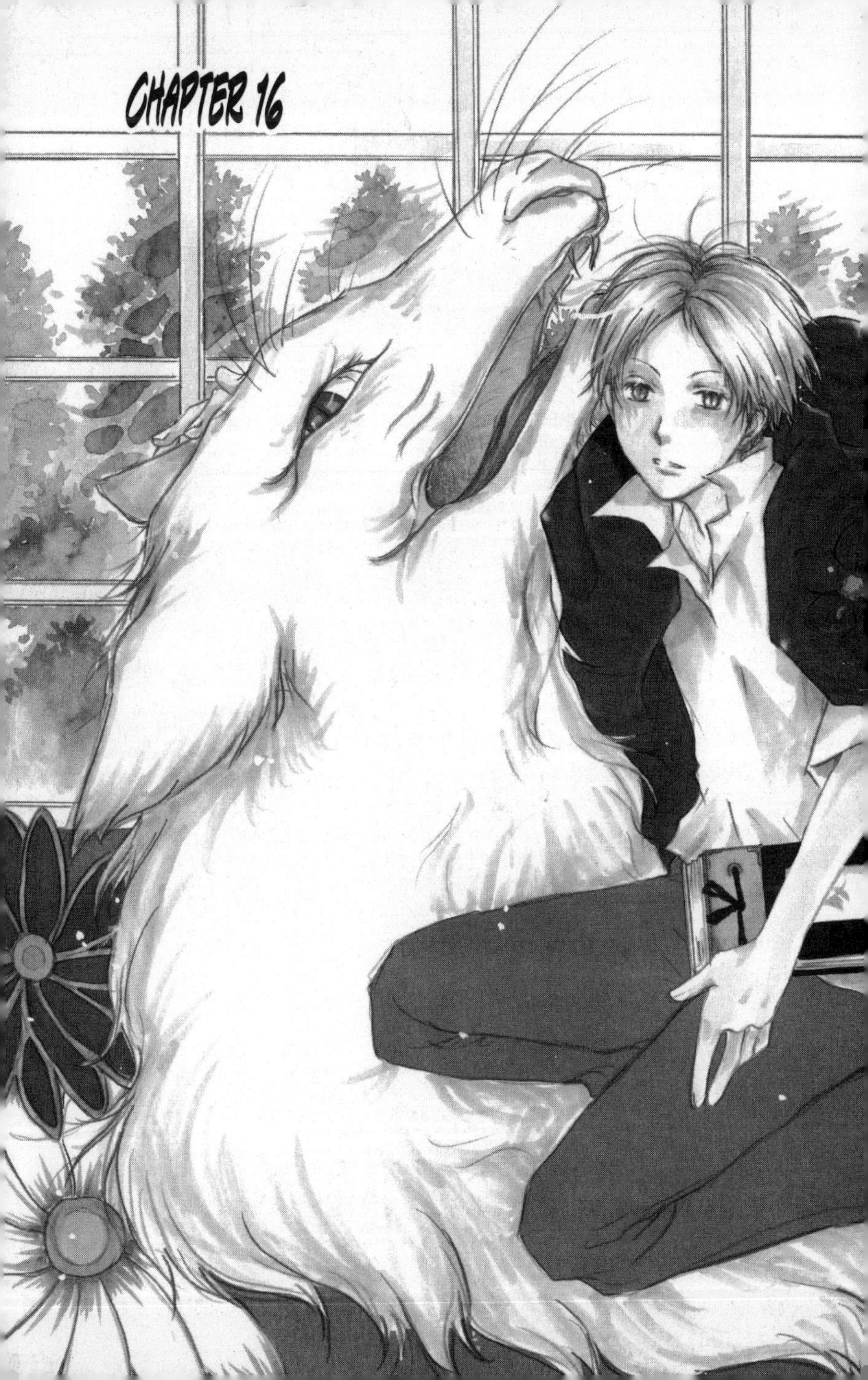
CHAPTER 16

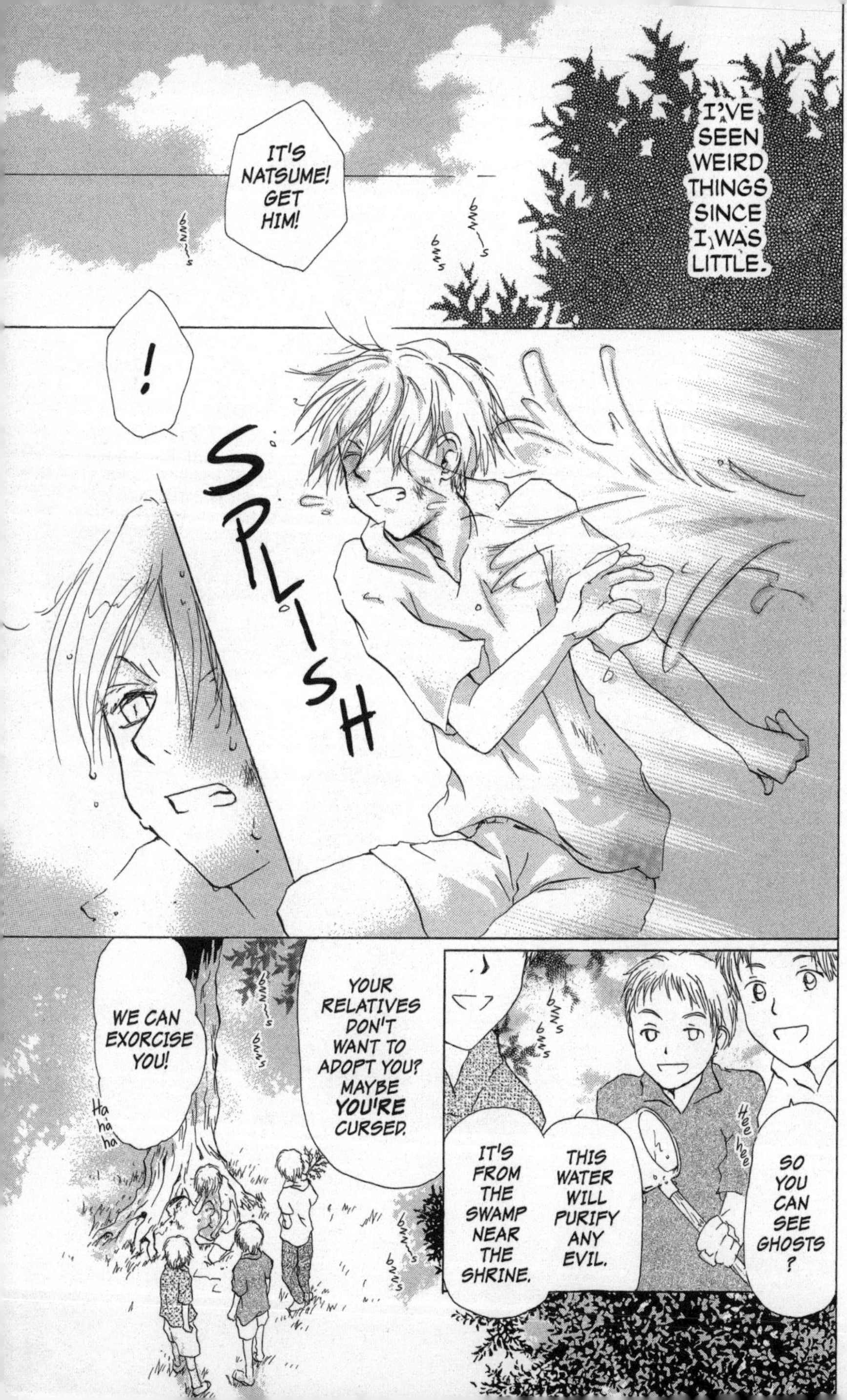
I'VE SEEN WEIRD THINGS SINCE I WAS LITTLE.
bzzz
IT'S NATSUME! GET HIM!
bzzz
!
SPLISH
SO YOU CAN SEE GHOSTS?
Hee hee
THIS WATER WILL PURIFY ANY EVIL.
IT'S FROM THE SWAMP NEAR THE SHRINE.
bzzz
YOUR RELATIVES DON'T WANT TO ADOPT YOU? MAYBE YOU'RE CURSED.
WE CAN EXORCISE YOU!
Ha ha ha
bzzz

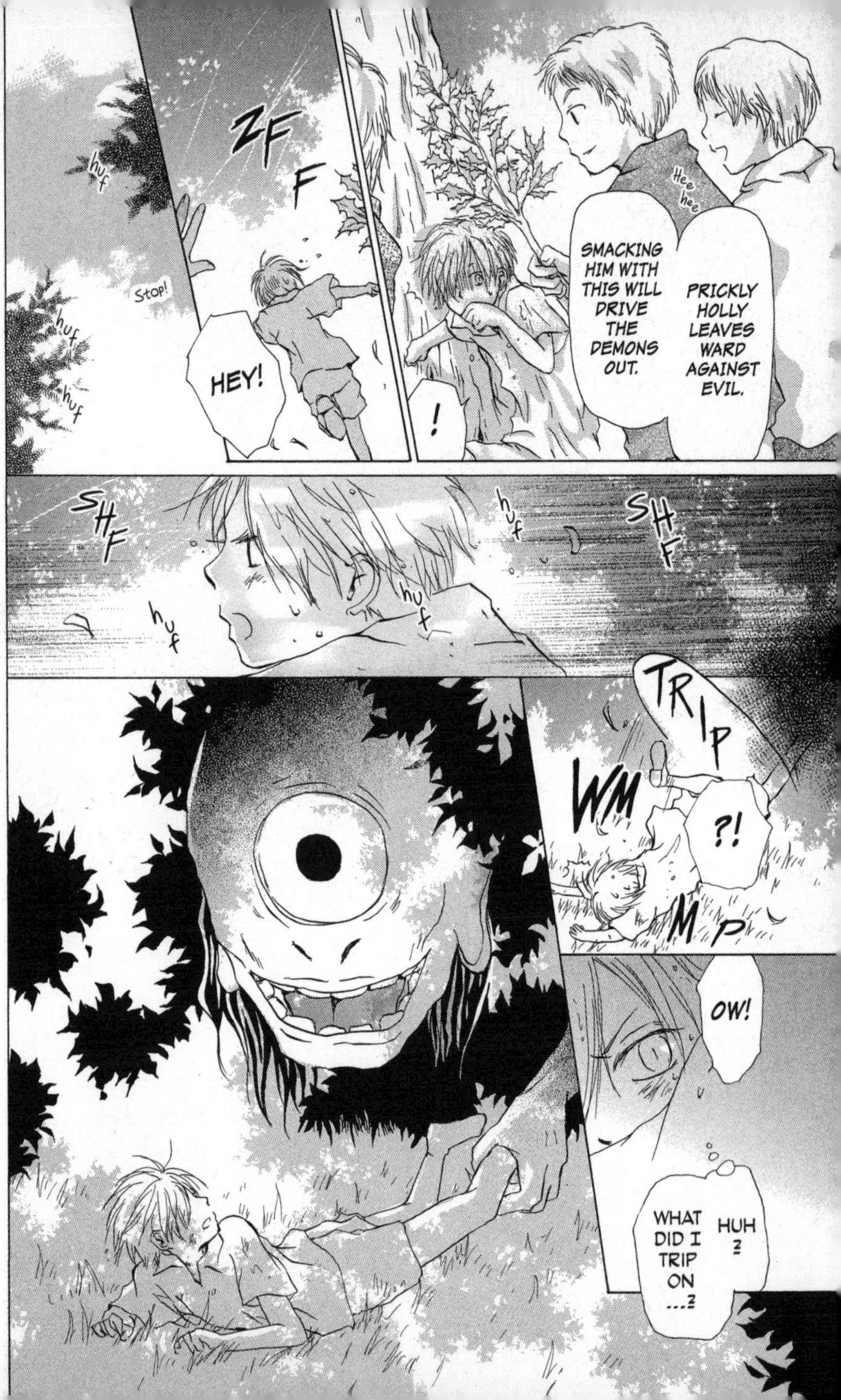
Hee hee
PRICKLY HOLLY LEAVES WARD AGAINST EVIL.
SMACKING HIM WITH THIS WILL DRIVE THE DEMONS OUT.
!
ZF F
HEY!
Stop!
huf
huf
huf
SHF
huf
huf
huf
SHF
TRIP
WM
?!
MP
OW!
HUH?
WHAT DID I TRIP ON...?

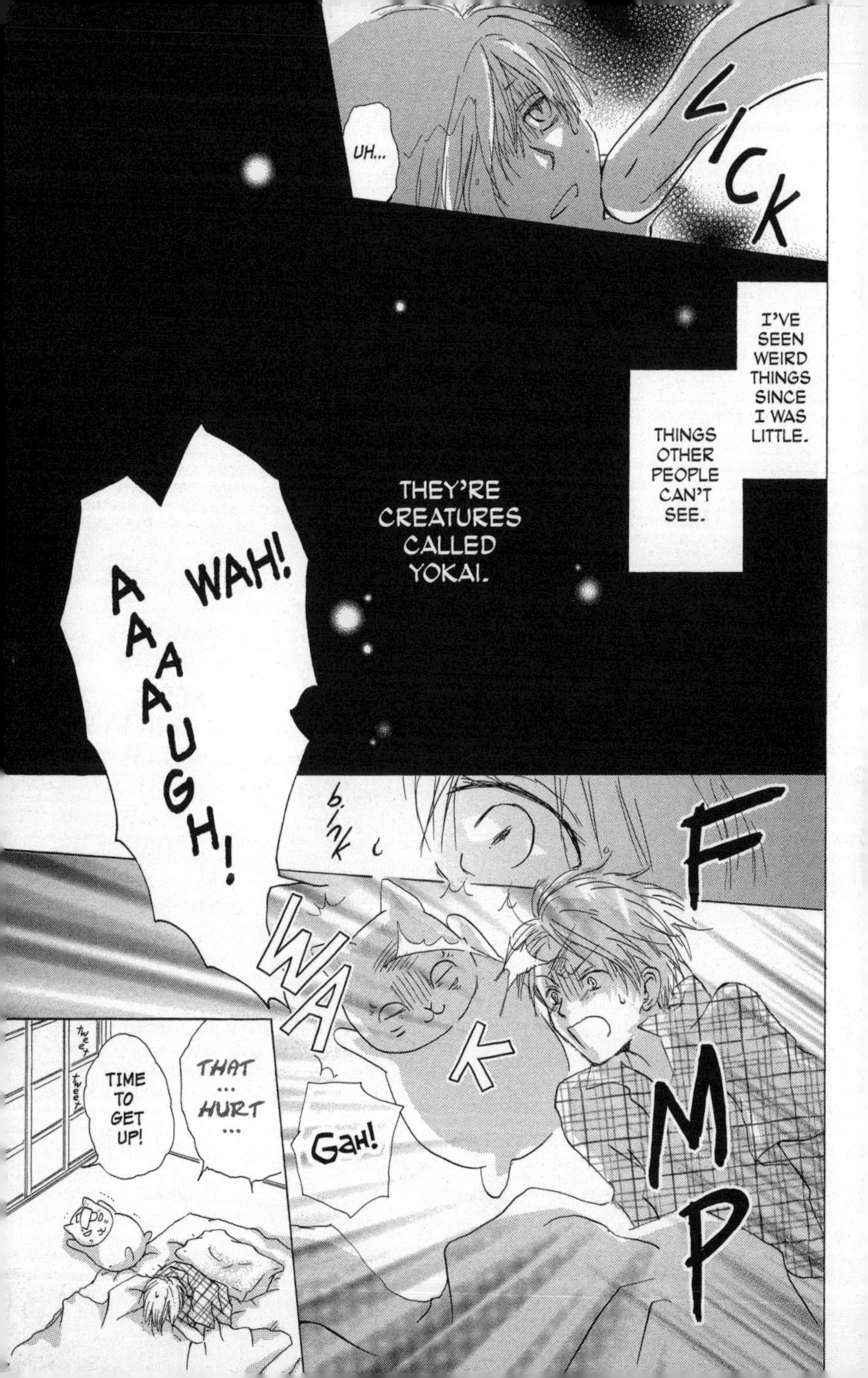
UH...
LICK
I'VE SEEN WEIRD THINGS SINCE I WAS LITTLE.
THINGS OTHER PEOPLE CAN'T SEE.
THEY'RE CREATURES CALLED YOKAI.
WAH! AAAAUGH!
FMP
blink
WAK
Gah!
tweet tweet
THAT ... HURT ...
TIME TO GET UP!

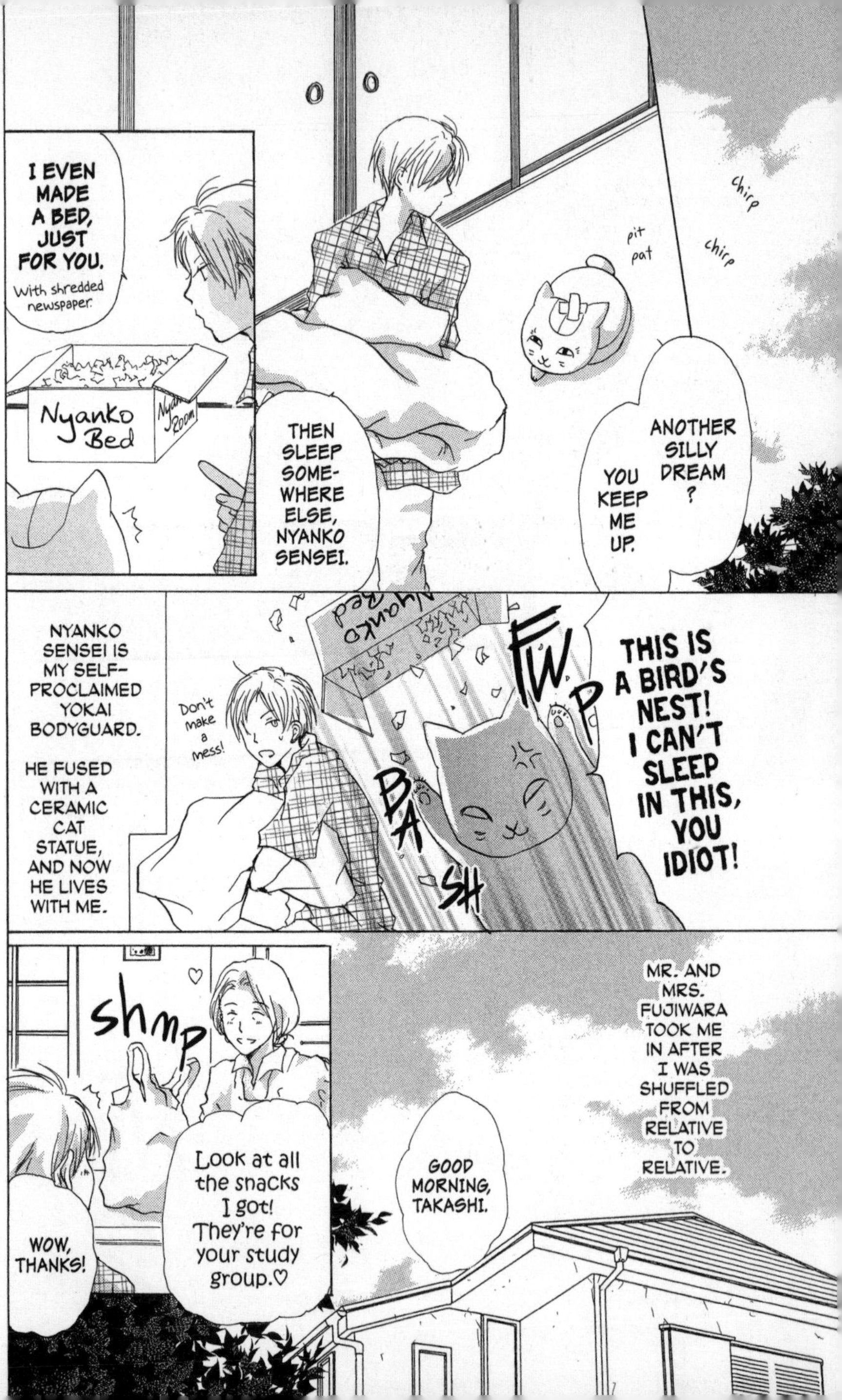
chirp
chirp
pit pat
ANOTHER SILLY DREAM? YOU KEEP ME UP.
THEN SLEEP SOMEWHERE ELSE, NYANKO SENSEI.
I EVEN MADE A BED, JUST FOR YOU.
With shredded newspaper.
Nyanko Bed
Nyanko Room
THIS IS A BIRD'S NEST! I CAN'T SLEEP IN THIS, YOU IDIOT!
FWP
BASH
Don't make a mess!
NYANKO SENSEI IS MY SELF-PROCLAIMED YOKAI BODYGUARD.
HE FUSED WITH A CERAMIC CAT STATUE, AND NOW HE LIVES WITH ME.
MR. AND MRS. FUJIWARA TOOK ME IN AFTER I WAS SHUFFLED FROM RELATIVE TO RELATIVE.
GOOD MORNING, TAKASHI.
shmp
Look at all the snacks I got! They're for your study group.♡
WOW, THANKS!

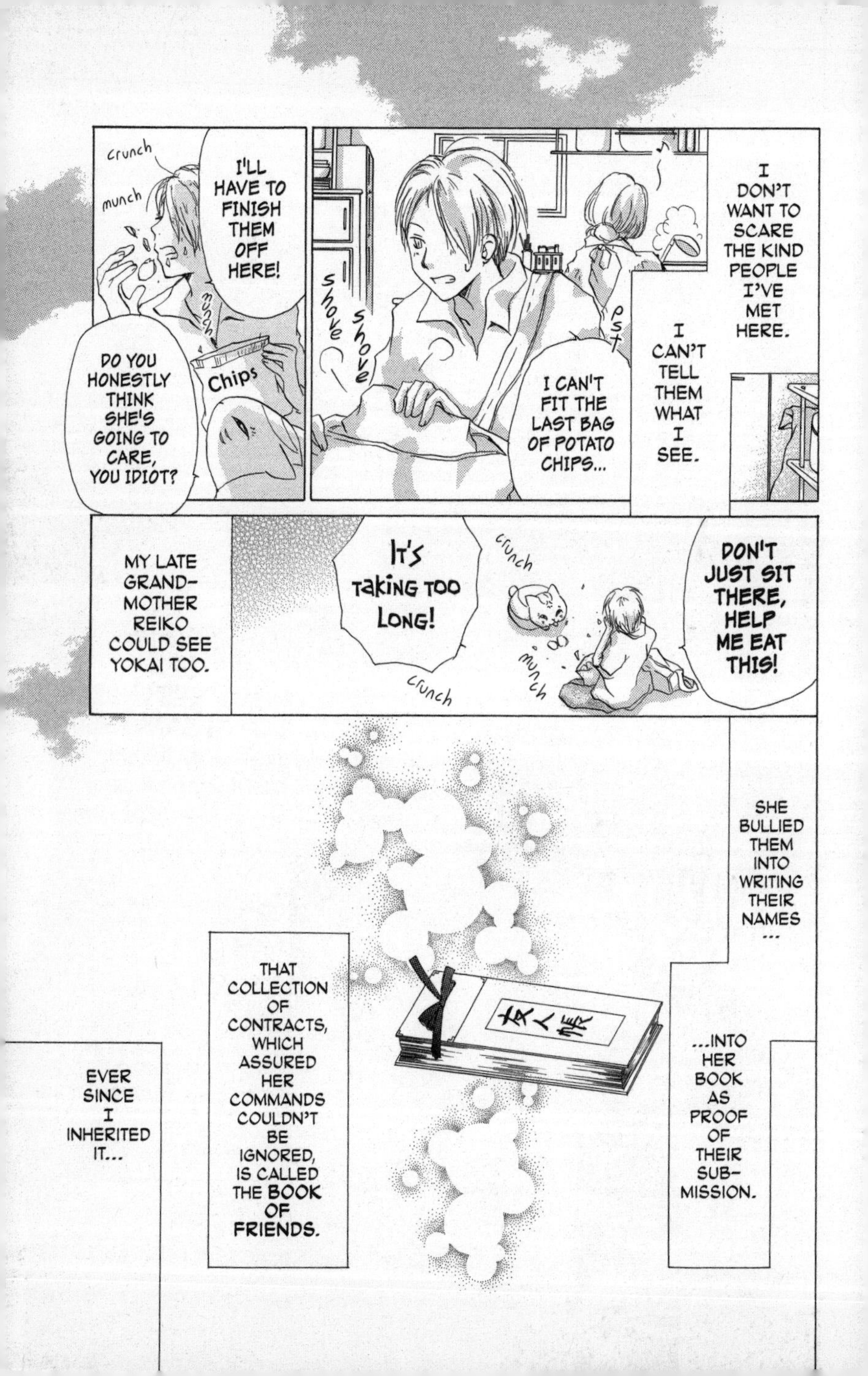
I DON'T WANT TO SCARE THE KIND PEOPLE I'VE MET HERE.
I CAN'T TELL THEM WHAT I SEE.
pst
I CAN'T FIT THE LAST BAG OF POTATO CHIPS...
shove shove
I'LL HAVE TO FINISH THEM OFF HERE!
crunch
munch
munch
Chips
DO YOU HONESTLY THINK SHE'S GOING TO CARE, YOU IDIOT?
DON'T JUST SIT THERE, HELP ME EAT THIS!
crunch
munch
IT'S TAKING TOO LONG!
crunch
MY LATE GRANDMOTHER REIKO COULD SEE YOKAI TOO.
SHE BULLIED THEM INTO WRITING THEIR NAMES...
...INTO HER BOOK AS PROOF OF THEIR SUBMISSION.
友人帳
THAT COLLECTION OF CONTRACTS, WHICH ASSURED HER COMMANDS COULDN'T BE IGNORED, IS CALLED THE BOOK OF FRIENDS.
EVER SINCE I INHERITED IT...

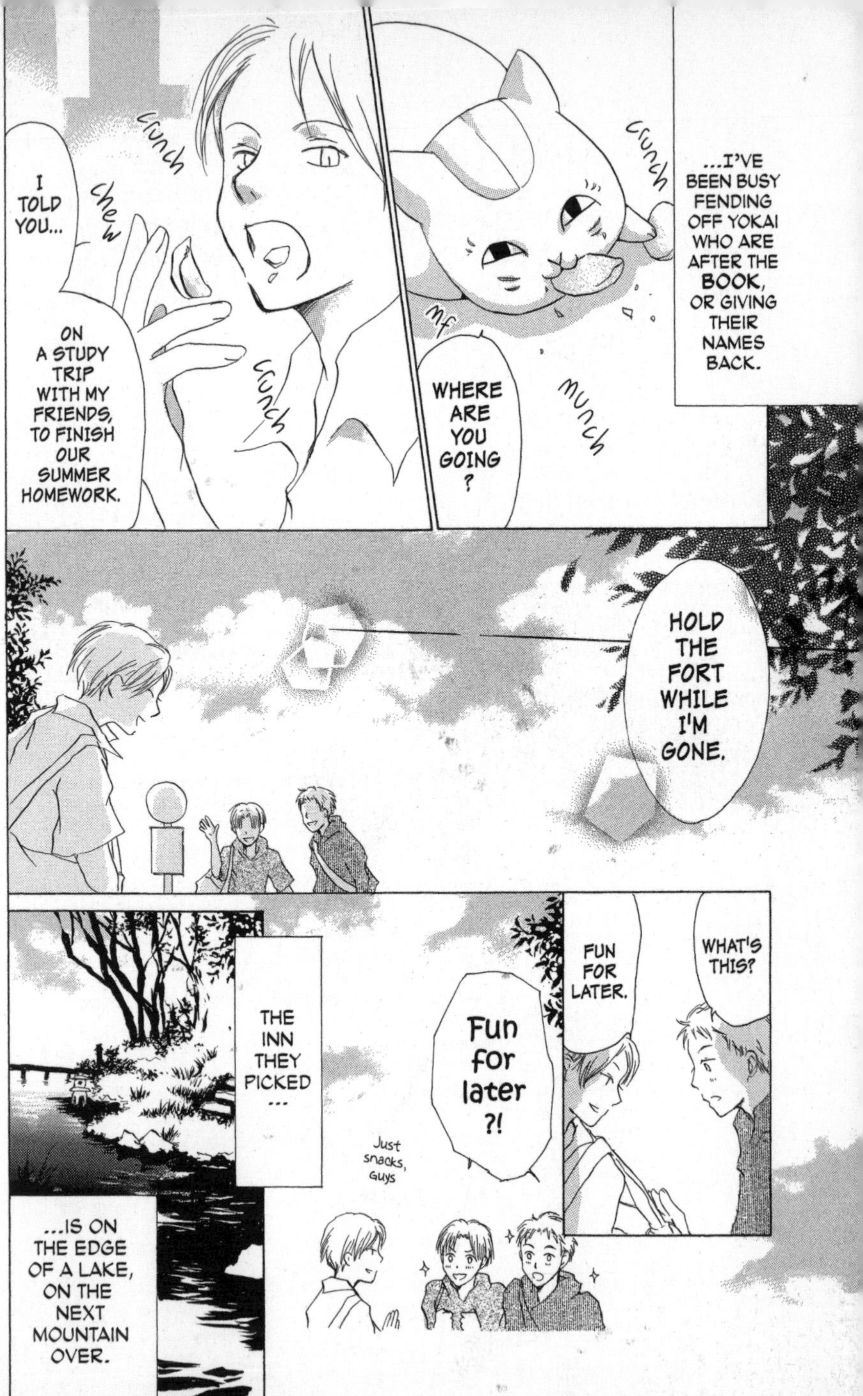
...I'VE BEEN BUSY FENDING OFF YOKAI WHO ARE AFTER THE BOOK, OR GIVING THEIR NAMES BACK.
crunch
mf
munch
WHERE ARE YOU GOING?
crunch
chew
I TOLD YOU...
ON A STUDY TRIP WITH MY FRIENDS, TO FINISH OUR SUMMER HOMEWORK.
crunch
HOLD THE FORT WHILE I'M GONE.
WHAT'S THIS?
FUN FOR LATER.
Fun for later?!
Just snacks, Guys
THE INN THEY PICKED...
...IS ON THE EDGE OF A LAKE, ON THE NEXT MOUNTAIN OVER.

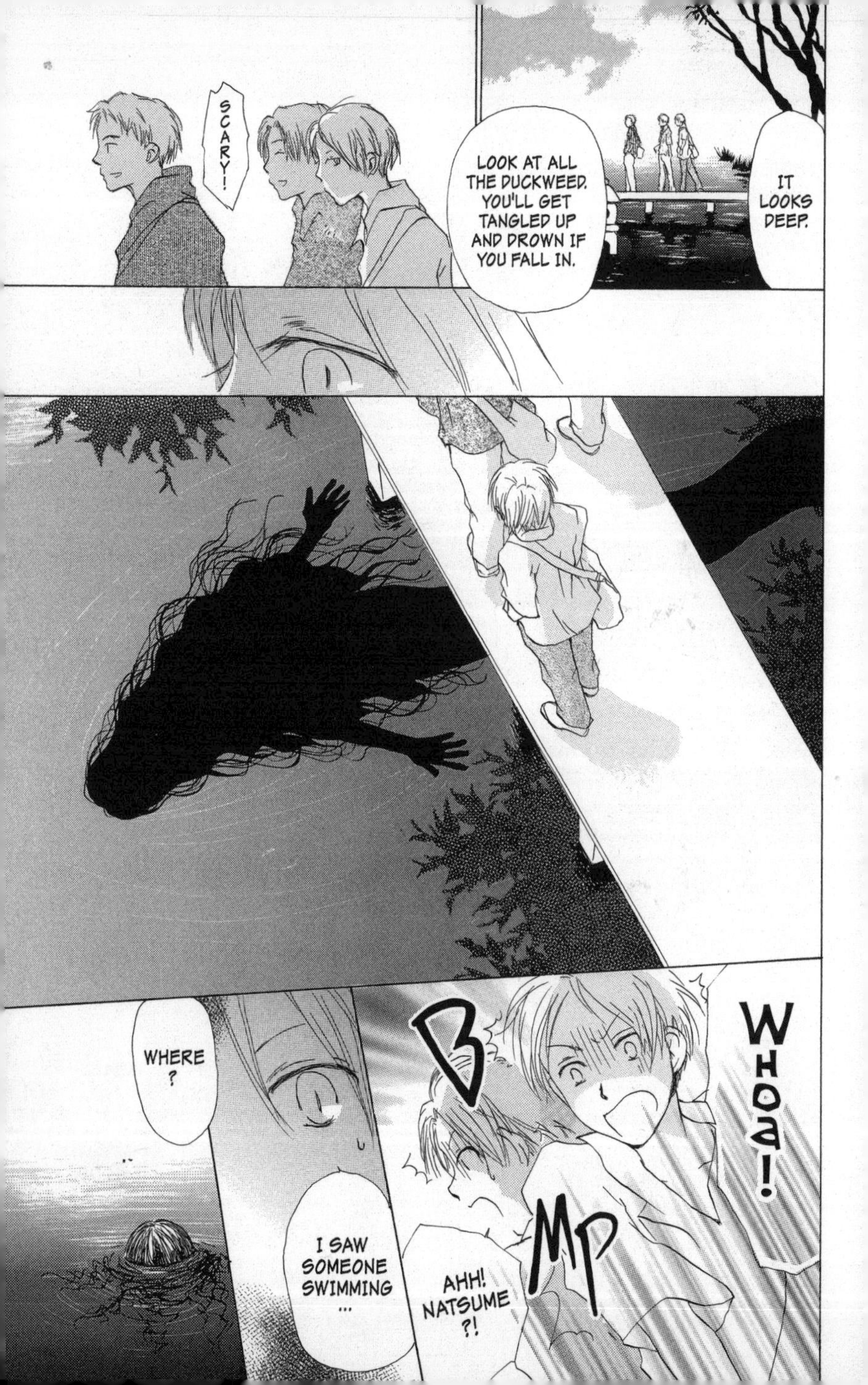
IT LOOKS DEEP.
LOOK AT ALL THE DUCKWEED. YOU'LL GET TANGLED UP AND DROWN IF YOU FALL IN.
SCARY!
WHOA!
B
MP
AHH! NATSUME?!
WHERE?
I SAW SOMEONE SWIMMING...

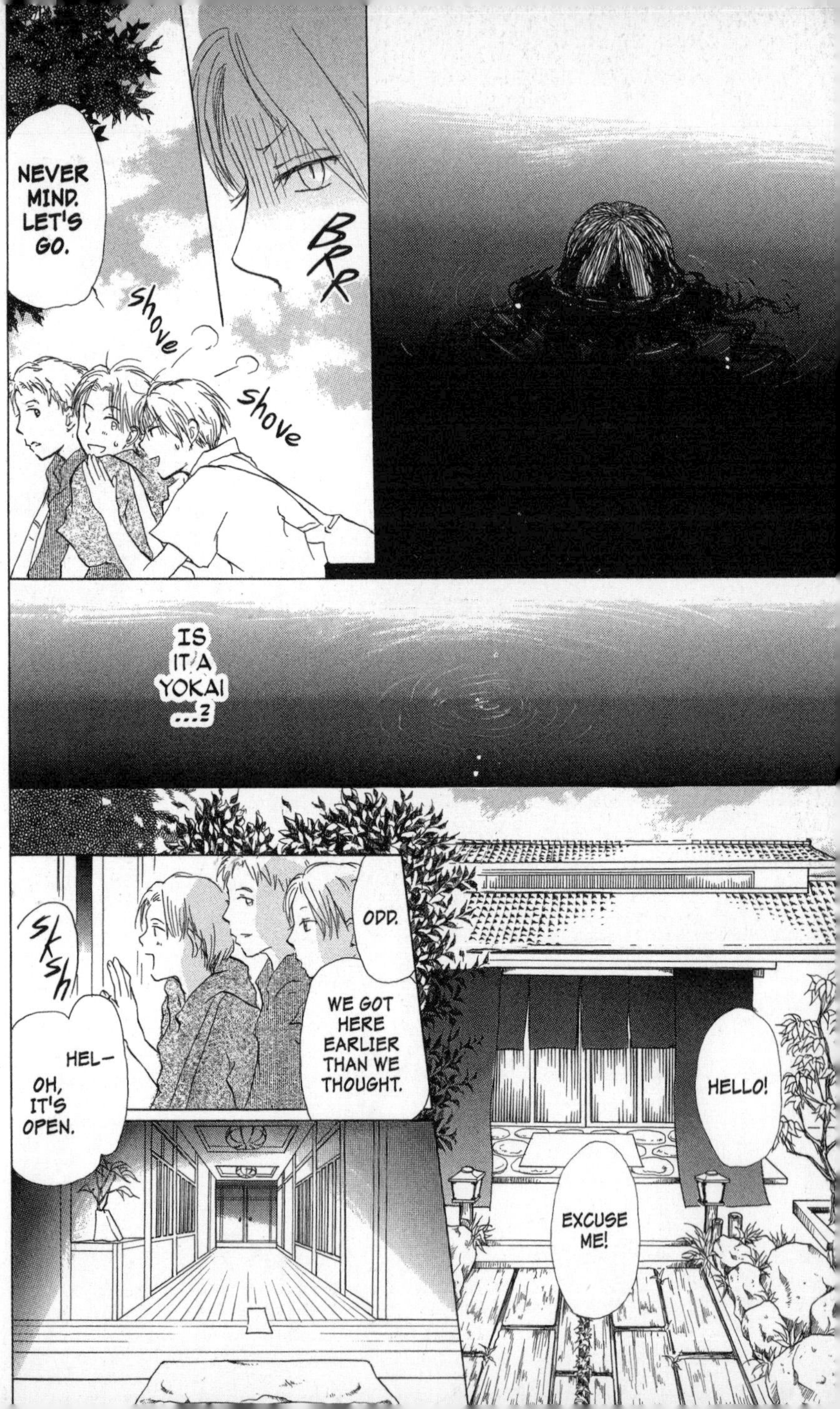
BRR
NEVER MIND. LET'S GO.
shove
shove
IS IT A YOKAI ...?
HELLO!
EXCUSE ME!
ODD.
WE GOT HERE EARLIER THAN WE THOUGHT.
SKSH
HEL— OH, IT'S OPEN.

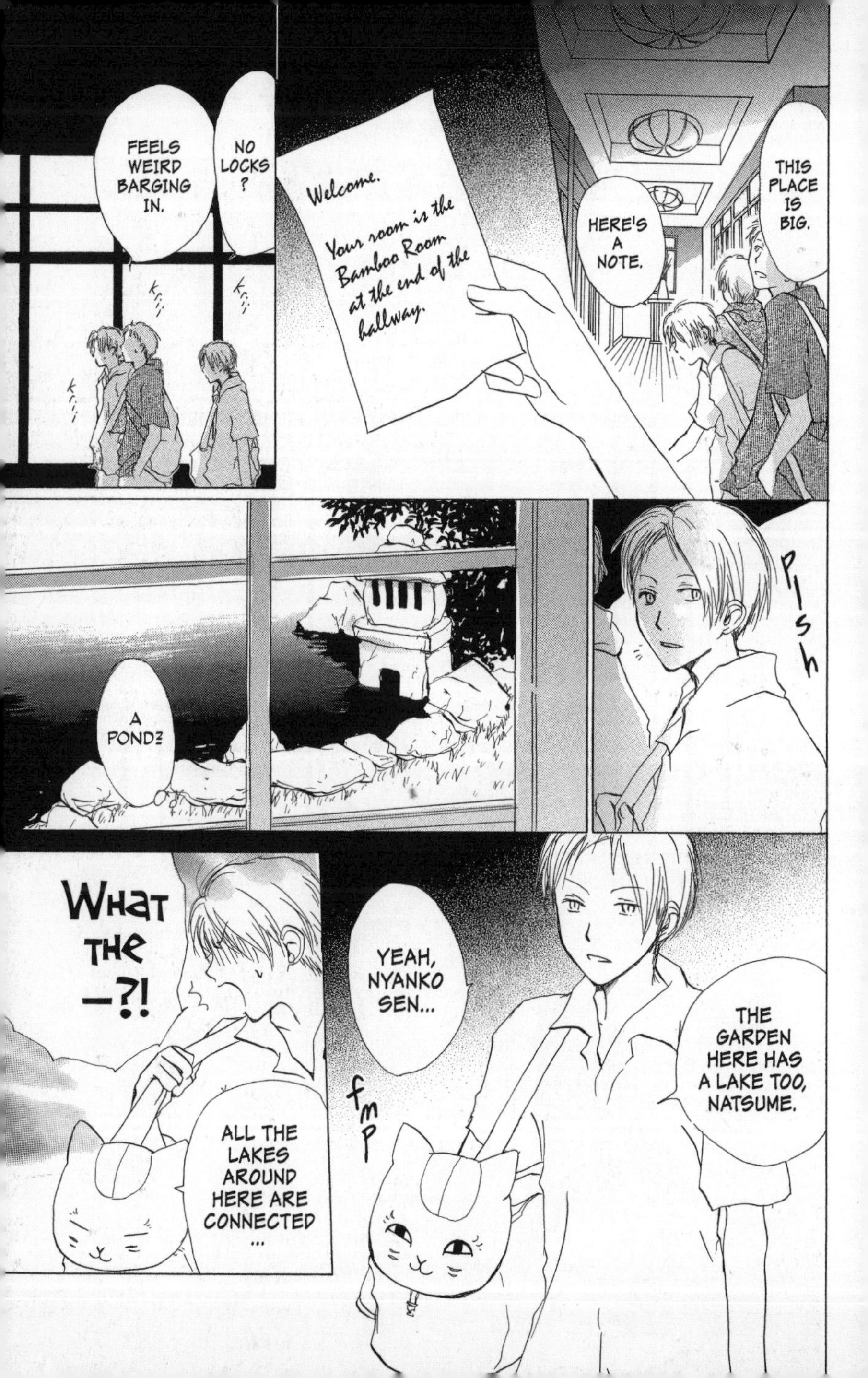
THIS PLACE IS BIG.
HERE'S A NOTE.
Welcome.
Your room is the Bamboo Room at the end of the hallway.
NO LOCKS?
FEELS WEIRD BARGING IN.
Pish
A POND?
THE GARDEN HERE HAS A LAKE TOO, NATSUME.
YEAH, NYANKO SEN...
fmp
WHAT THE—?!
ALL THE LAKES AROUND HERE ARE CONNECTED...

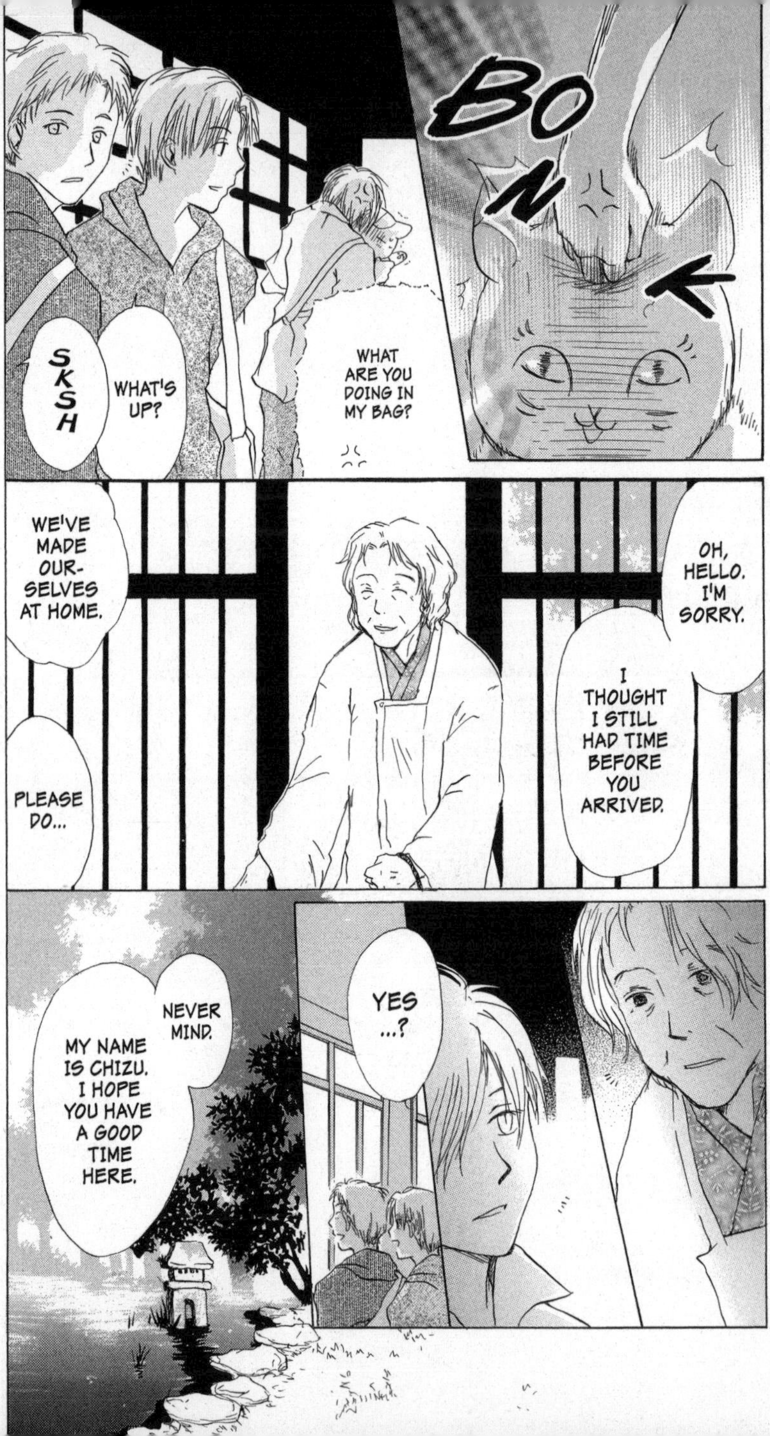
BONK
WHAT ARE YOU DOING IN MY BAG?
WHAT'S UP?
SKSH
OH, HELLO. I'M SORRY.
I THOUGHT I STILL HAD TIME BEFORE YOU ARRIVED.
WE'VE MADE OURSELVES AT HOME.
PLEASE DO...
YES ...?
NEVER MIND.
MY NAME IS CHIZU. I HOPE YOU HAVE A GOOD TIME HERE.

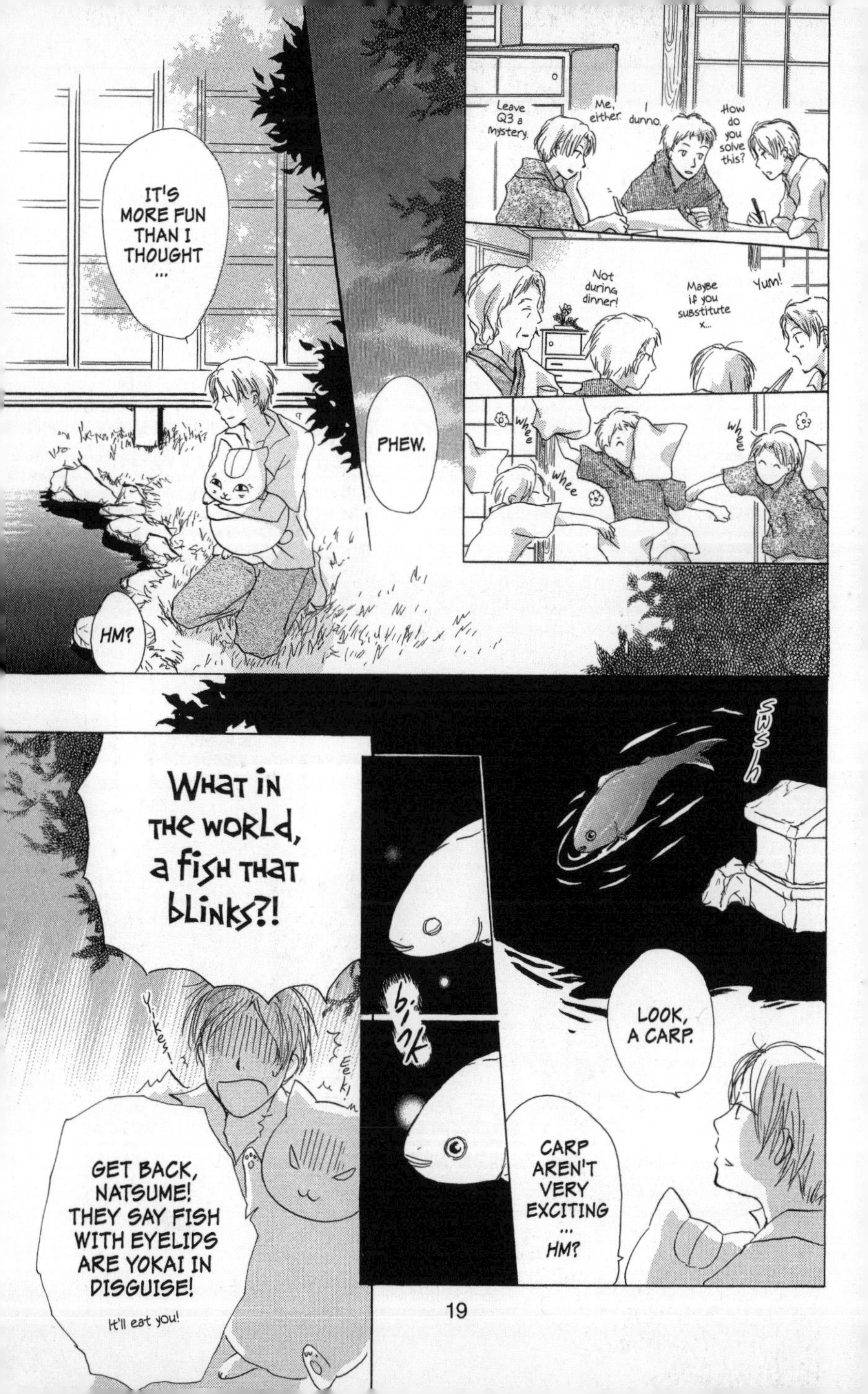
How do you solve this?
I dunno.
Me, either.
Leave Q3 a mystery.
Yum!
Maybe if you substitute x...
Not during dinner!
whee
whee
whee
IT'S MORE FUN THAN I THOUGHT ...
PHEW.
HM?
SWSH
LOOK, A CARP.
CARP AREN'T VERY EXCITING ... HM?
blink
What in the world, a fish that blinks?!
Eek!
Yikes!
GET BACK, NATSUME! THEY SAY FISH WITH EYELIDS ARE YOKAI IN DISGUISE!
It'll eat you!

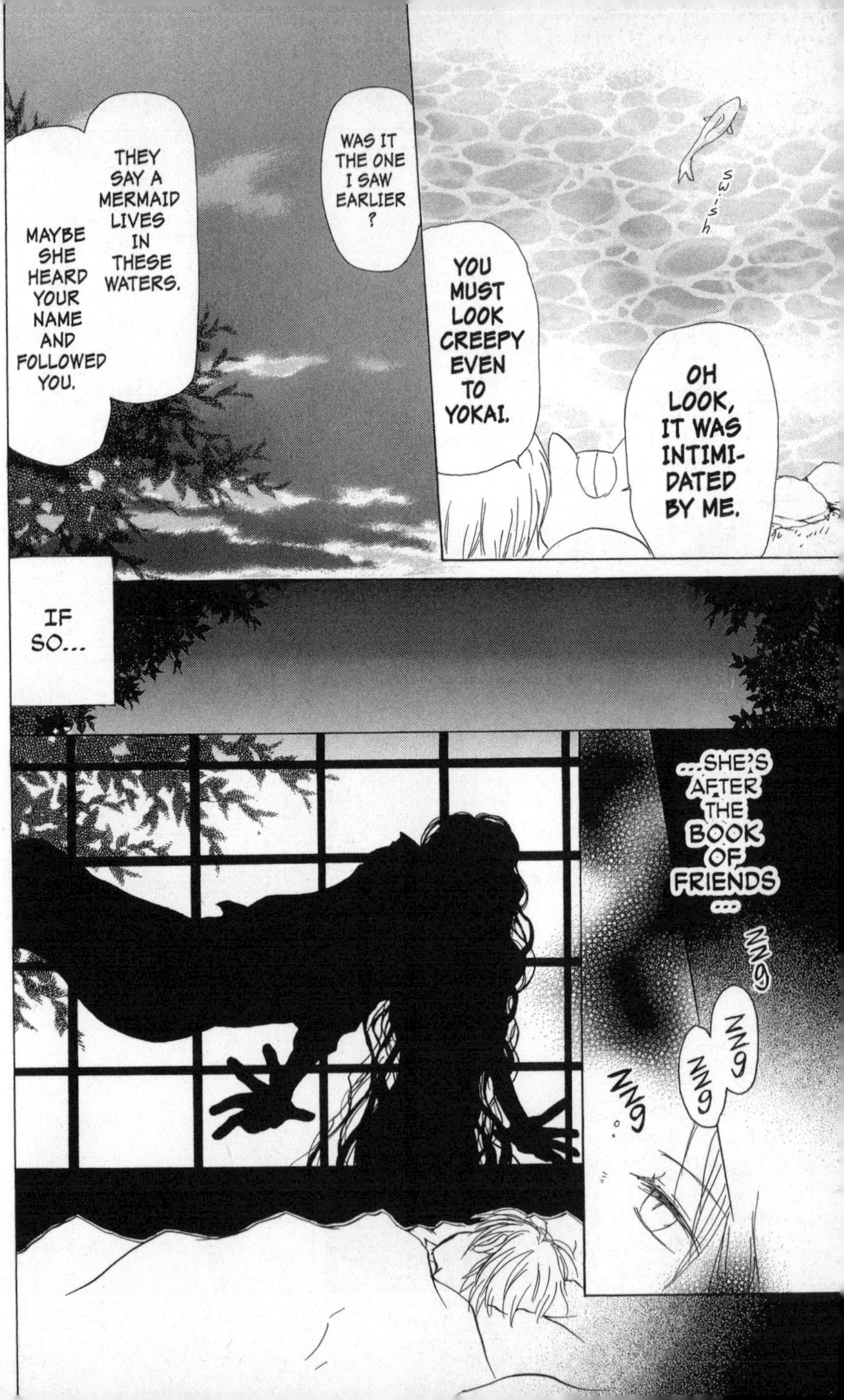
swish
OH LOOK, IT WAS INTIMIDATED BY ME.
YOU MUST LOOK CREEPY EVEN TO YOKAI.
WAS IT THE ONE I SAW EARLIER?
THEY SAY A MERMAID LIVES IN THESE WATERS.
MAYBE SHE HEARD YOUR NAME AND FOLLOWED YOU.
IF SO...
...SHE'S AFTER THE BOOK OF FRIENDS...
GNN
GNN GNN
GNN...

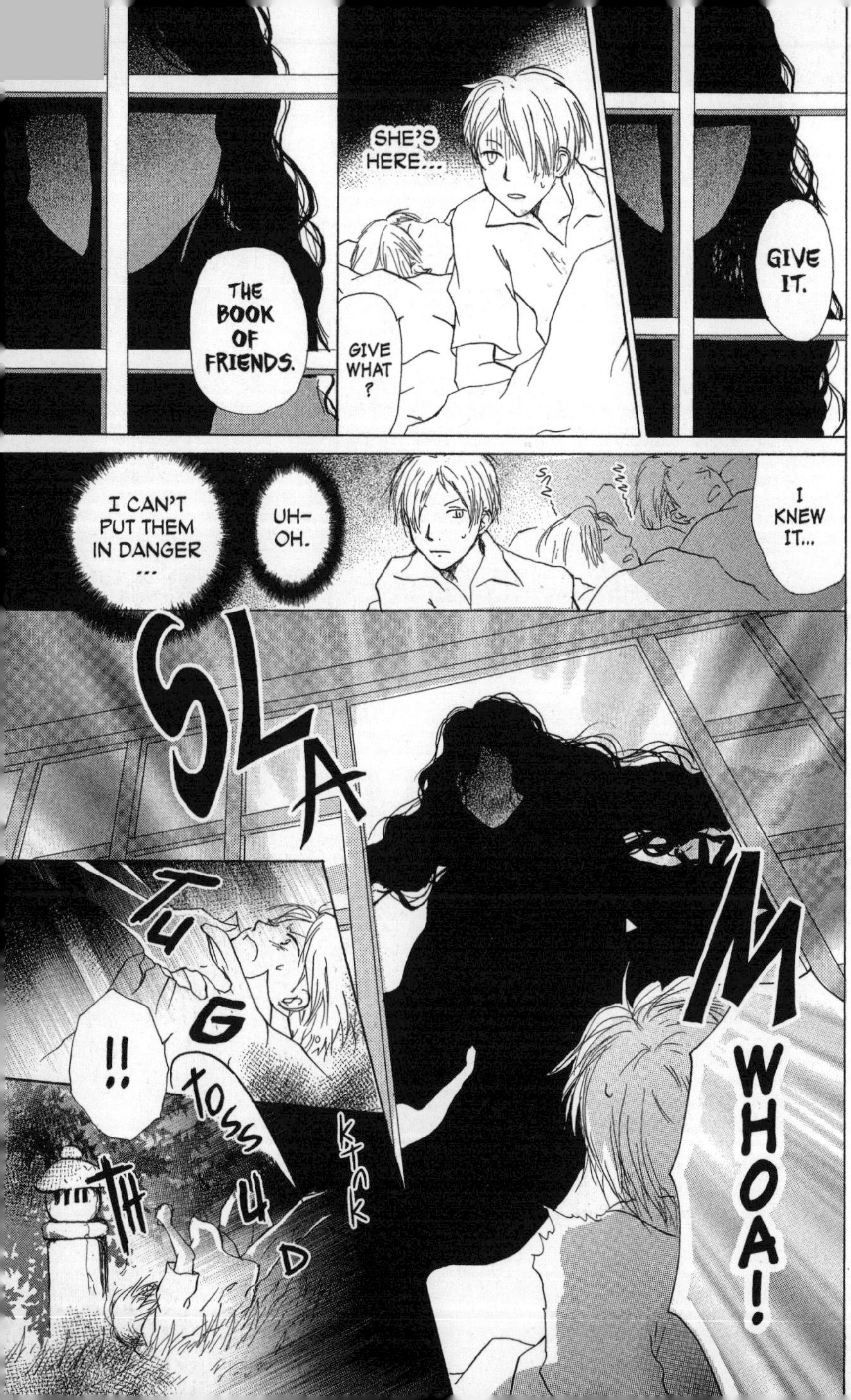
GIVE IT.
SHE'S HERE...
GIVE WHAT?
THE BOOK OF FRIENDS.
I KNEW IT...
UH-OH.
I CAN'T PUT THEM IN DANGER...
SLAM
WHOA!
TUG
!!
TOSS
KTNK
THUD

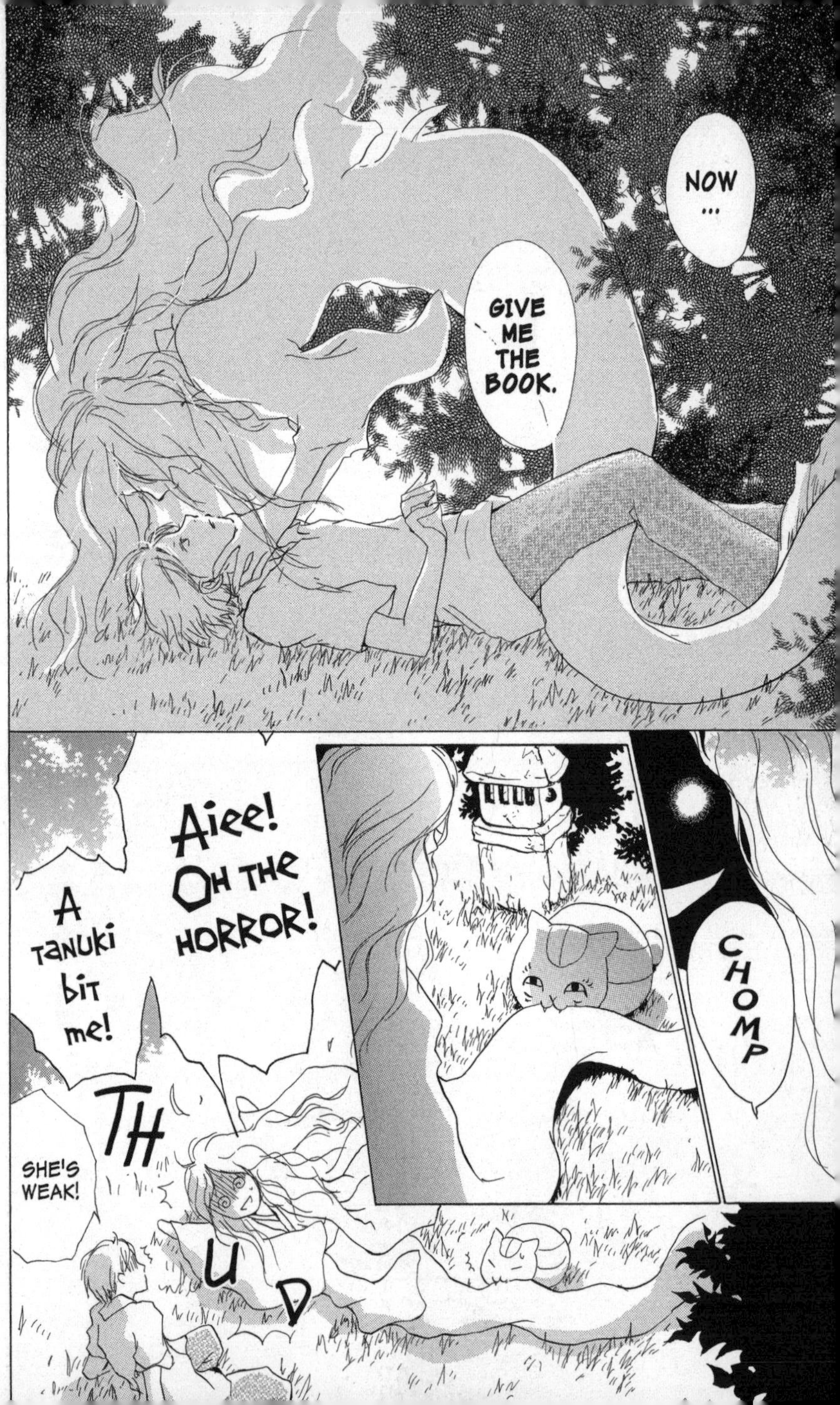
NOW ...
GIVE ME THE BOOK.
CHOMP
Aiee! Oh the horror!
A tanuki bit me!
THUD
SHE'S WEAK!

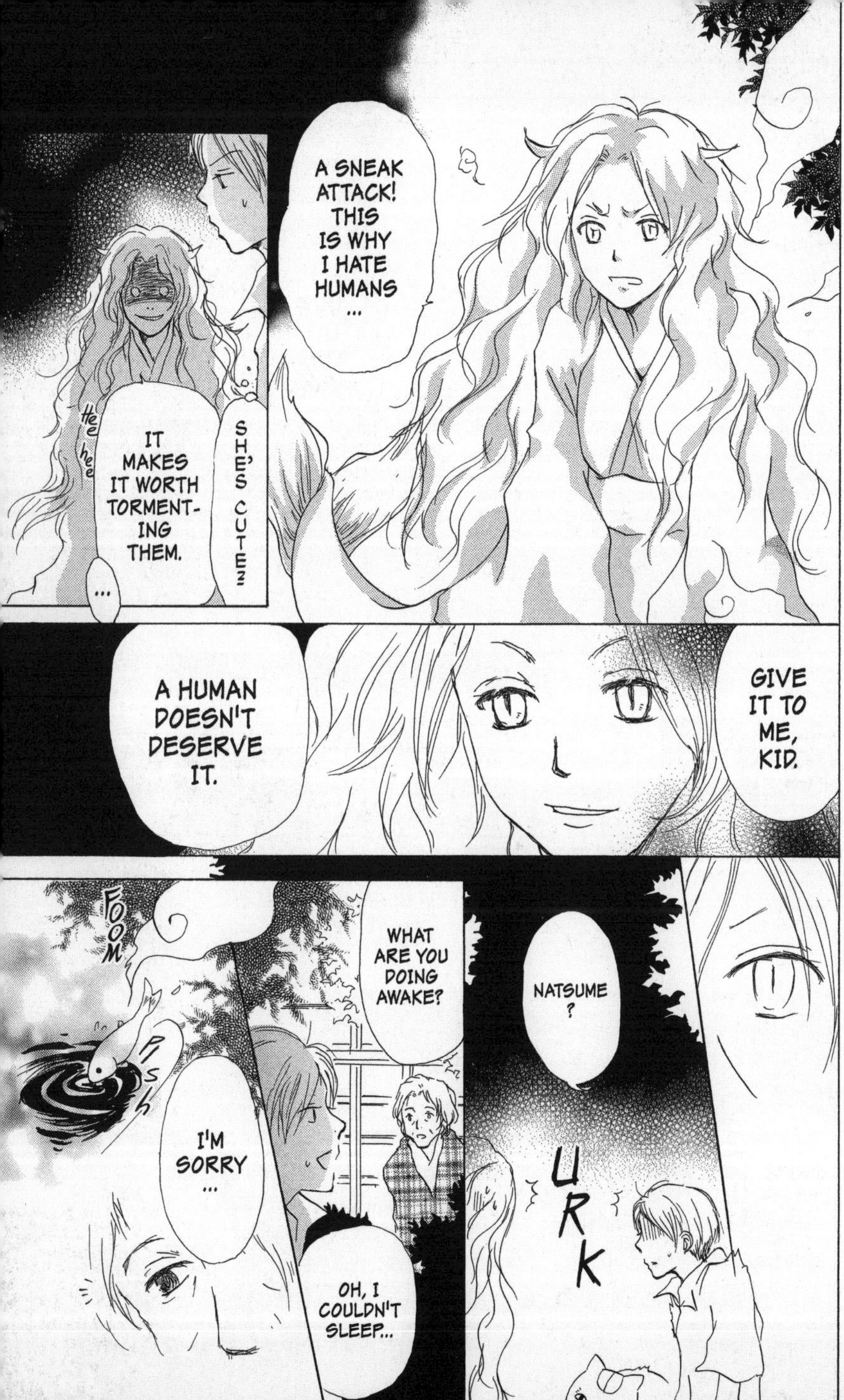
A SNEAK ATTACK! THIS IS WHY I HATE HUMANS ...
SHE'S CUTE?
IT MAKES IT WORTH TORMENT-ING THEM.
HEE HEE
...
GIVE IT TO ME, KID.
A HUMAN DOESN'T DESERVE IT.
NATSUME ?
URK
WHAT ARE YOU DOING AWAKE?
FOOM
PISH
I'M SORRY ...
OH, I COULDN'T SLEEP...

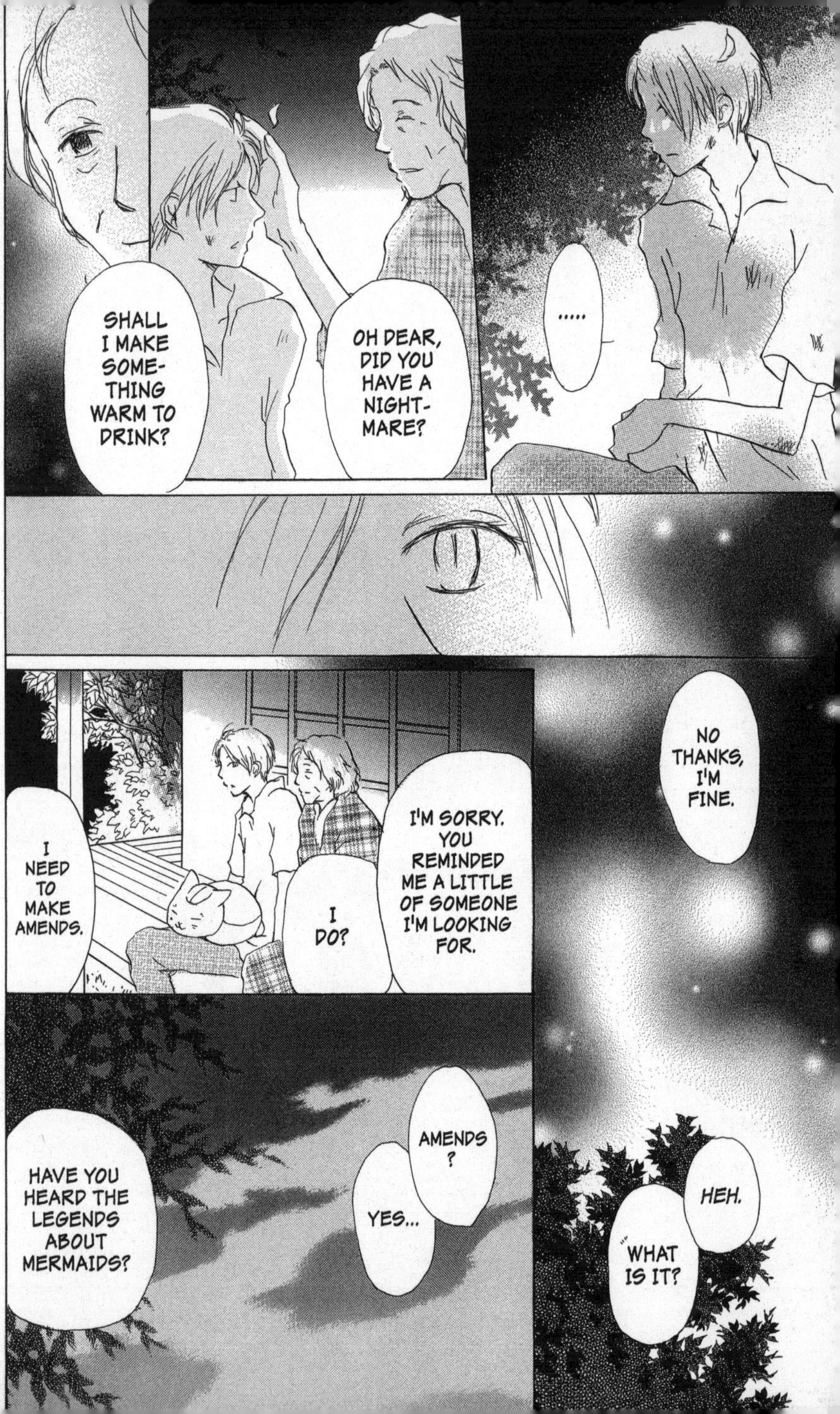
.....
OH DEAR, DID YOU HAVE A NIGHT-MARE?
SHALL I MAKE SOME-THING WARM TO DRINK?
NO THANKS, I'M FINE.
I'M SORRY. YOU REMINDED ME A LITTLE OF SOMEONE I'M LOOKING FOR.
I DO?
I NEED TO MAKE AMENDS.
HEH.
WHAT IS IT?
AMENDS?
YES...
HAVE YOU HEARD THE LEGENDS ABOUT MERMAIDS?

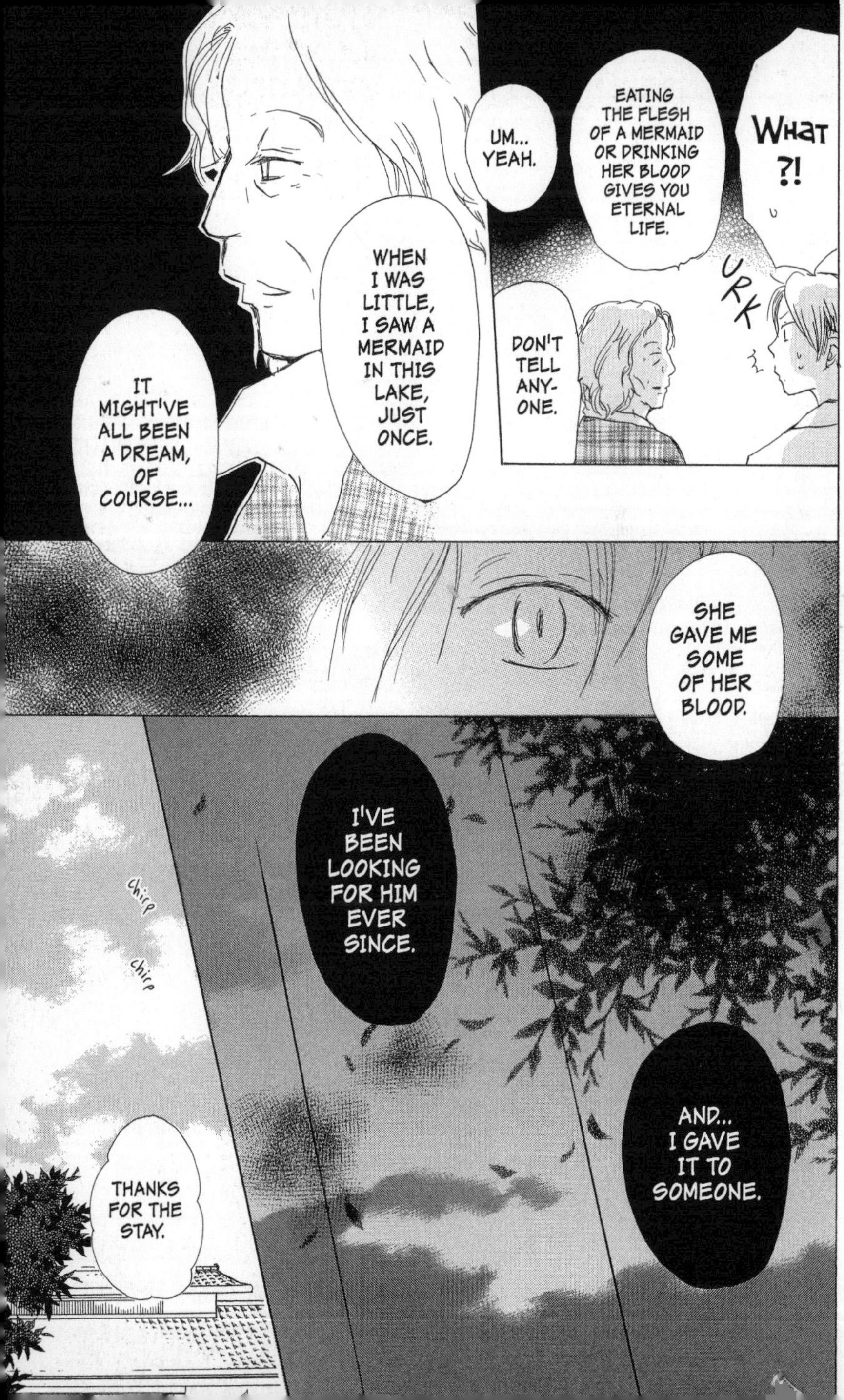
WHAT?!
EATING THE FLESH OF A MERMAID OR DRINKING HER BLOOD GIVES YOU ETERNAL LIFE.
URK
DON'T TELL ANY-ONE.
UM... YEAH.
WHEN I WAS LITTLE, I SAW A MERMAID IN THIS LAKE, JUST ONCE.
IT MIGHT'VE ALL BEEN A DREAM, OF COURSE...
SHE GAVE ME SOME OF HER BLOOD.
I'VE BEEN LOOKING FOR HIM EVER SINCE.
AND... I GAVE IT TO SOMEONE.
chirp
chirp
THANKS FOR THE STAY.

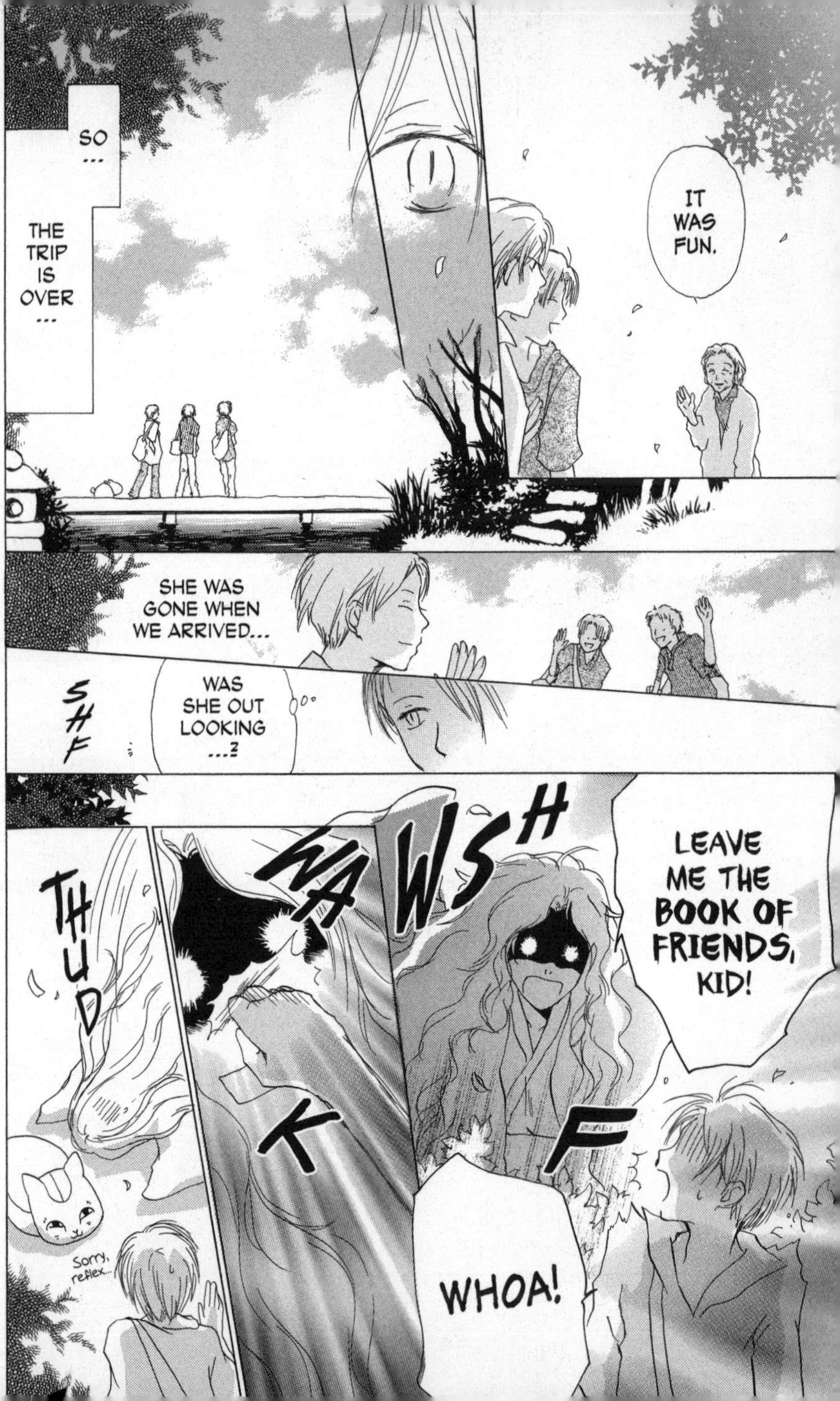
IT WAS FUN.
SO ... THE TRIP IS OVER ...
SHE WAS GONE WHEN WE ARRIVED...
WAS SHE OUT LOOKING ...?
SHF
WAWSH
LEAVE ME THE BOOK OF FRIENDS, KID!
THUD
F
K
WHOA!
Sorry, reflex...

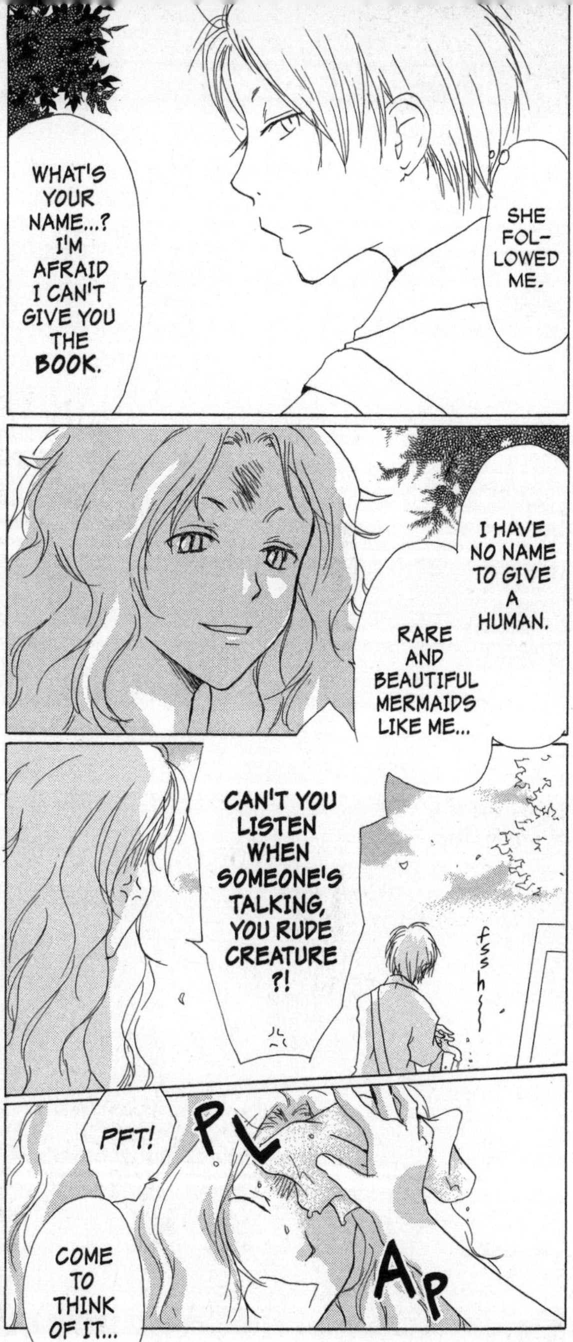
SHE FOL-LOWED ME.
WHAT'S YOUR NAME...? I'M AFRAID I CAN'T GIVE YOU THE BOOK.
I HAVE NO NAME TO GIVE A HUMAN.
RARE AND BEAUTIFUL MERMAIDS LIKE ME...
fssh~
CAN'T YOU LISTEN WHEN SOMEONE'S TALKING, YOU RUDE CREATURE?!
PLAP
PFT!
COME TO THINK OF IT...

01

Hello, I'm Midorikawa. This is my 13th ever graphic novel. I would like to thank the readers who are picking this up for the first time, as well as those who have been with me from the beginning.

I'll work hard so you'll keep reading. Please continue with your support!

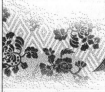

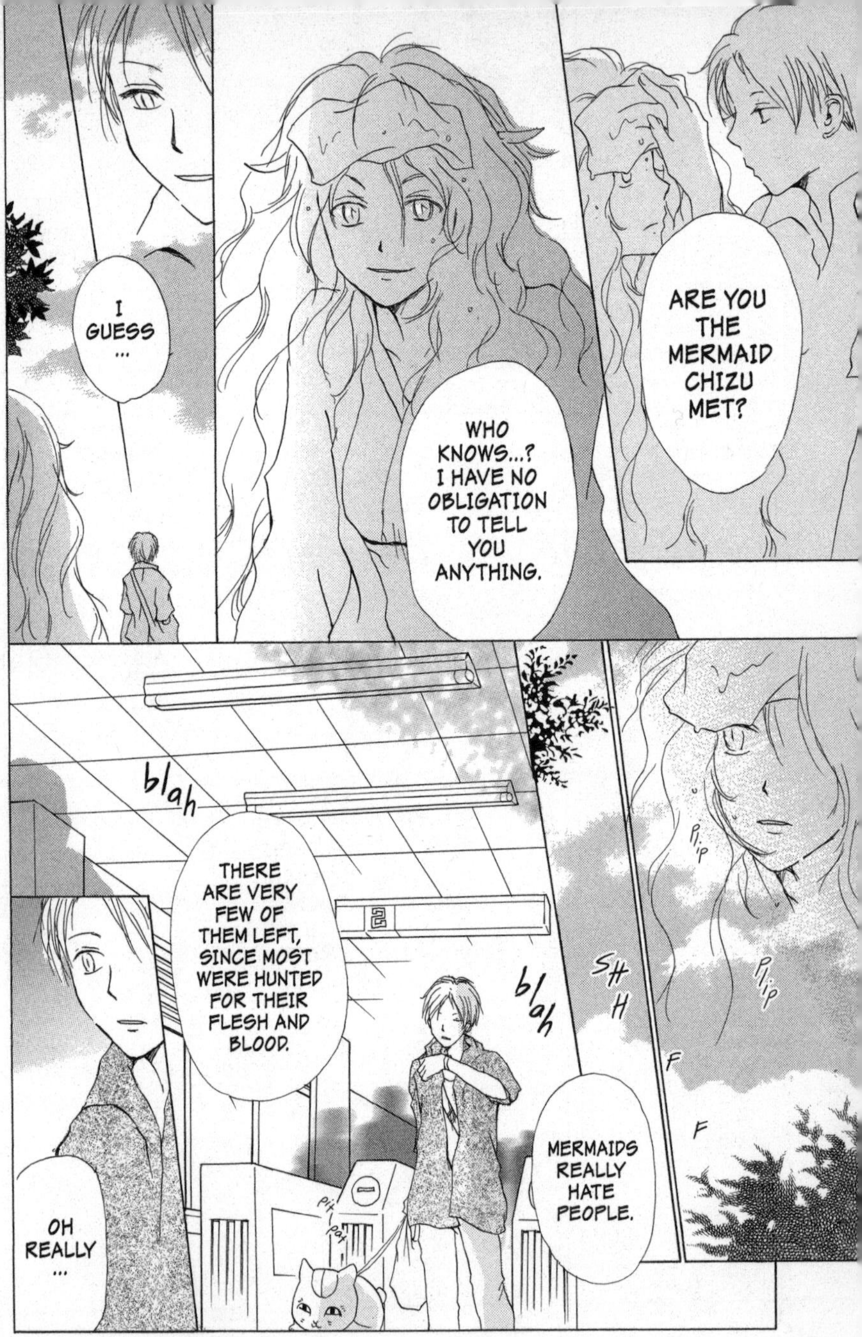
ARE YOU THE MERMAID CHIZU MET?
WHO KNOWS...? I HAVE NO OBLIGATION TO TELL YOU ANYTHING.
I GUESS ...
Plip
Plip
SHH
F
F
blah
MERMAIDS REALLY HATE PEOPLE.
blah
THERE ARE VERY FEW OF THEM LEFT, SINCE MOST WERE HUNTED FOR THEIR FLESH AND BLOOD.
pit pat
OH REALLY ...

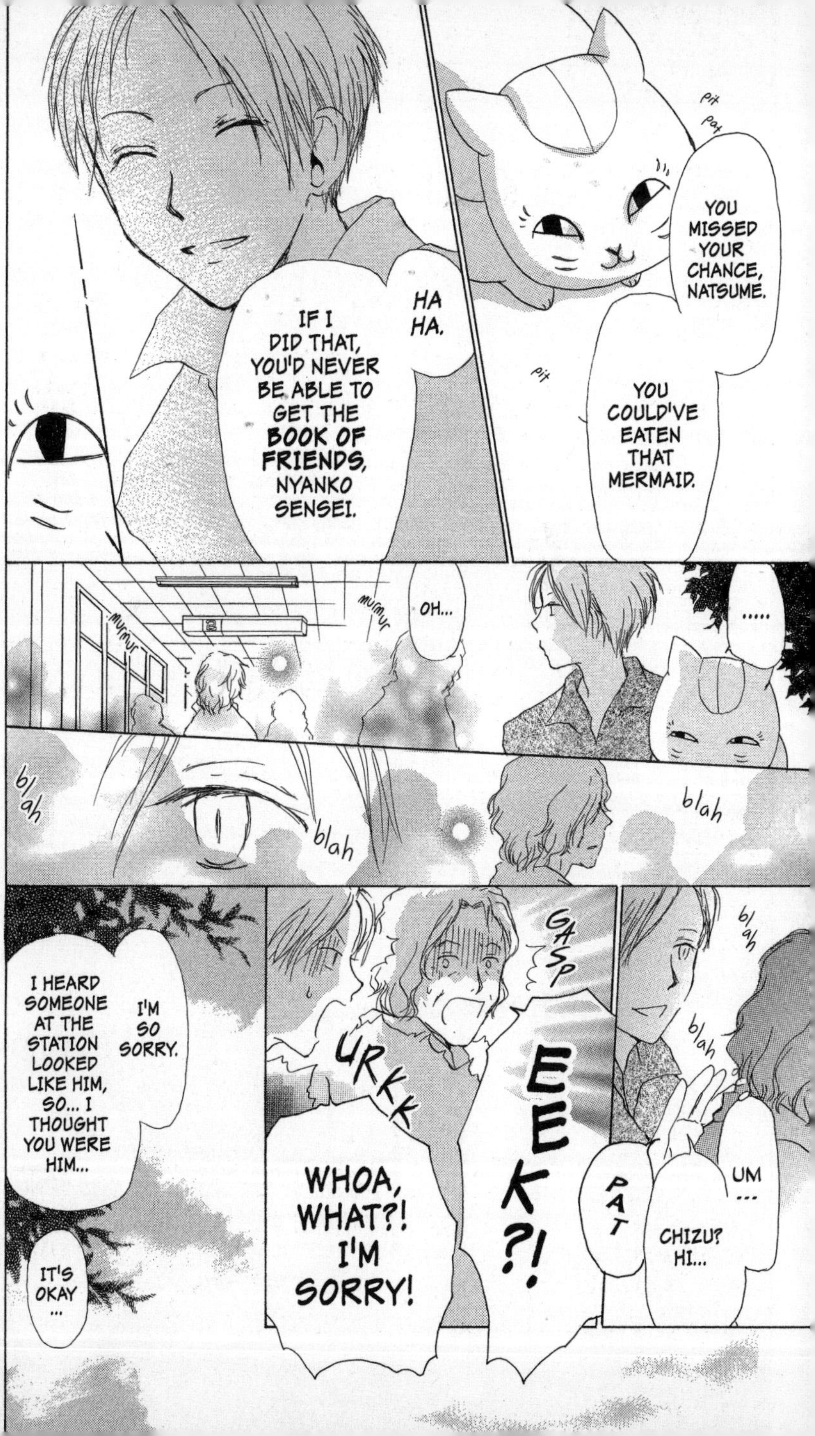
pit
pat
YOU MISSED YOUR CHANCE, NATSUME.
pit
YOU COULD'VE EATEN THAT MERMAID.
HA HA.
IF I DID THAT, YOU'D NEVER BE ABLE TO GET THE BOOK OF FRIENDS, NYANKO SENSEI.
.....
OH...
murmur
murmur
blah
blah
blah
blah
blah
UM ...
CHIZU? HI...
PAT
GASP
EEK?!
URKK
WHOA, WHAT?! I'M SORRY!
I'M SO SORRY.
I HEARD SOMEONE AT THE STATION LOOKED LIKE HIM, SO... I THOUGHT YOU WERE HIM...
IT'S OKAY ...

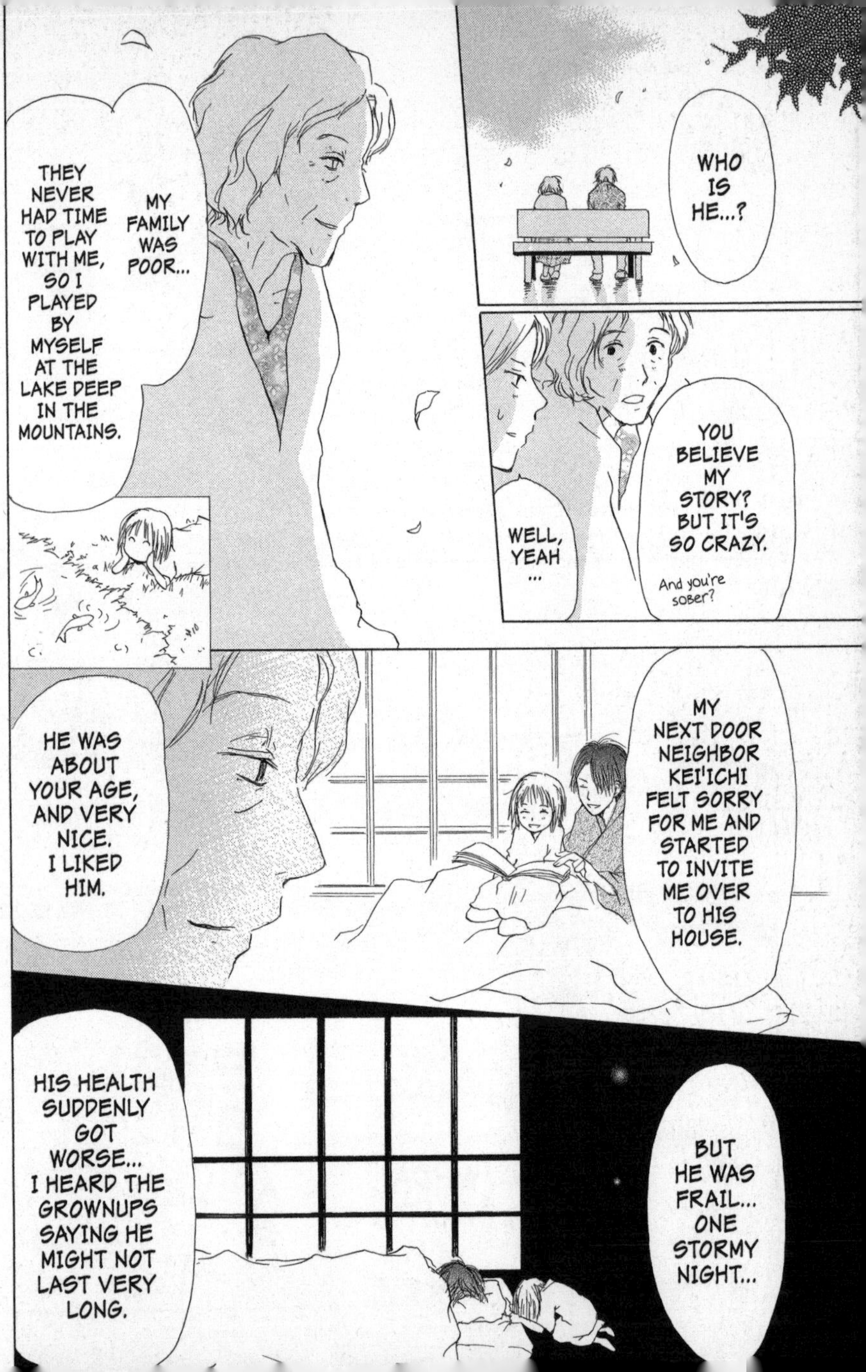
WHO IS HE...?
YOU BELIEVE MY STORY? BUT IT'S SO CRAZY.
And you're sober?
WELL, YEAH ...
MY FAMILY WAS POOR...
THEY NEVER HAD TIME TO PLAY WITH ME, SO I PLAYED BY MYSELF AT THE LAKE DEEP IN THE MOUNTAINS.
MY NEXT DOOR NEIGHBOR KEI'ICHI FELT SORRY FOR ME AND STARTED TO INVITE ME OVER TO HIS HOUSE.
HE WAS ABOUT YOUR AGE, AND VERY NICE. I LIKED HIM.
BUT HE WAS FRAIL... ONE STORMY NIGHT...
HIS HEALTH SUDDENLY GOT WORSE... I HEARD THE GROWNUPS SAYING HE MIGHT NOT LAST VERY LONG.

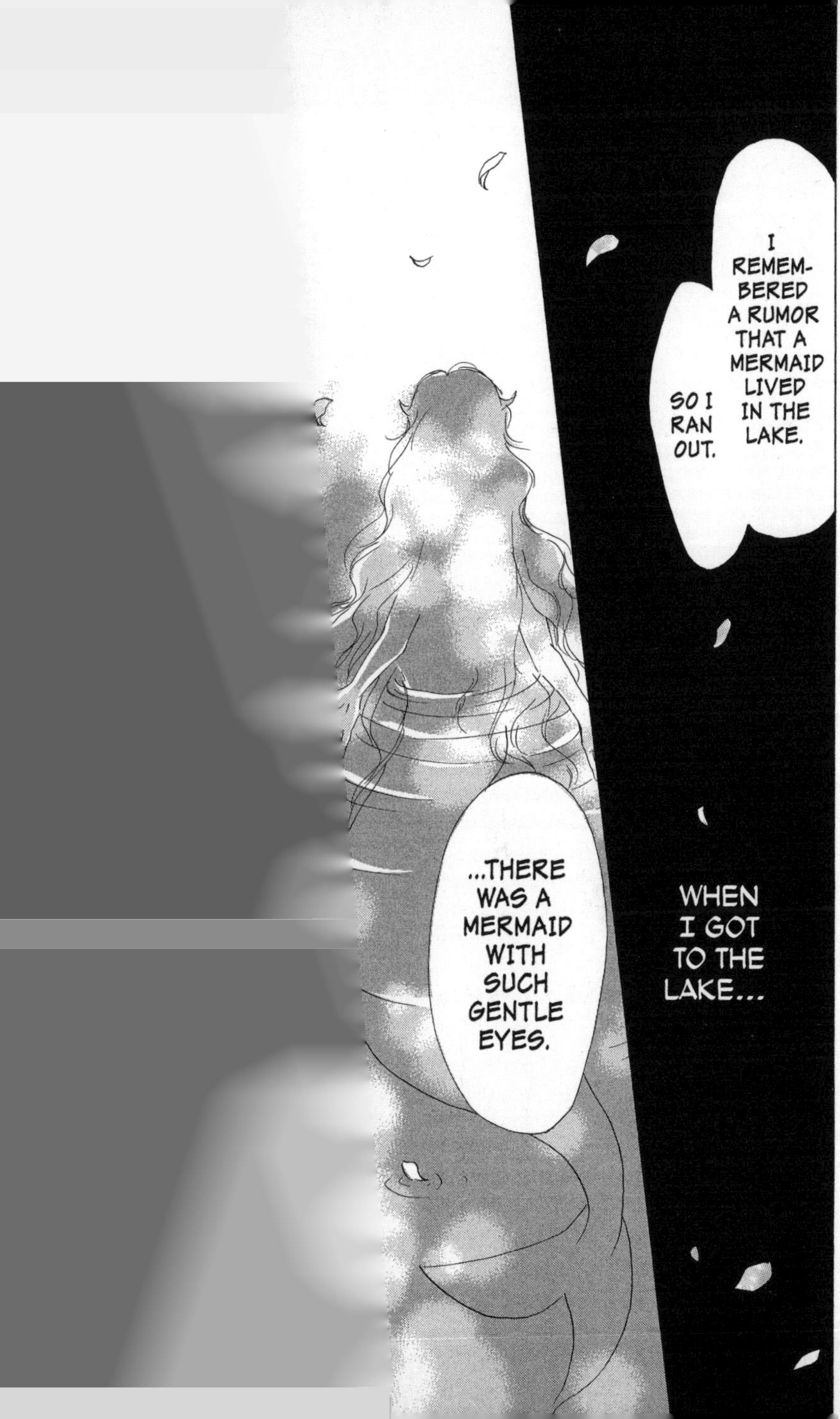
I REMEMBERED A RUMOR THAT A MERMAID LIVED IN THE LAKE.
SO I RAN OUT.
WHEN I GOT TO THE LAKE...
...THERE WAS A MERMAID WITH SUCH GENTLE EYES.

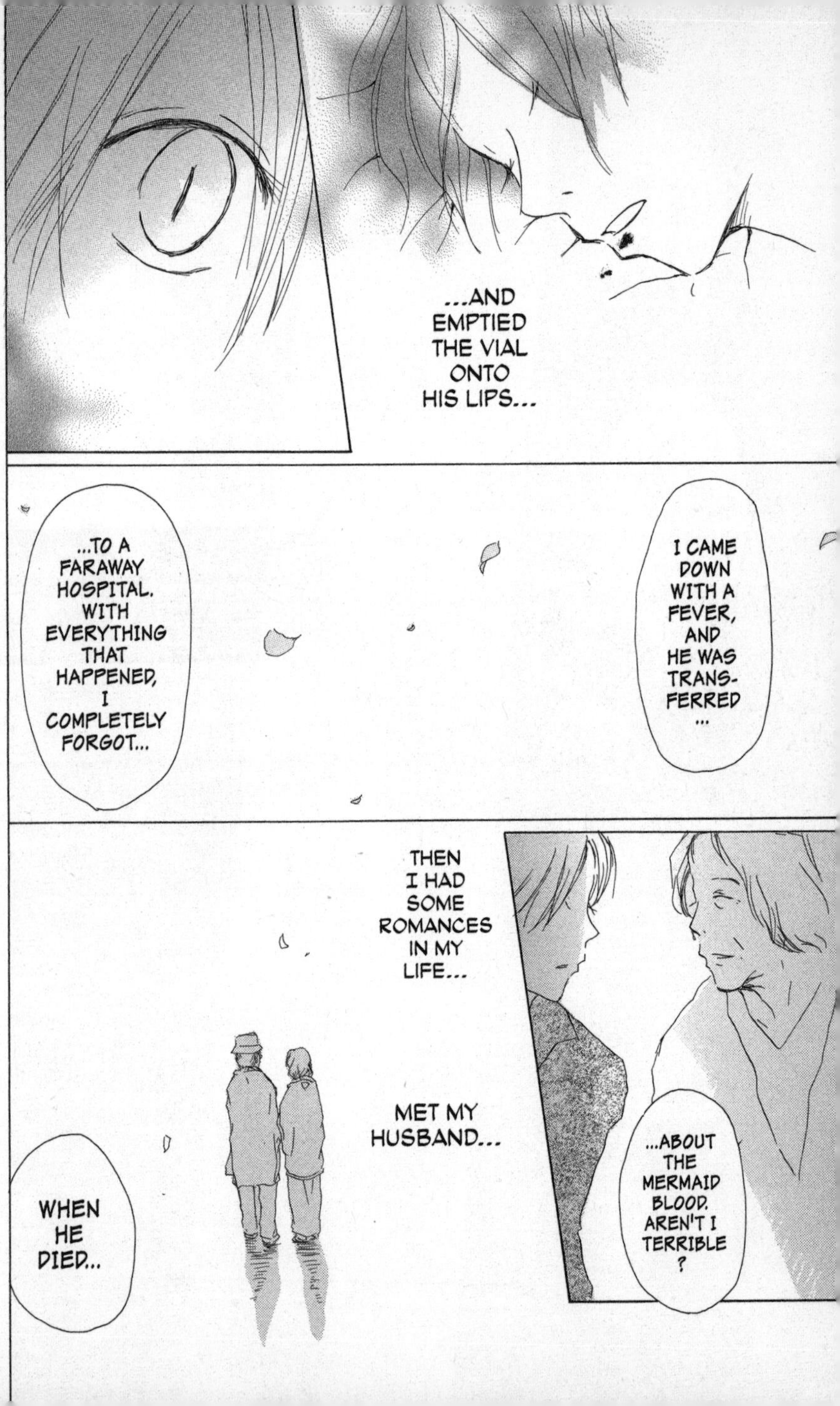
...AND EMPTIED THE VIAL ONTO HIS LIPS...
I CAME DOWN WITH A FEVER, AND HE WAS TRANSFERRED ...
...TO A FARAWAY HOSPITAL. WITH EVERYTHING THAT HAPPENED, I COMPLETELY FORGOT...
...ABOUT THE MERMAID BLOOD. AREN'T I TERRIBLE?
THEN I HAD SOME ROMANCES IN MY LIFE...
MET MY HUSBAND...
WHEN HE DIED...

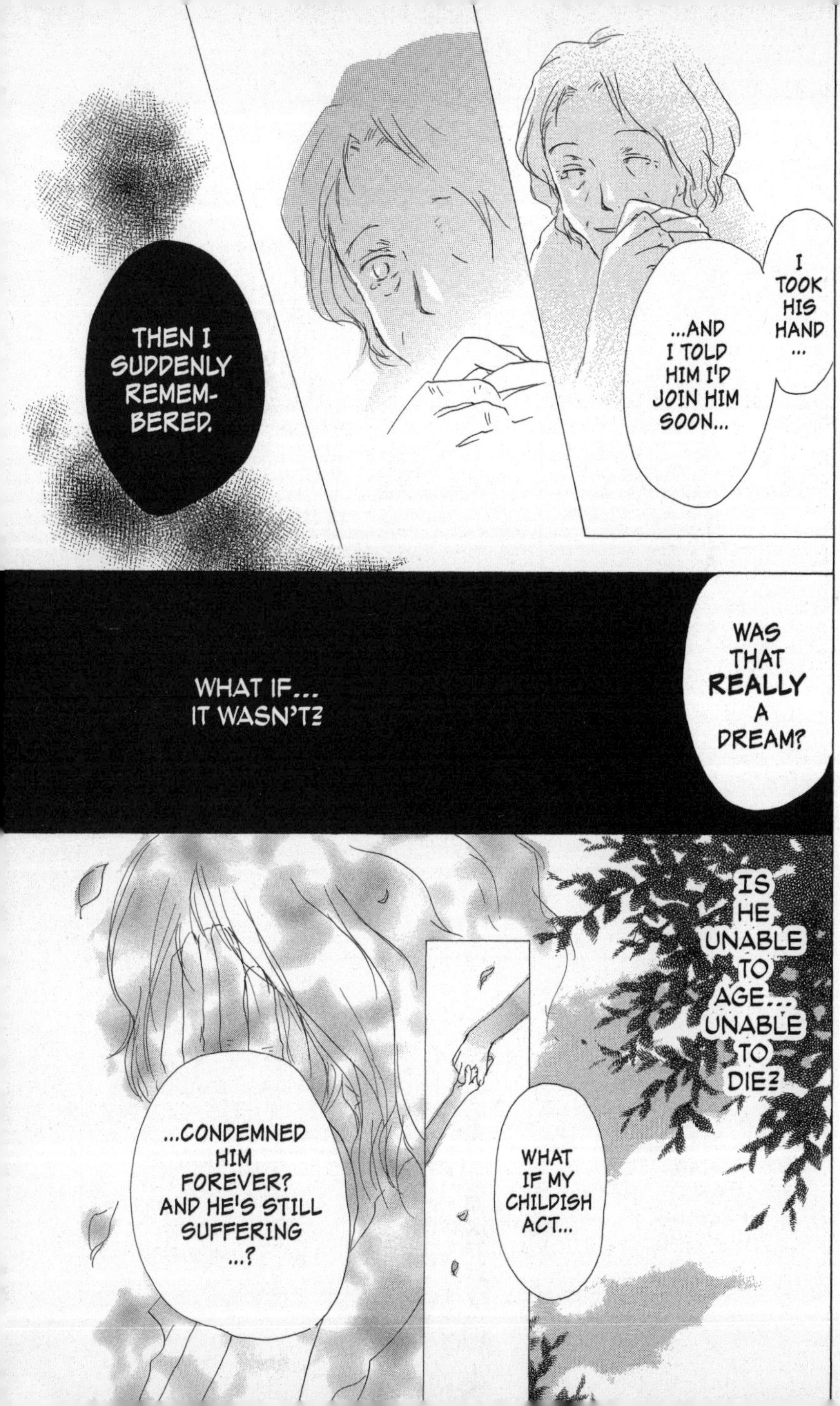
I TOOK HIS HAND...
...AND I TOLD HIM I'D JOIN HIM SOON...
THEN I SUDDENLY REMEM-BERED.
WAS THAT **REALLY** A DREAM?
WHAT IF... IT WASN'T?
IS HE UNABLE TO AGE... UNABLE TO DIE?
WHAT IF MY CHILDISH ACT...
...CONDEMNED HIM FOREVER? AND HE'S STILL SUFFERING...?

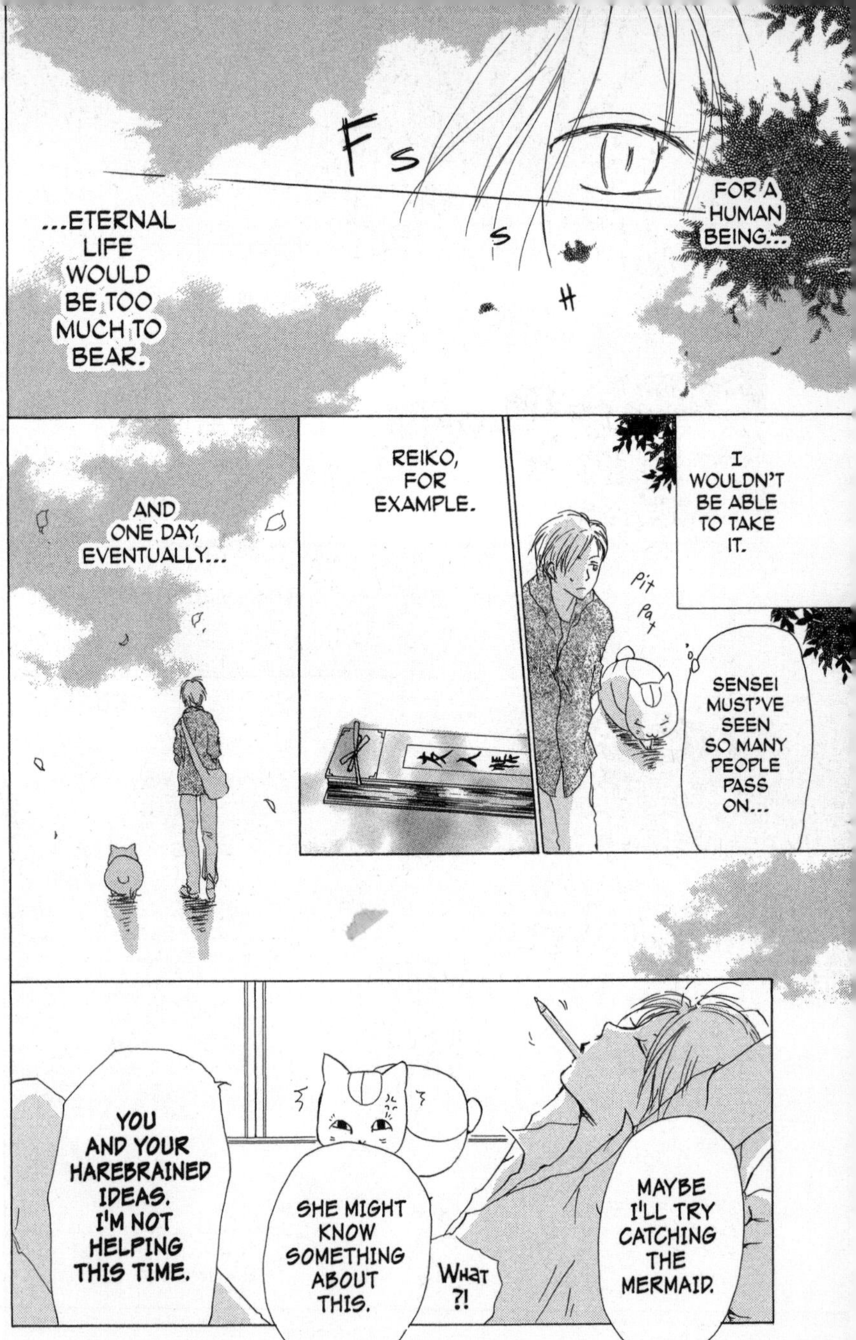
FOR A HUMAN BEING...
FSSH
...ETERNAL LIFE WOULD BE TOO MUCH TO BEAR.
I WOULDN'T BE ABLE TO TAKE IT.
Pit Pat
SENSEI MUST'VE SEEN SO MANY PEOPLE PASS ON...
REIKO, FOR EXAMPLE.
AND ONE DAY, EVENTUALLY...
MAYBE I'LL TRY CATCHING THE MERMAID.
WHAT ?!
SHE MIGHT KNOW SOMETHING ABOUT THIS.
YOU AND YOUR HAREBRAINED IDEAS. I'M NOT HELPING THIS TIME.

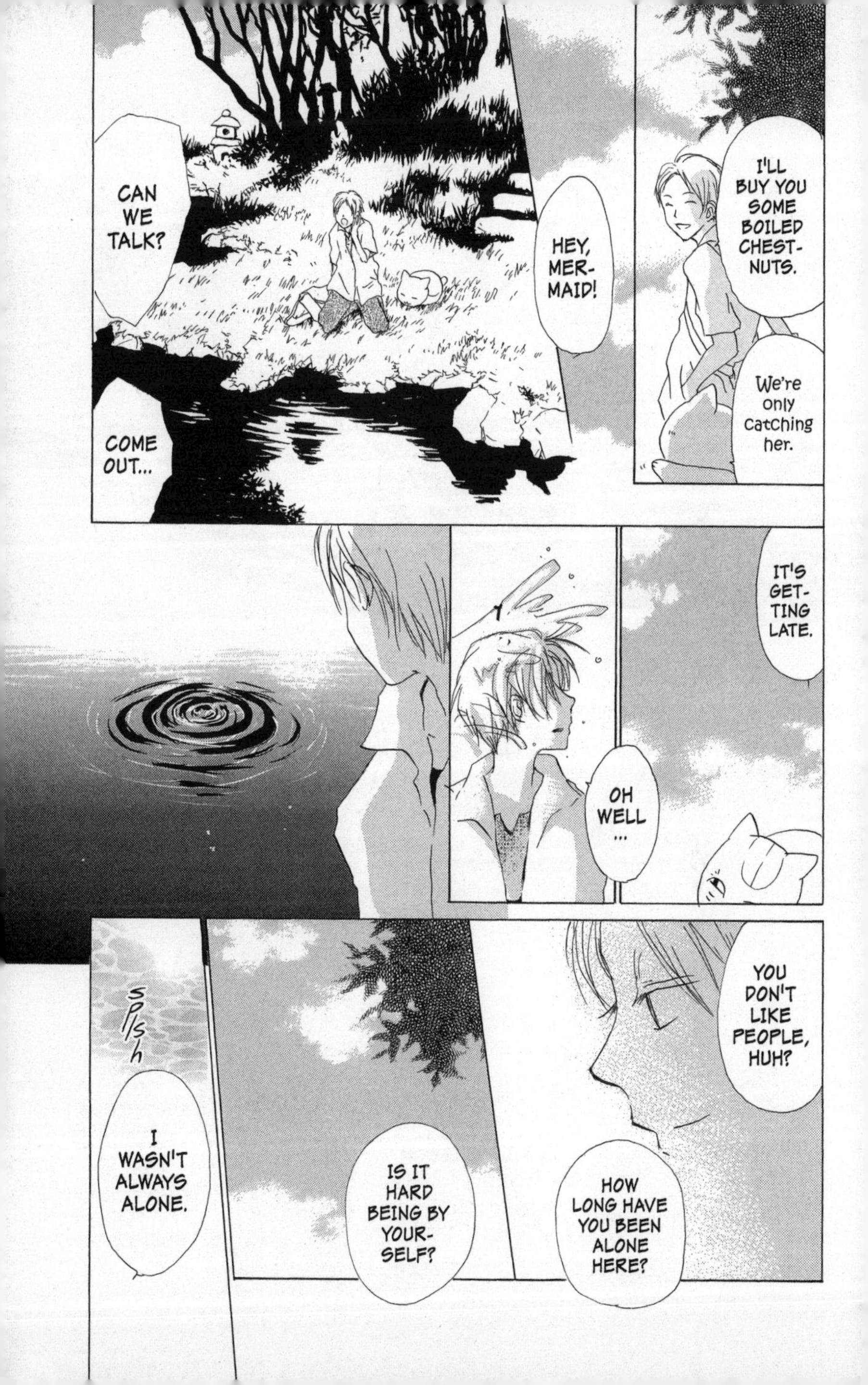
I'LL BUY YOU SOME BOILED CHEST-NUTS.
We're only catching her.
HEY, MER-MAID!
CAN WE TALK?
COME OUT...
IT'S GET-TING LATE.
OH WELL ...
YOU DON'T LIKE PEOPLE, HUH?
HOW LONG HAVE YOU BEEN ALONE HERE?
IS IT HARD BEING BY YOUR-SELF?
SPLSH
I WASN'T ALWAYS ALONE.

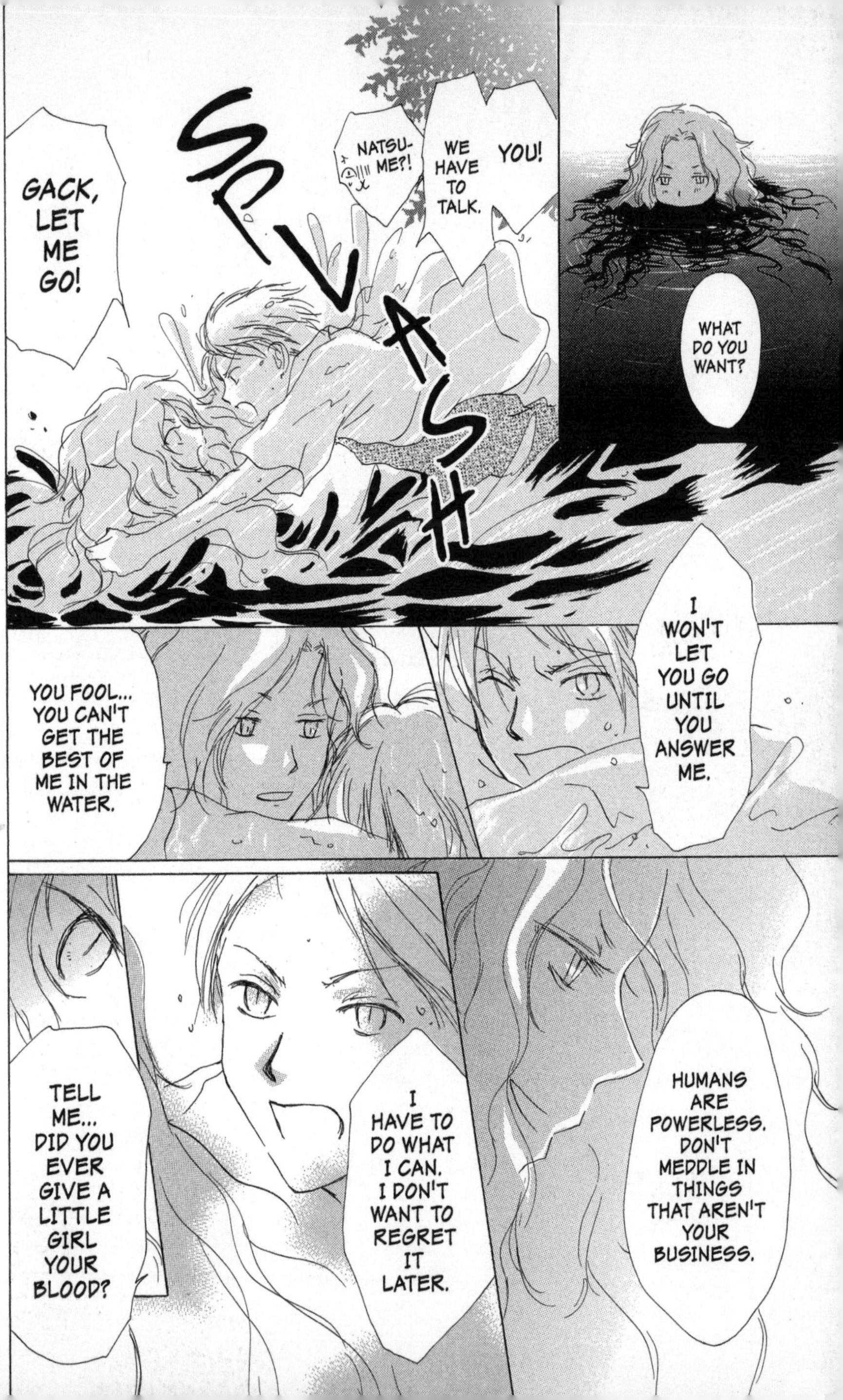
WHAT DO YOU WANT?
YOU!
WE HAVE TO TALK.
NATSU-ME?!
SPLASH
GACK, LET ME GO!
I WON'T LET YOU GO UNTIL YOU ANSWER ME.
YOU FOOL... YOU CAN'T GET THE BEST OF ME IN THE WATER.
HUMANS ARE POWERLESS. DON'T MEDDLE IN THINGS THAT AREN'T YOUR BUSINESS.
I HAVE TO DO WHAT I CAN. I DON'T WANT TO REGRET IT LATER.
TELL ME... DID YOU EVER GIVE A LITTLE GIRL YOUR BLOOD?

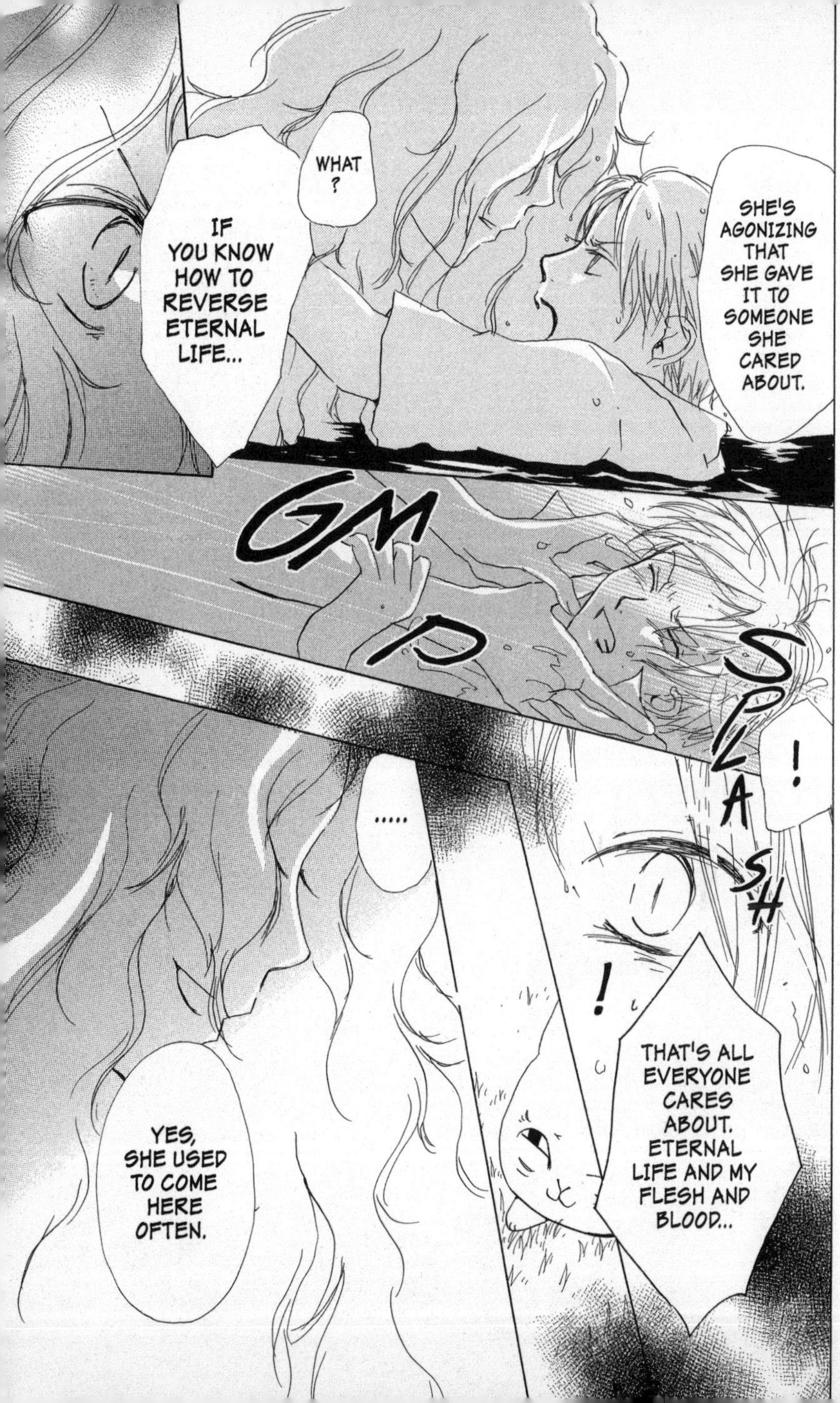
SHE'S AGONIZING THAT SHE GAVE IT TO SOMEONE SHE CARED ABOUT.
WHAT?
IF YOU KNOW HOW TO REVERSE ETERNAL LIFE...
GMP
SPLASH
!
!
THAT'S ALL EVERYONE CARES ABOUT. ETERNAL LIFE AND MY FLESH AND BLOOD...
......
YES, SHE USED TO COME HERE OFTEN.

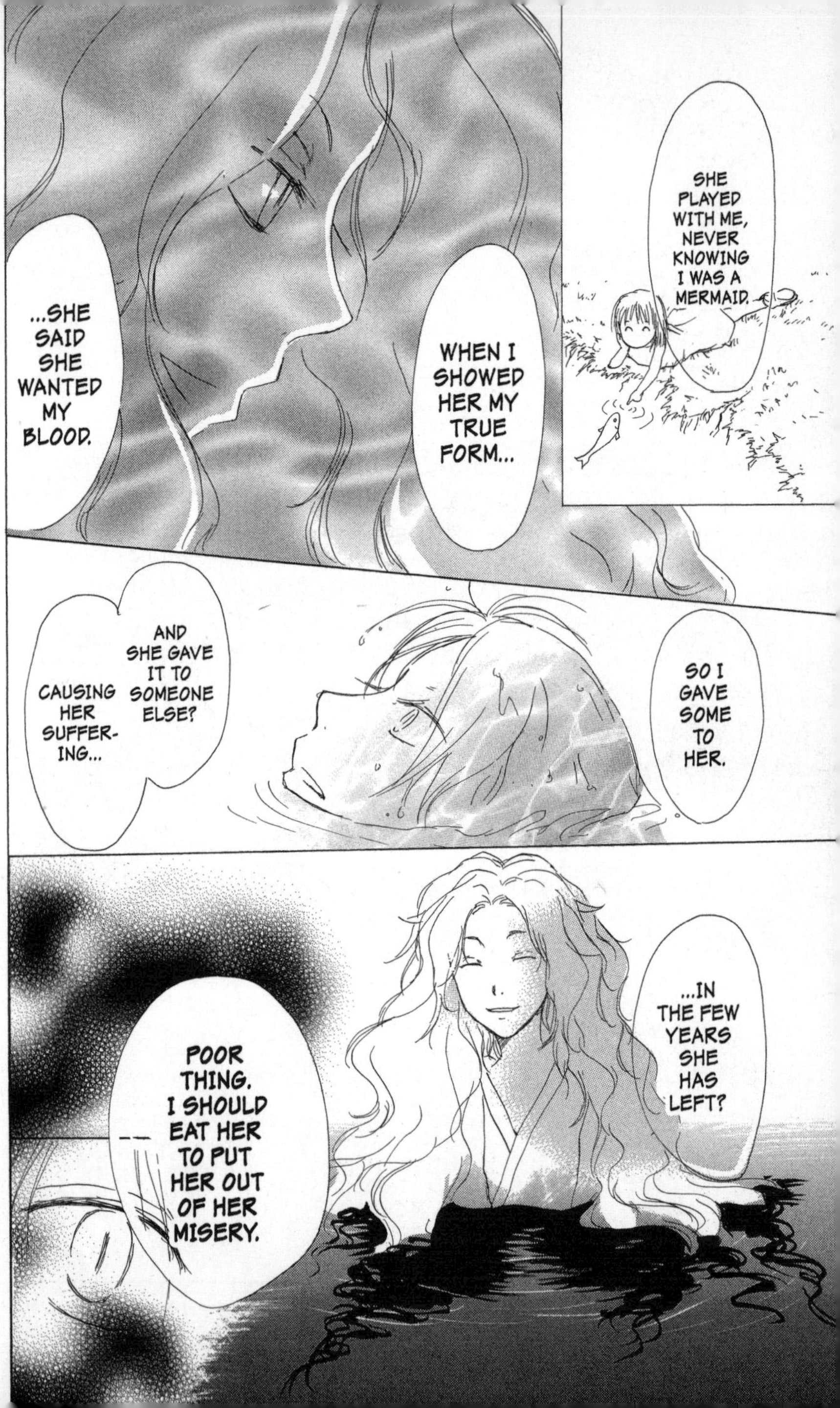
SHE PLAYED WITH ME, NEVER KNOWING I WAS A MERMAID.
WHEN I SHOWED HER MY TRUE FORM...
...SHE SAID SHE WANTED MY BLOOD.
SO I GAVE SOME TO HER.
AND SHE GAVE IT TO SOMEONE ELSE?
CAUSING HER SUFFER-ING...
...IN THE FEW YEARS SHE HAS LEFT?
POOR THING. I SHOULD EAT HER TO PUT HER OUT OF HER MISERY.

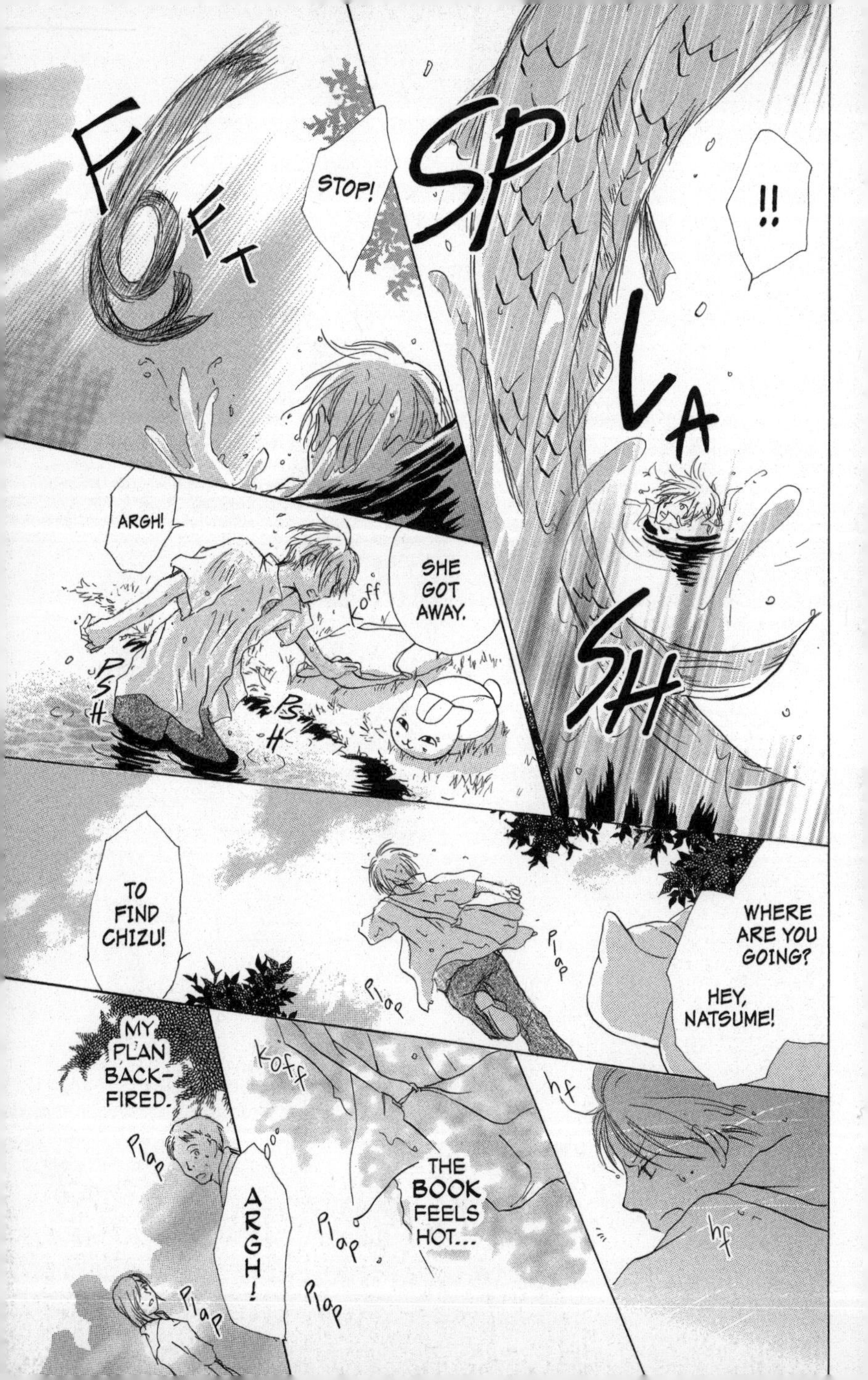
!!
SPLASH
FOFFT
STOP!
SHE GOT AWAY.
koff
ARGH!
PSH
PSH
WHERE ARE YOU GOING?
HEY, NATSUME!
Plap
TO FIND CHIZU!
Plap
hf
hf
koff
THE BOOK FEELS HOT...
Plap
Plap
MY PLAN BACKFIRED.
ARGH!
Plap
Plap

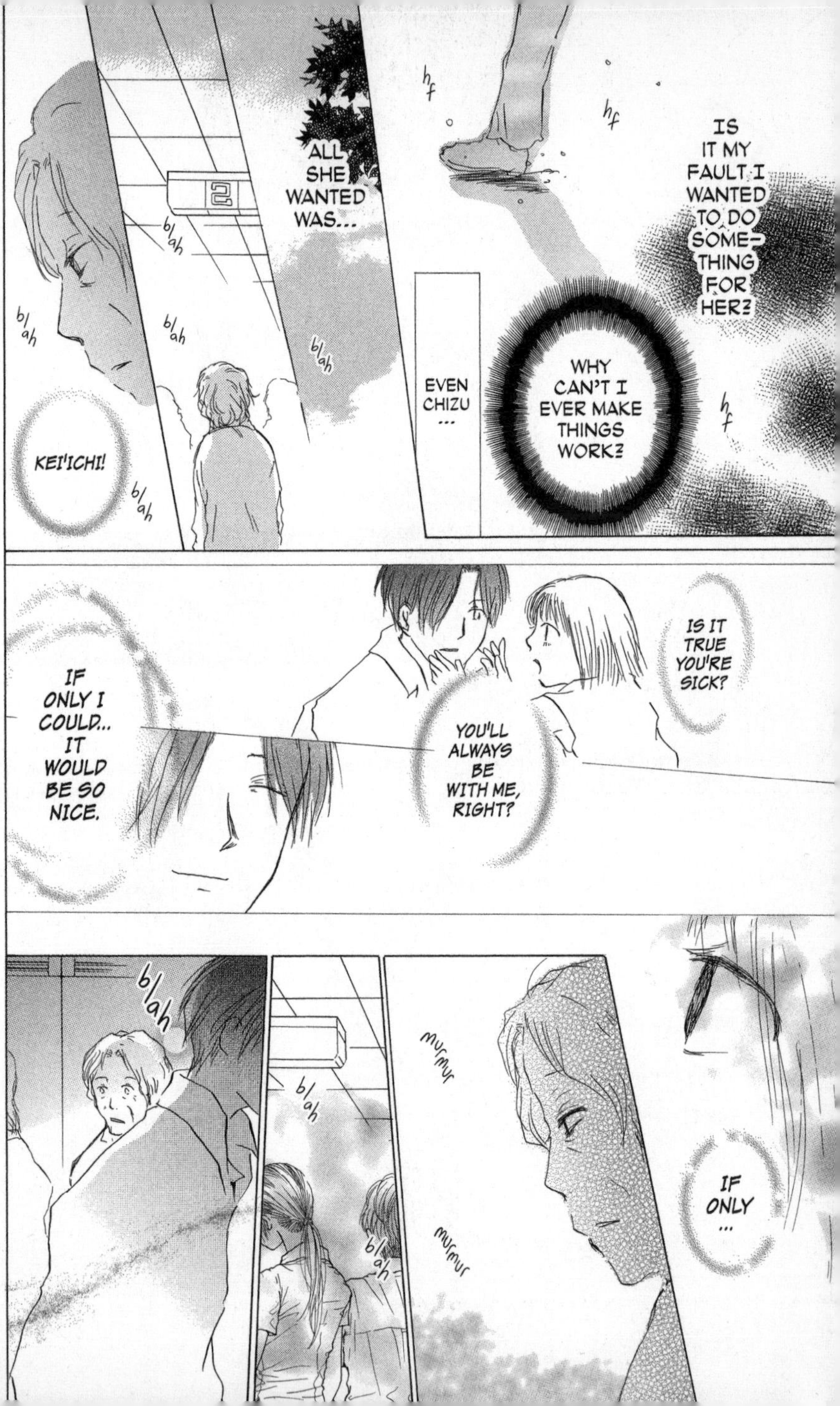
hf
hf
IS IT MY FAULT I WANTED TO DO SOME-THING FOR HER?
WHY CAN'T I EVER MAKE THINGS WORK?
hf
EVEN CHIZU ...
ALL SHE WANTED WAS...
blah
blah
blah
blah
KEI'ICHI!
blah
IS IT TRUE YOU'RE SICK?
YOU'LL ALWAYS BE WITH ME, RIGHT?
IF ONLY I COULD... IT WOULD BE SO NICE.
IF ONLY ...
murmur
murmur
blah
blah
blah

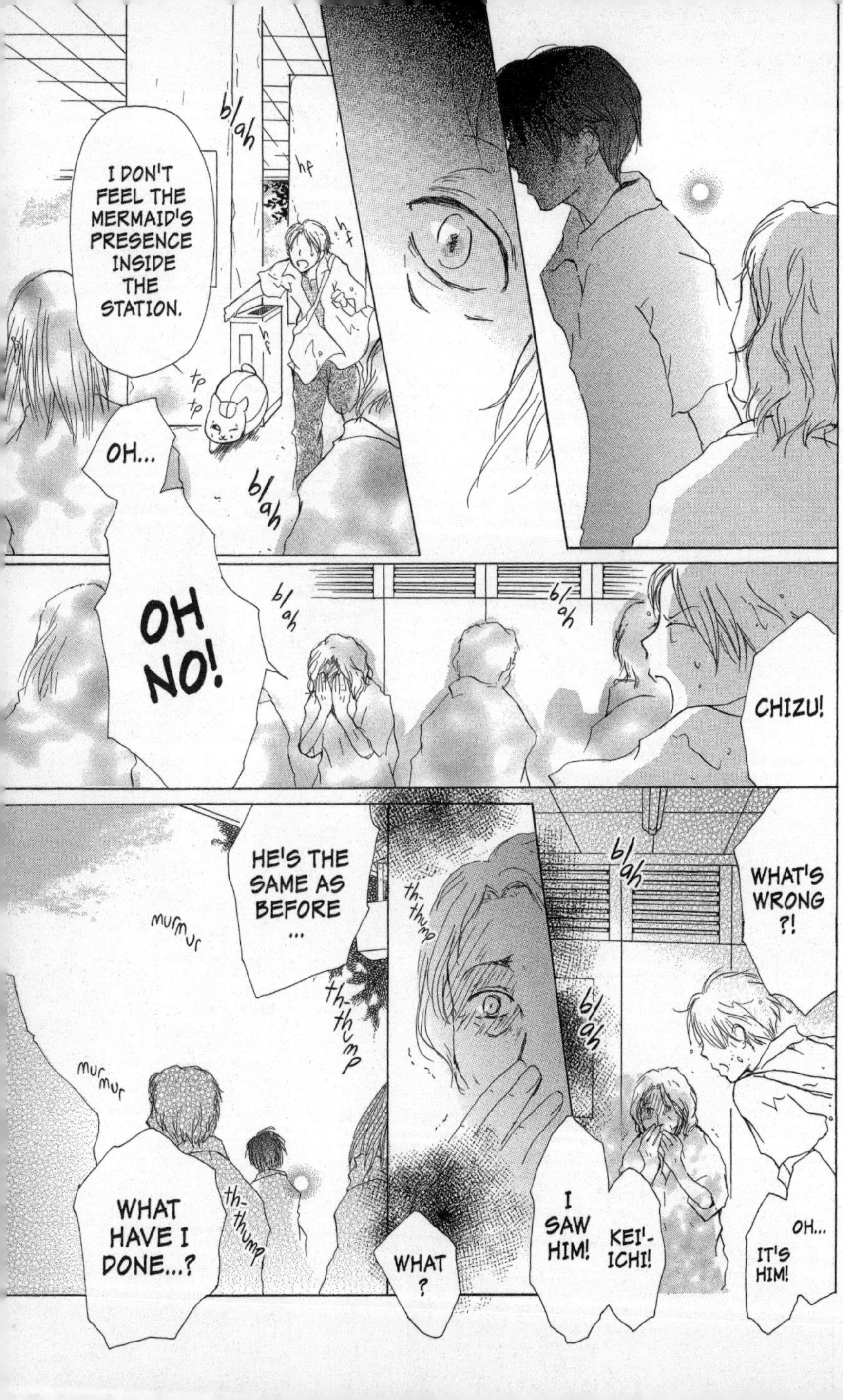
blah
hf
I DON'T FEEL THE MERMAID'S PRESENCE INSIDE THE STATION.
hf
hf
xp
xp
OH...
blah
CHIZU!
blah
blah
OH NO!
WHAT'S WRONG?!
blah
blah
OH...
IT'S HIM!
KEI'-ICHI!
I SAW HIM!
th-thump
WHAT?
HE'S THE SAME AS BEFORE...
murmur
th-thump
murmur
WHAT HAVE I DONE...?
th-thump

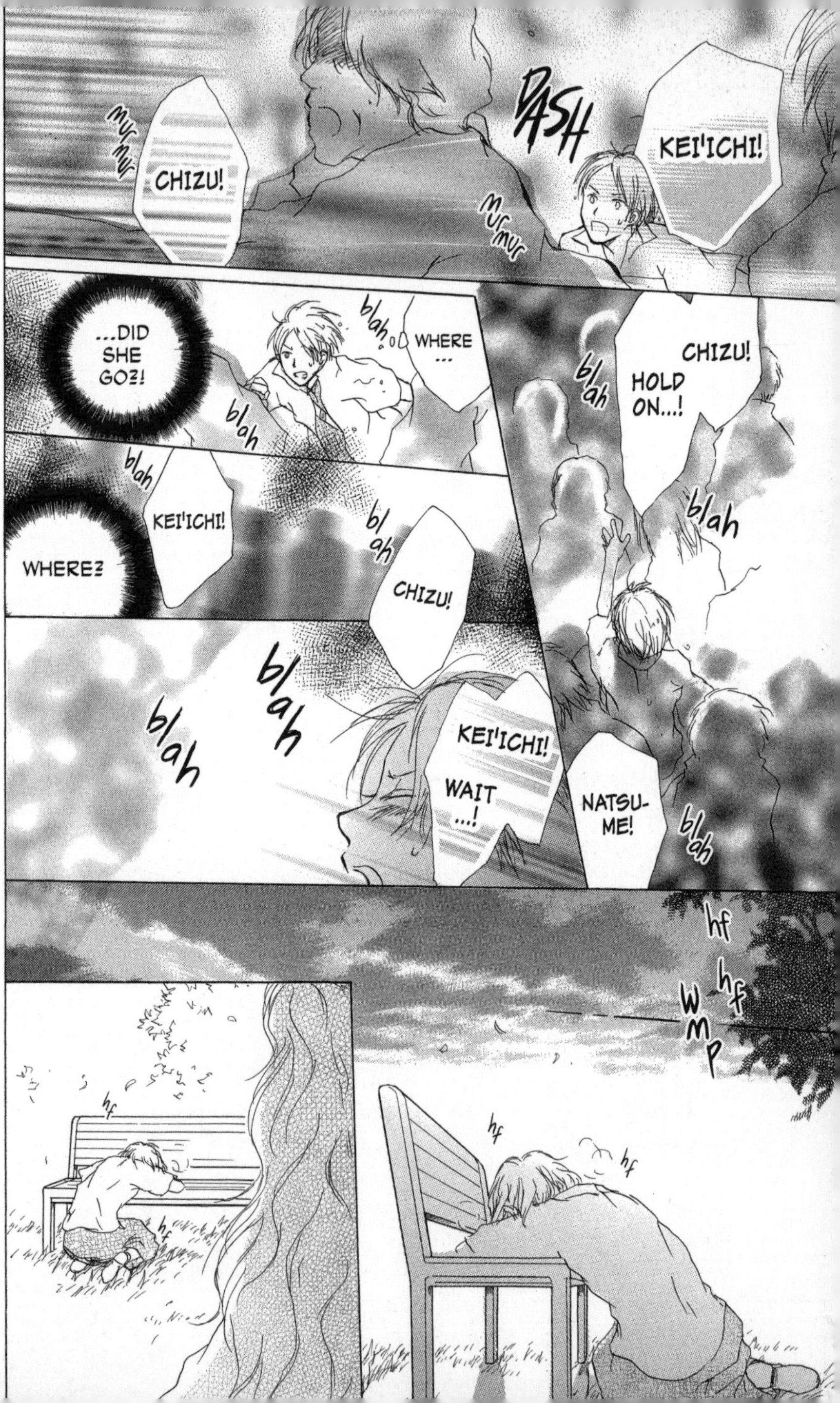
DASH
KEI'ICHI!
murmur
CHIZU!
murmur
CHIZU!
HOLD ON...!
blah
blah
blah
WHERE ...
...DID SHE GO?!
blah
blah
blah
CHIZU!
KEI'ICHI!
WHERE?
blah
NATSUME!
KEI'ICHI!
WAIT ...!
blah
blah
hf
hf
wmp
hf
hf
hf
hf

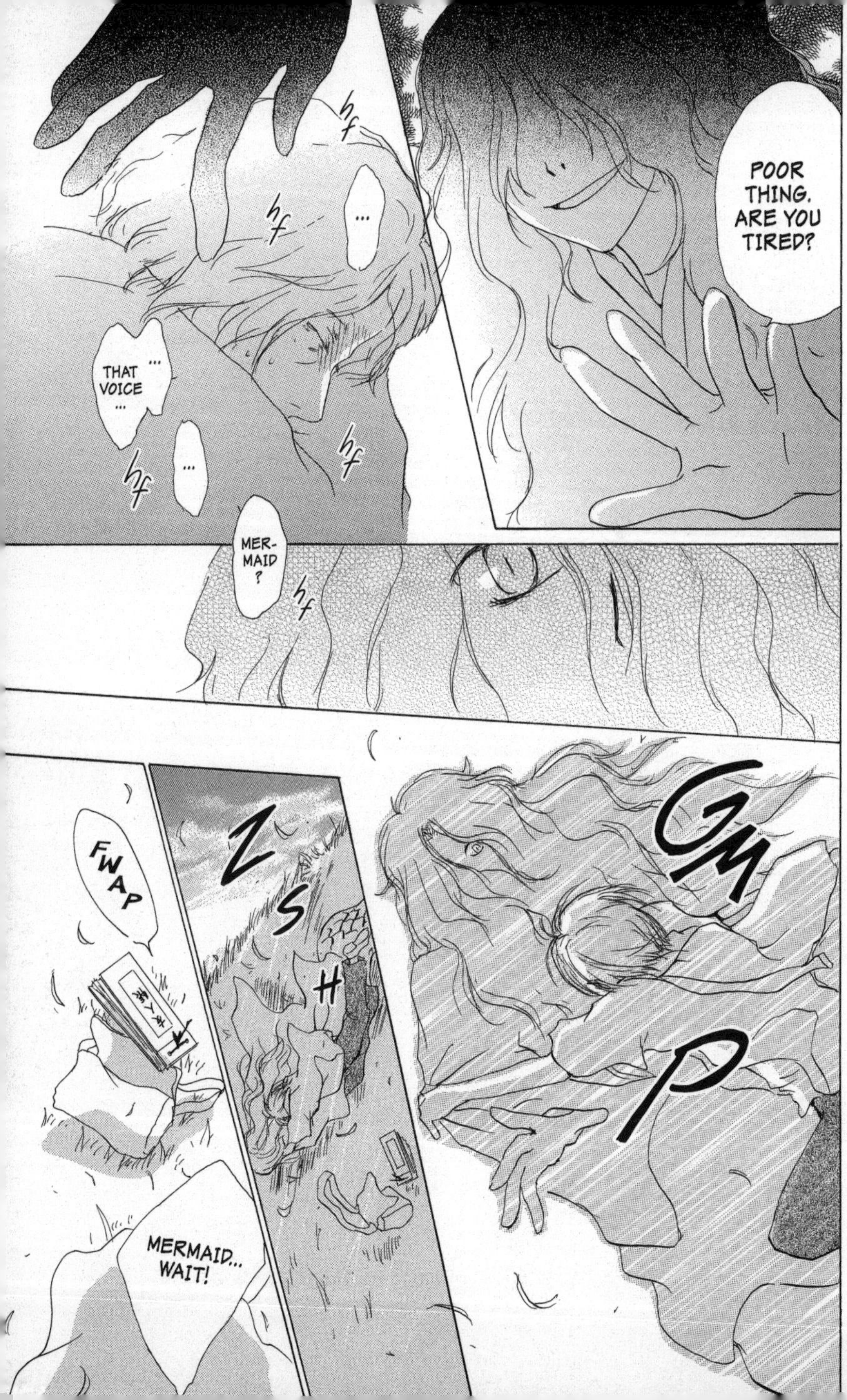
POOR THING. ARE YOU TIRED?
hf
...
hf
... THAT VOICE ...
hf
...
hf
MER-MAID?
hf
GMP
ZSSH
FWAP
MERMAID... WAIT!

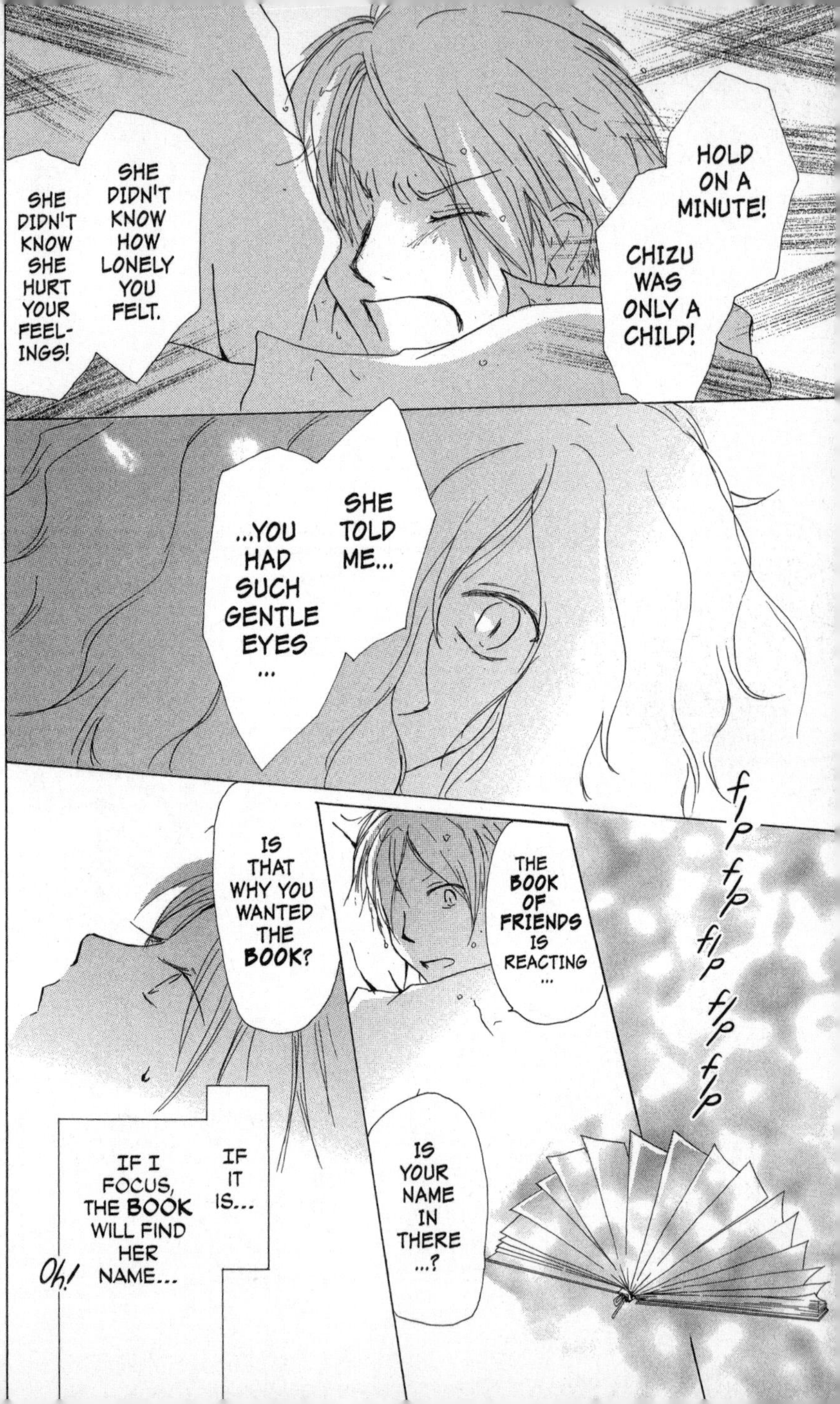
HOLD ON A MINUTE!
CHIZU WAS ONLY A CHILD!
SHE DIDN'T KNOW HOW LONELY YOU FELT.
SHE DIDN'T KNOW SHE HURT YOUR FEEL-INGS!
SHE TOLD ME...
...YOU HAD SUCH GENTLE EYES...
flip flip flip flip flip
THE BOOK OF FRIENDS IS REACTING...
IS THAT WHY YOU WANTED THE BOOK?
IS YOUR NAME IN THERE...?
IF IT IS...
IF I FOCUS, THE BOOK WILL FIND HER NAME...
Oh!

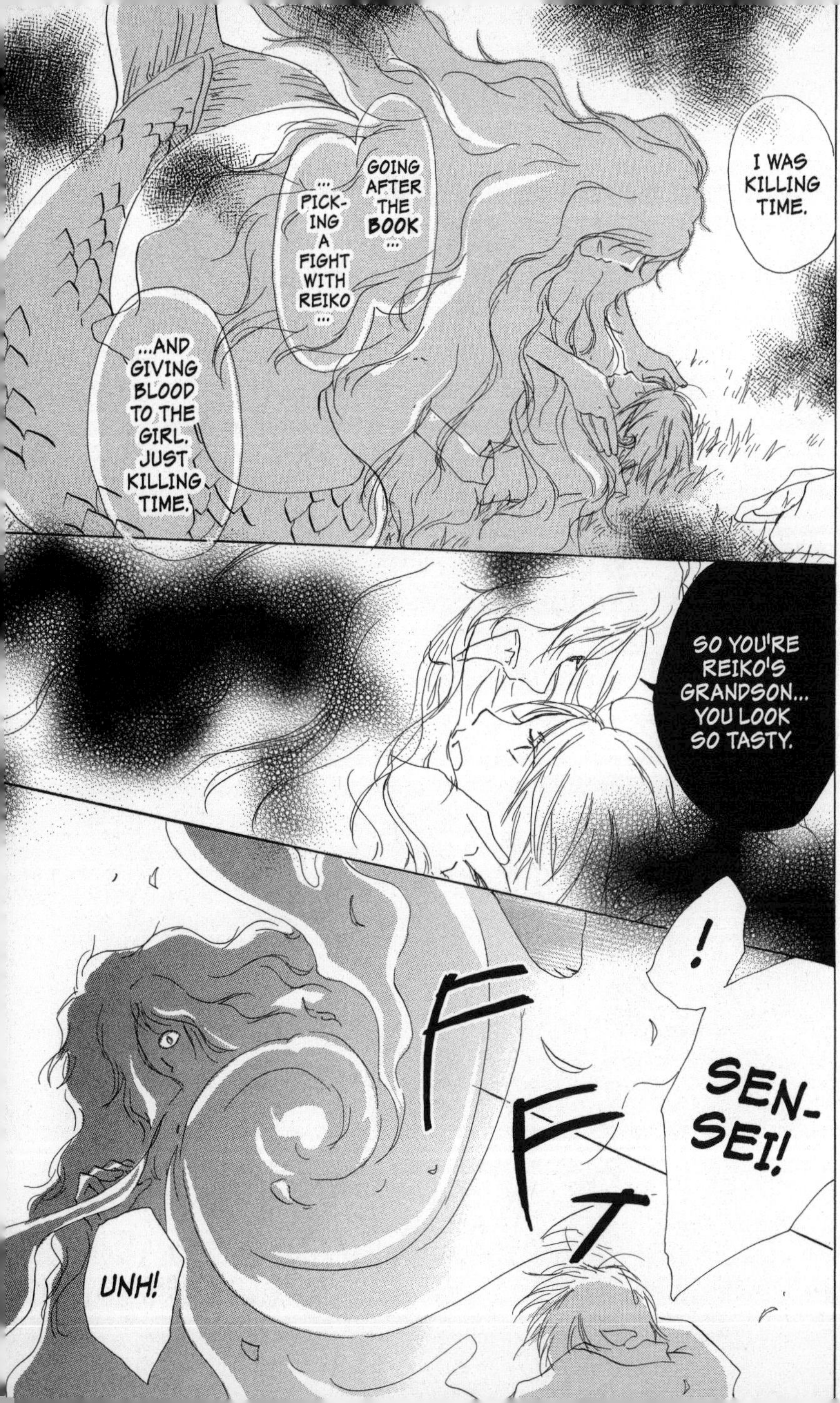
I WAS KILLING TIME.
GOING AFTER THE BOOK...
...PICKING A FIGHT WITH REIKO...
...AND GIVING BLOOD TO THE GIRL. JUST KILLING TIME.
SO YOU'RE REIKO'S GRANDSON... YOU LOOK SO TASTY.
!
SEN-SEI!
FFT
UNH!

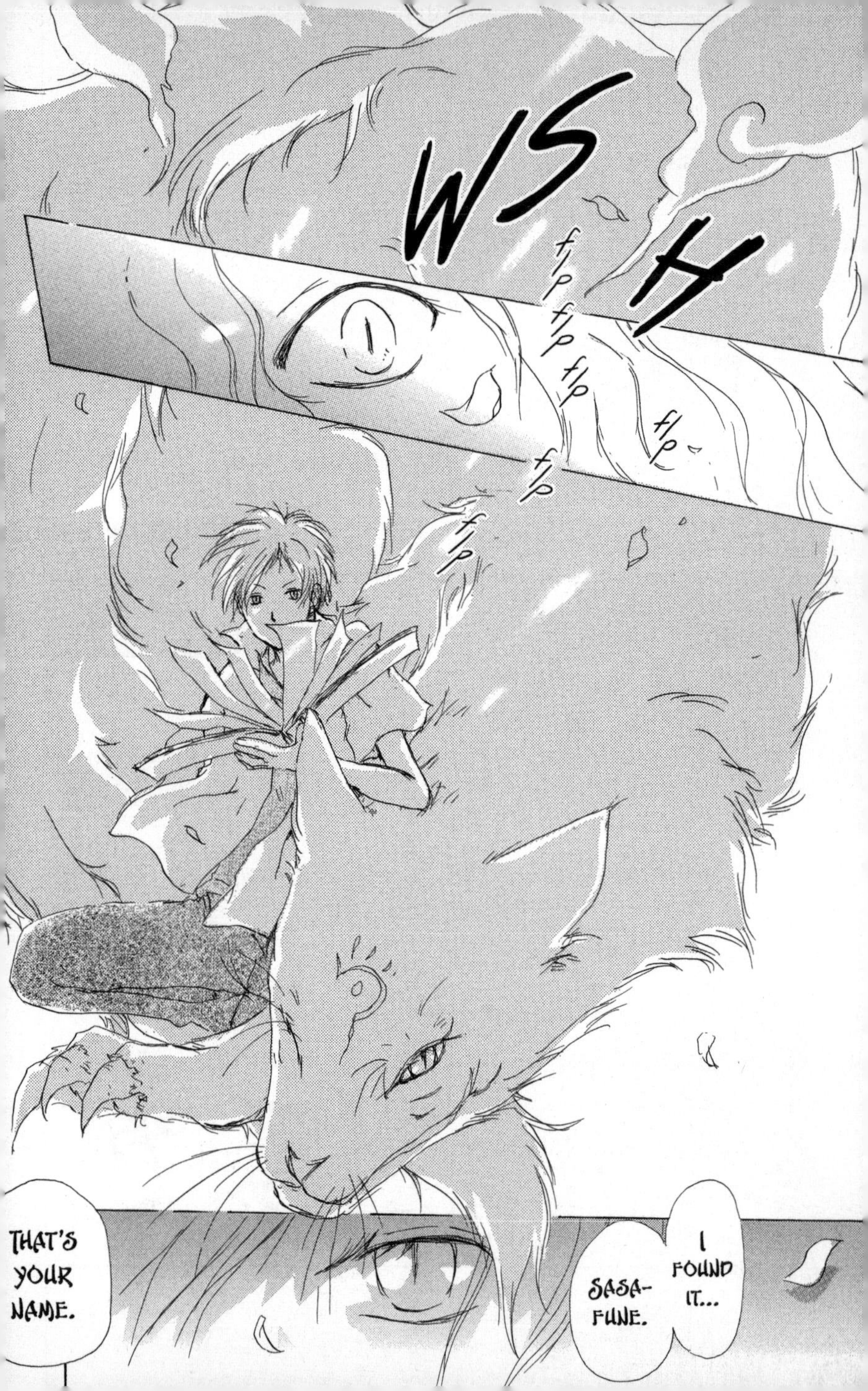
WSH
flip flip flip flip
flip
flip
flip
I FOUND IT...
SASA-FUNE.
THAT'S YOUR NAME.

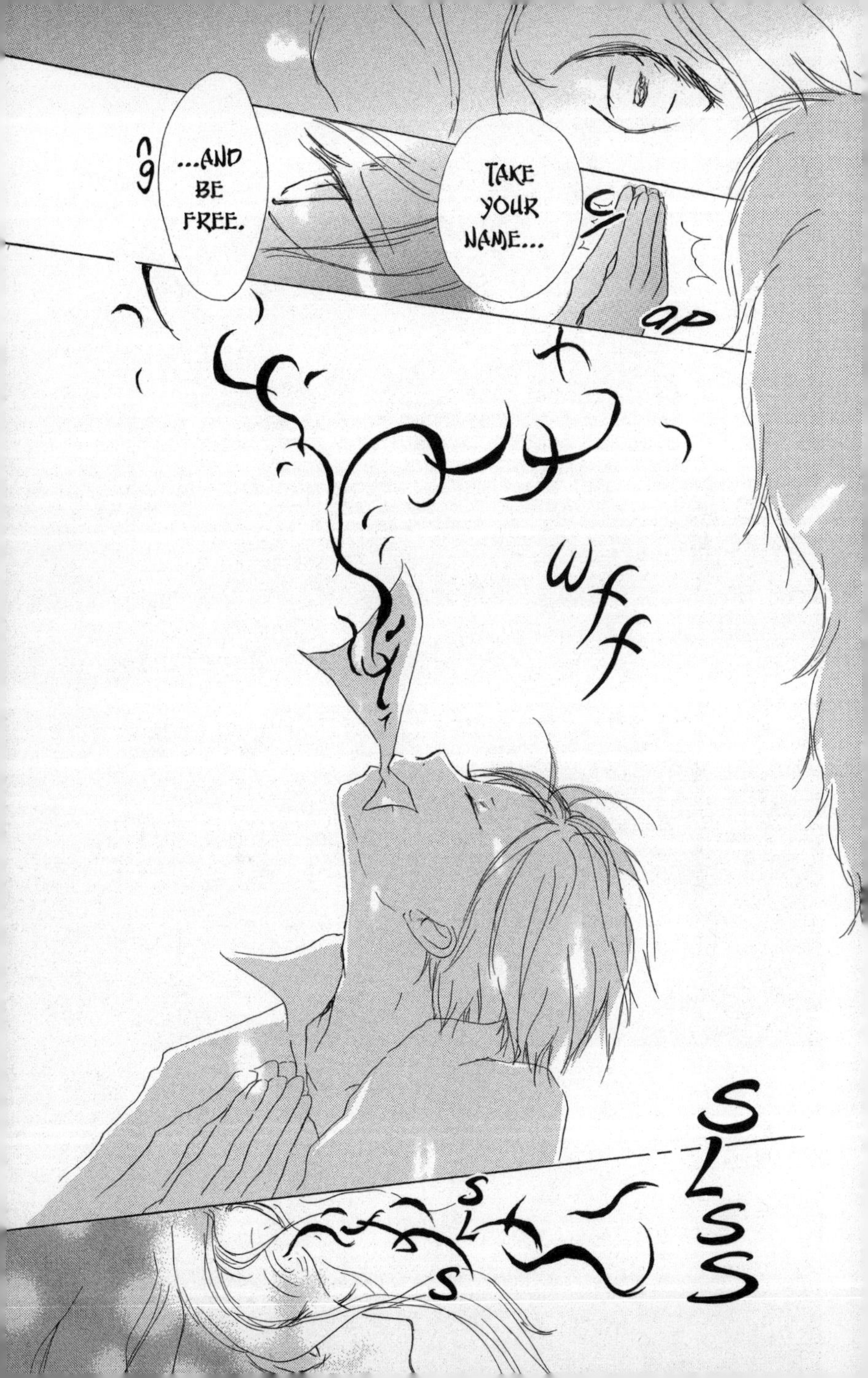
TAKE YOUR NAME...
...AND BE FREE.
SLSS
SLSS

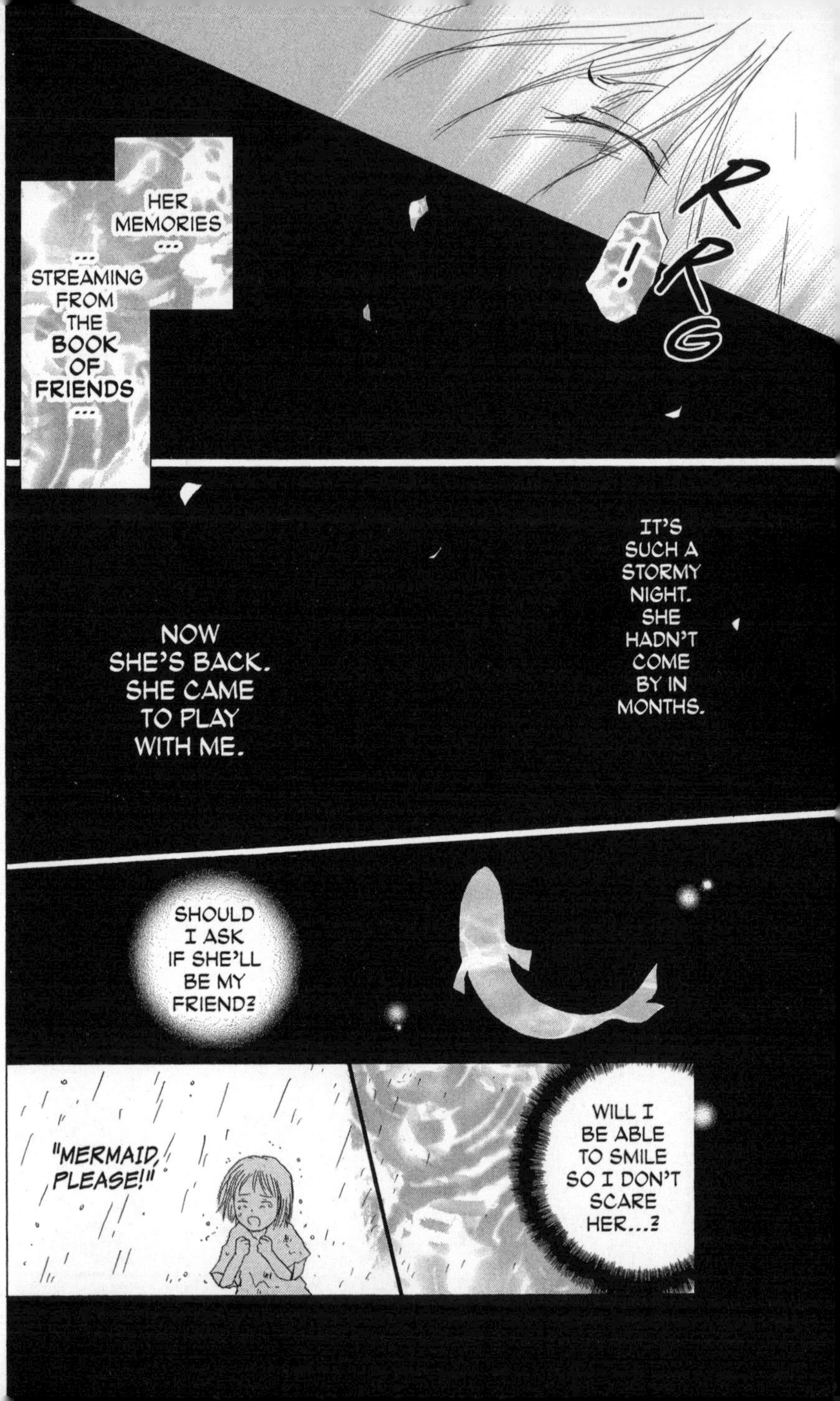
RRG
!
HER MEMORIES... ...STREAMING FROM THE BOOK OF FRIENDS...
IT'S SUCH A STORMY NIGHT. SHE HADN'T COME BY IN MONTHS.
NOW SHE'S BACK. SHE CAME TO PLAY WITH ME.
SHOULD I ASK IF SHE'LL BE MY FRIEND?
WILL I BE ABLE TO SMILE SO I DON'T SCARE HER...?
"MERMAID, PLEASE!"

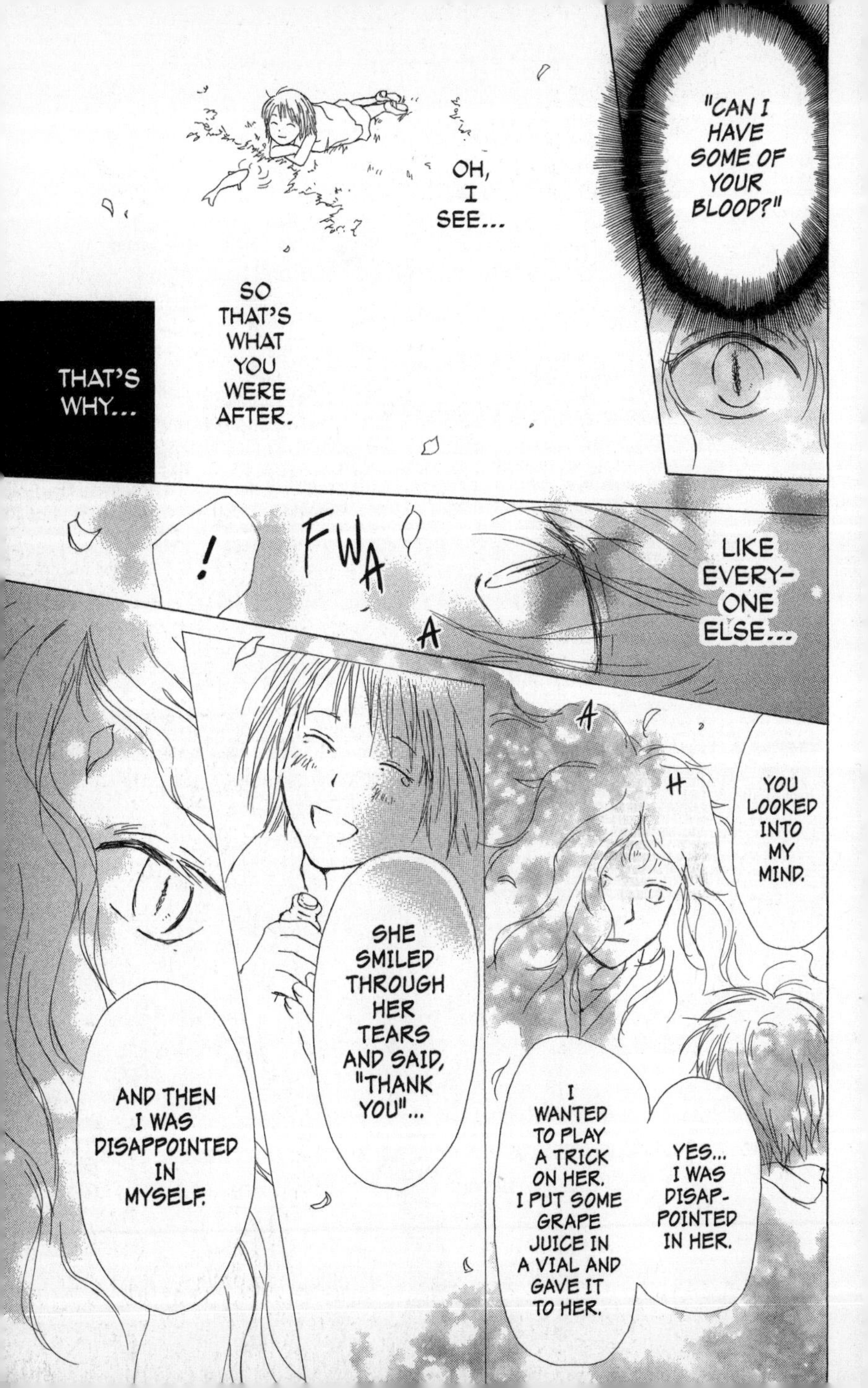
"CAN I HAVE SOME OF YOUR BLOOD?"
OH, I SEE...
SO THAT'S WHAT YOU WERE AFTER.
THAT'S WHY...
LIKE EVERY-ONE ELSE...
!
FWAAAH
YOU LOOKED INTO MY MIND.
YES... I WAS DISAP-POINTED IN HER.
I WANTED TO PLAY A TRICK ON HER. I PUT SOME GRAPE JUICE IN A VIAL AND GAVE IT TO HER.
SHE SMILED THROUGH HER TEARS AND SAID, "THANK YOU"...
AND THEN I WAS DISAPPOINTED IN MYSELF.

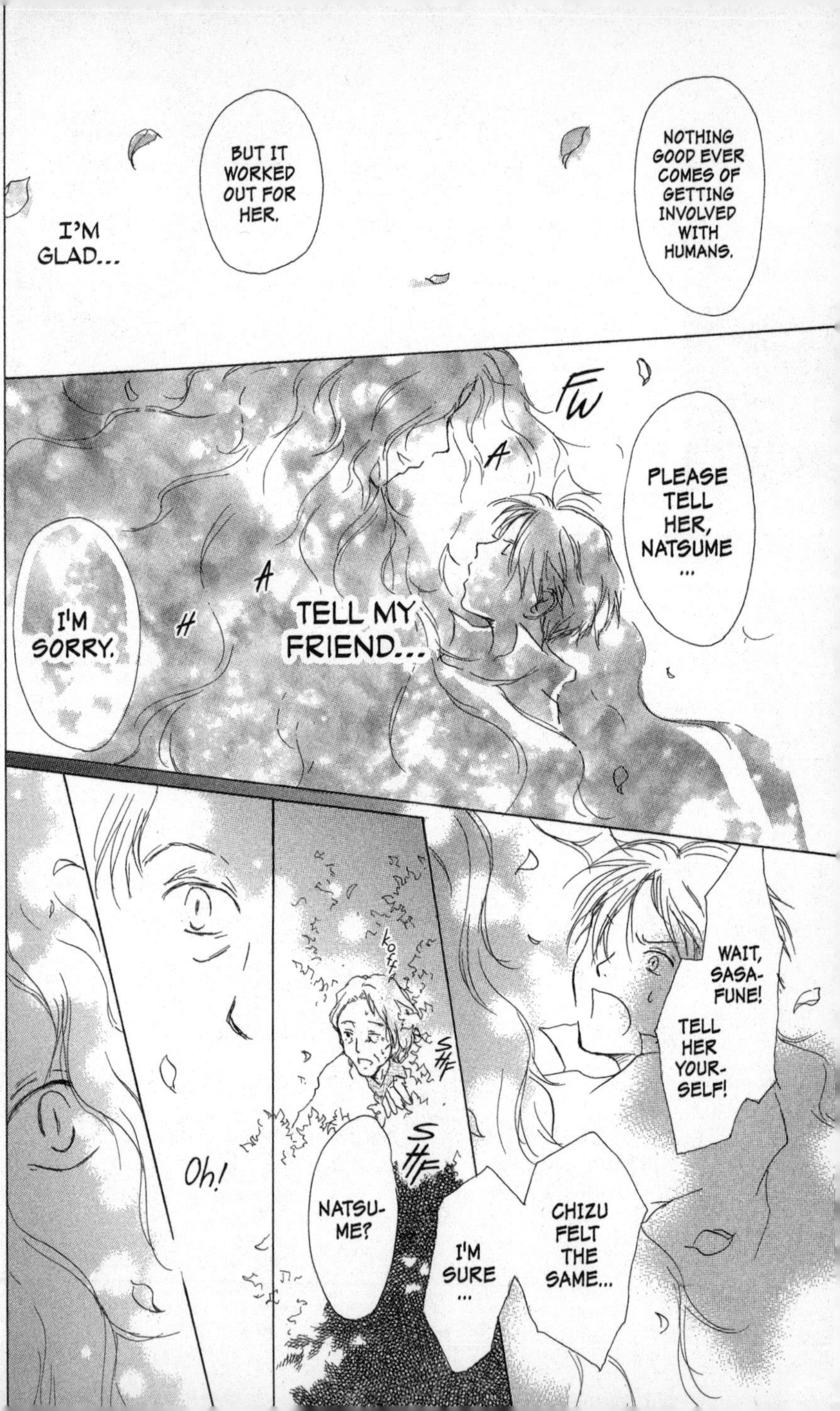
NOTHING GOOD EVER COMES OF GETTING INVOLVED WITH HUMANS.
BUT IT WORKED OUT FOR HER.
I'M GLAD...
FW
PLEASE TELL HER, NATSUME ...
A
A
H
TELL MY FRIEND...
I'M SORRY.
WAIT, SASA-FUNE!
TELL HER YOUR-SELF!
CHIZU FELT THE SAME...
I'M SURE ...
koff
SHF
SHF
NATSU-ME?
Oh!

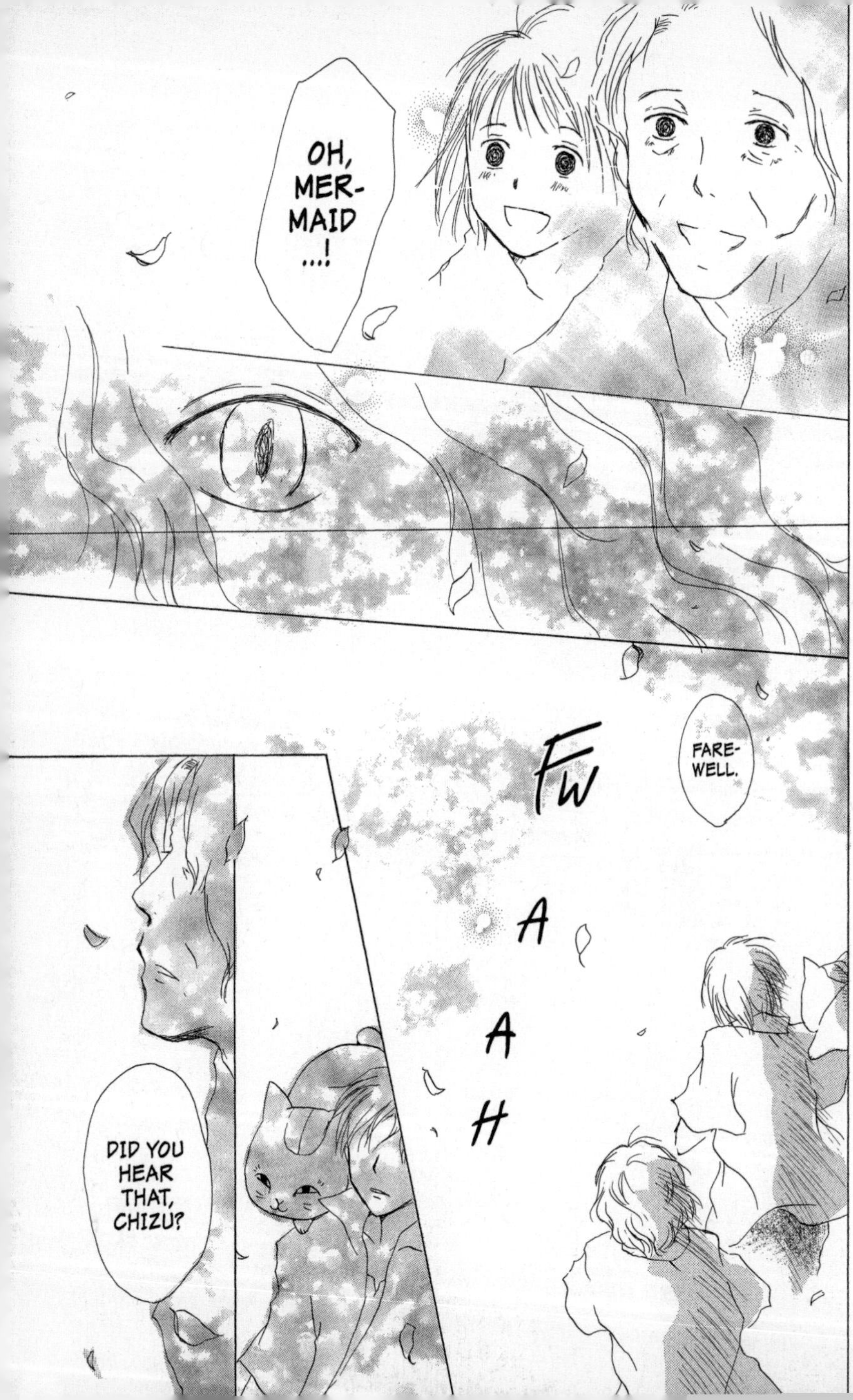
OH, MER-MAID ...!
FARE-WELL.
FWAAH
DID YOU HEAR THAT, CHIZU?

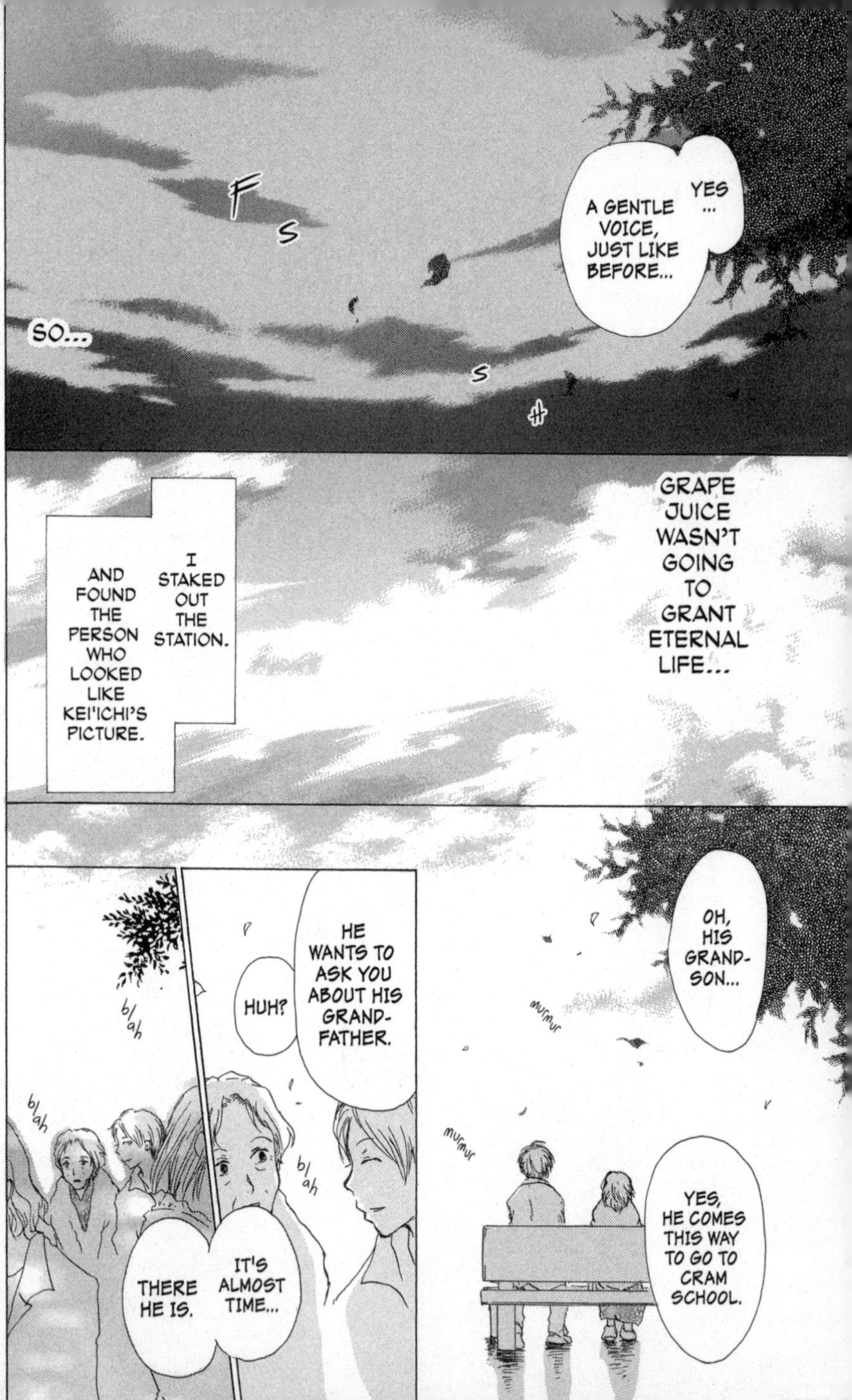
YES...
A GENTLE VOICE, JUST LIKE BEFORE...
FSSH
SO...
GRAPE JUICE WASN'T GOING TO GRANT ETERNAL LIFE...
I STAKED OUT THE STATION.
AND FOUND THE PERSON WHO LOOKED LIKE KEI'ICHI'S PICTURE.
OH, HIS GRANDSON...
murmur
YES, HE COMES THIS WAY TO GO TO CRAM SCHOOL.
murmur
HE WANTS TO ASK YOU ABOUT HIS GRANDFATHER.
HUH?
blah
blah
blah
IT'S ALMOST TIME...
THERE HE IS.

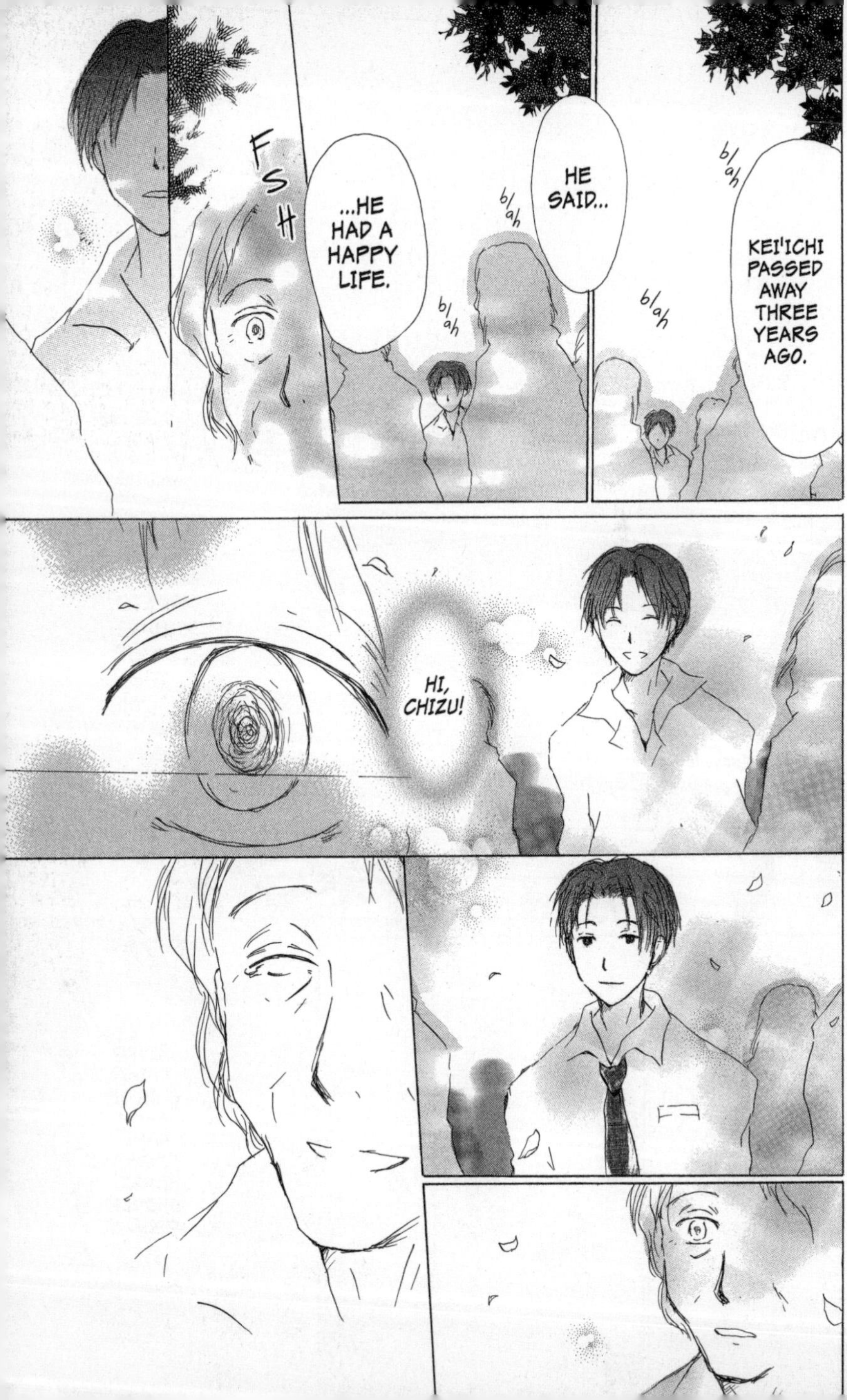
blah
KEI'ICHI PASSED AWAY THREE YEARS AGO.
blah
blah
HE SAID...
...HE HAD A HAPPY LIFE.
blah
FSH
HI, CHIZU!

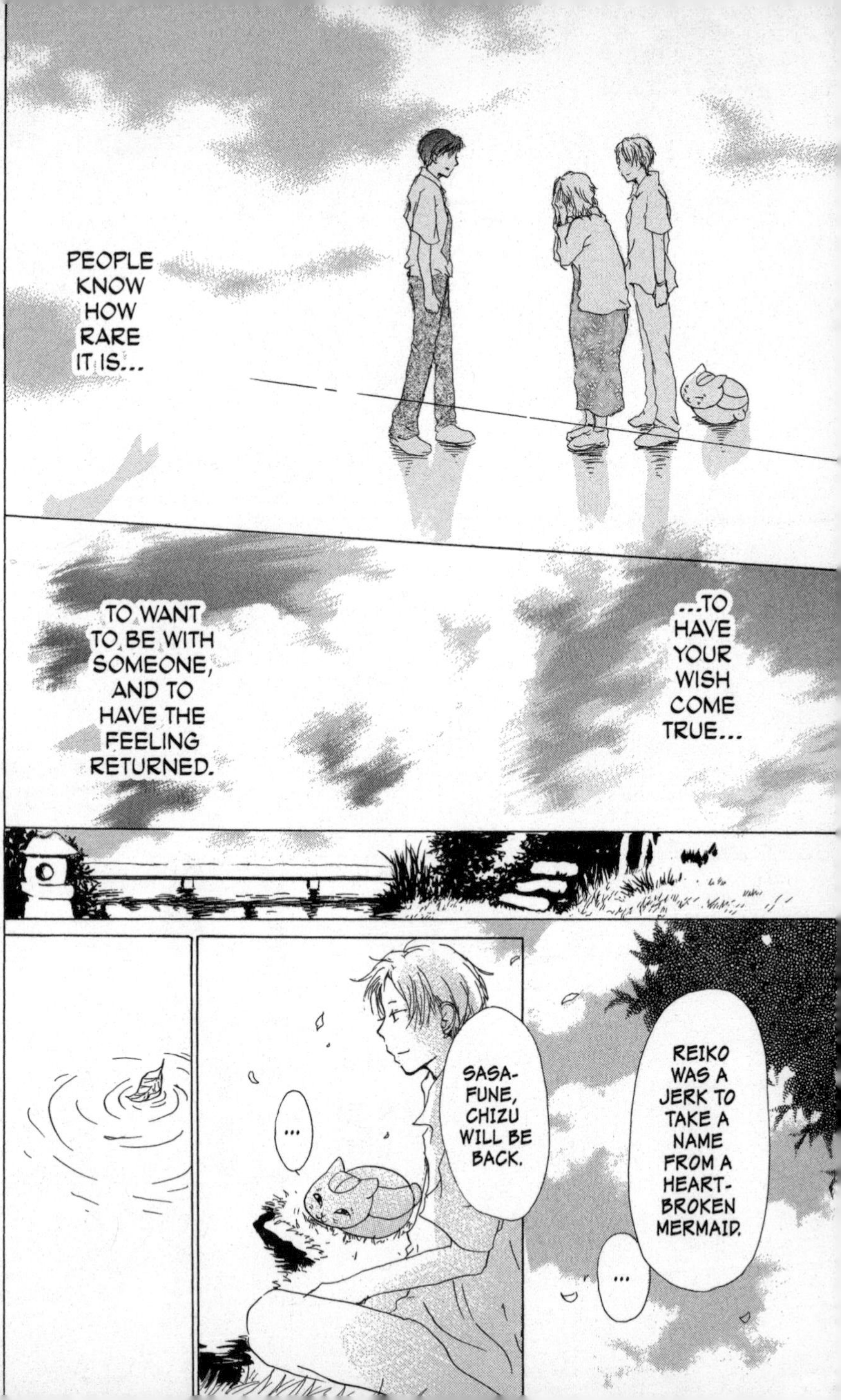
PEOPLE KNOW HOW RARE IT IS...
...TO HAVE YOUR WISH COME TRUE...
TO WANT TO BE WITH SOMEONE, AND TO HAVE THE FEELING RETURNED.
REIKO WAS A JERK TO TAKE A NAME FROM A HEART-BROKEN MERMAID.
...
SASA-FUNE, CHIZU WILL BE BACK.
...

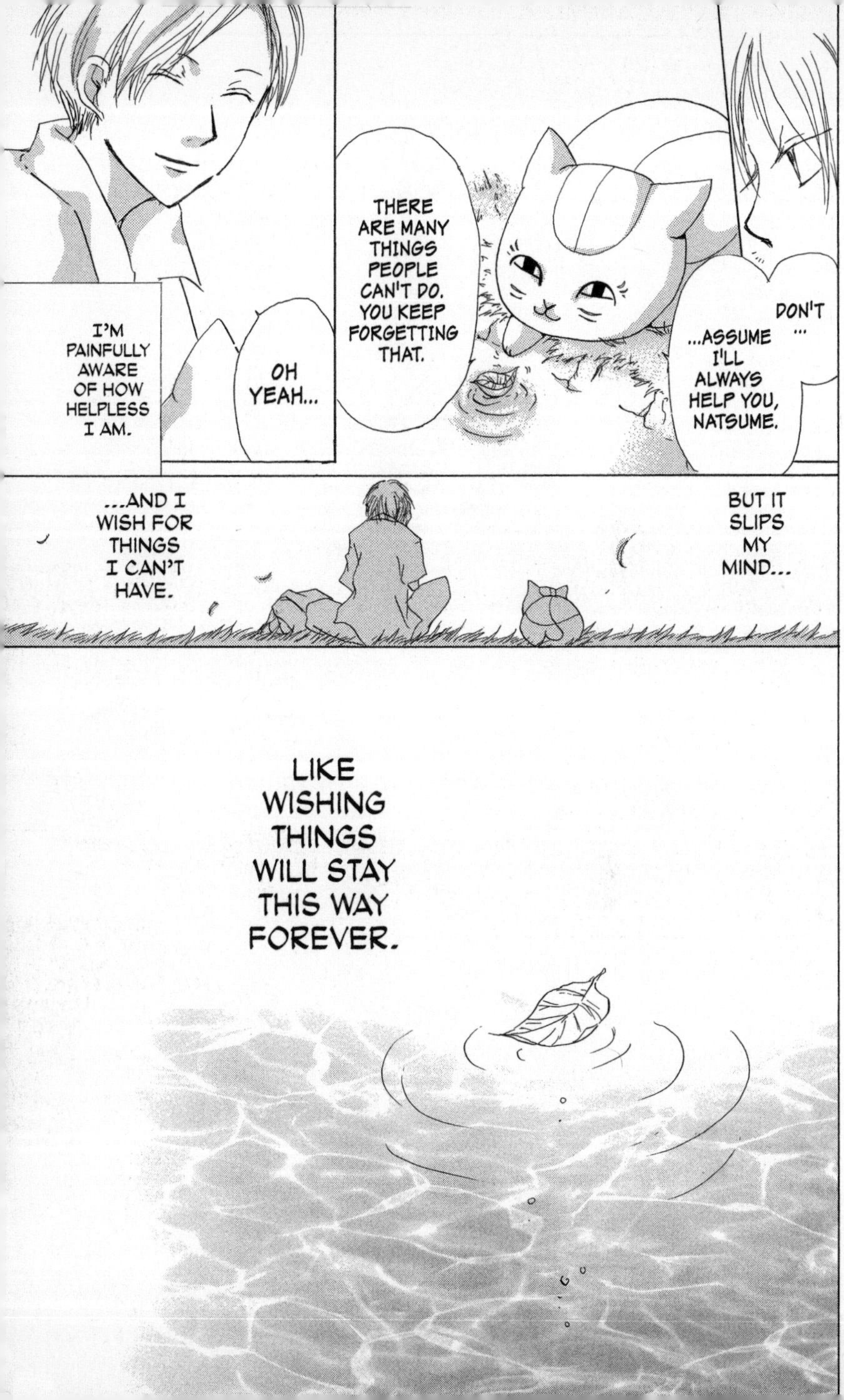
DON'T ...
...ASSUME I'LL ALWAYS HELP YOU, NATSUME.
THERE ARE MANY THINGS PEOPLE CAN'T DO. YOU KEEP FORGETTING THAT.
OH YEAH...
I'M PAINFULLY AWARE OF HOW HELPLESS I AM.
BUT IT SLIPS MY MIND...
...AND I WISH FOR THINGS I CAN'T HAVE.
LIKE WISHING THINGS WILL STAY THIS WAY FOREVER.

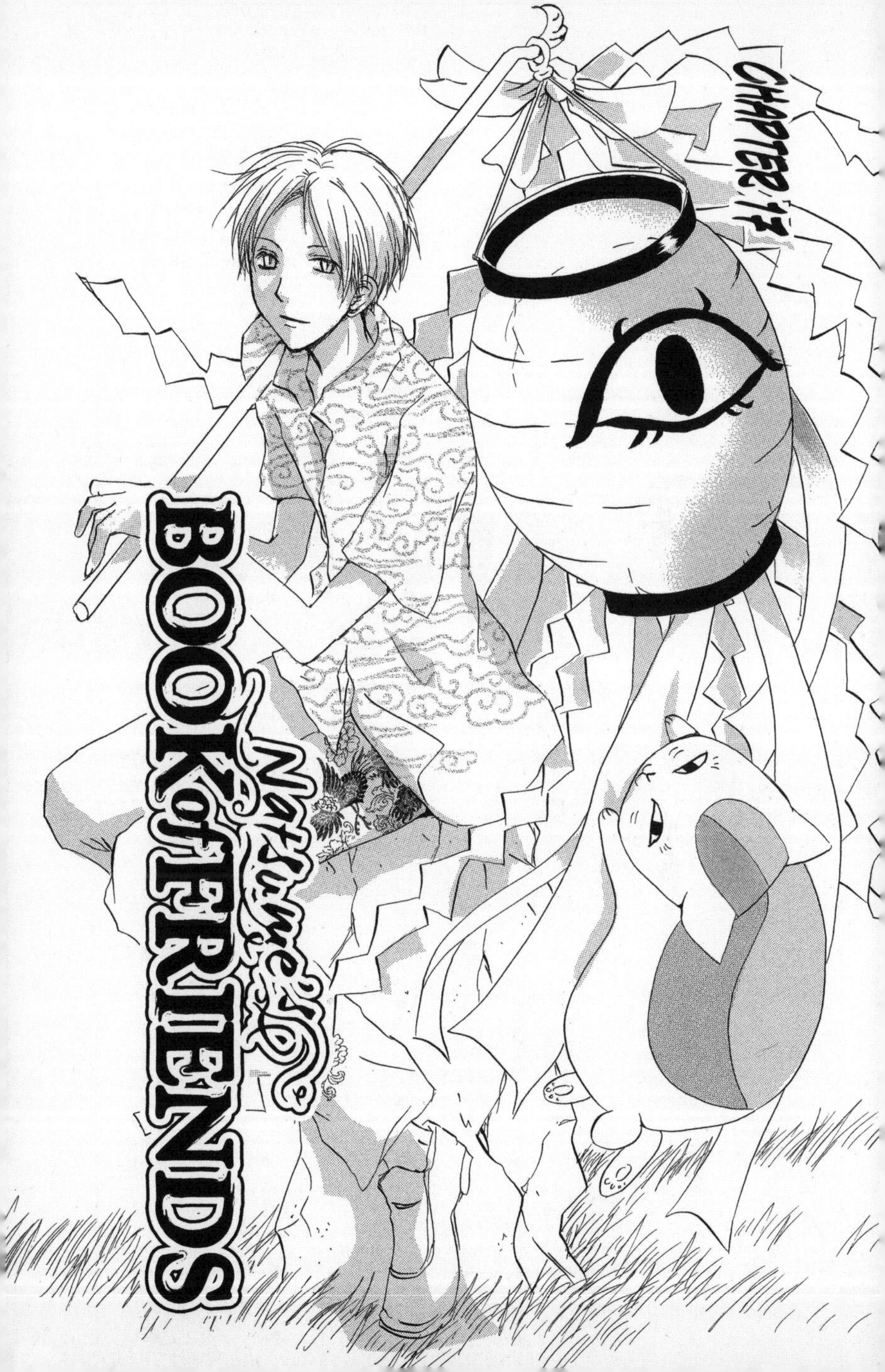
CHAPTER 17
Natsume's
BOOK of FRIENDS

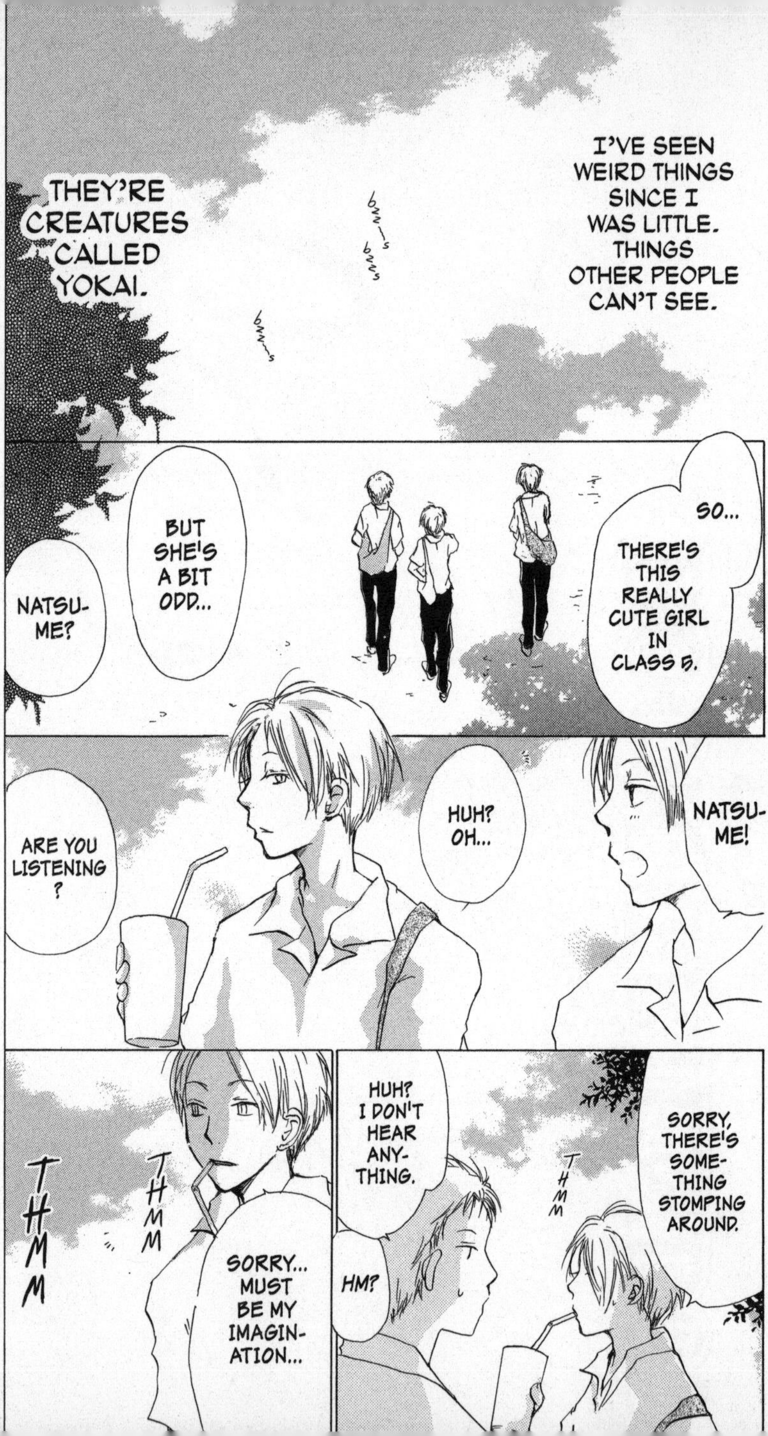
I'VE SEEN WEIRD THINGS SINCE I WAS LITTLE. THINGS OTHER PEOPLE CAN'T SEE.
bzzs
bzzs
bzzs
THEY'RE CREATURES CALLED YOKAI.
SO...
THERE'S THIS REALLY CUTE GIRL IN CLASS 5.
BUT SHE'S A BIT ODD...
NATSUME?
NATSUME!
HUH? OH...
ARE YOU LISTENING?
SORRY, THERE'S SOMETHING STOMPING AROUND.
THMM
HUH? I DON'T HEAR ANYTHING.
HM?
THMM
THMM
SORRY... MUST BE MY IMAGINATION...

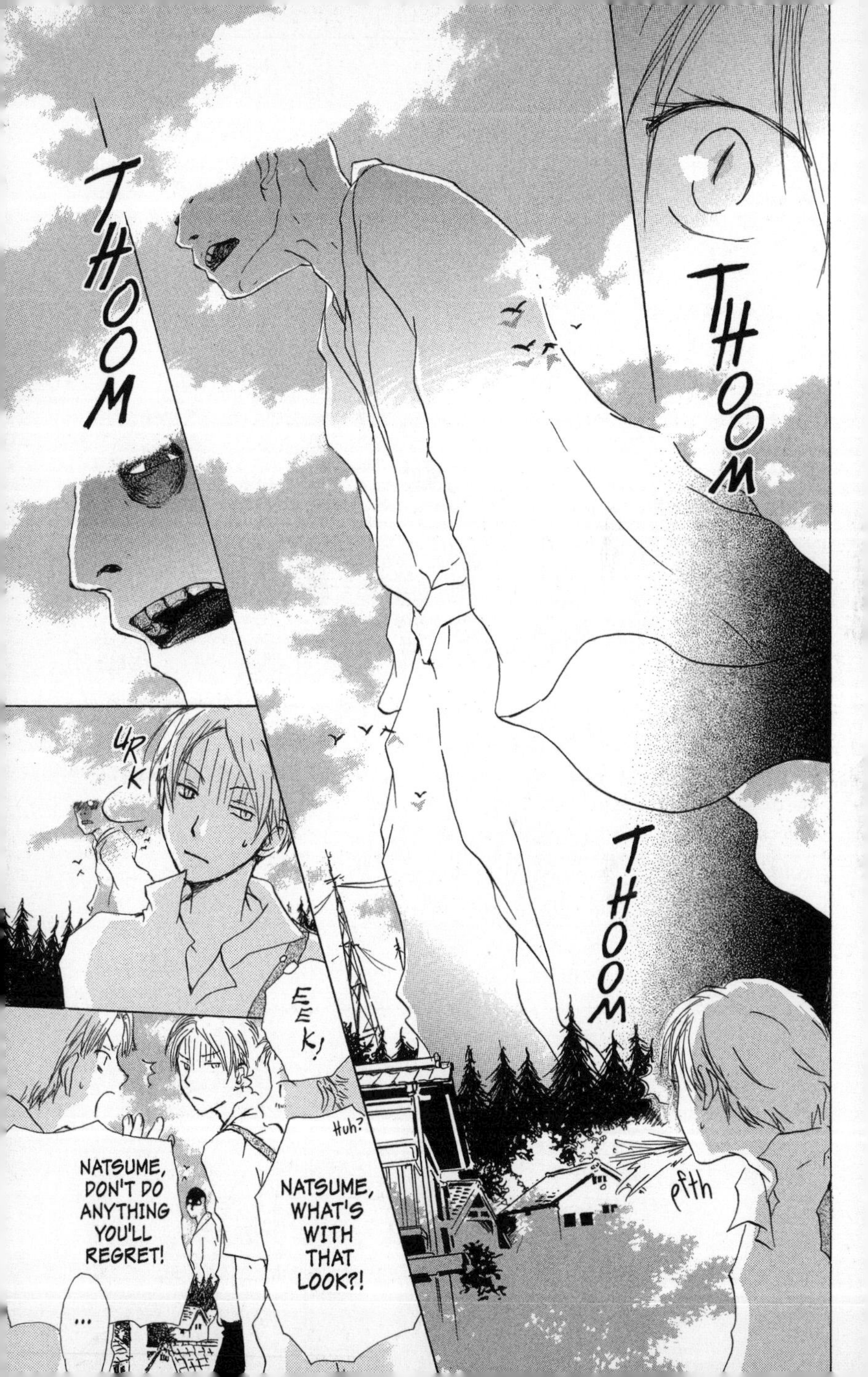
THOOM
THOOM
pfth
THOOM
URK
EEK!
Huh?
NATSUME, WHAT'S WITH THAT LOOK?!
NATSUME, DON'T DO ANYTHING YOU'LL REGRET!
...

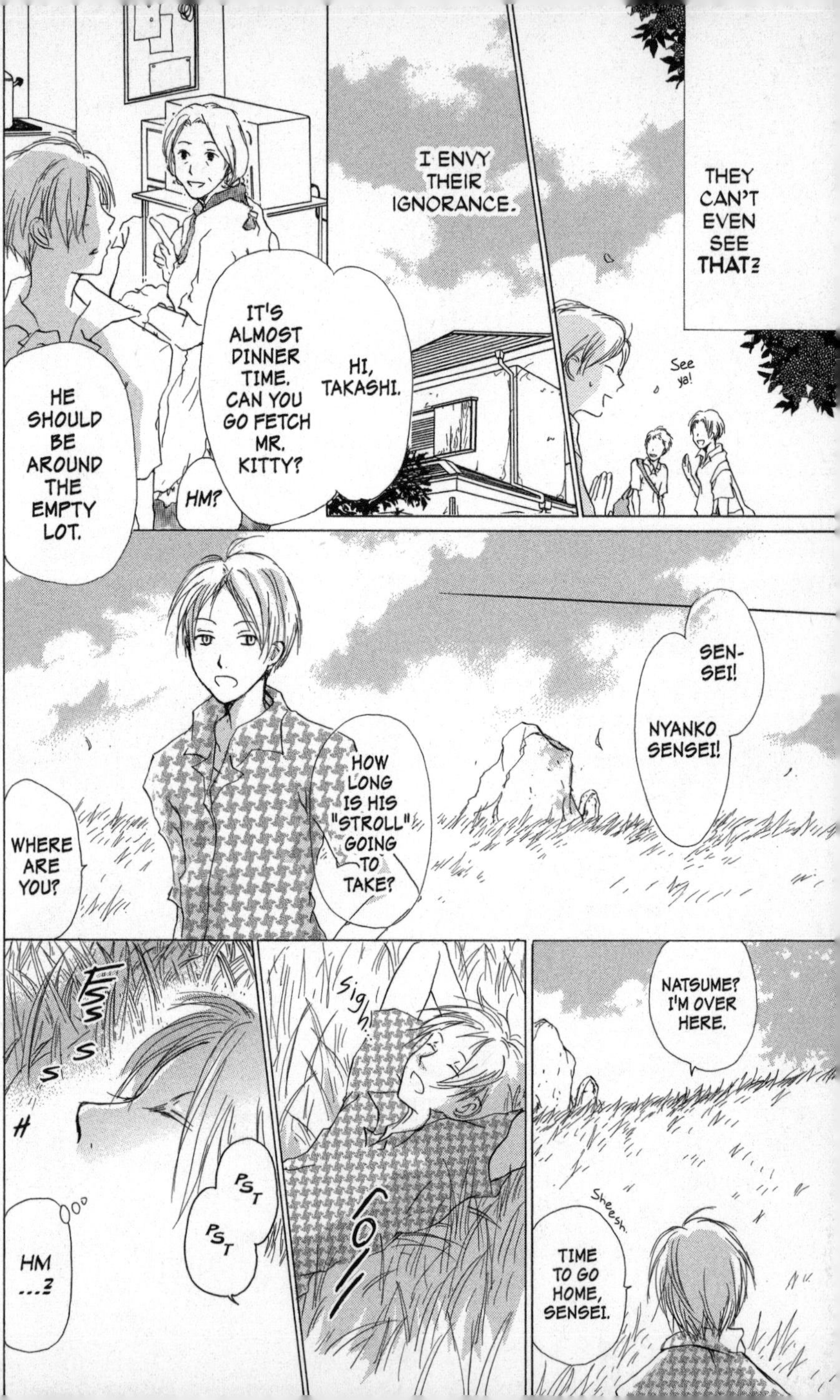
THEY CAN'T EVEN SEE THAT?
See ya!
I ENVY THEIR IGNORANCE.
HI, TAKASHI.
IT'S ALMOST DINNER TIME. CAN YOU GO FETCH MR. KITTY?
HM?
HE SHOULD BE AROUND THE EMPTY LOT.
SEN-SEI!
NYANKO SENSEI!
HOW LONG IS HIS "STROLL" GOING TO TAKE?
WHERE ARE YOU?
NATSUME? I'M OVER HERE.
Sheesh.
TIME TO GO HOME, SENSEI.
Sigh...
PST
PST
FSSSH
HM...?

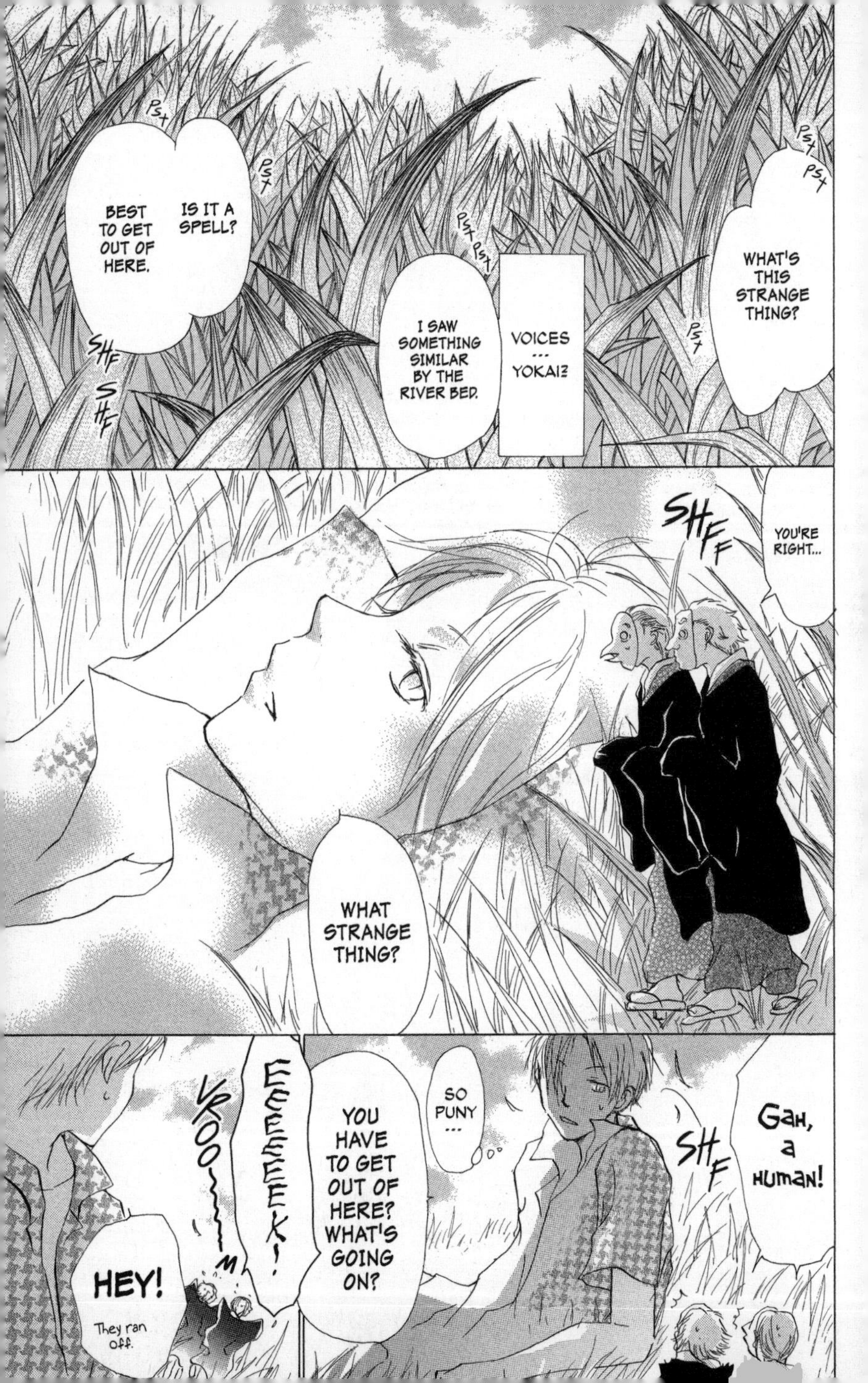
Pst
Pst
WHAT'S THIS STRANGE THING?
Pst
VOICES ... YOKAI?
Pst Pst
I SAW SOMETHING SIMILAR BY THE RIVER BED.
Pst
IS IT A SPELL?
Pst
BEST TO GET OUT OF HERE.
SHF
SHF
YOU'RE RIGHT...
SHFF
WHAT STRANGE THING?
Gah, a human!
SHF
SO PUNY ...
YOU HAVE TO GET OUT OF HERE? WHAT'S GOING ON?
EEEEEEK!
VROO~~~M
HEY!
They ran off.

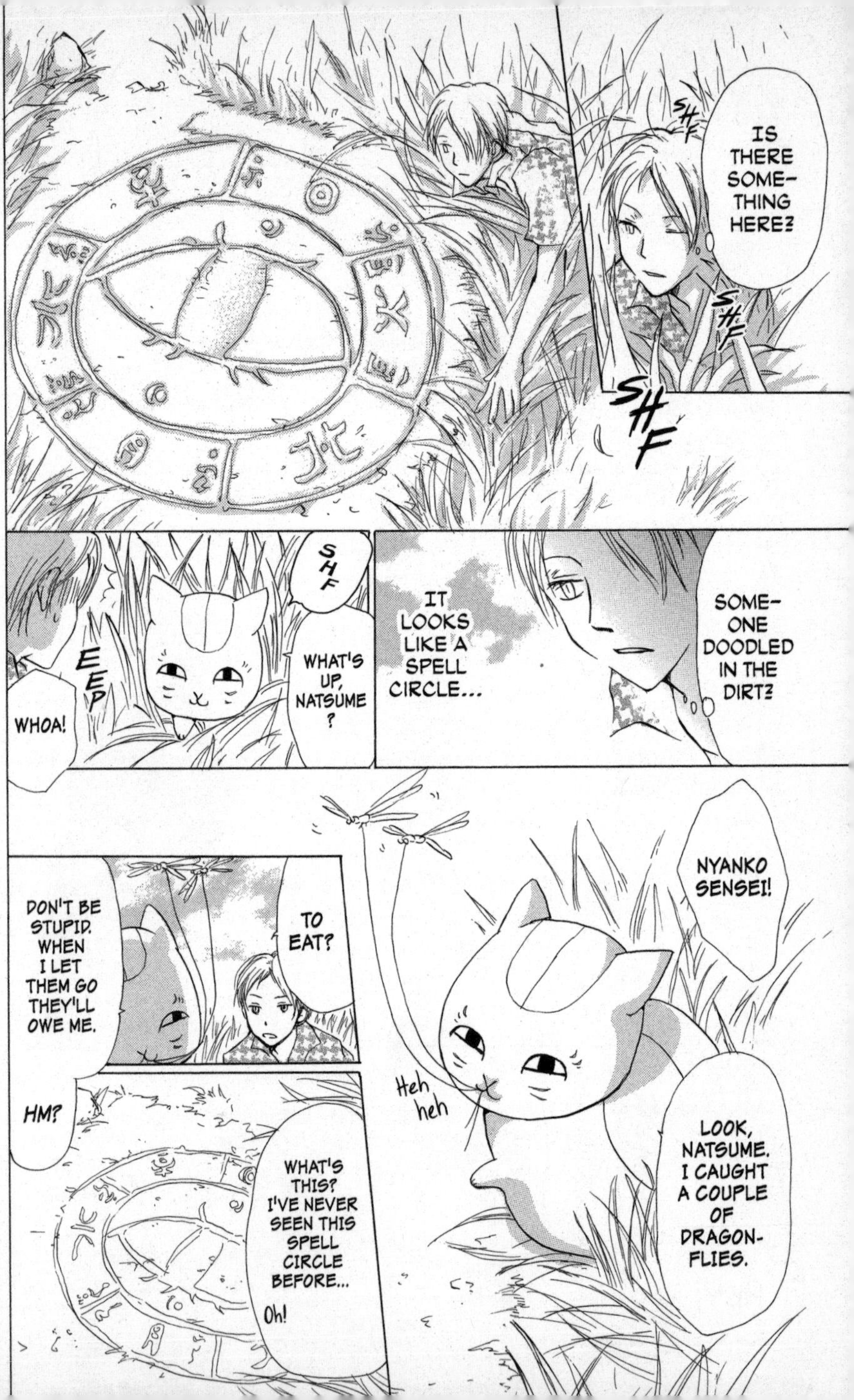

SHF
IS THERE SOMETHING HERE?
SHF
SHF
SOMEONE DOODLED IN THE DIRT?
IT LOOKS LIKE A SPELL CIRCLE...
SHF
WHAT'S UP, NATSUME?
EEP
WHOA!
NYANKO SENSEI!
LOOK, NATSUME. I CAUGHT A COUPLE OF DRAGONFLIES.
Heh heh
TO EAT?
DON'T BE STUPID. WHEN I LET THEM GO THEY'LL OWE ME.
HM?
WHAT'S THIS? I'VE NEVER SEEN THIS SPELL CIRCLE BEFORE...
Oh!

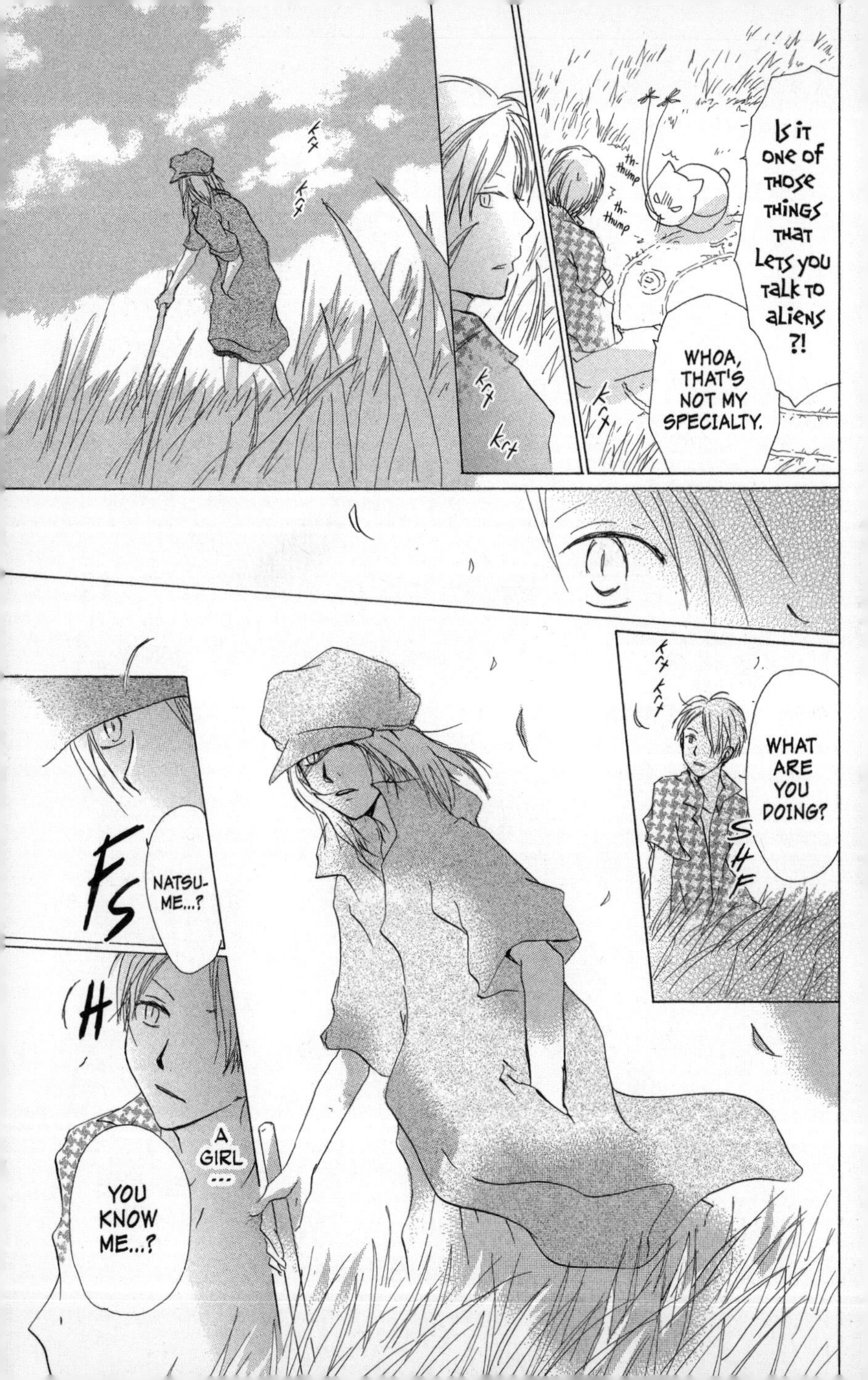
Is it one of those things that Lets you talk to aliens?!
th-thump
th-thump
krt
WHOA, THAT'S NOT MY SPECIALTY.
krt krt
krt krt
krt krt
WHAT ARE YOU DOING?
SHF
NATSU-ME...?
FS
H
A GIRL ...
YOU KNOW ME...?

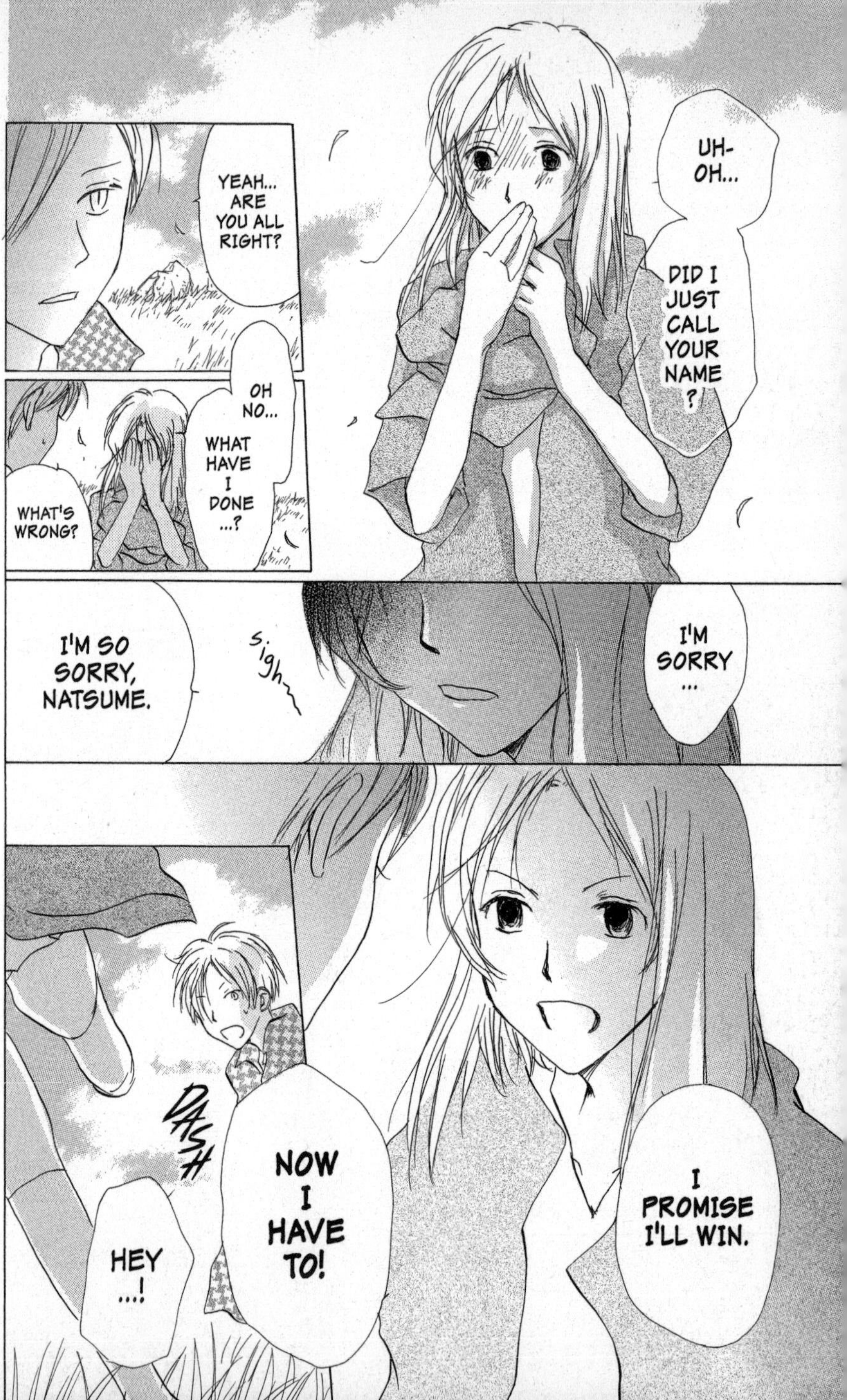
UH-OH...
DID I JUST CALL YOUR NAME?
YEAH... ARE YOU ALL RIGHT?
OH NO...
WHAT HAVE I DONE...?
WHAT'S WRONG?
I'M SORRY...
sigh
I'M SO SORRY, NATSUME.
I PROMISE I'LL WIN.
NOW I HAVE TO!
DASH
HEY...!

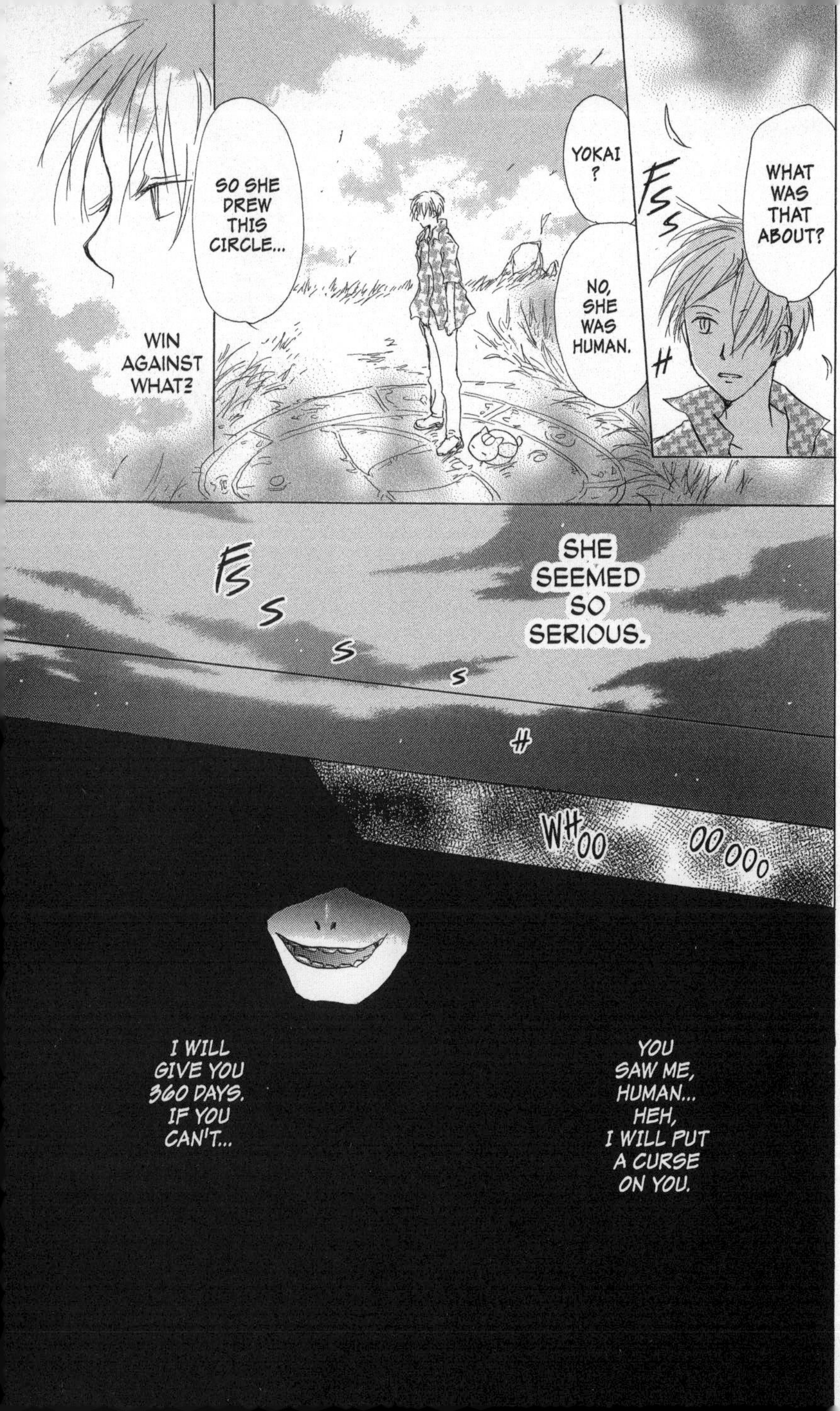
WHAT WAS THAT ABOUT?
FSS
H
YOKAI?
NO, SHE WAS HUMAN.
SO SHE DREW THIS CIRCLE...
WIN AGAINST WHAT?
SHE SEEMED SO SERIOUS.
FSSSSH
WHOOOOOOO
YOU SAW ME, HUMAN... HEH, I WILL PUT A CURSE ON YOU.
I WILL GIVE YOU 360 DAYS. IF YOU CAN'T...

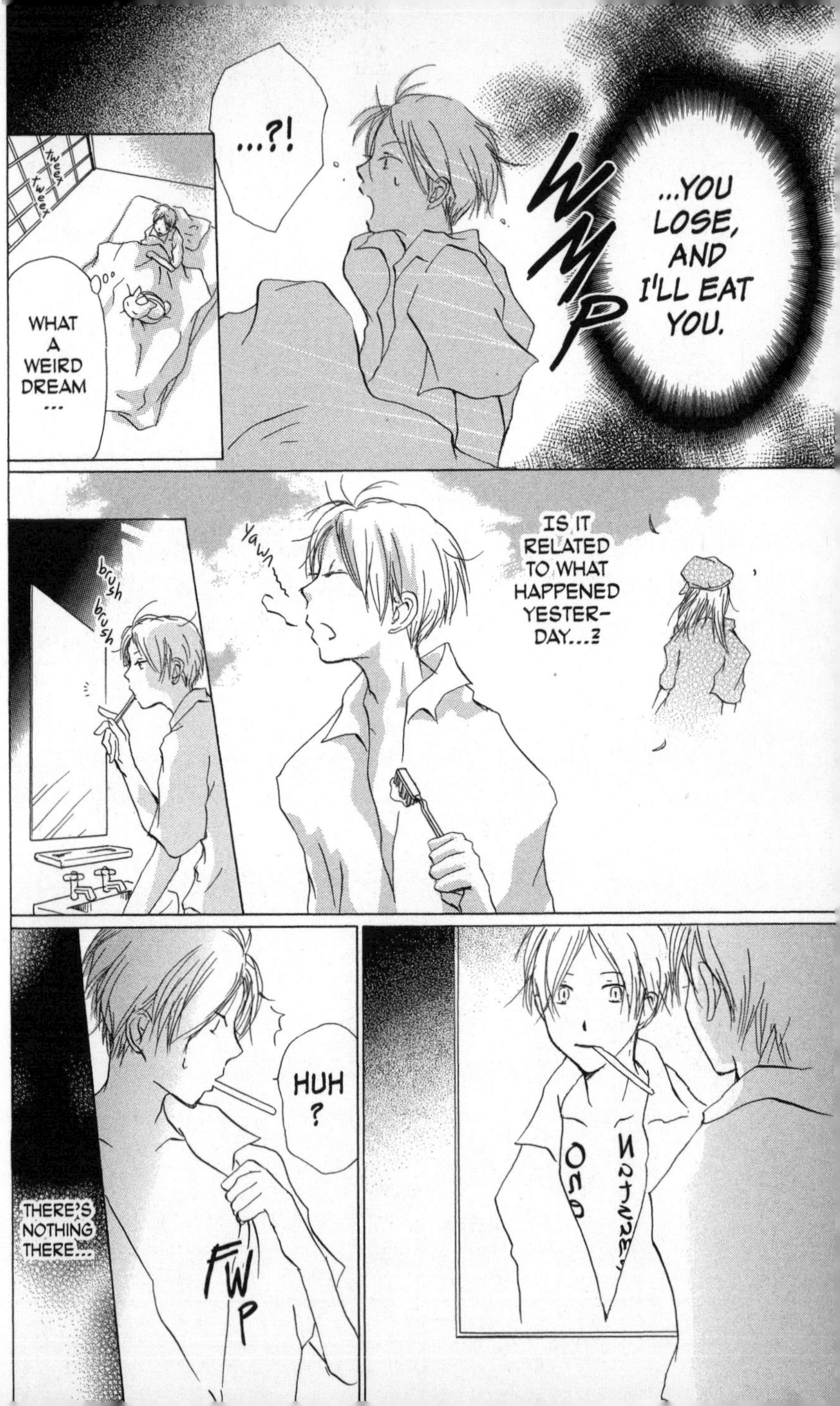
...YOU LOSE, AND I'LL EAT YOU.
WMP
...?!
tweet tweet
WHAT A WEIRD DREAM...
IS IT RELATED TO WHAT HAPPENED YESTER-DAY...?
Yawn
brush brush
HUH?
THERE'S NOTHING THERE...
FWP

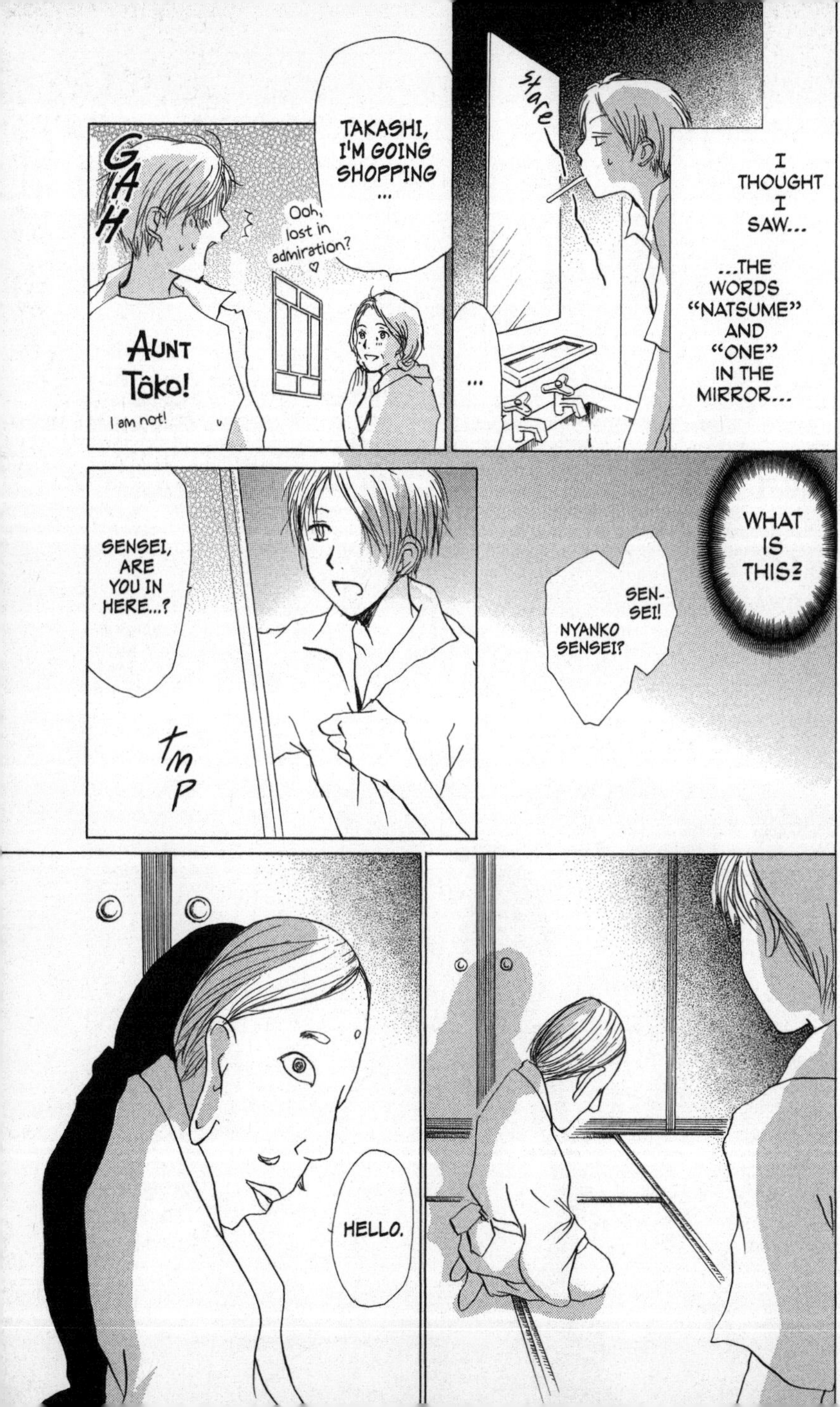
stare
...
I THOUGHT I SAW...
...THE WORDS "NATSUME" AND "ONE" IN THE MIRROR...
TAKASHI, I'M GOING SHOPPING ...
Ooh, lost in admiration? ♡
GAH
AUNT TÔKO!
I am not!
WHAT IS THIS?
SEN-SEI!
NYANKO SENSEI?
SENSEI, ARE YOU IN HERE...?
tmp
HELLO.

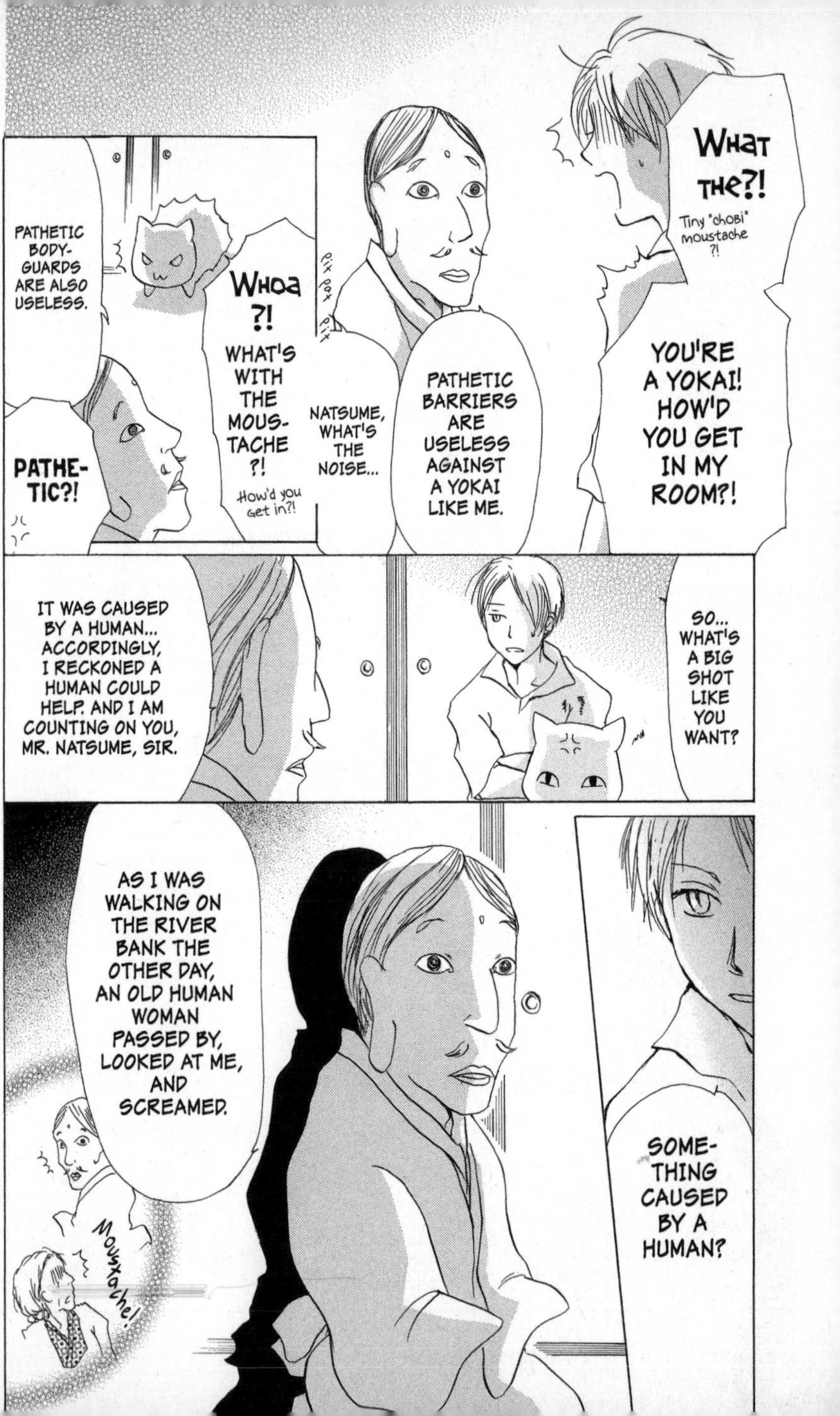
WHAT THE?!
Tiny "chobi" moustache ?!
YOU'RE A YOKAI! HOW'D YOU GET IN MY ROOM?!
PATHETIC BARRIERS ARE USELESS AGAINST A YOKAI LIKE ME.
pit pat pit
NATSUME, WHAT'S THE NOISE...
WHOA ?!
WHAT'S WITH THE MOUS-TACHE ?!
How'd you get in?!
PATHETIC BODY-GUARDS ARE ALSO USELESS.
PATHE-TIC?!
SO... WHAT'S A BIG SHOT LIKE YOU WANT?
IT WAS CAUSED BY A HUMAN... ACCORDINGLY, I RECKONED A HUMAN COULD HELP. AND I AM COUNTING ON YOU, MR. NATSUME, SIR.
SOME-THING CAUSED BY A HUMAN?
AS I WAS WALKING ON THE RIVER BANK THE OTHER DAY, AN OLD HUMAN WOMAN PASSED BY, LOOKED AT ME, AND SCREAMED.
Moustache!

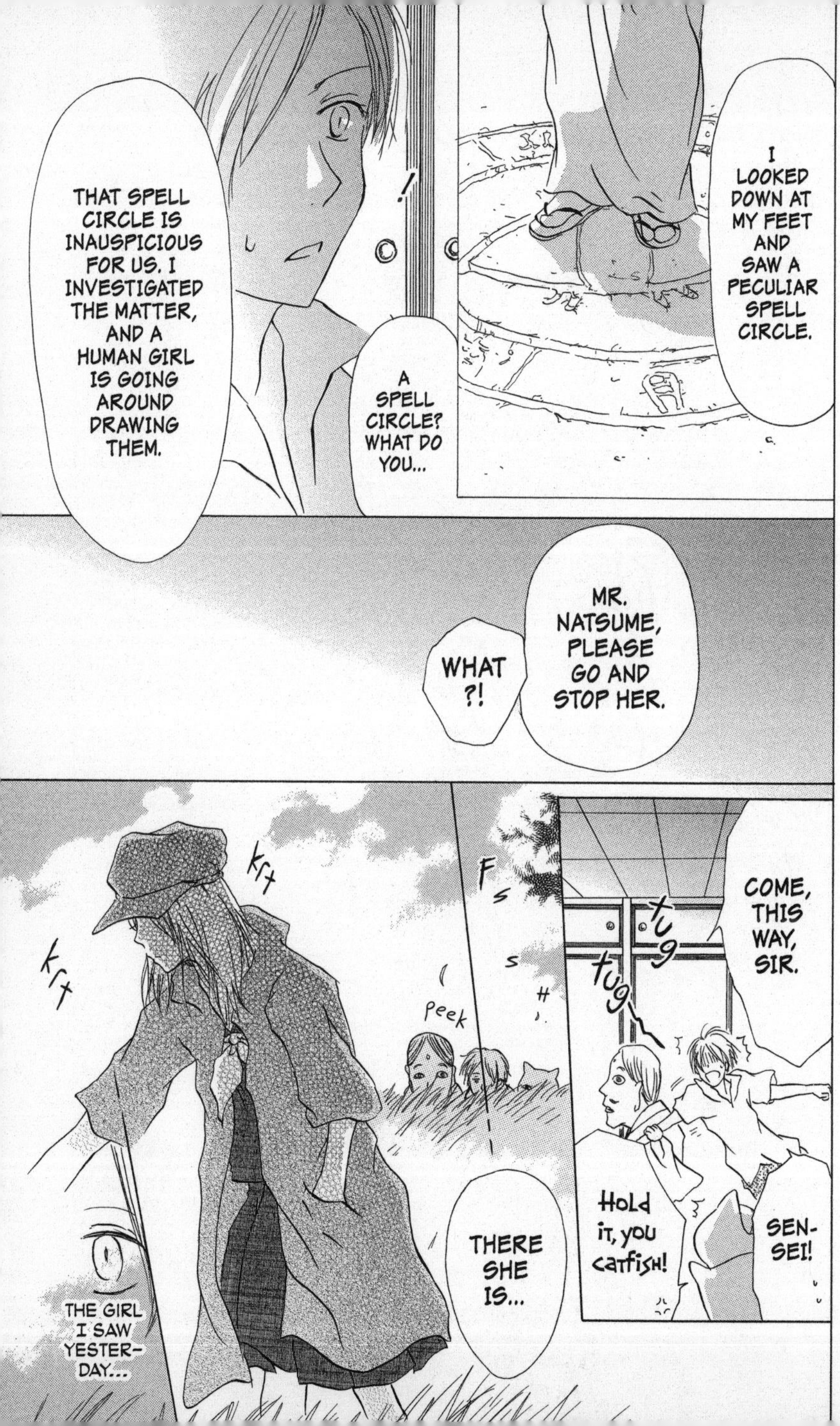
I LOOKED DOWN AT MY FEET AND SAW A PECULIAR SPELL CIRCLE.
A SPELL CIRCLE? WHAT DO YOU...
!
THAT SPELL CIRCLE IS INAUSPICIOUS FOR US. I INVESTIGATED THE MATTER, AND A HUMAN GIRL IS GOING AROUND DRAWING THEM.
MR. NATSUME, PLEASE GO AND STOP HER.
WHAT?!
COME, THIS WAY, SIR.
tug tug
SEN-SEI!
Hold it, you catfish!
FssH
peek
THERE SHE IS...
krt
krt
THE GIRL I SAW YESTER-DAY...

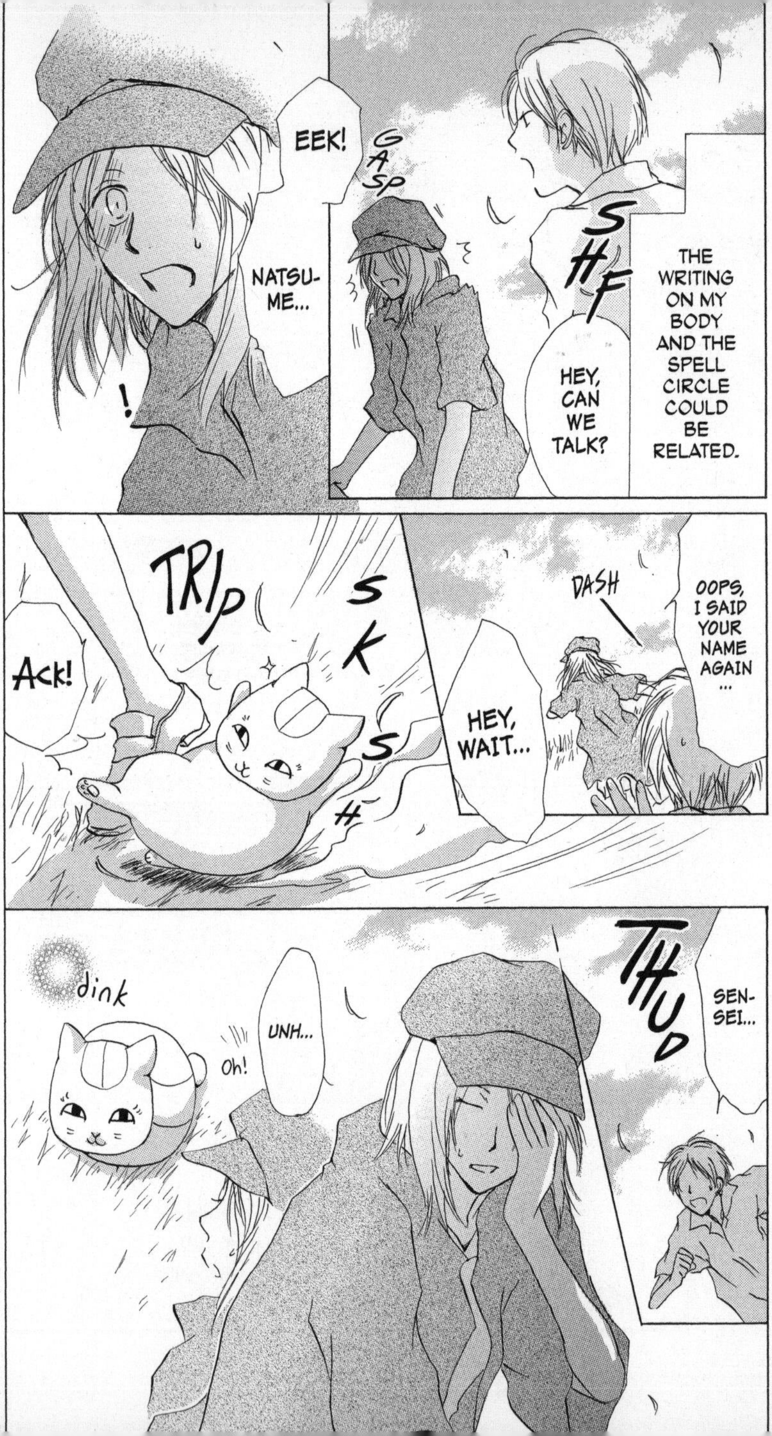
THE WRITING ON MY BODY AND THE SPELL CIRCLE COULD BE RELATED.
SHF
HEY, CAN WE TALK?
GASP
EEK!
NATSU-ME...
!
OOPS, I SAID YOUR NAME AGAIN...
DASH
HEY, WAIT...
SKSSH
TRIP
Ack!
THUD
SEN-SEI...
UNH...
Oh!
dink

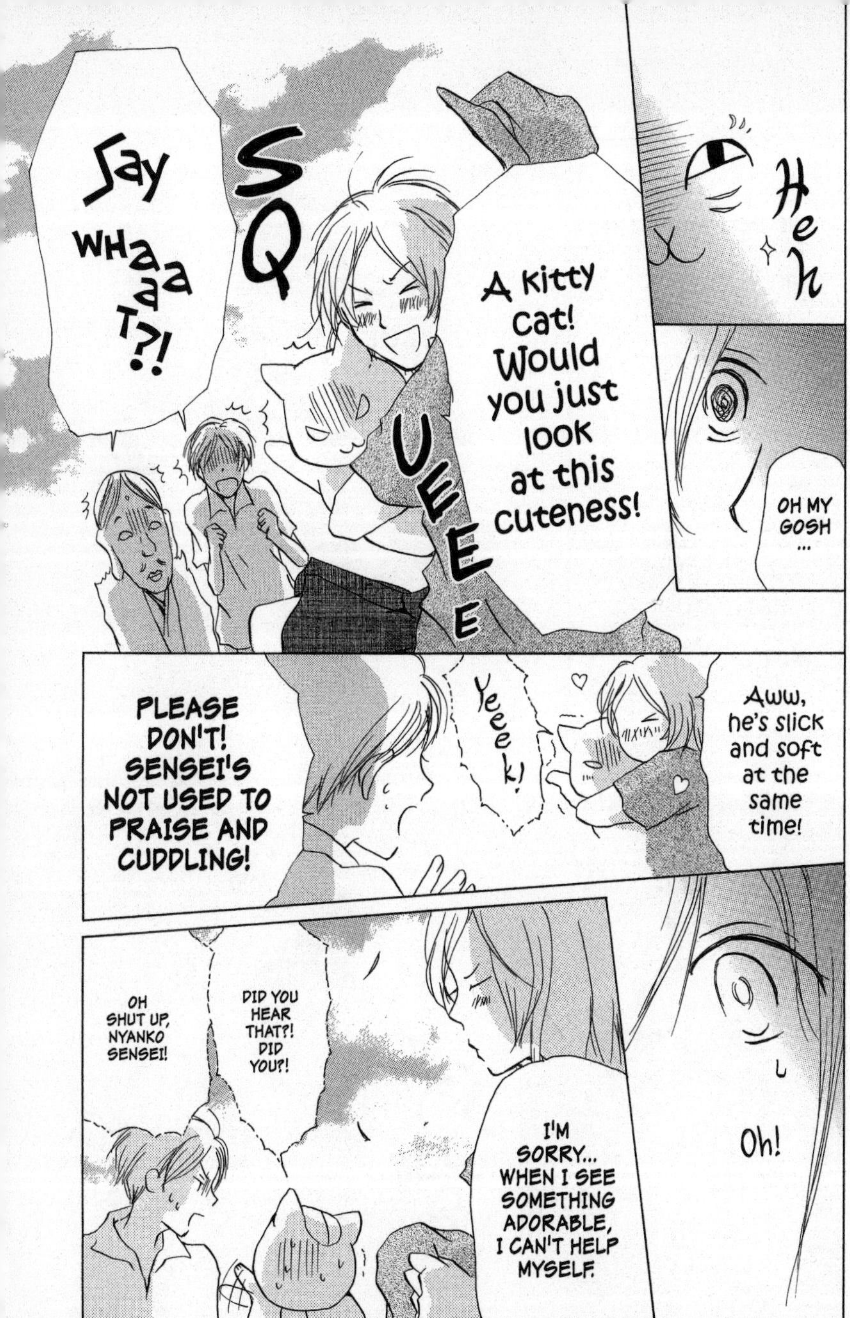
Heh
OH MY GOSH...
A kitty cat! Would you just look at this cuteness!
SQUEEEE
Say whaaaaT?!
Aww, he's slick and soft at the same time!
Yeeeek!
PLEASE DON'T! SENSEI'S NOT USED TO PRAISE AND CUDDLING!
Oh!
I'M SORRY... WHEN I SEE SOMETHING ADORABLE, I CAN'T HELP MYSELF.
DID YOU HEAR THAT?! DID YOU?!
OH SHUT UP, NYANKO SENSEI!

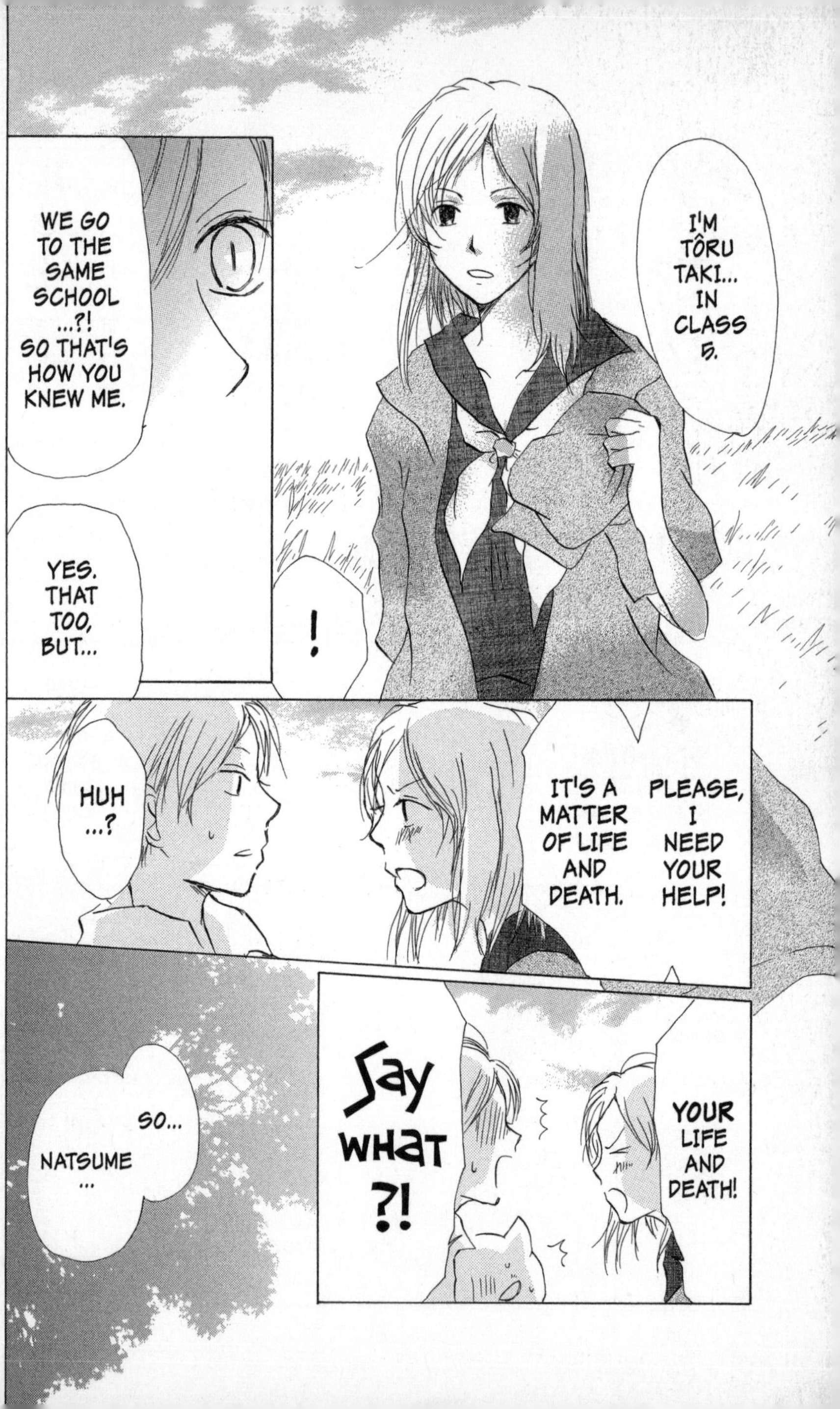
I'M TÔRU TAKI... IN CLASS 5.
WE GO TO THE SAME SCHOOL ...?! SO THAT'S HOW YOU KNEW ME.
!
YES. THAT TOO, BUT...
PLEASE, I NEED YOUR HELP!
IT'S A MATTER OF LIFE AND DEATH.
HUH ...?
YOUR LIFE AND DEATH!
Say WHAT ?!
SO...
NATSUME ...

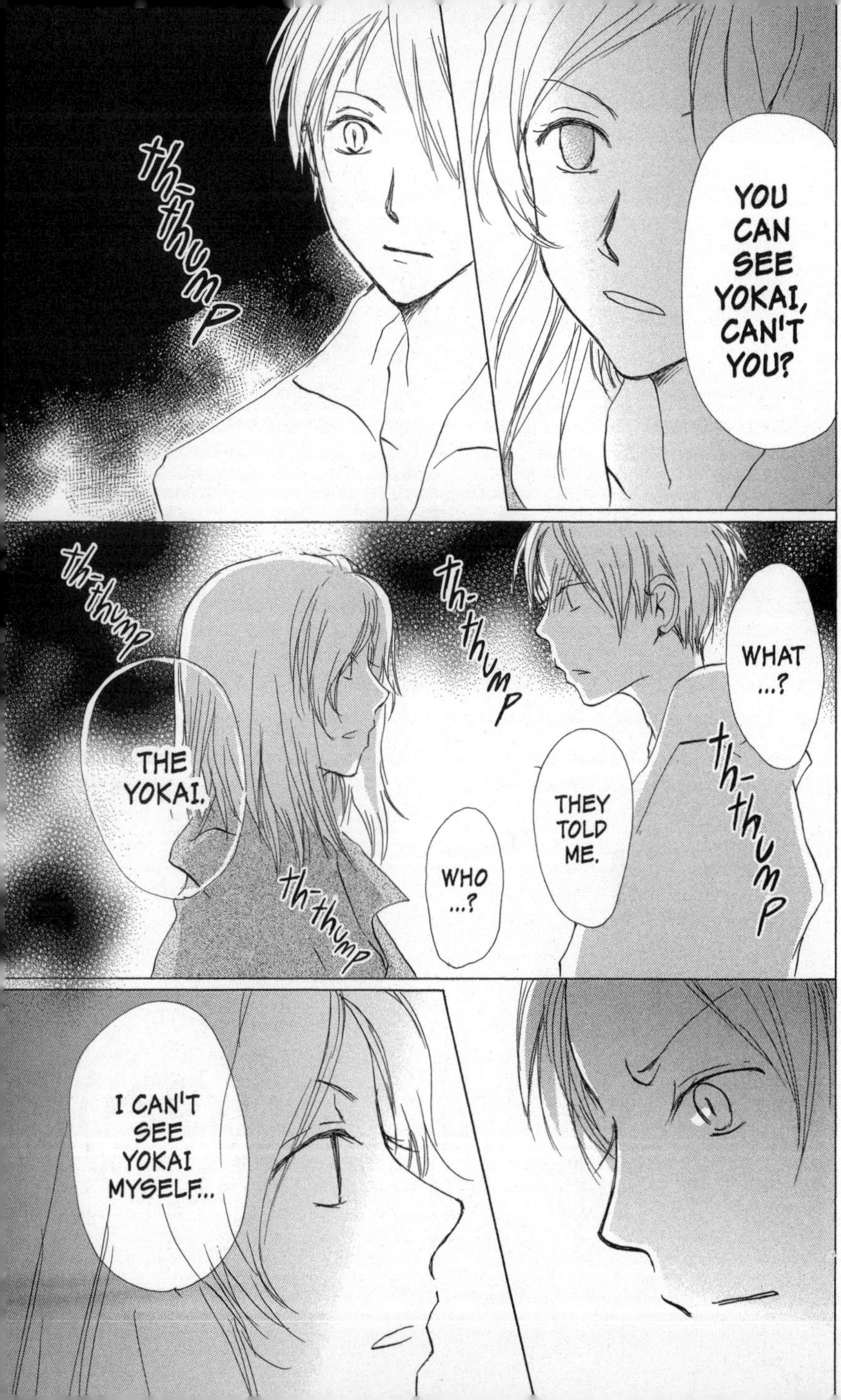
YOU CAN SEE YOKAI, CAN'T YOU?
th-thump
WHAT ...?
th-thump
th-thump
THEY TOLD ME.
WHO ...?
th-thump
THE YOKAI.
th-thump
I CAN'T SEE YOKAI MYSELF...

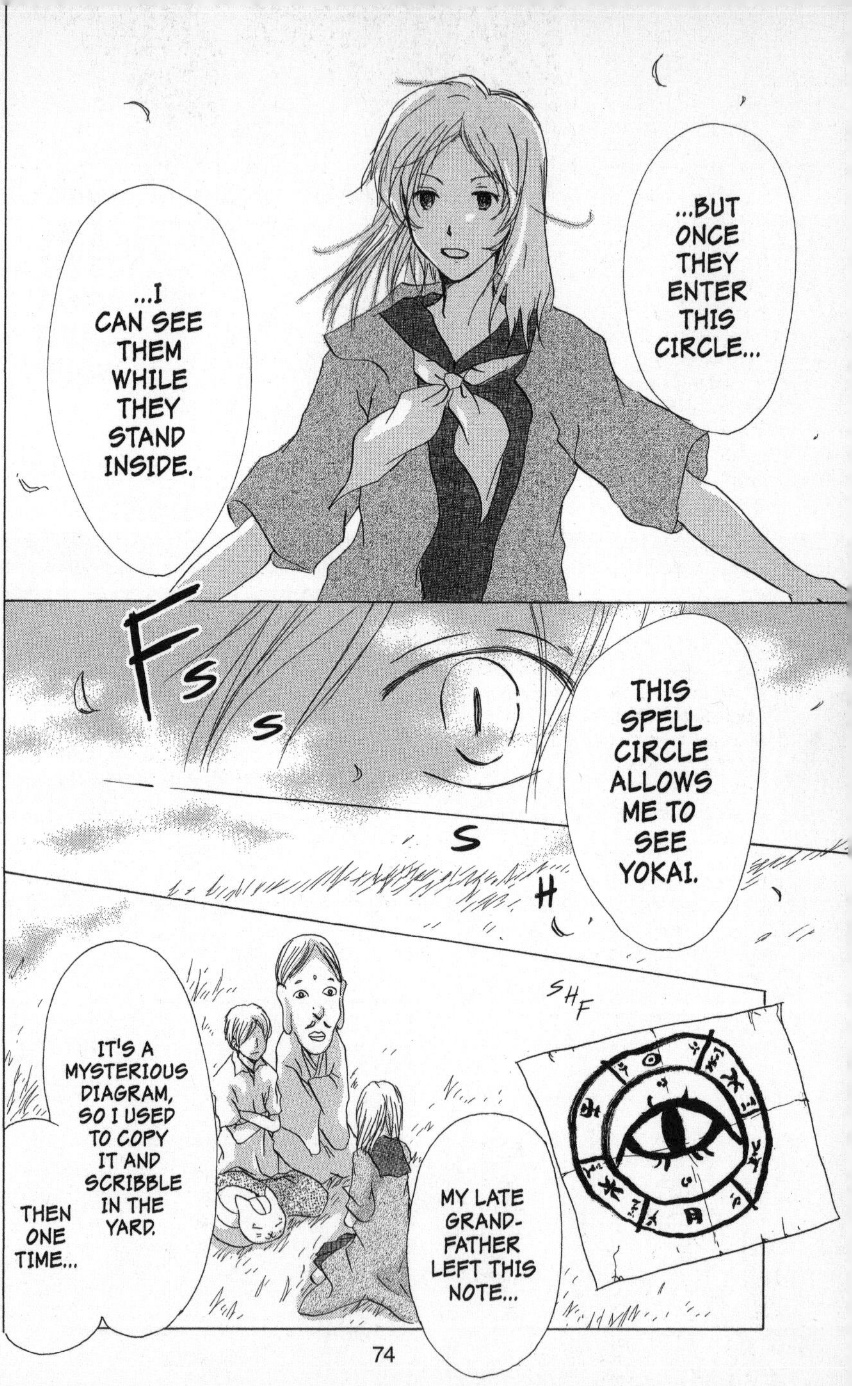
...BUT ONCE THEY ENTER THIS CIRCLE...
...I CAN SEE THEM WHILE THEY STAND INSIDE.
THIS SPELL CIRCLE ALLOWS ME TO SEE YOKAI.
FSSSH
SHF
MY LATE GRANDFATHER LEFT THIS NOTE...
IT'S A MYSTERIOUS DIAGRAM, SO I USED TO COPY IT AND SCRIBBLE IN THE YARD.
THEN ONE TIME...

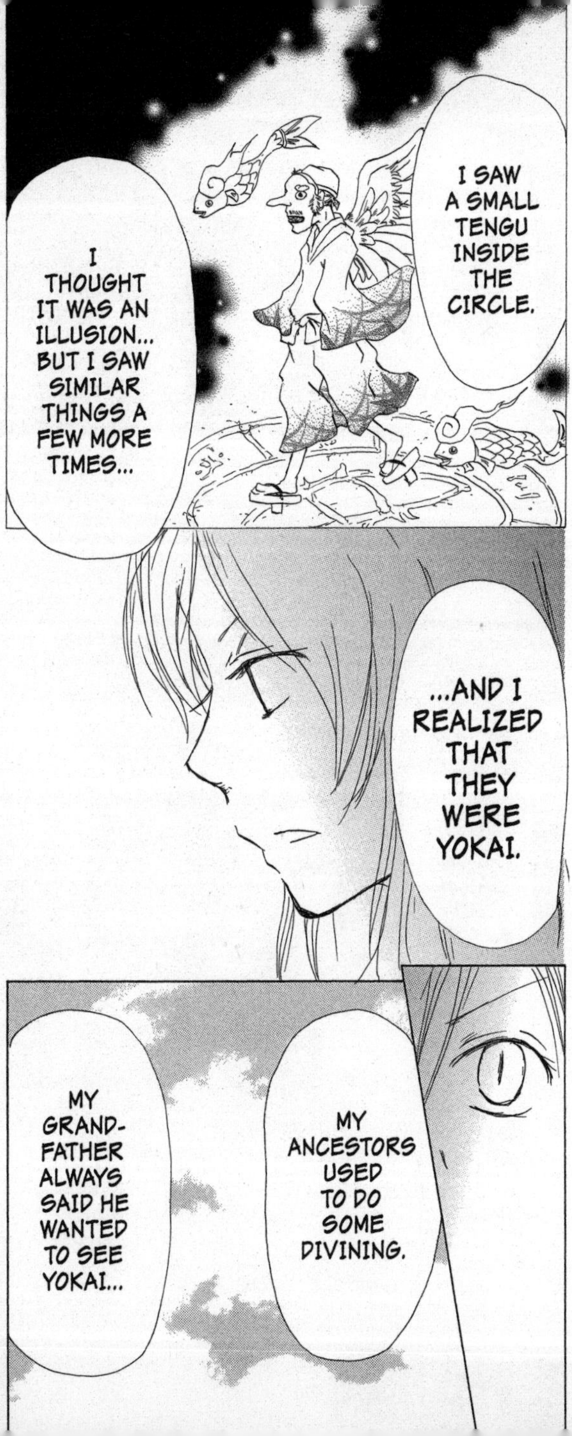
I SAW A SMALL TENGU INSIDE THE CIRCLE.
I THOUGHT IT WAS AN ILLUSION... BUT I SAW SIMILAR THINGS A FEW MORE TIMES...
...AND I REALIZED THAT THEY WERE YOKAI.
MY ANCESTORS USED TO DO SOME DIVINING.
MY GRANDFATHER ALWAYS SAID HE WANTED TO SEE YOKAI...

02

❋ Drama CD

I wrote about this a little in vol. 4, but they made a drama CD. They cast so many famous voice actors. I thought some of the lines would be weird when said out loud, but they expressed them so naturally, and I was so impressed. They tweaked the parts that didn't make sense without visuals, and they used sound effects that added ambiance, and then my characters started talking. I was so happy, but at the same time, I noticed some things I hadn't realized before, so it was a learning experience. I'm so grateful for this opportunity.

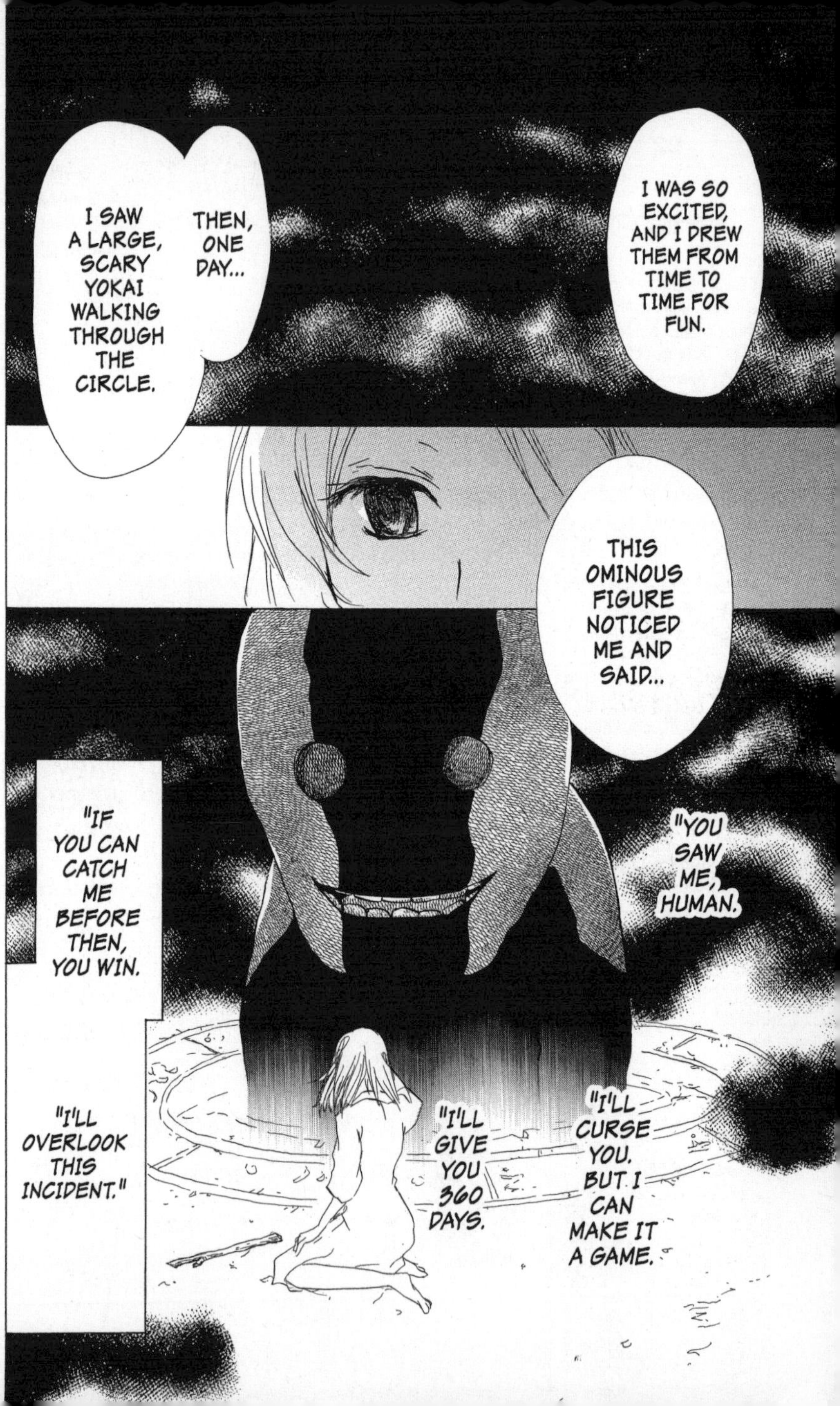
I WAS SO EXCITED, AND I DREW THEM FROM TIME TO TIME FOR FUN.
THEN, ONE DAY...
I SAW A LARGE, SCARY YOKAI WALKING THROUGH THE CIRCLE.
THIS OMINOUS FIGURE NOTICED ME AND SAID...
"YOU SAW ME, HUMAN.
"I'LL CURSE YOU. BUT I CAN MAKE IT A GAME.
"I'LL GIVE YOU 360 DAYS.
"IF YOU CAN CATCH ME BEFORE THEN, YOU WIN.
"I'LL OVERLOOK THIS INCIDENT."

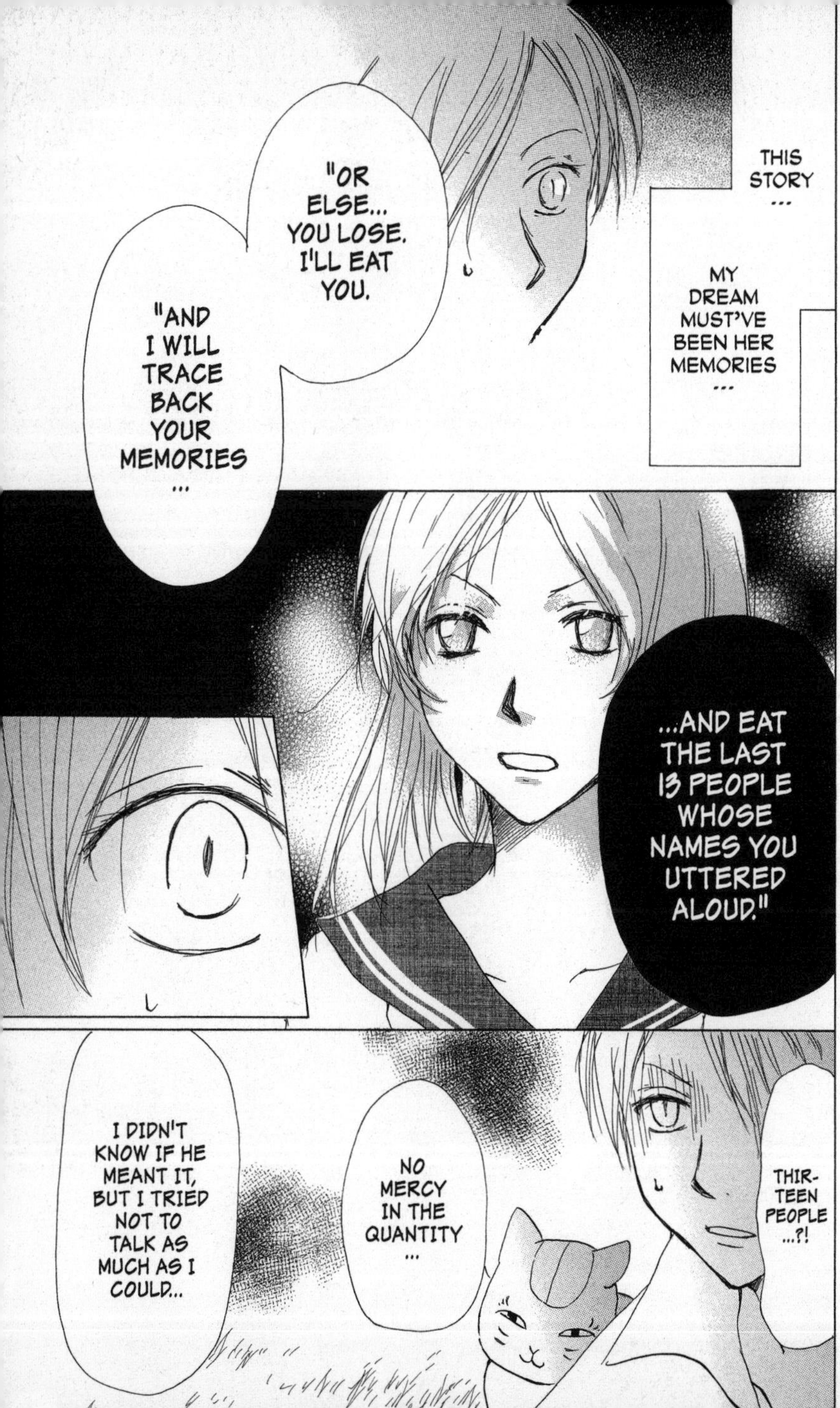
THIS STORY ...
MY DREAM MUST'VE BEEN HER MEMORIES ...
"OR ELSE... YOU LOSE. I'LL EAT YOU.
"AND I WILL TRACE BACK YOUR MEMORIES ...
...AND EAT THE LAST 13 PEOPLE WHOSE NAMES YOU UTTERED ALOUD."
THIR-TEEN PEOPLE ...?!
NO MERCY IN THE QUANTITY ...
I DIDN'T KNOW IF HE MEANT IT, BUT I TRIED NOT TO TALK AS MUCH AS I COULD...

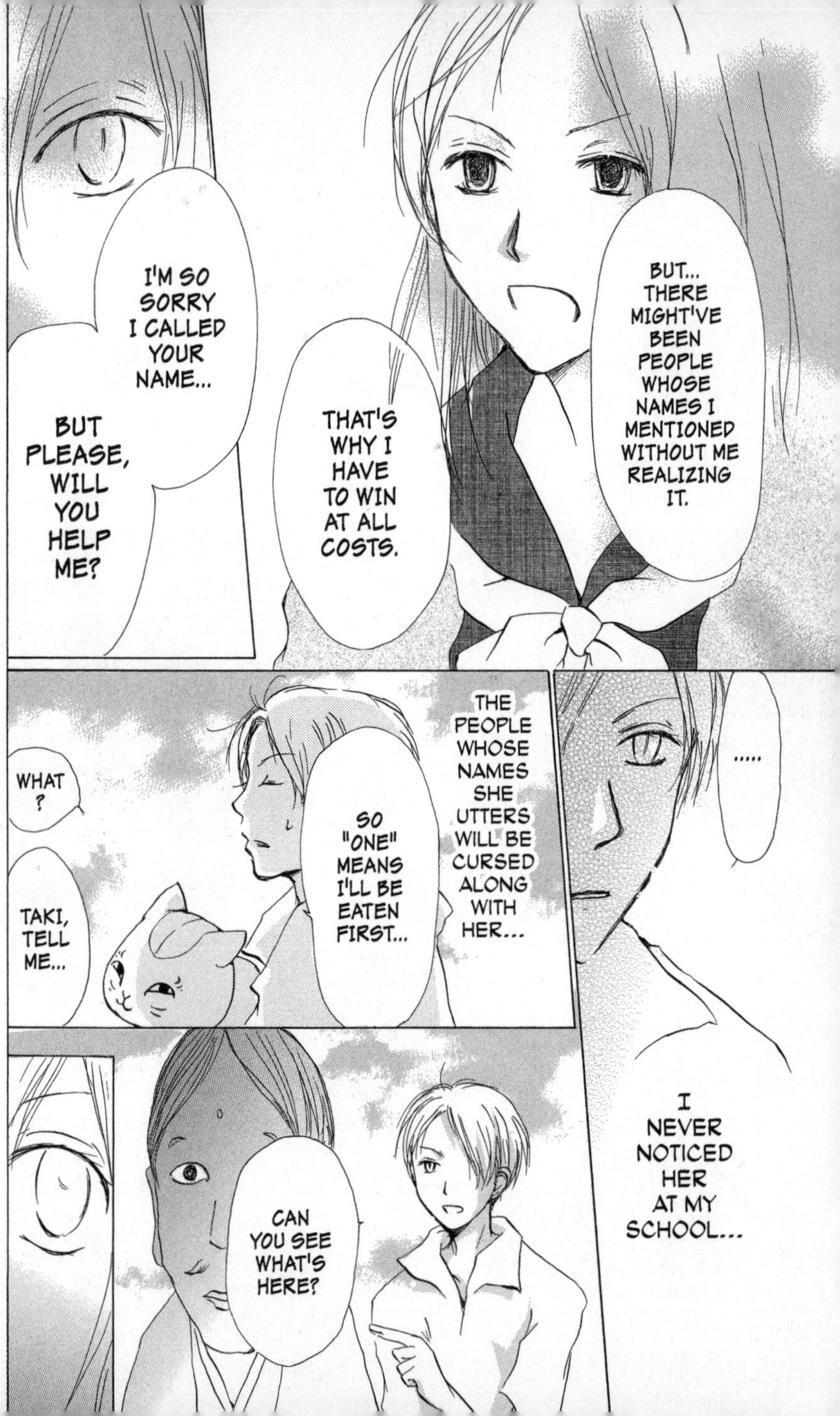
BUT... THERE MIGHT'VE BEEN PEOPLE WHOSE NAMES I MENTIONED WITHOUT ME REALIZING IT.
THAT'S WHY I HAVE TO WIN AT ALL COSTS.
I'M SO SORRY I CALLED YOUR NAME...
BUT PLEASE, WILL YOU HELP ME?
.....
I NEVER NOTICED HER AT MY SCHOOL...
THE PEOPLE WHOSE NAMES SHE UTTERS WILL BE CURSED ALONG WITH HER...
SO "ONE" MEANS I'LL BE EATEN FIRST...
WHAT ?
TAKI, TELL ME...
CAN YOU SEE WHAT'S HERE?

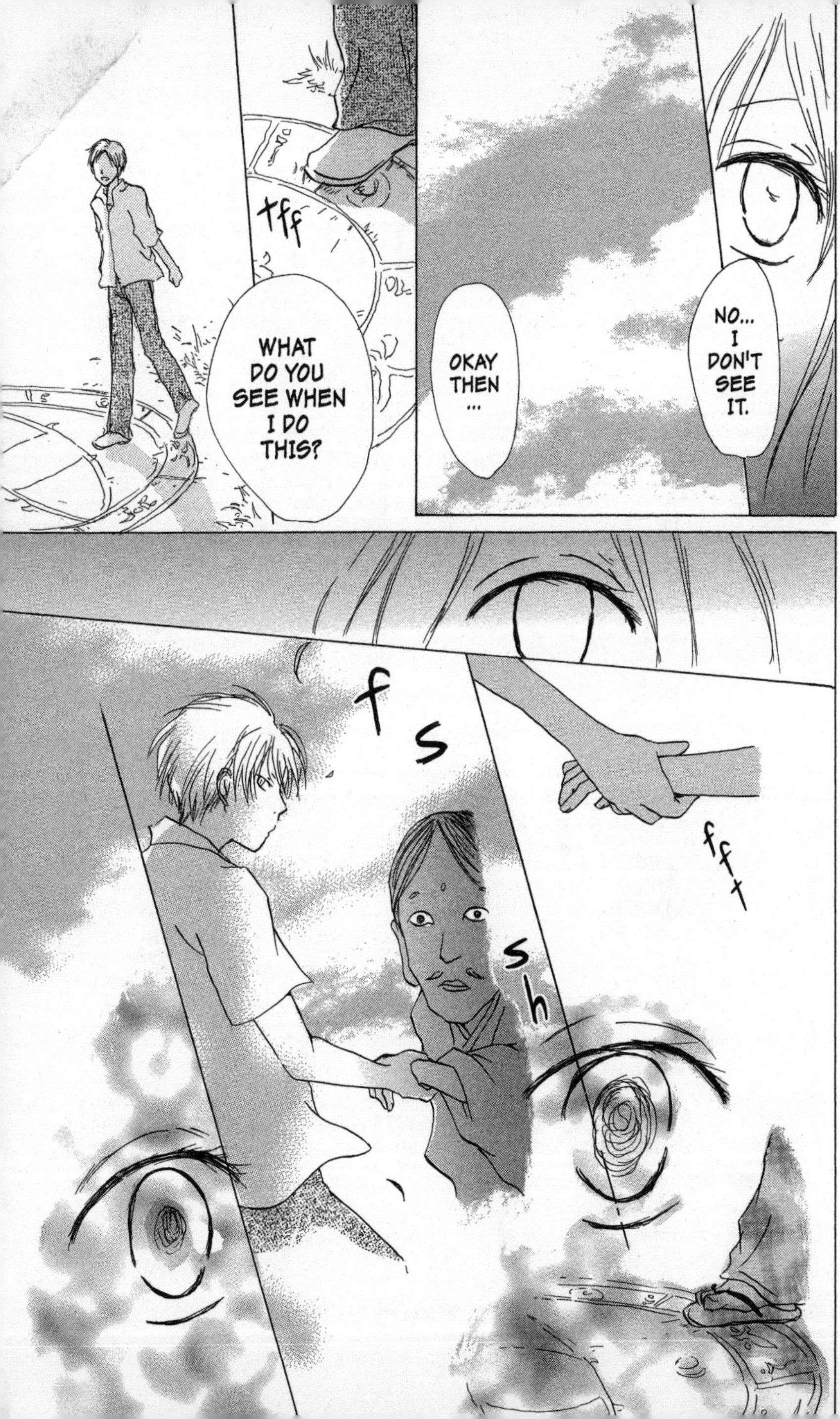
NO... I DON'T SEE IT.
OKAY THEN ...
tff
WHAT DO YOU SEE WHEN I DO THIS?
fft
f s
sh

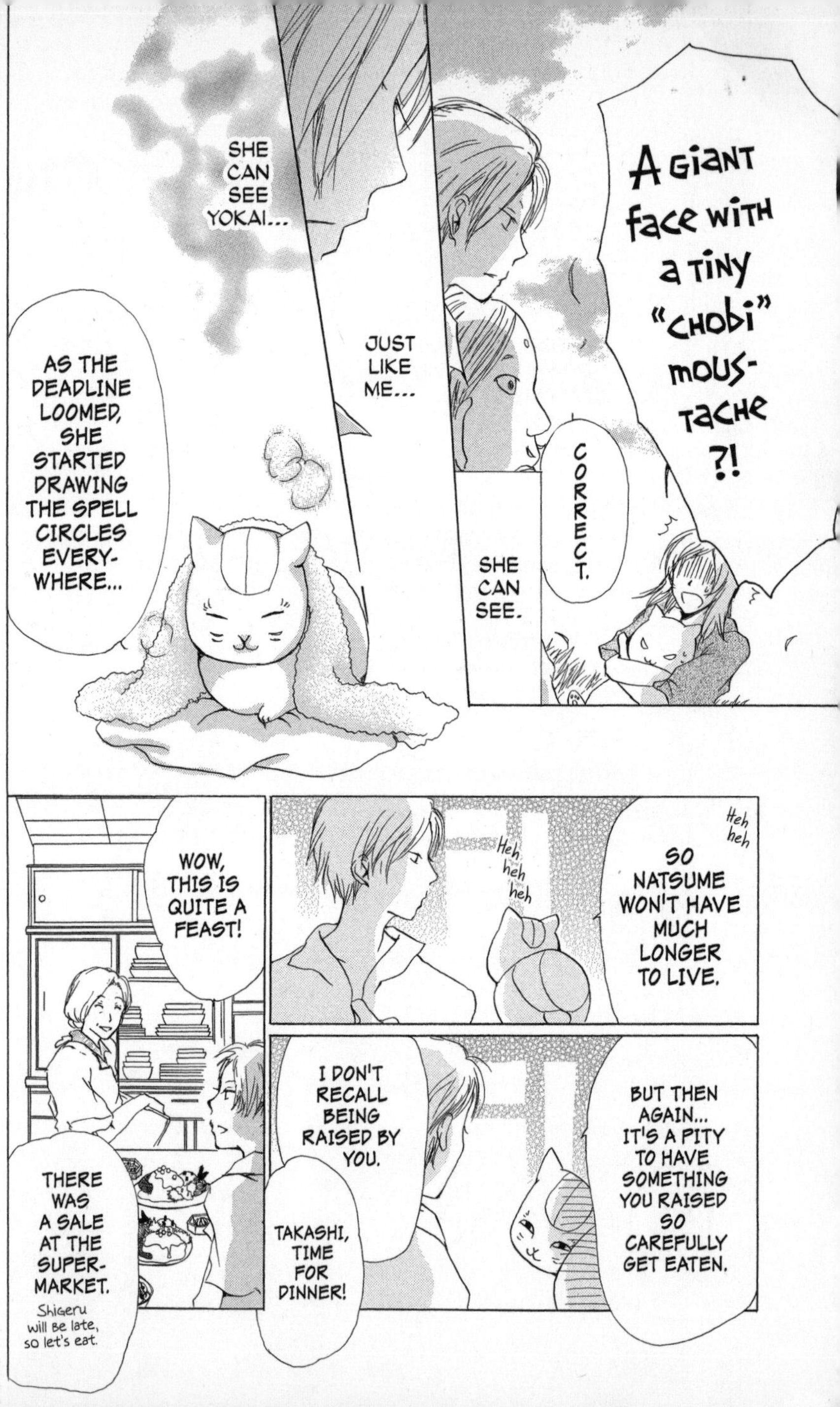
A GIANT FACE WITH A TINY "CHOBI" MOUSTACHE ?!
CORRECT.
SHE CAN SEE.
JUST LIKE ME...
SHE CAN SEE YOKAI...
AS THE DEADLINE LOOMED, SHE STARTED DRAWING THE SPELL CIRCLES EVERYWHERE...
Heh heh
SO NATSUME WON'T HAVE MUCH LONGER TO LIVE.
Heh heh heh
BUT THEN AGAIN... IT'S A PITY TO HAVE SOMETHING YOU RAISED SO CAREFULLY GET EATEN.
I DON'T RECALL BEING RAISED BY YOU.
TAKASHI, TIME FOR DINNER!
WOW, THIS IS QUITE A FEAST!
THERE WAS A SALE AT THE SUPERMARKET.
Shigeru will be late, so let's eat.

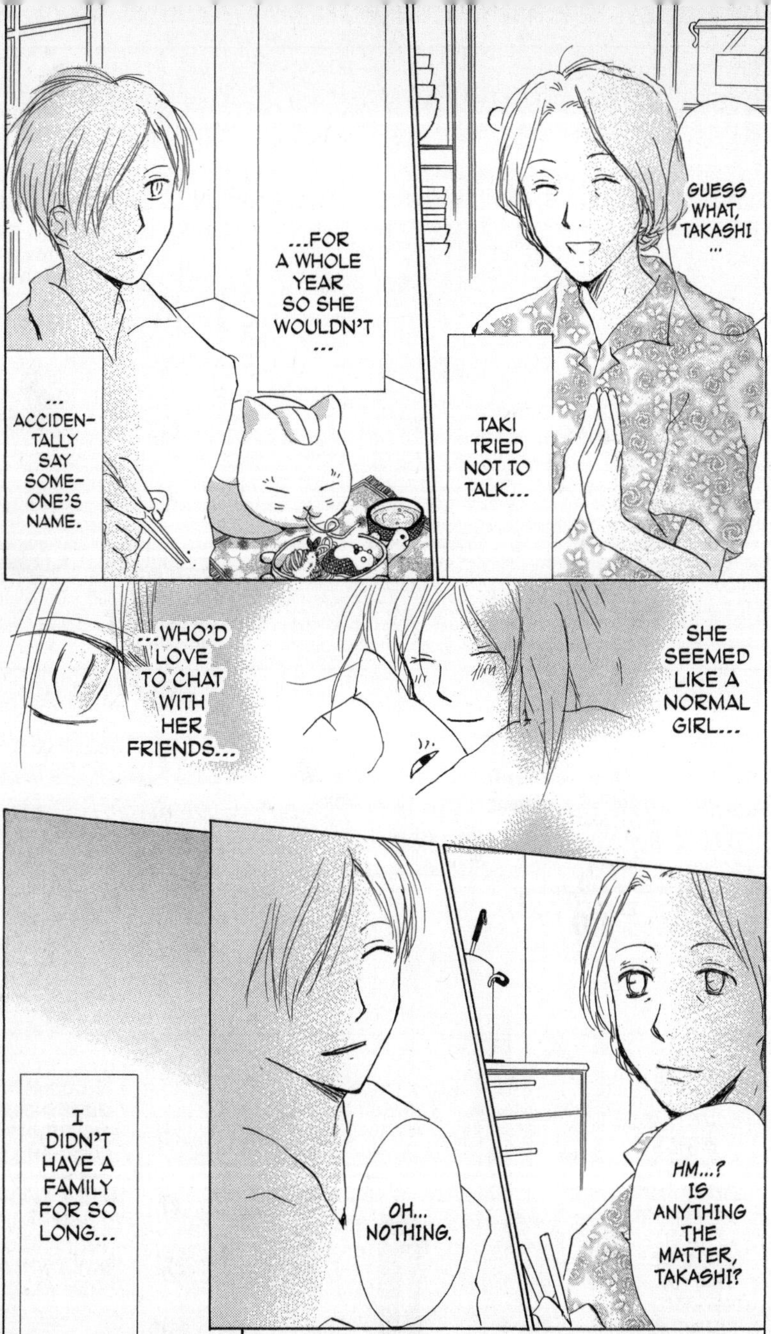
GUESS WHAT, TAKASHI...
TAKI TRIED NOT TO TALK...
...FOR A WHOLE YEAR SO SHE WOULDN'T...
...ACCIDENTALLY SAY SOMEONE'S NAME.
SHE SEEMED LIKE A NORMAL GIRL...
...WHO'D LOVE TO CHAT WITH HER FRIENDS...
HM...? IS ANYTHING THE MATTER, TAKASHI?
OH... NOTHING.
I DIDN'T HAVE A FAMILY FOR SO LONG...

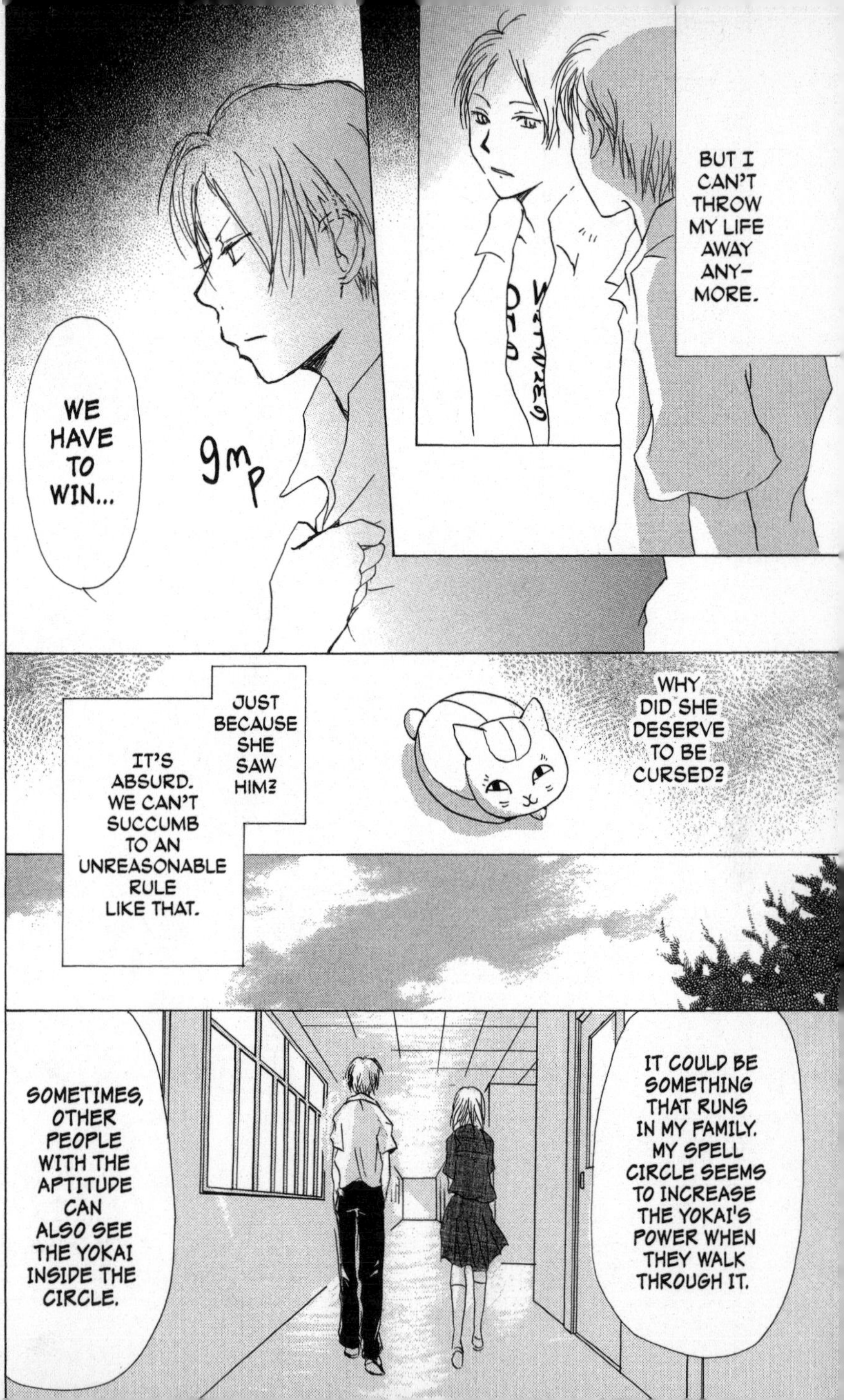
BUT I CAN'T THROW MY LIFE AWAY ANYMORE.
WE HAVE TO WIN...
gmp
WHY DID SHE DESERVE TO BE CURSED?
JUST BECAUSE SHE SAW HIM?
IT'S ABSURD. WE CAN'T SUCCUMB TO AN UNREASONABLE RULE LIKE THAT.
IT COULD BE SOMETHING THAT RUNS IN MY FAMILY. MY SPELL CIRCLE SEEMS TO INCREASE THE YOKAI'S POWER WHEN THEY WALK THROUGH IT.
SOMETIMES, OTHER PEOPLE WITH THE APTITUDE CAN ALSO SEE THE YOKAI INSIDE THE CIRCLE.

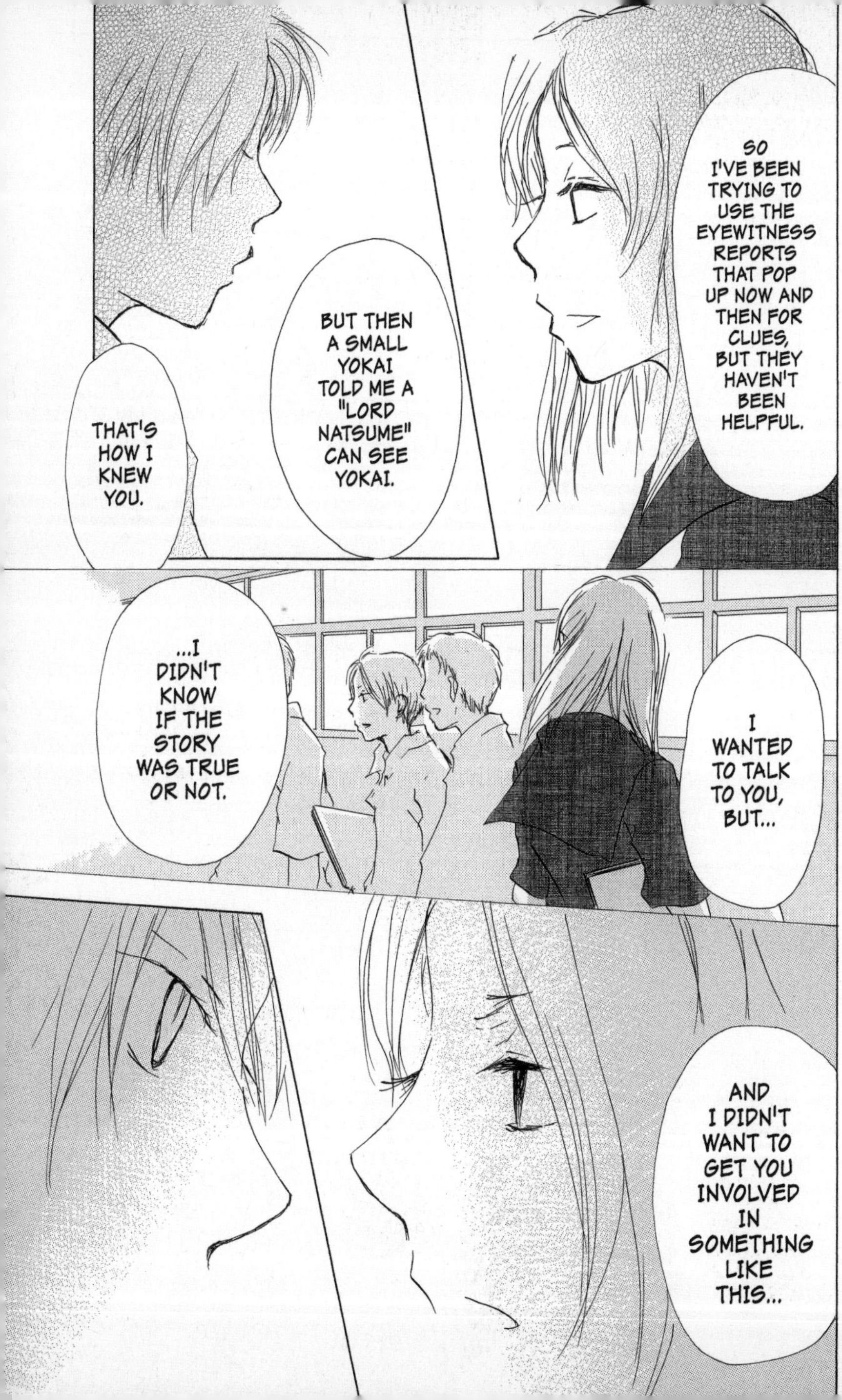
SO I'VE BEEN TRYING TO USE THE EYEWITNESS REPORTS THAT POP UP NOW AND THEN FOR CLUES, BUT THEY HAVEN'T BEEN HELPFUL.
BUT THEN A SMALL YOKAI TOLD ME A "LORD NATSUME" CAN SEE YOKAI.
THAT'S HOW I KNEW YOU.
I WANTED TO TALK TO YOU, BUT...
...I DIDN'T KNOW IF THE STORY WAS TRUE OR NOT.
AND I DIDN'T WANT TO GET YOU INVOLVED IN SOMETHING LIKE THIS...

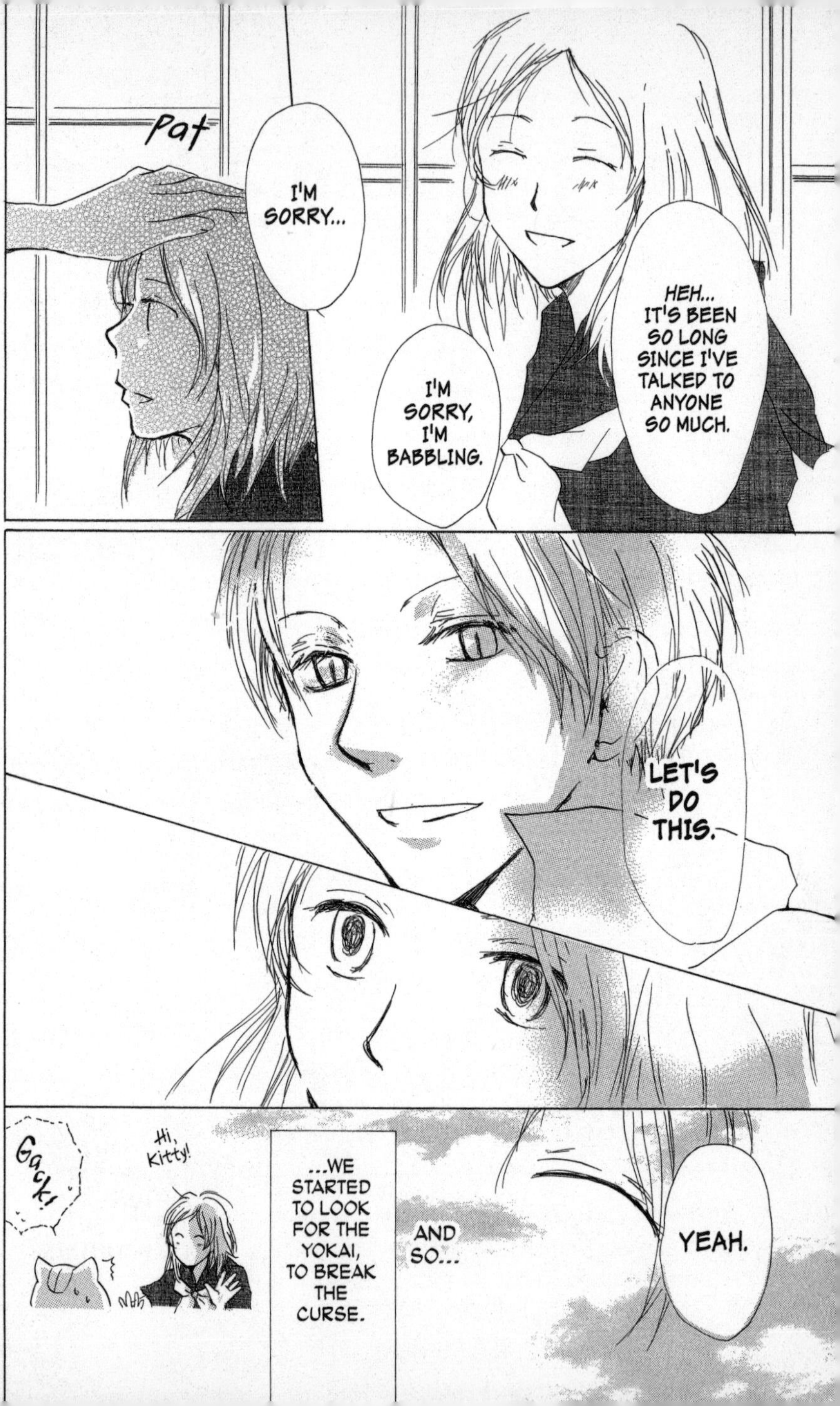
HEH... IT'S BEEN SO LONG SINCE I'VE TALKED TO ANYONE SO MUCH.
I'M SORRY, I'M BABBLING.
I'M SORRY...
Pat
LET'S DO THIS.
YEAH.
AND SO...
...WE STARTED TO LOOK FOR THE YOKAI, TO BREAK THE CURSE.
Hi, Kitty!
Gack!

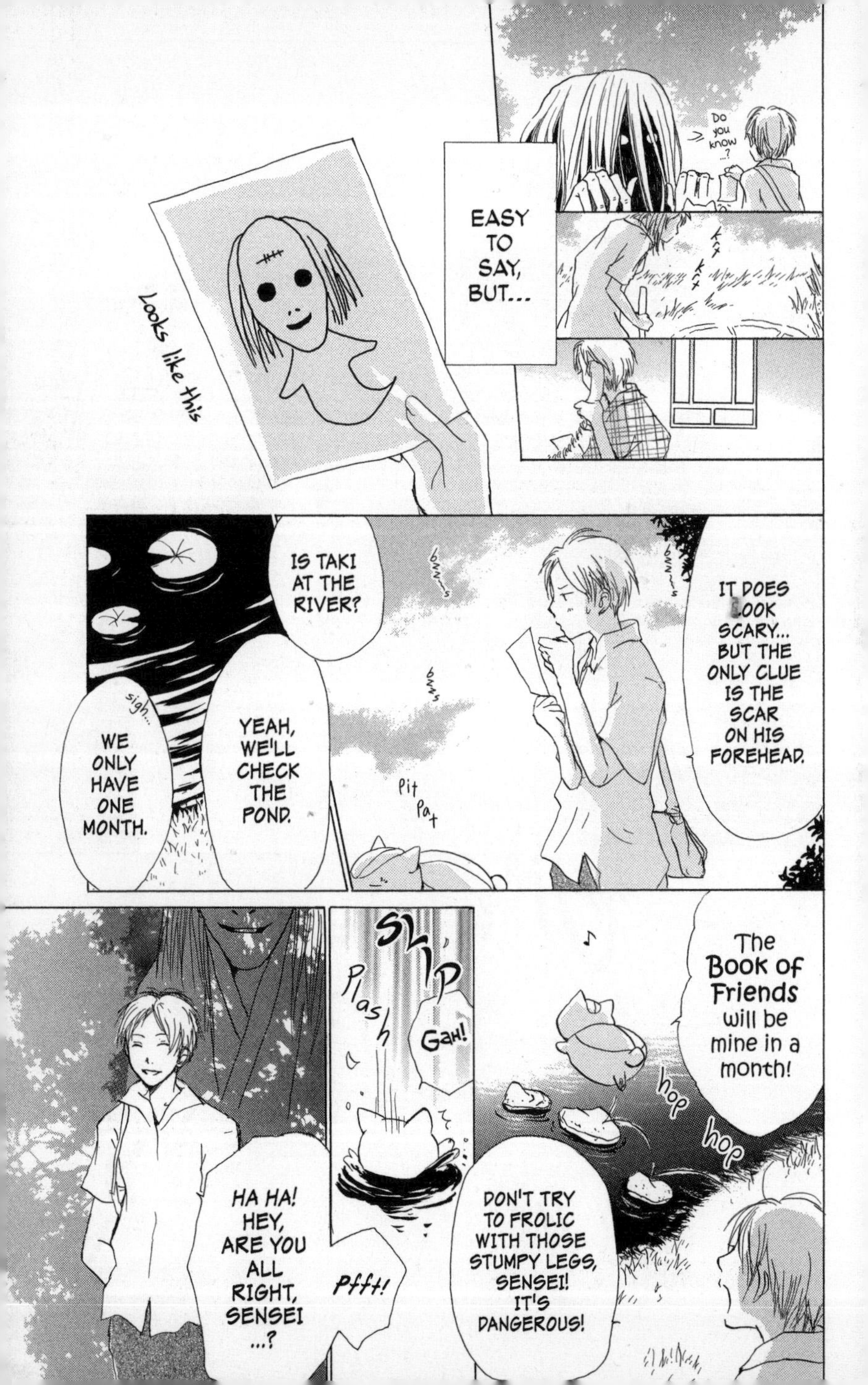
Do you know ...?
EASY TO SAY, BUT...
krt krt
Looks like this
IT DOES LOOK SCARY... BUT THE ONLY CLUE IS THE SCAR ON HIS FOREHEAD.
bzzzz
bzzzz
IS TAKI AT THE RIVER?
bzzzz
YEAH, WE'LL CHECK THE POND.
Pit Pat
sigh...
WE ONLY HAVE ONE MONTH.
The Book of Friends will be mine in a month!
hop hop
DON'T TRY TO FROLIC WITH THOSE STUMPY LEGS, SENSEI! IT'S DANGEROUS!
SLIP
Plash
GAH!
HA HA! HEY, ARE YOU ALL RIGHT, SENSEI ...?
Pfft!

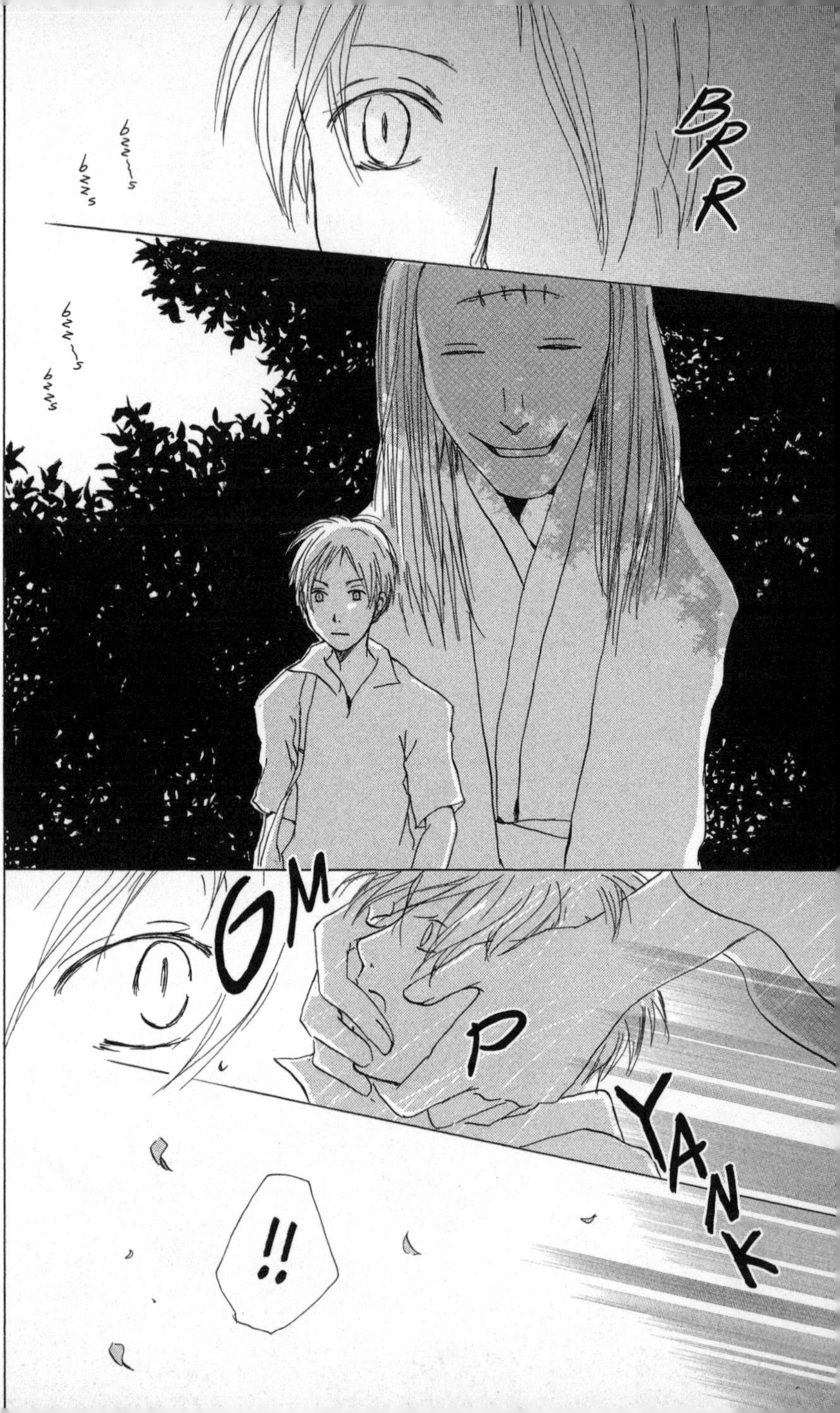
BRRR
bzz~s
bzzs
bzz~s
bzzs
GMP
YANK
!!

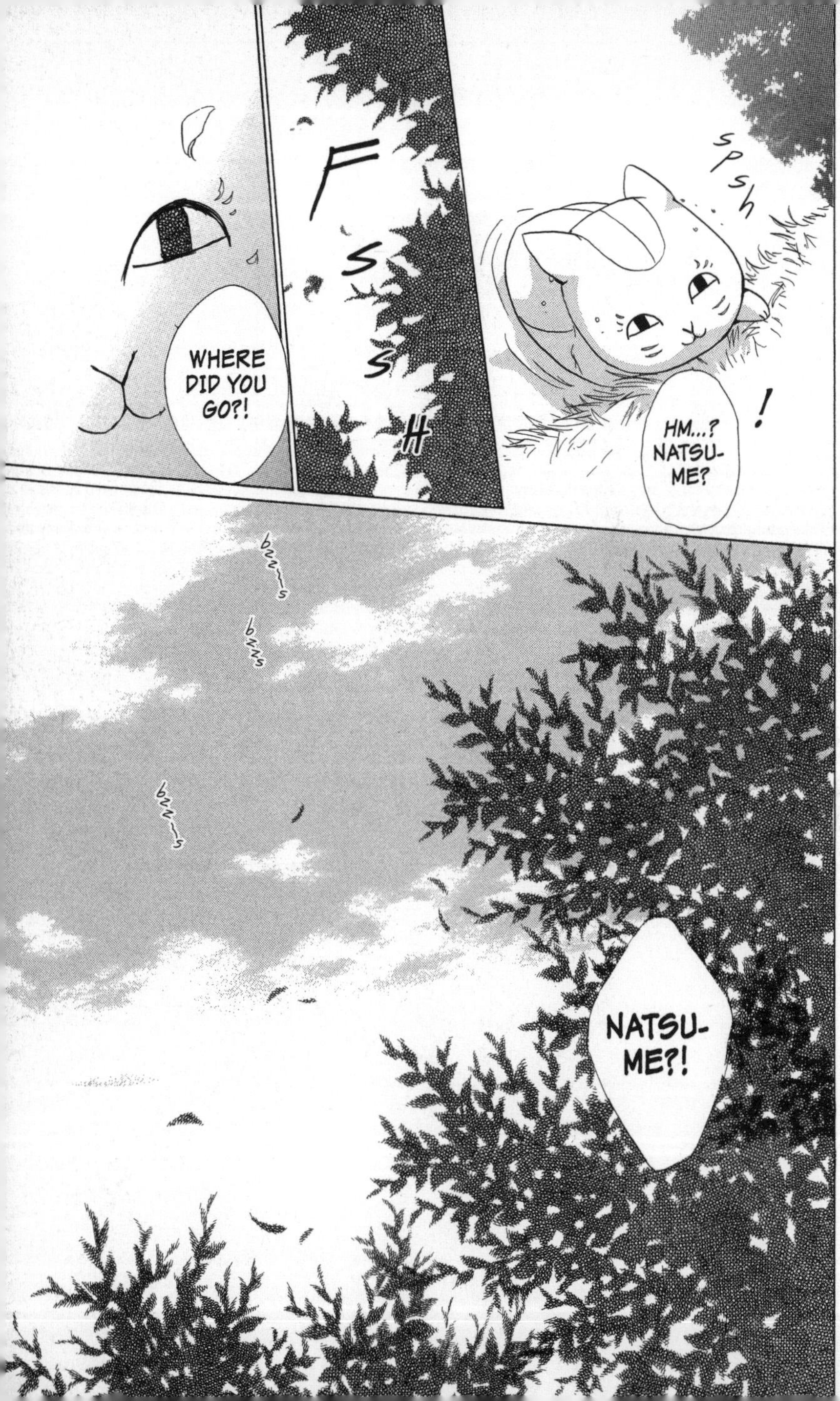
spsh
HM...? NATSU-ME?
!
FSSH
WHERE DID YOU GO?!
bzz~s
bzzs
bzz~s
NATSU-ME?!

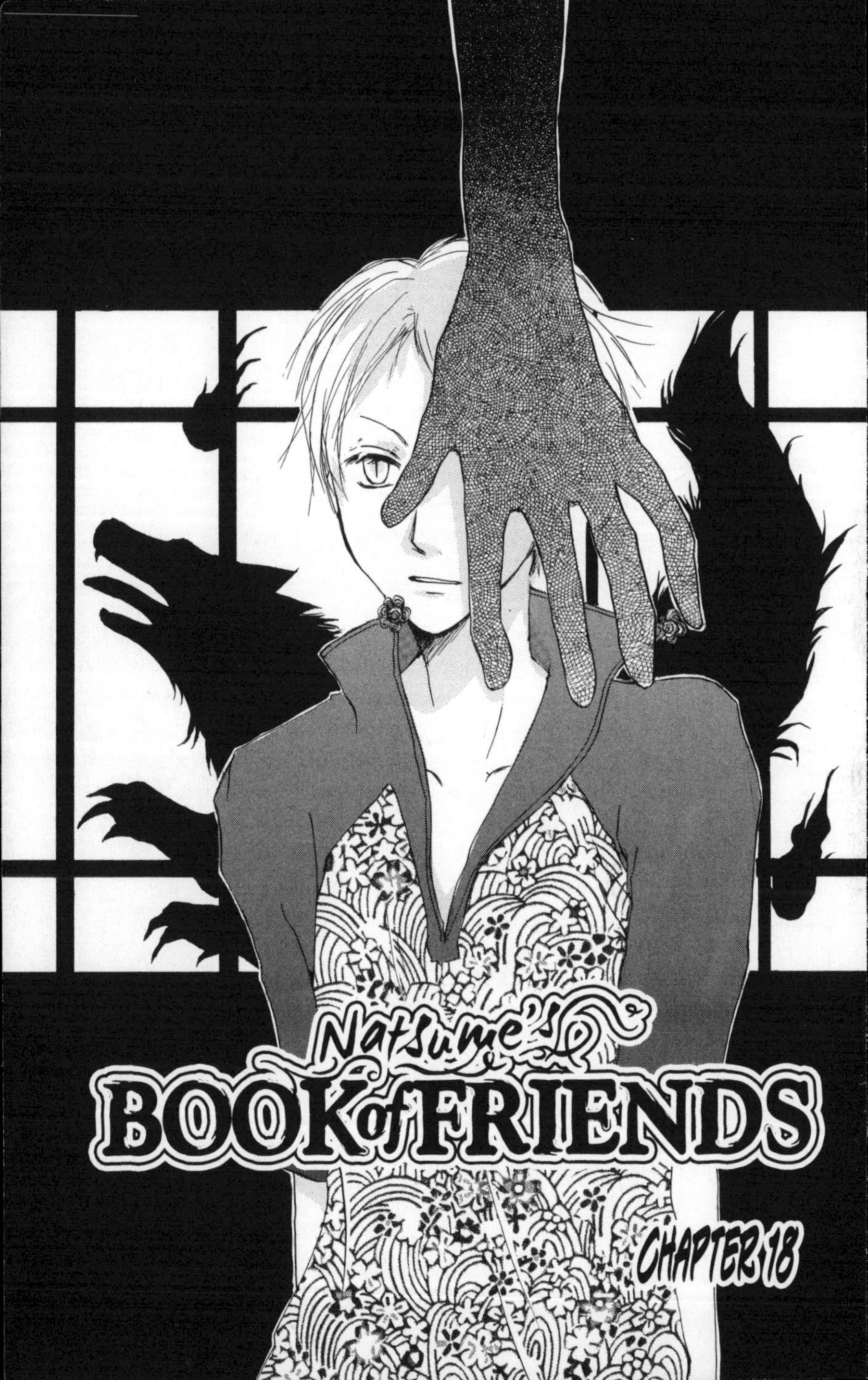
Natsume's
BOOK of FRIENDS
CHAPTER 18

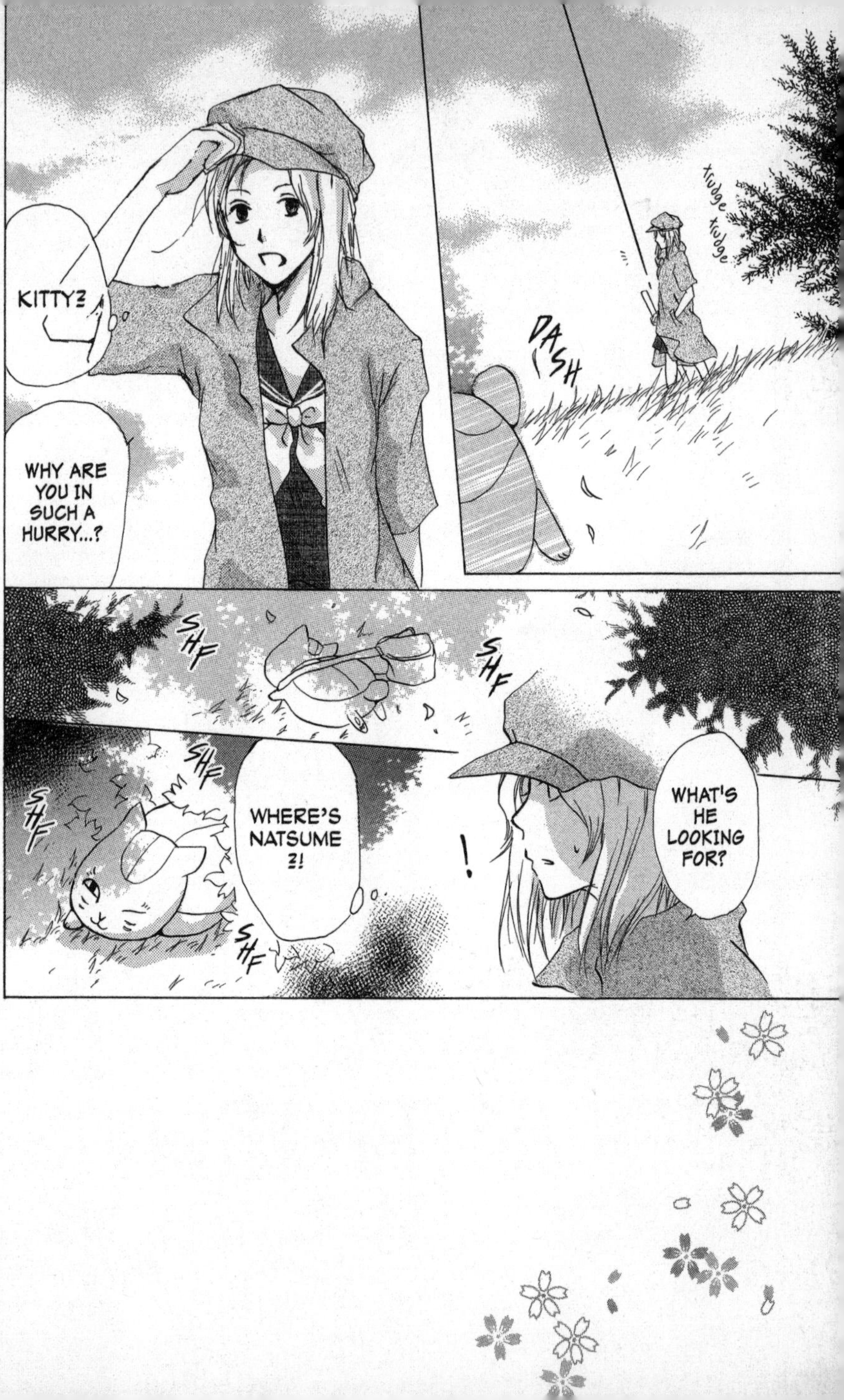
trudge trudge
DASH
KITTY?
WHY ARE YOU IN SUCH A HURRY...?
SHF
SHF
WHAT'S HE LOOKING FOR?
!
WHERE'S NATSUME ?!
SHF
SHF
SHF

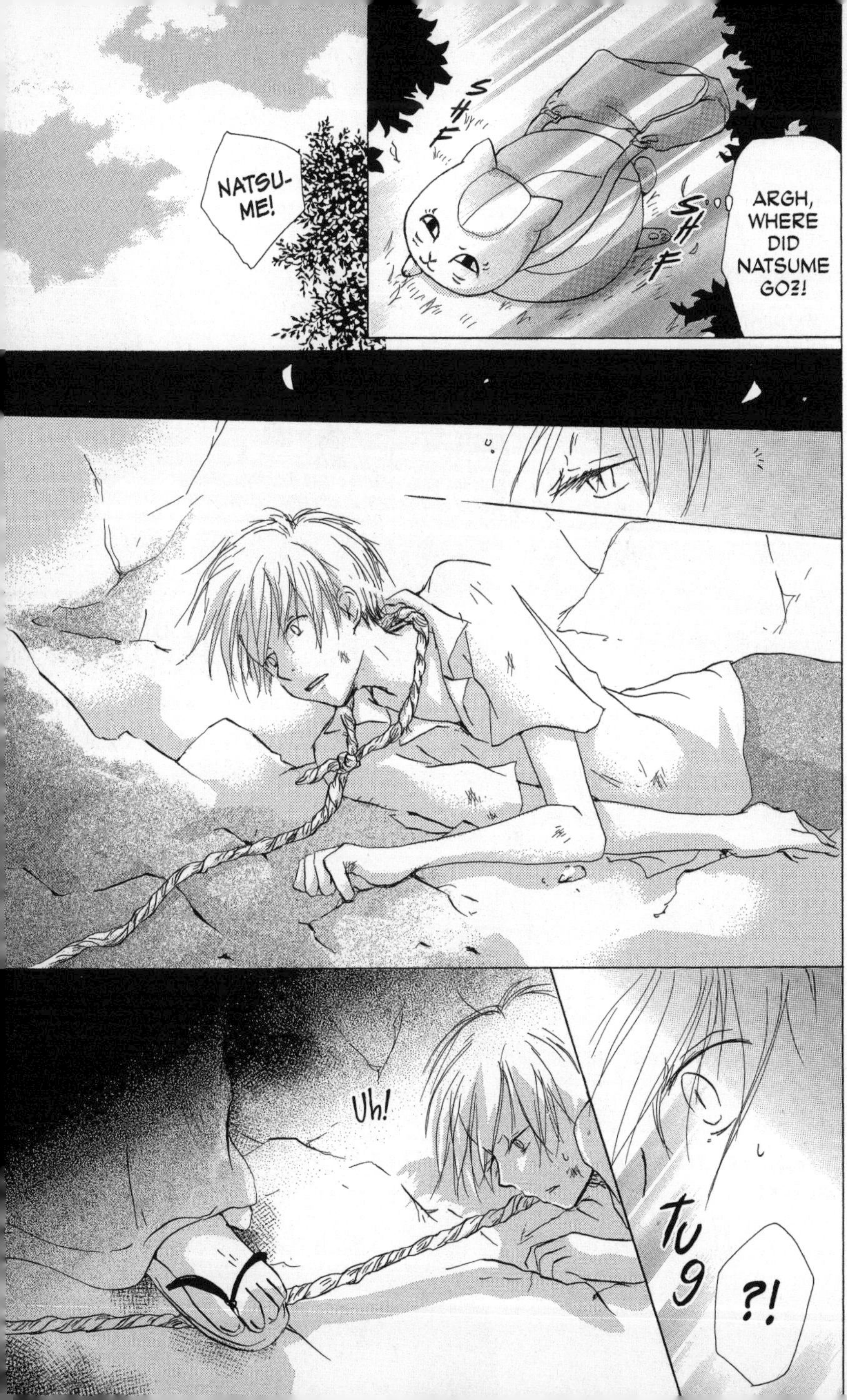
ARGH, WHERE DID NATSUME GO?!
SHF
SHF
NATSU-ME!
TUG
?!
Uh!

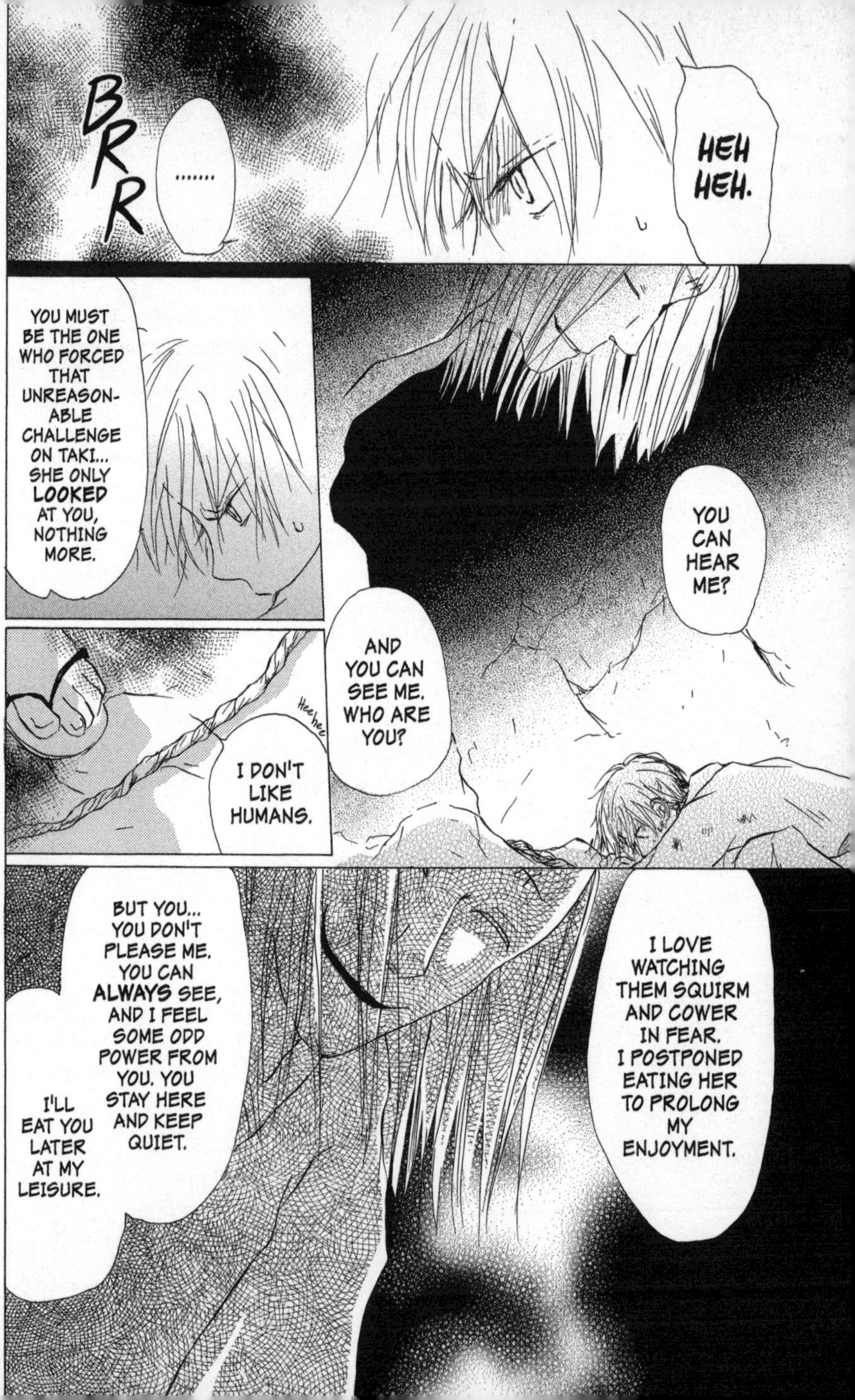
HEH HEH.
....
BRR
YOU CAN HEAR ME?
AND YOU CAN SEE ME. WHO ARE YOU?
YOU MUST BE THE ONE WHO FORCED THAT UNREASON-ABLE CHALLENGE ON TAKI... SHE ONLY LOOKED AT YOU, NOTHING MORE.
Hee hee
I DON'T LIKE HUMANS.
I LOVE WATCHING THEM SQUIRM AND COWER IN FEAR. I POSTPONED EATING HER TO PROLONG MY ENJOYMENT.
BUT YOU... YOU DON'T PLEASE ME. YOU CAN ALWAYS SEE, AND I FEEL SOME ODD POWER FROM YOU. YOU STAY HERE AND KEEP QUIET.
I'LL EAT YOU LATER AT MY LEISURE.

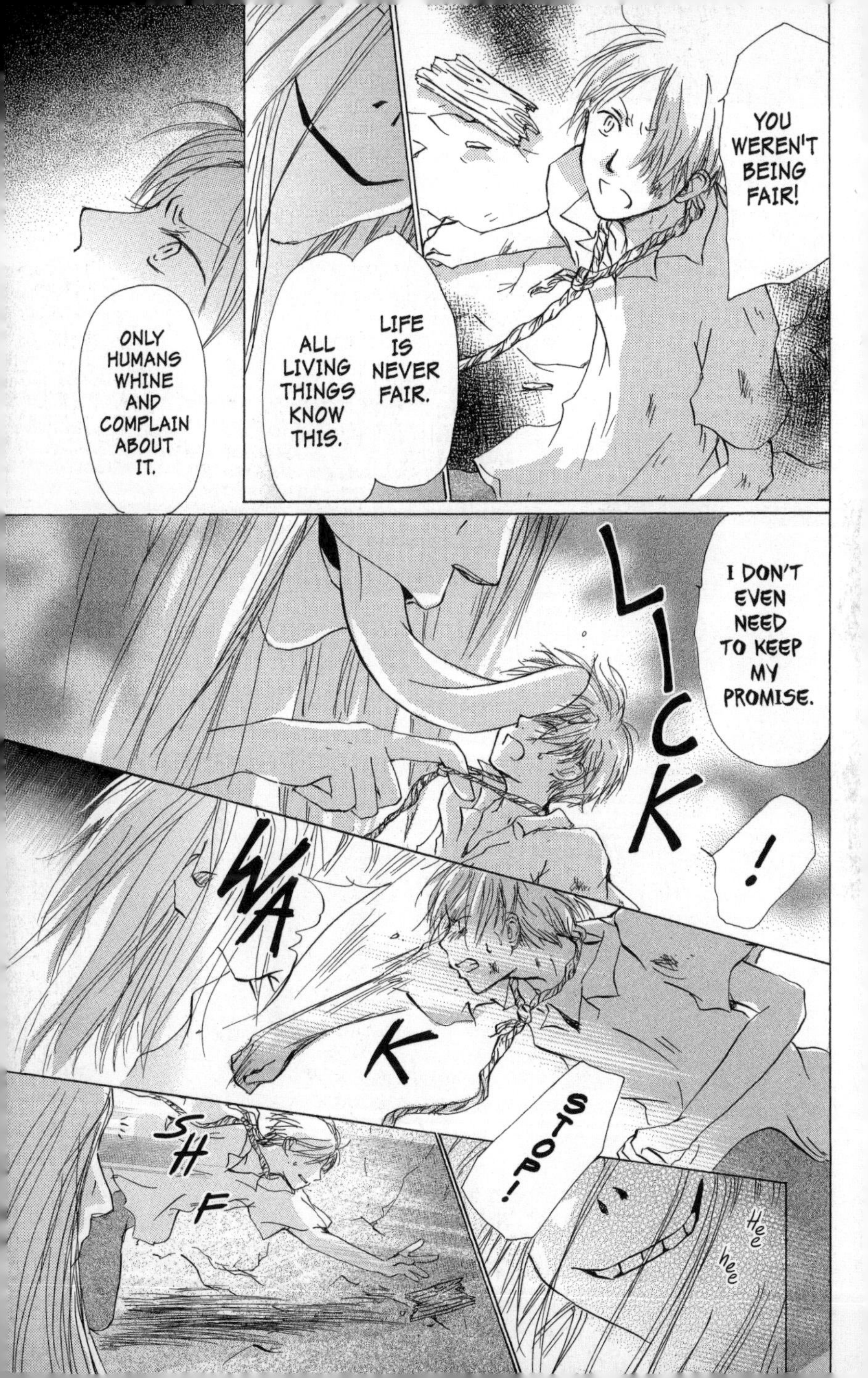
YOU WEREN'T BEING FAIR!
LIFE IS NEVER FAIR.
ALL LIVING THINGS KNOW THIS.
ONLY HUMANS WHINE AND COMPLAIN ABOUT IT.
I DON'T EVEN NEED TO KEEP MY PROMISE.
LICK
!
WAK
STOP!
Hee hee
SHF

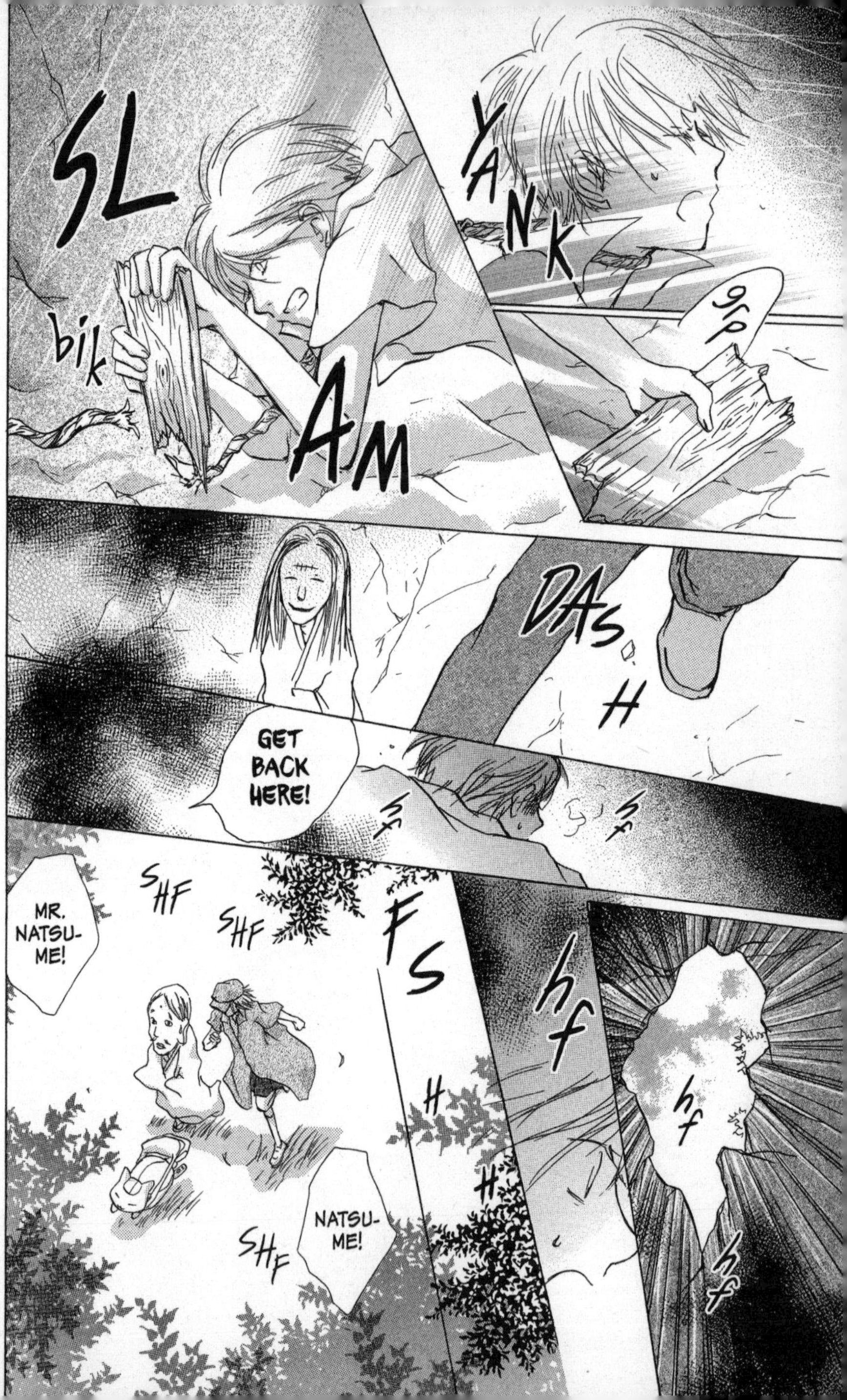
YANK
grp
SLAM
bik
DASH
GET BACK HERE!
hf
hf
hf
hf
hf
FS
H
H
MR. NATSU-ME!
SHF
SHF
NATSU-ME!
SHF

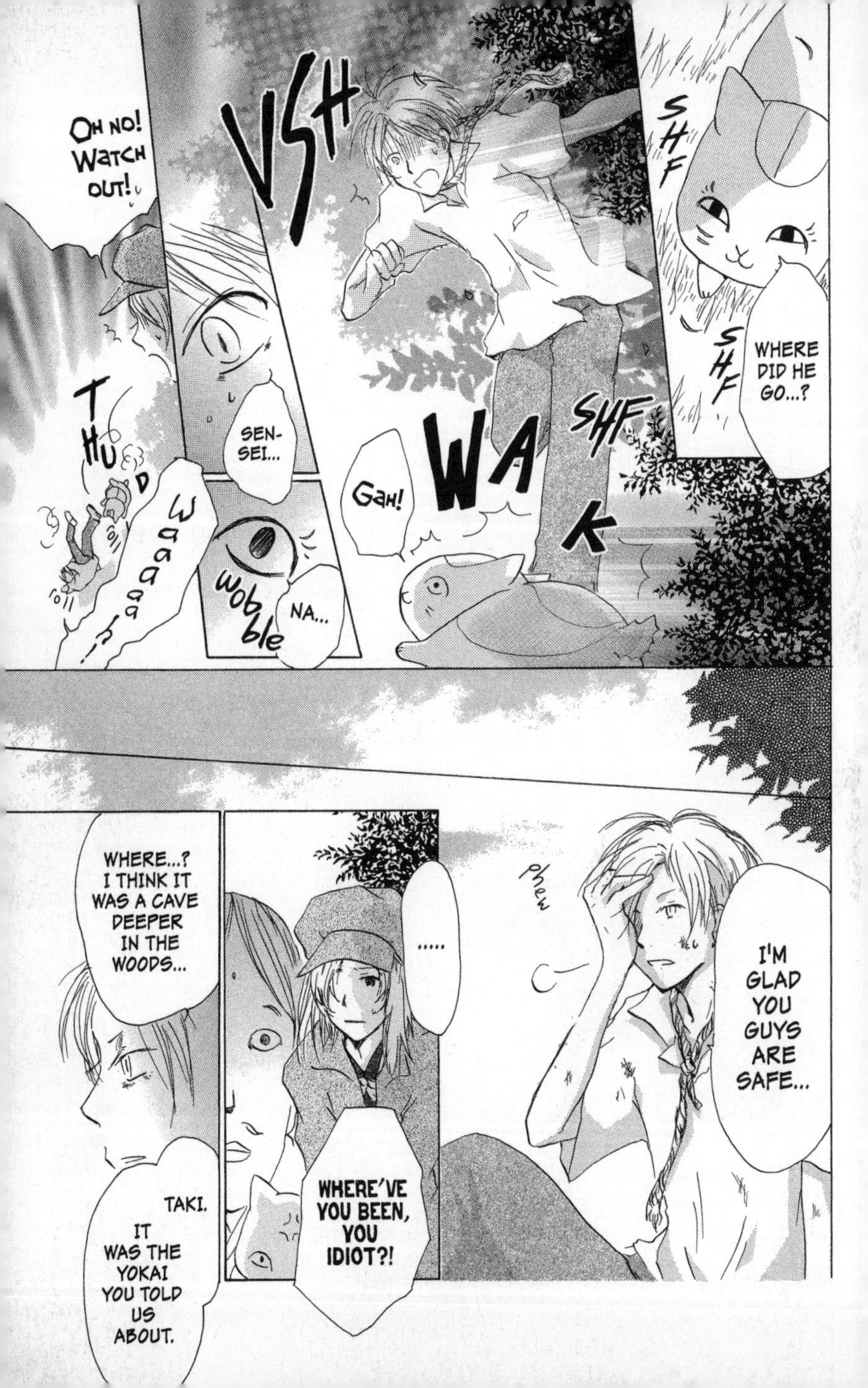
SHF
SHF
WHERE DID HE GO...?
VSH
SHF
WA K
GAH!
SEN-SEI...
NA...
wobble
OH NO! WATCH OUT!
THUD
roll
roll
Waaaaah!?
I'M GLAD YOU GUYS ARE SAFE...
phew
.....
WHERE'VE YOU BEEN, YOU IDIOT?!
WHERE...? I THINK IT WAS A CAVE DEEPER IN THE WOODS...
TAKI.
IT WAS THE YOKAI YOU TOLD US ABOUT.

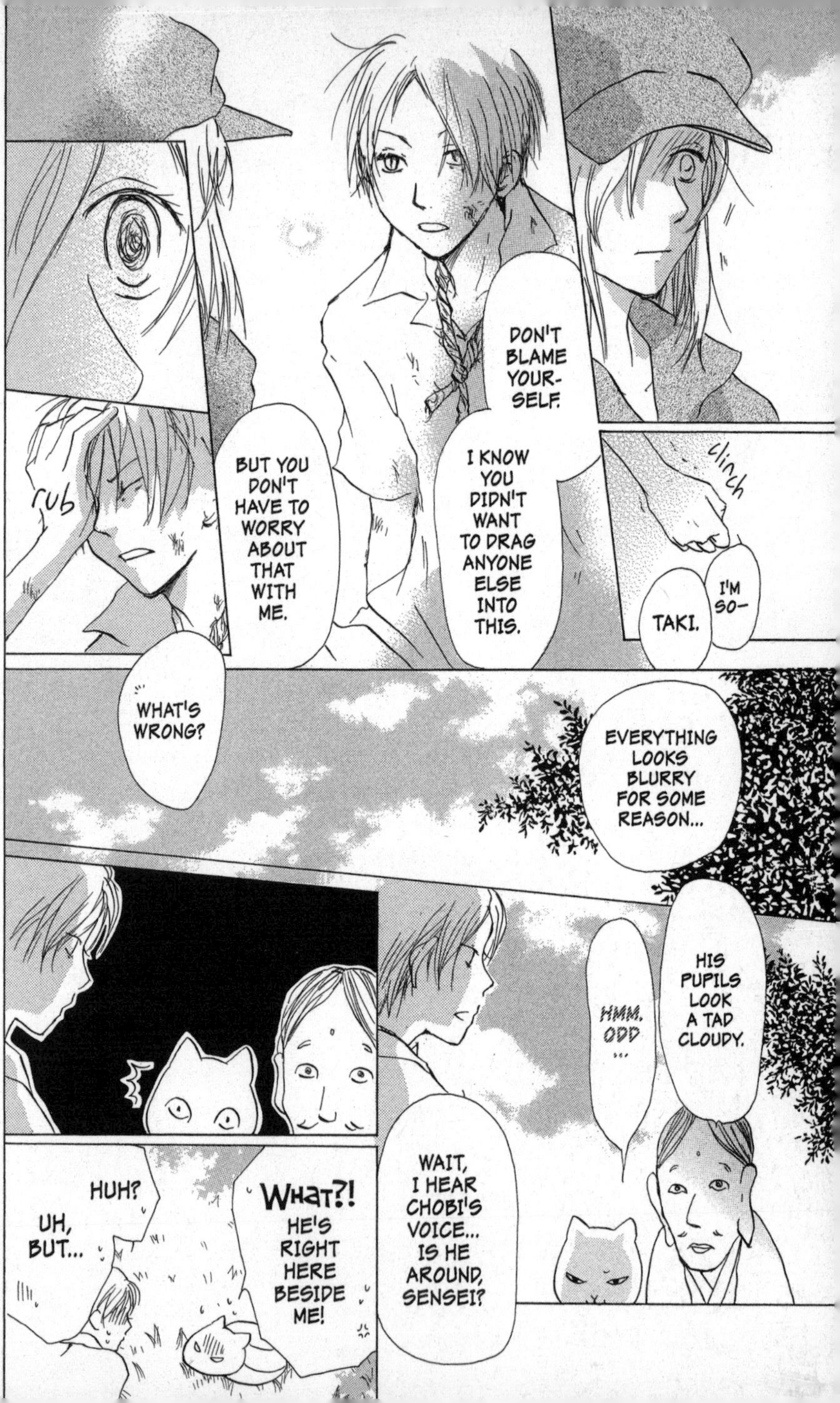
clinch
I'M SO—
TAKI.
DON'T BLAME YOURSELF.
I KNOW YOU DIDN'T WANT TO DRAG ANYONE ELSE INTO THIS.
rub
BUT YOU DON'T HAVE TO WORRY ABOUT THAT WITH ME.
WHAT'S WRONG?
EVERYTHING LOOKS BLURRY FOR SOME REASON...
HIS PUPILS LOOK A TAD CLOUDY.
HMM. ODD...
WAIT, I HEAR CHOBI'S VOICE... IS HE AROUND, SENSEI?
WHAT?! HE'S RIGHT HERE BESIDE ME!
HUH?
UH, BUT...

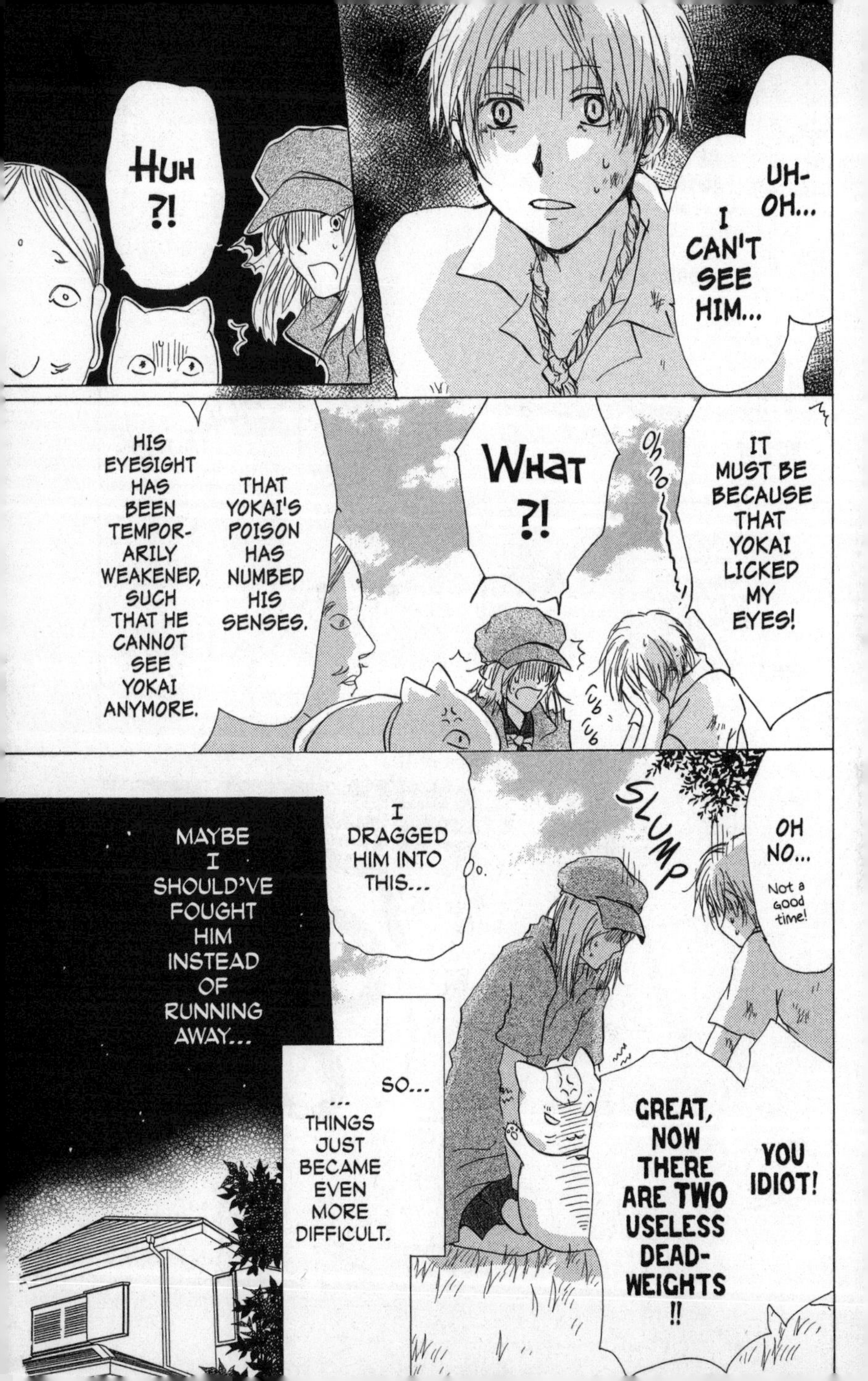

UH-OH... I CAN'T SEE HIM...
HUH ?!
IT MUST BE BECAUSE THAT YOKAI LICKED MY EYES!
Oh no~
WHAT ?!
THAT YOKAI'S POISON HAS NUMBED HIS SENSES.
HIS EYESIGHT HAS BEEN TEMPORARILY WEAKENED, SUCH THAT HE CANNOT SEE YOKAI ANYMORE.
OH NO...
Not a good time!
SLUMP
I DRAGGED HIM INTO THIS...
YOU IDIOT!
GREAT, NOW THERE ARE TWO USELESS DEAD-WEIGHTS !!
MAYBE I SHOULD'VE FOUGHT HIM INSTEAD OF RUNNING AWAY...
SO...
...THINGS JUST BECAME EVEN MORE DIFFICULT.

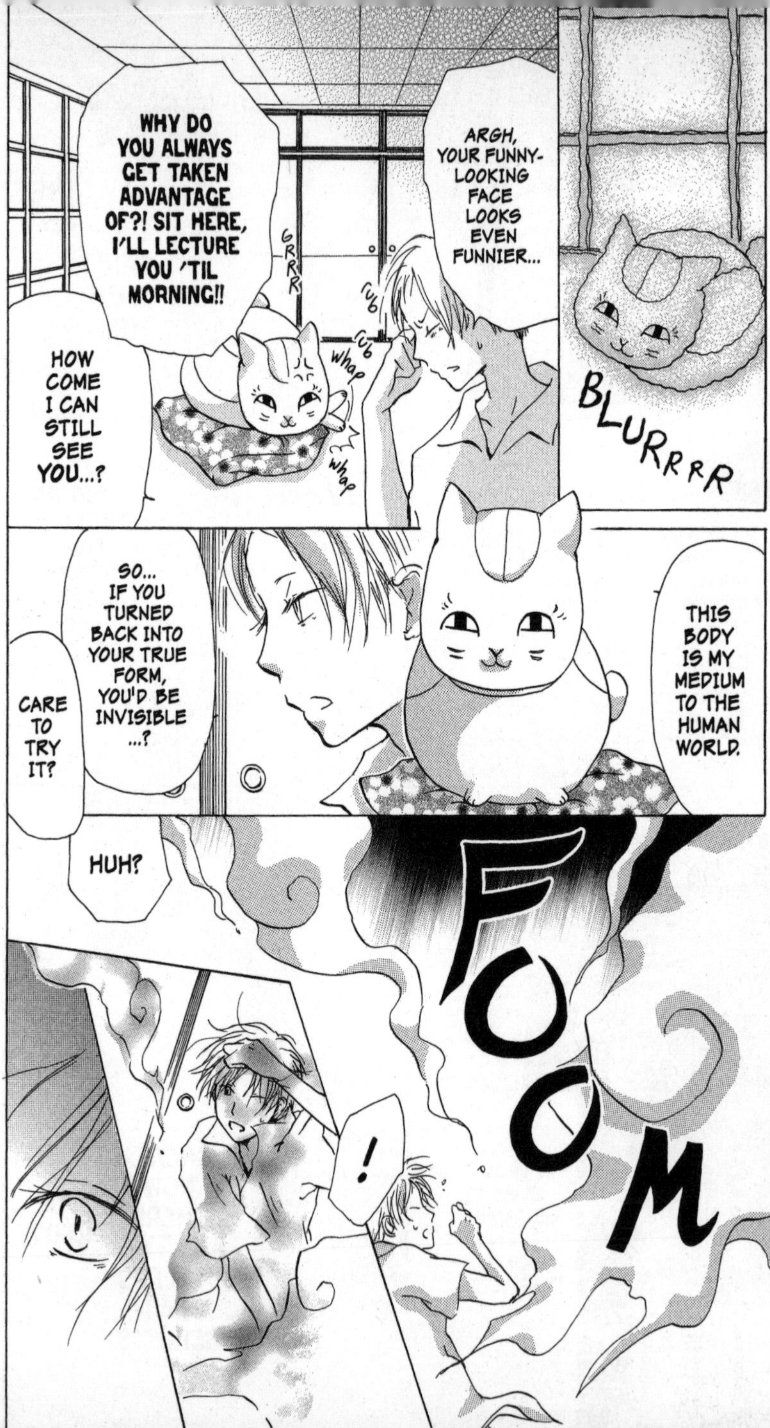
BLURRRRR
ARGH, YOUR FUNNY-LOOKING FACE LOOKS EVEN FUNNIER...
rub rub
whap whap
GRRR
WHY DO YOU ALWAYS GET TAKEN ADVANTAGE OF?! SIT HERE, I'LL LECTURE YOU 'TIL MORNING!!
HOW COME I CAN STILL SEE YOU...?
THIS BODY IS MY MEDIUM TO THE HUMAN WORLD.
SO... IF YOU TURNED BACK INTO YOUR TRUE FORM, YOU'D BE INVISIBLE ...?
CARE TO TRY IT?
HUH?
FOOOM
!

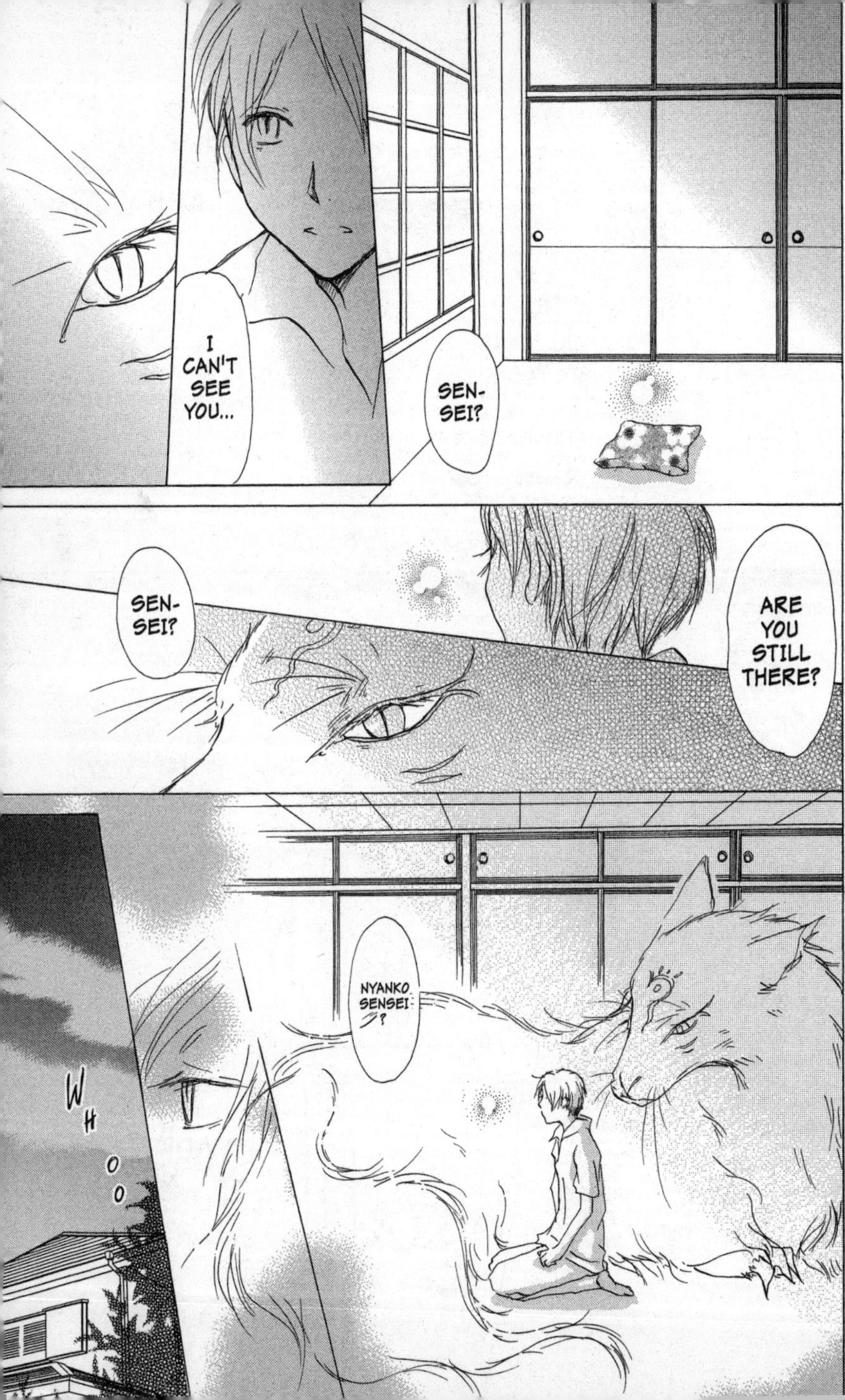
SEN-SEI?
I CAN'T SEE YOU...
ARE YOU STILL THERE?
SEN-SEI?
NYANKO SENSEI...?
WHOO

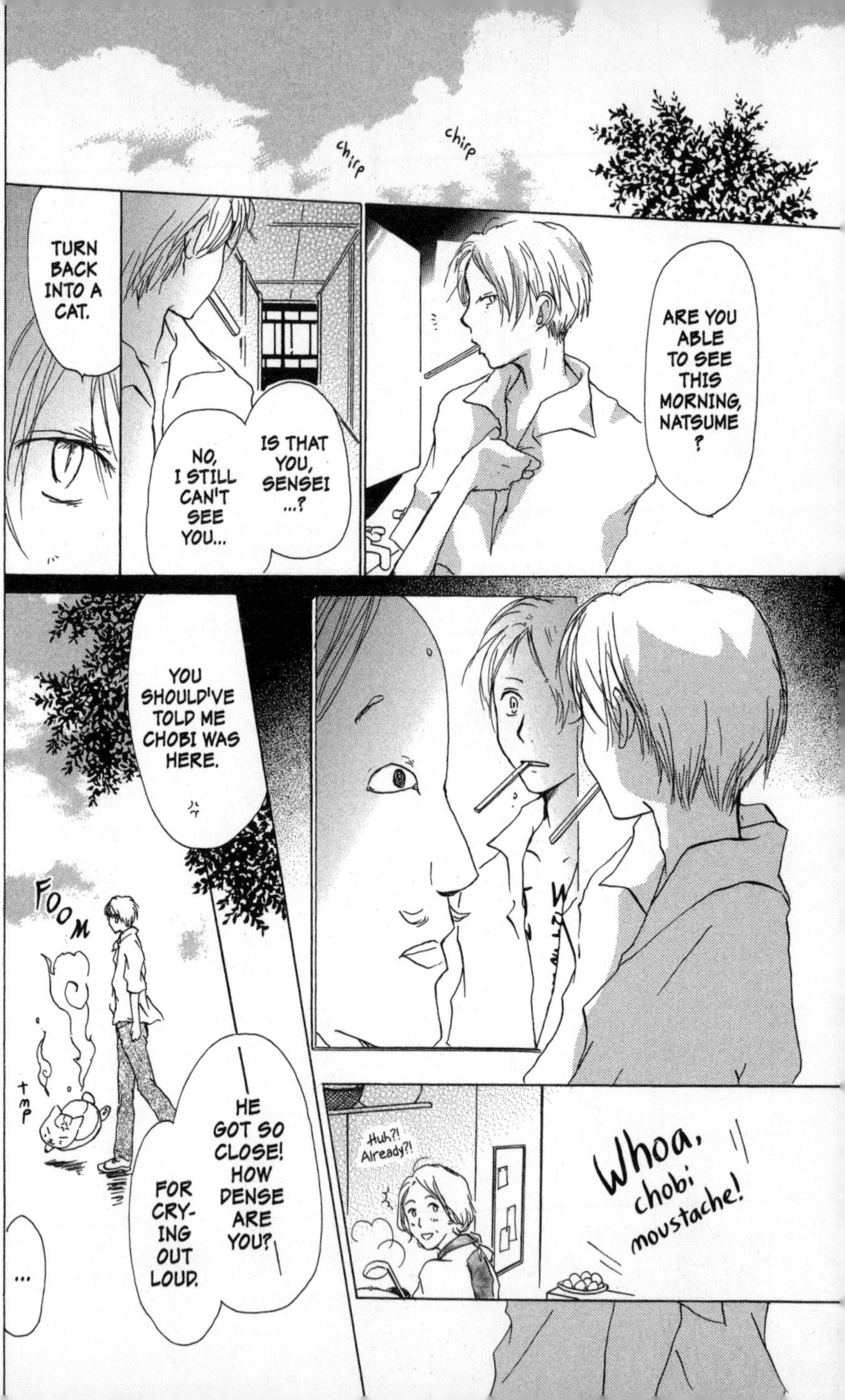
chirp
chirp
ARE YOU ABLE TO SEE THIS MORNING, NATSUME?
NO, I STILL CAN'T SEE YOU...
IS THAT YOU, SENSEI...?
TURN BACK INTO A CAT.
Whoa, chobi moustache!
Huh?! Already?!
YOU SHOULD'VE TOLD ME CHOBI WAS HERE.
FOOM
tmp
HE GOT SO CLOSE! HOW DENSE ARE YOU?
FOR CRYING OUT LOUD.
...

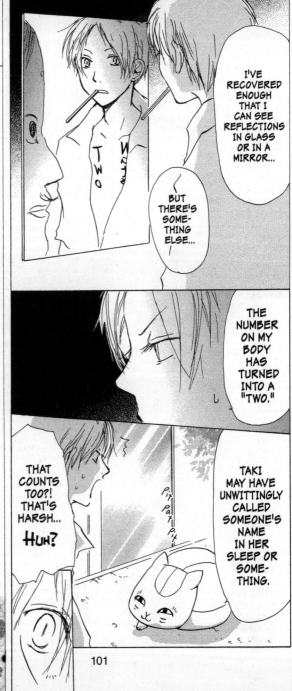

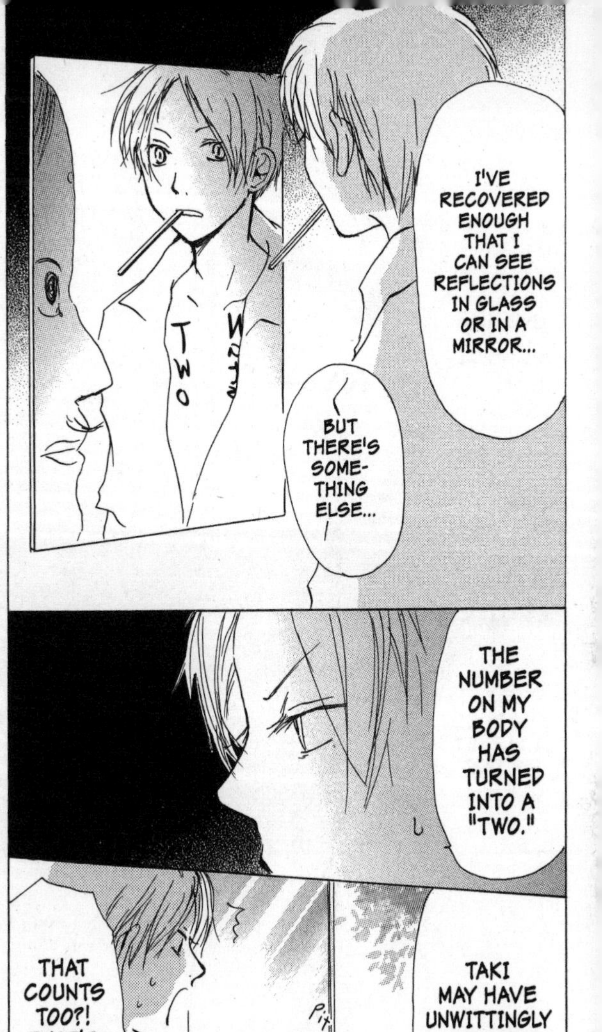
I'VE RECOVERED ENOUGH THAT I CAN SEE REFLECTIONS IN GLASS OR IN A MIRROR...
TWO
BUT THERE'S SOME-THING ELSE...
THE NUMBER ON MY BODY HAS TURNED INTO A "TWO."
TAKI MAY HAVE UNWITTINGLY CALLED SOMEONE'S NAME IN HER SLEEP OR SOME-THING.
Pit Pat Pit
THAT COUNTS TOO?! THAT'S HARSH...
HUH?

03

❋ Screentone of traditional Japanese patterns

After I started working on Natsume's Book of Friends I started to really enjoy browsing through Japanese patterned screentones. Natsume is a guy, and the yokai don't particularly tend to be fashionable, so I have few opportunities to use it. I hope to one day work on a story where I can use these screentones liberally. There are so many beautiful patterns available these days.

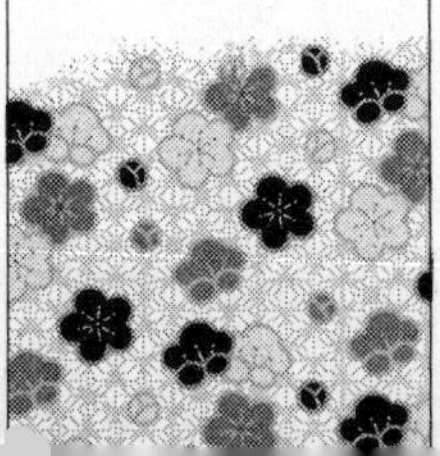

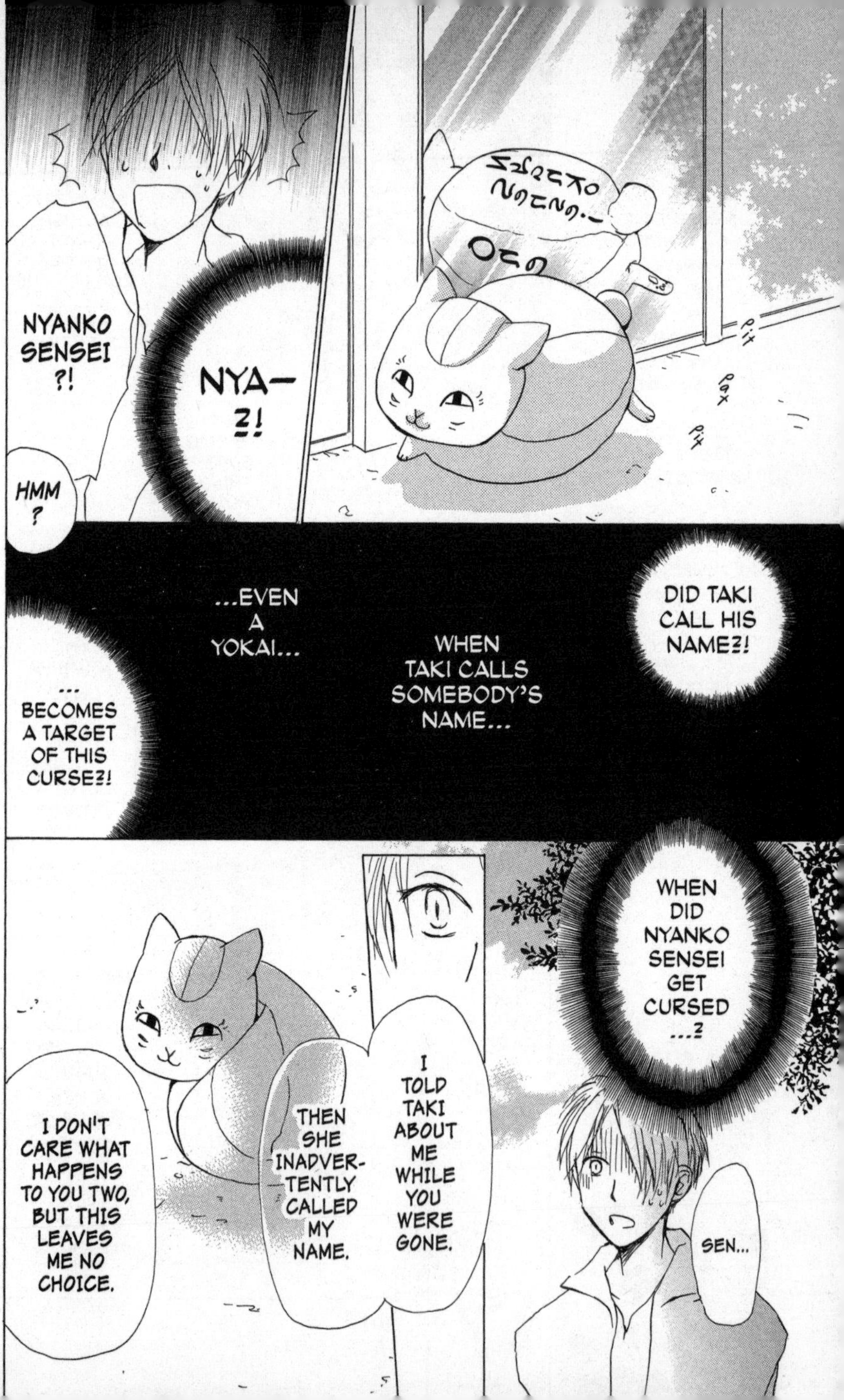
Pit
Pat
Pit
NYA-?!
NYANKO SENSEI ?!
HMM ?
DID TAKI CALL HIS NAME?!
WHEN TAKI CALLS SOMEBODY'S NAME...
...EVEN A YOKAI...
...BECOMES A TARGET OF THIS CURSE?!
WHEN DID NYANKO SENSEI GET CURSED...?
SEN...
I TOLD TAKI ABOUT ME WHILE YOU WERE GONE.
THEN SHE INADVERTENTLY CALLED MY NAME.
I DON'T CARE WHAT HAPPENS TO YOU TWO, BUT THIS LEAVES ME NO CHOICE.

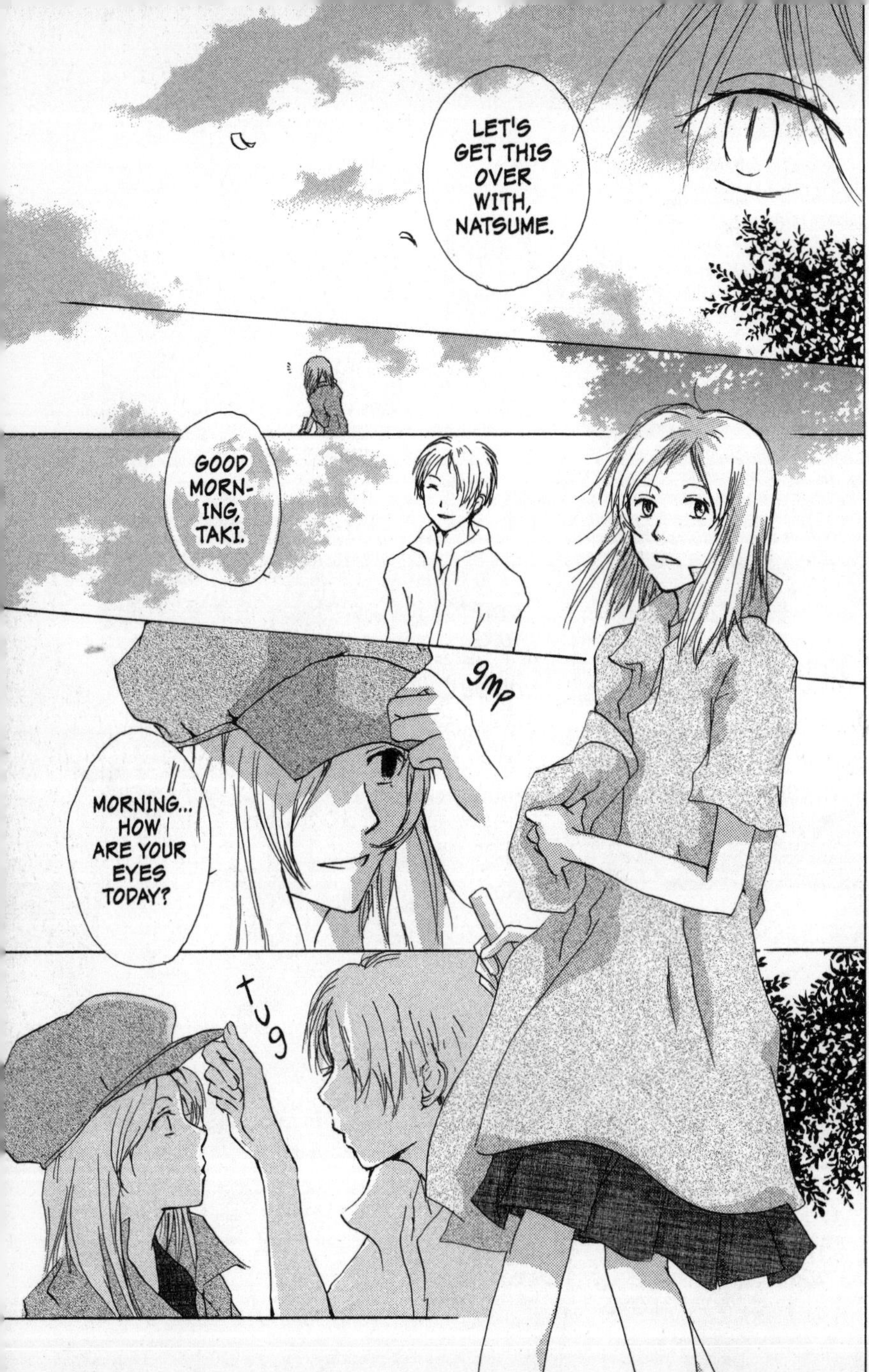
LET'S GET THIS OVER WITH, NATSUME.
GOOD MORN-ING, TAKI.
gmp
MORNING... HOW ARE YOUR EYES TODAY?
TUG

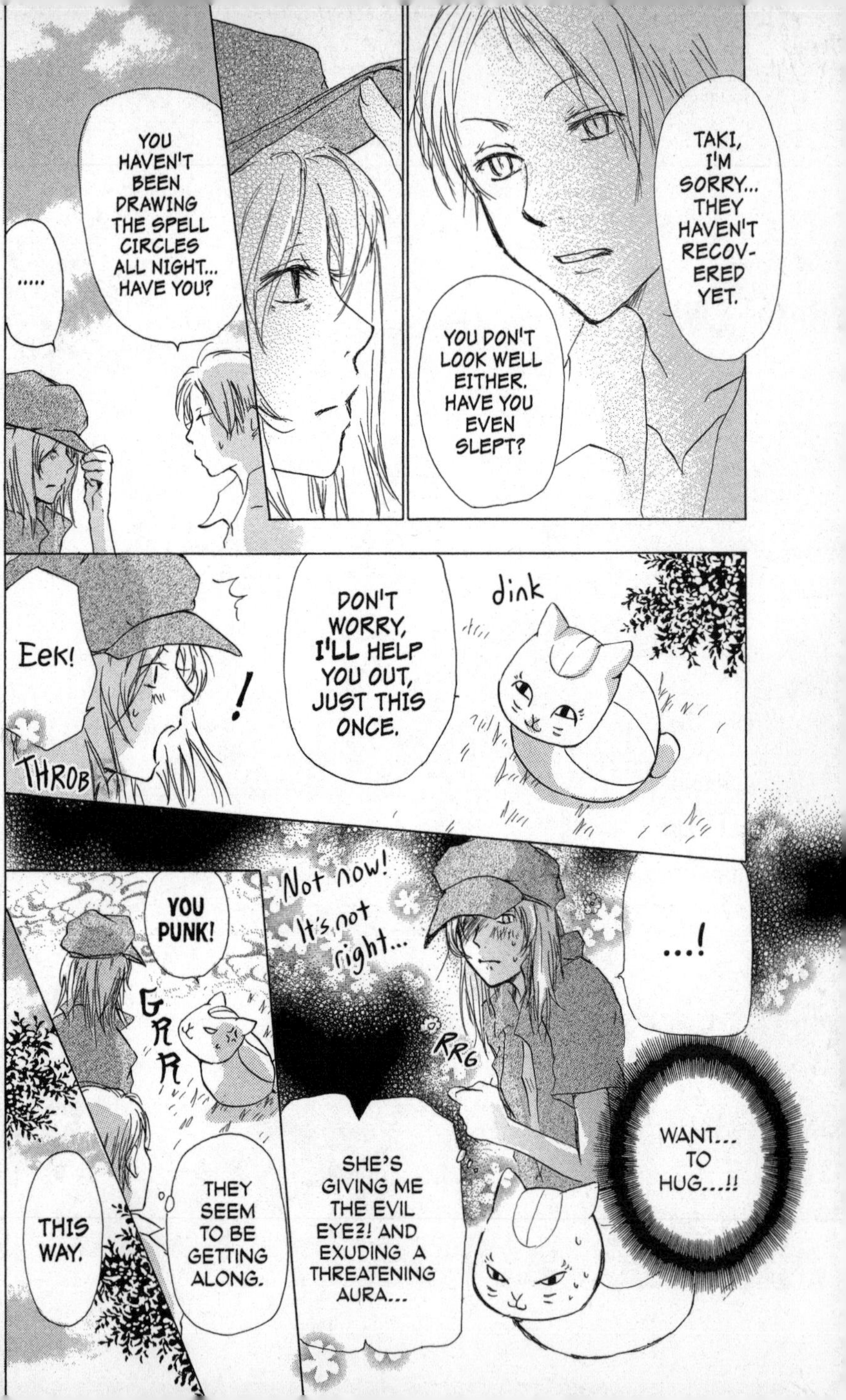
TAKI, I'M SORRY... THEY HAVEN'T RECOVERED YET.
YOU DON'T LOOK WELL EITHER. HAVE YOU EVEN SLEPT?
YOU HAVEN'T BEEN DRAWING THE SPELL CIRCLES ALL NIGHT... HAVE YOU?
.....
dink
DON'T WORRY, I'LL HELP YOU OUT, JUST THIS ONCE.
!
Eek!
THROB
...!
Not now! It's not right...
RRG
WANT... TO HUG...!!
SHE'S GIVING ME THE EVIL EYE?! AND EXUDING A THREATENING AURA...
YOU PUNK!
GRR
THEY SEEM TO BE GETTING ALONG.
THIS WAY.

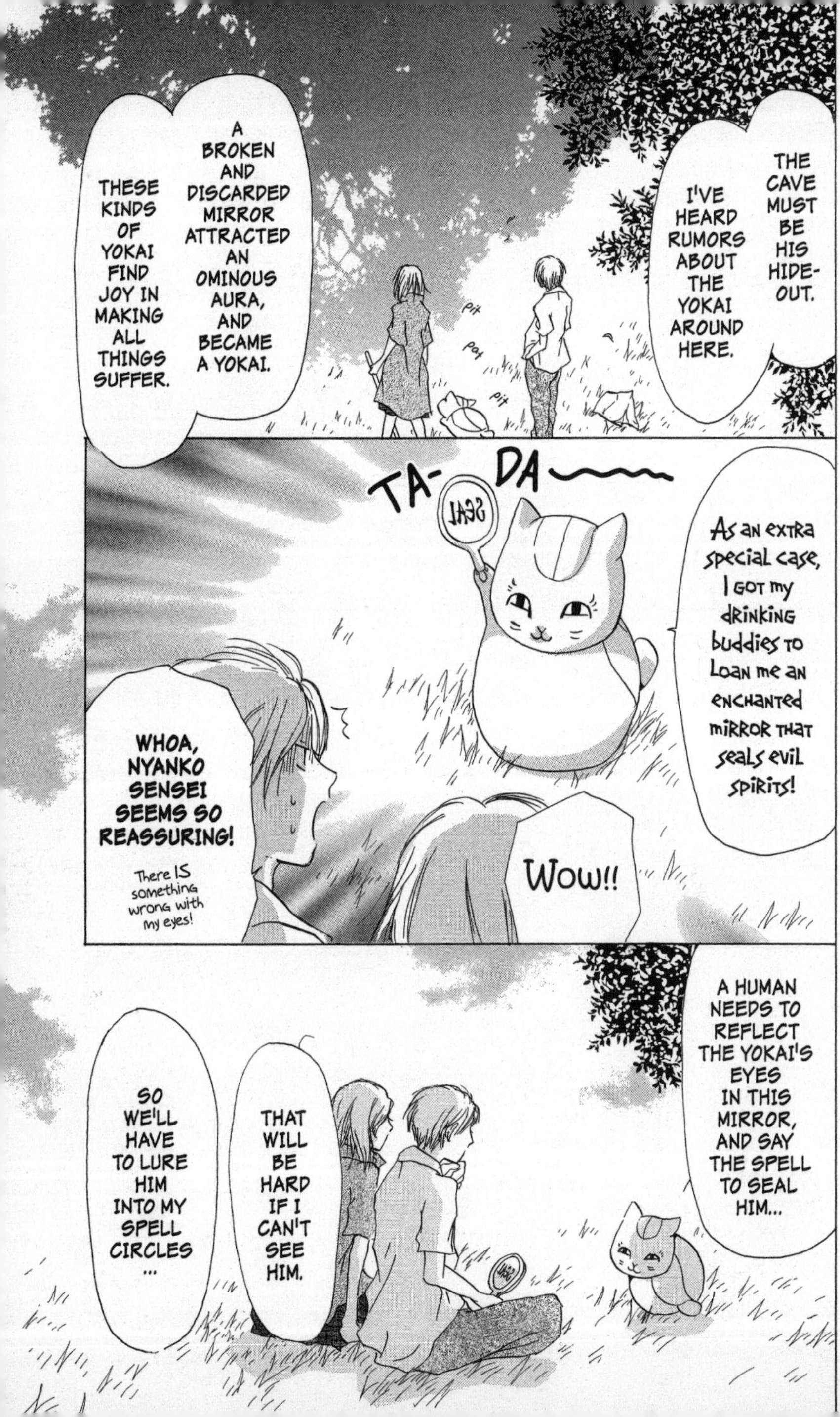
THE CAVE MUST BE HIS HIDE-OUT.
I'VE HEARD RUMORS ABOUT THE YOKAI AROUND HERE.
A BROKEN AND DISCARDED MIRROR ATTRACTED AN OMINOUS AURA, AND BECAME A YOKAI.
THESE KINDS OF YOKAI FIND JOY IN MAKING ALL THINGS SUFFER.
pit
pat
pit
TA- DA
SEAL
As an extra special case, I got my drinking buddies to loan me an enchanted mirror that seals evil spirits!
WOW!!
WHOA, NYANKO SENSEI SEEMS SO REASSURING!
There IS something wrong with my eyes!
A HUMAN NEEDS TO REFLECT THE YOKAI'S EYES IN THIS MIRROR, AND SAY THE SPELL TO SEAL HIM...
THAT WILL BE HARD IF I CAN'T SEE HIM.
SO WE'LL HAVE TO LURE HIM INTO MY SPELL CIRCLES ...

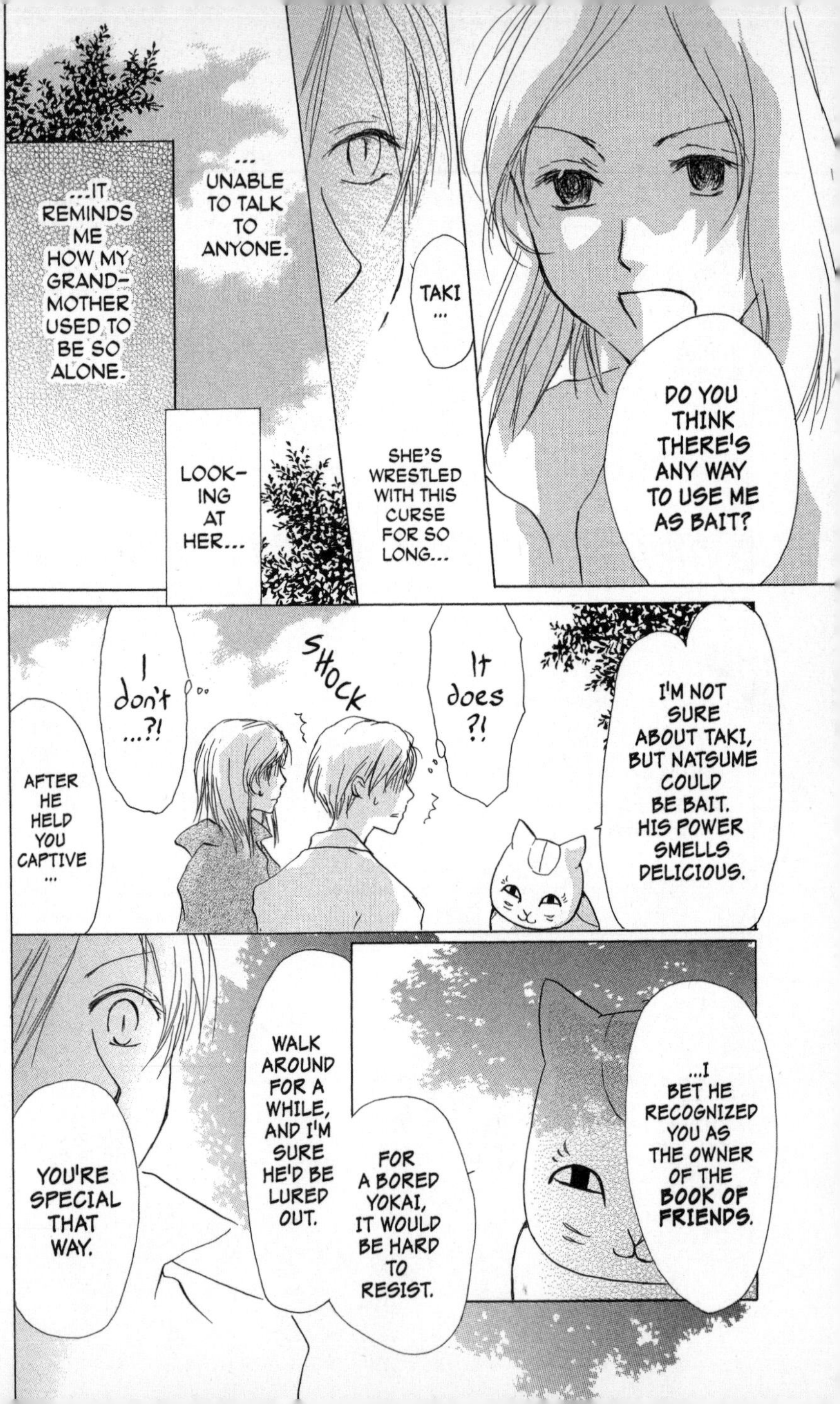

DO YOU THINK THERE'S ANY WAY TO USE ME AS BAIT?
TAKI ...
SHE'S WRESTLED WITH THIS CURSE FOR SO LONG...
...UNABLE TO TALK TO ANYONE.
LOOKING AT HER...
...IT REMINDS ME HOW MY GRANDMOTHER USED TO BE SO ALONE.
I'M NOT SURE ABOUT TAKI, BUT NATSUME COULD BE BAIT. HIS POWER SMELLS DELICIOUS.
It does?!
SHOCK
I don't ...?!
AFTER HE HELD YOU CAPTIVE ...
...I BET HE RECOGNIZED YOU AS THE OWNER OF THE BOOK OF FRIENDS.
FOR A BORED YOKAI, IT WOULD BE HARD TO RESIST.
WALK AROUND FOR A WHILE, AND I'M SURE HE'D BE LURED OUT.
YOU'RE SPECIAL THAT WAY.

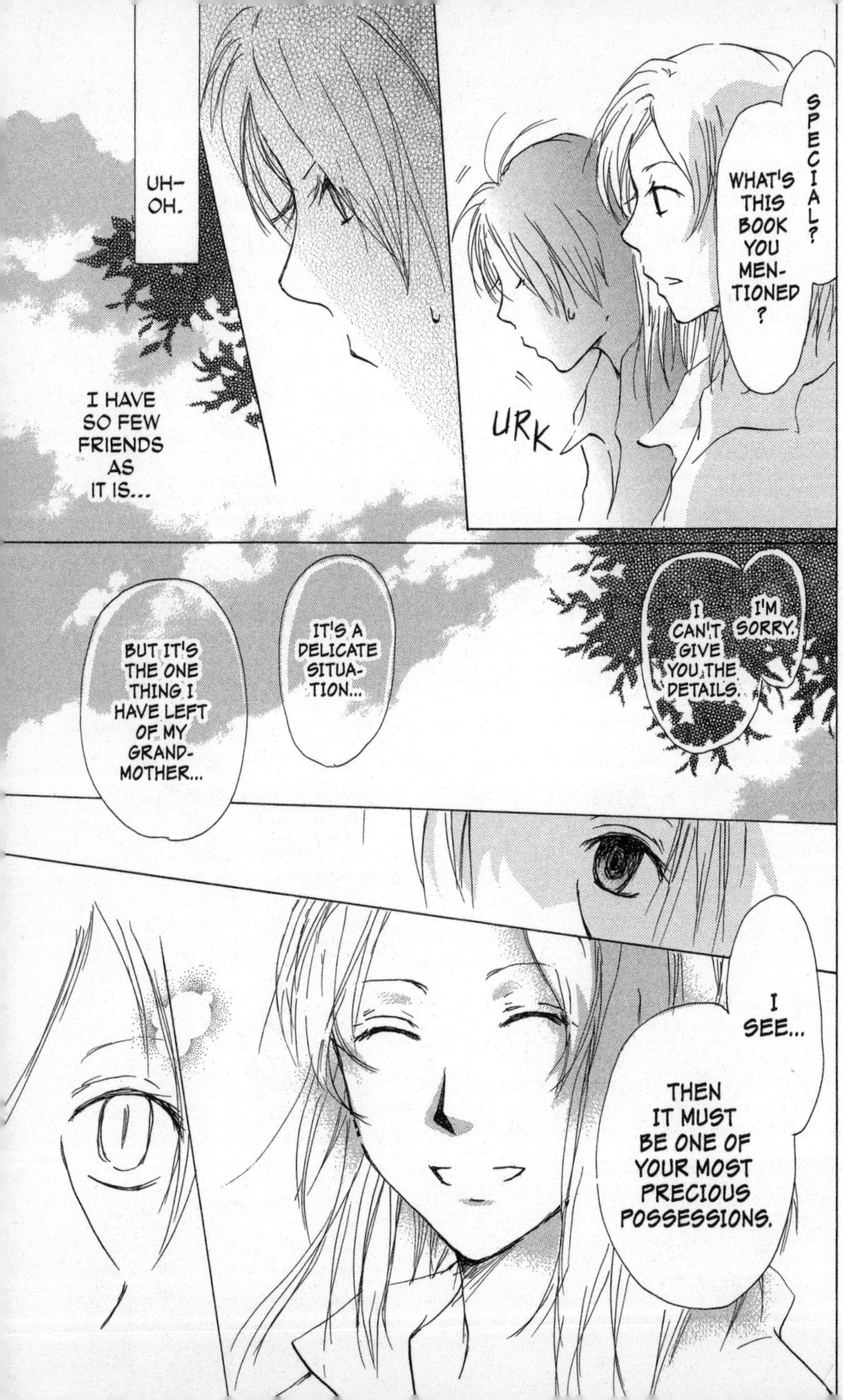
SPECIAL?
WHAT'S THIS BOOK YOU MENTIONED?
URK
UH-OH.
I HAVE SO FEW FRIENDS AS IT IS...
I'M SORRY.
I CAN'T GIVE YOU THE DETAILS.
IT'S A DELICATE SITUATION...
BUT IT'S THE ONE THING I HAVE LEFT OF MY GRANDMOTHER...
I SEE...
THEN IT MUST BE ONE OF YOUR MOST PRECIOUS POSSESSIONS.

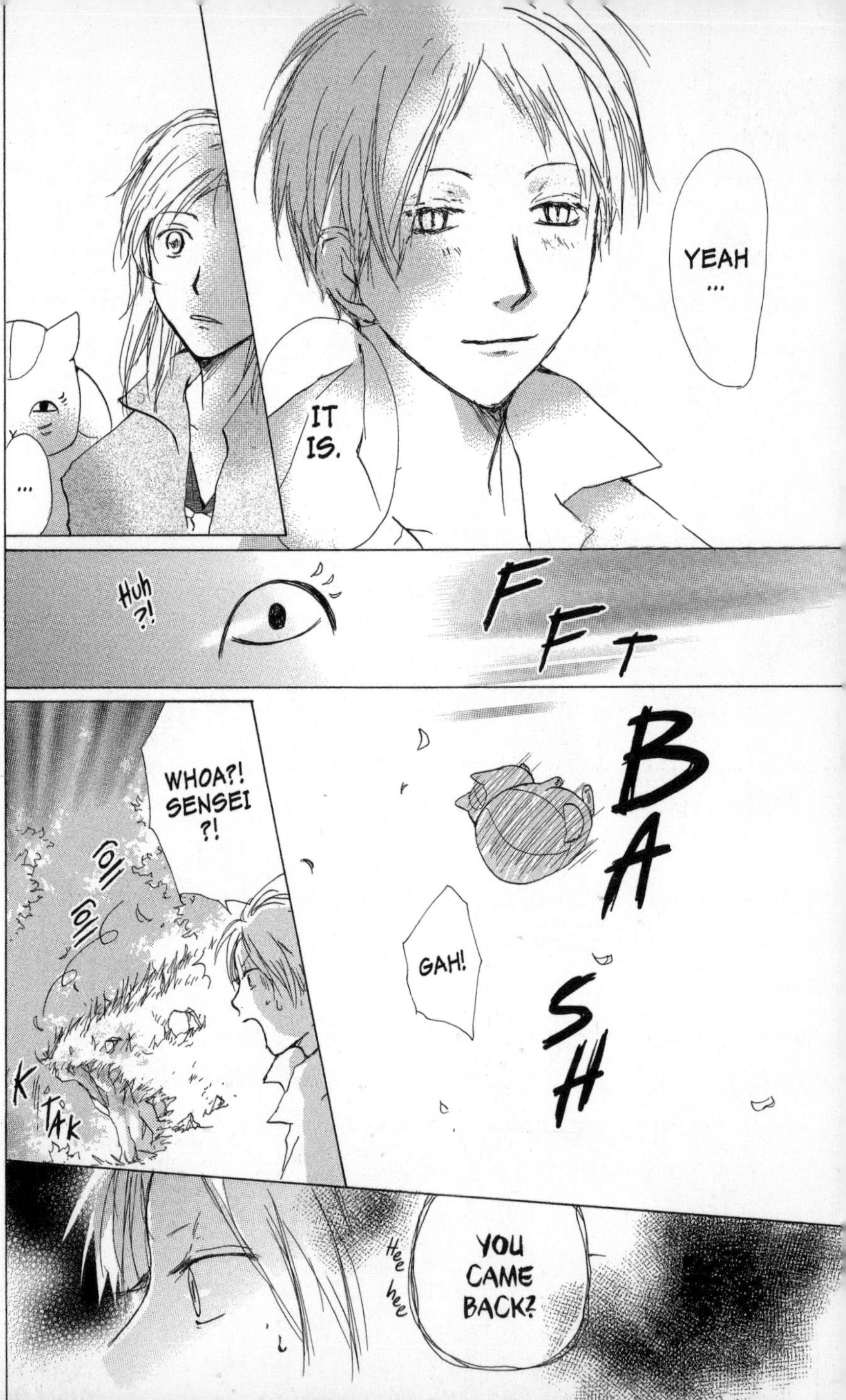
YEAH ...
IT IS.
...
FFT
Huh?!
BASH
GAH!
WHOA?! SENSEI?!
KTAK
YOU CAME BACK?
Hee hee

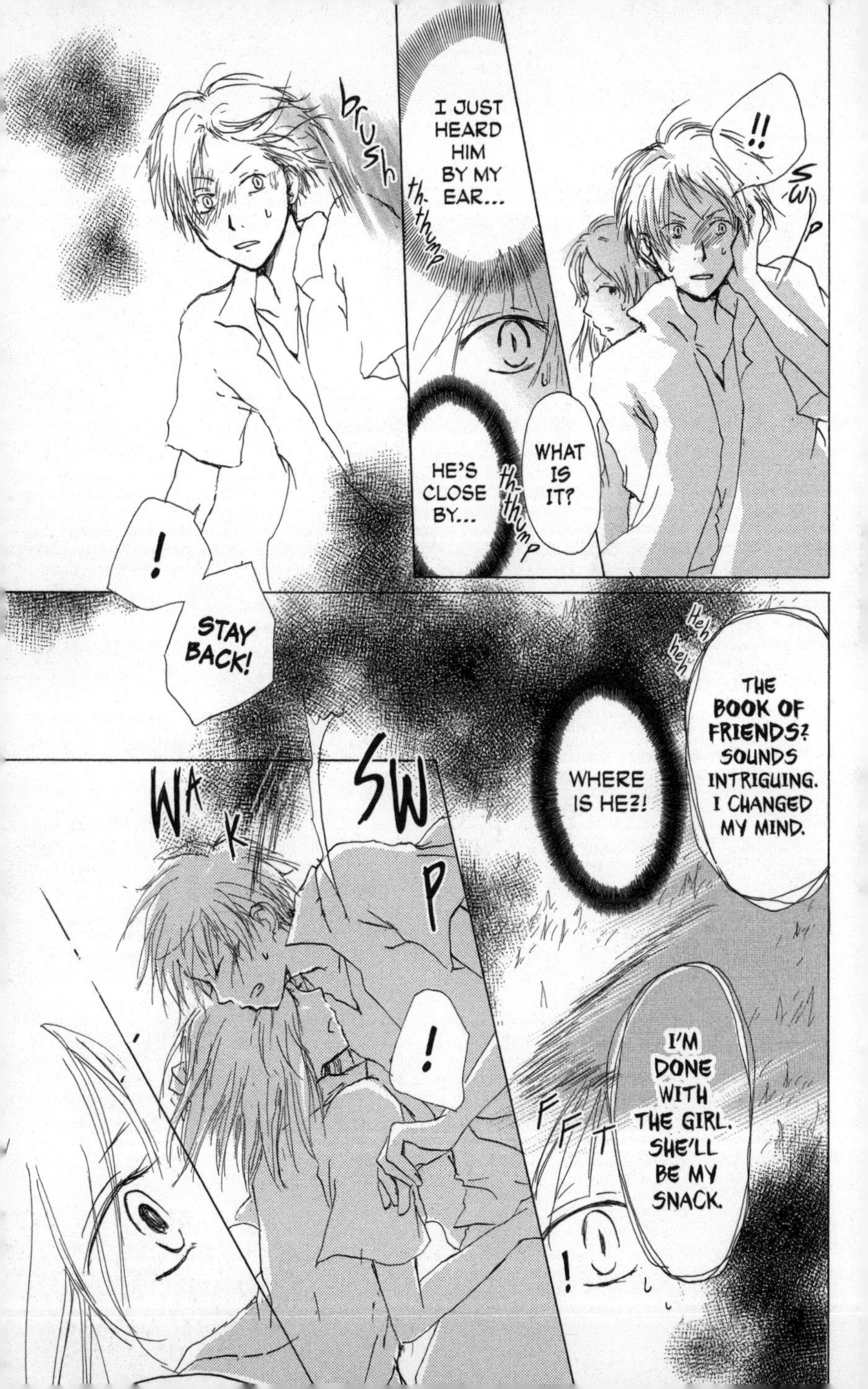
!!
SWP
WHAT IS IT?
I JUST HEARD HIM BY MY EAR...
th-thump
HE'S CLOSE BY...
th-thump
brush
!
Heh heh
THE BOOK OF FRIENDS? SOUNDS INTRIGUING. I CHANGED MY MIND.
WHERE IS HE?!
STAY BACK!
I'M DONE WITH THE GIRL. SHE'LL BE MY SNACK.
FFT
!
SWP
WAK
!

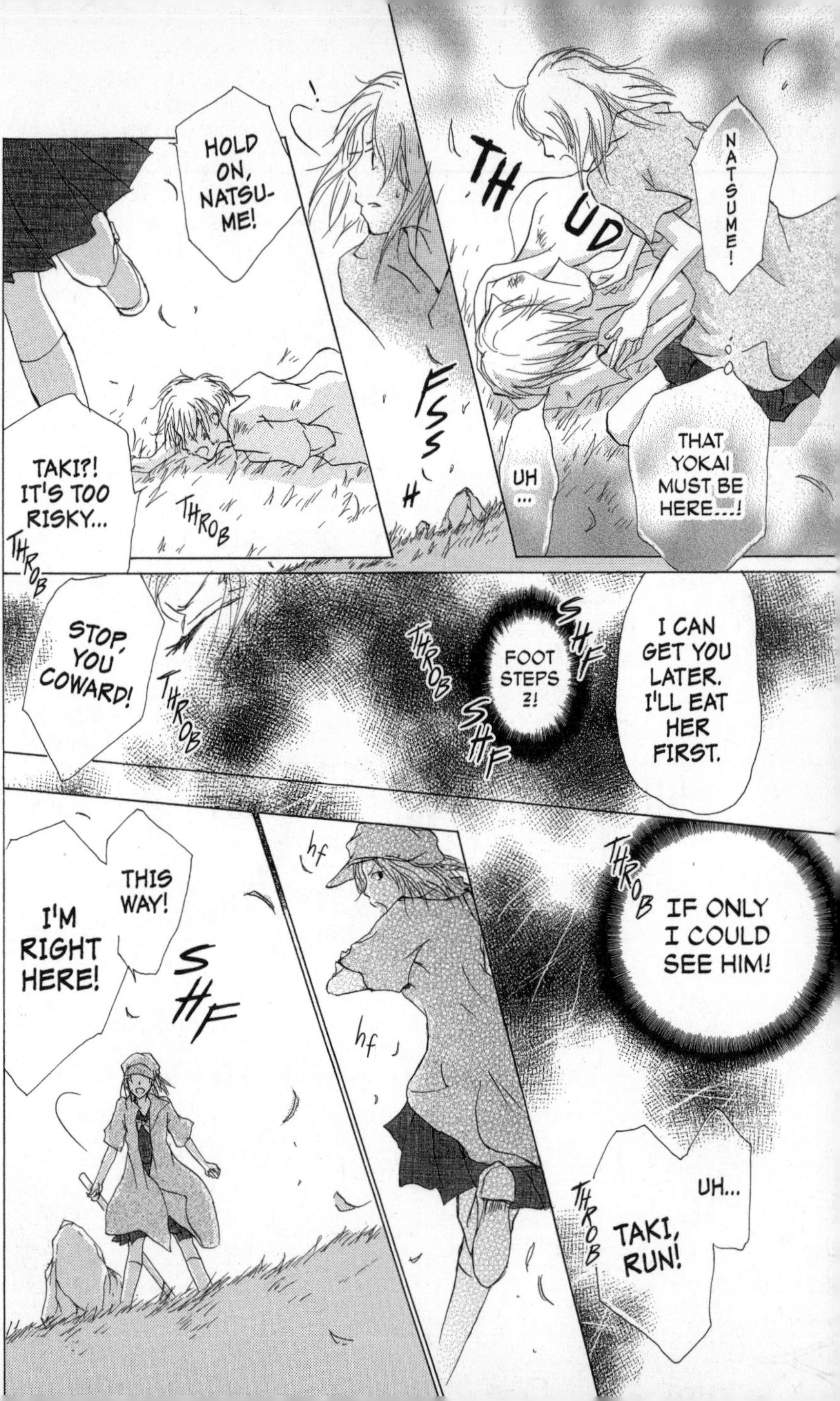
NATSUME!
THUD
THAT YOKAI MUST BE HERE...!
UH ...
!
FSSH
HOLD ON, NATSU-ME!
TAKI?! IT'S TOO RISKY...
THROB
THROB
I CAN GET YOU LATER. I'LL EAT HER FIRST.
SHF
FOOT STEPS?!
THROB
SHF
THROB
STOP, YOU COWARD!
THROB
IF ONLY I COULD SEE HIM!
THROB
UH...
TAKI, RUN!
THROB
hf
hf
THIS WAY!
I'M RIGHT HERE!
SHF

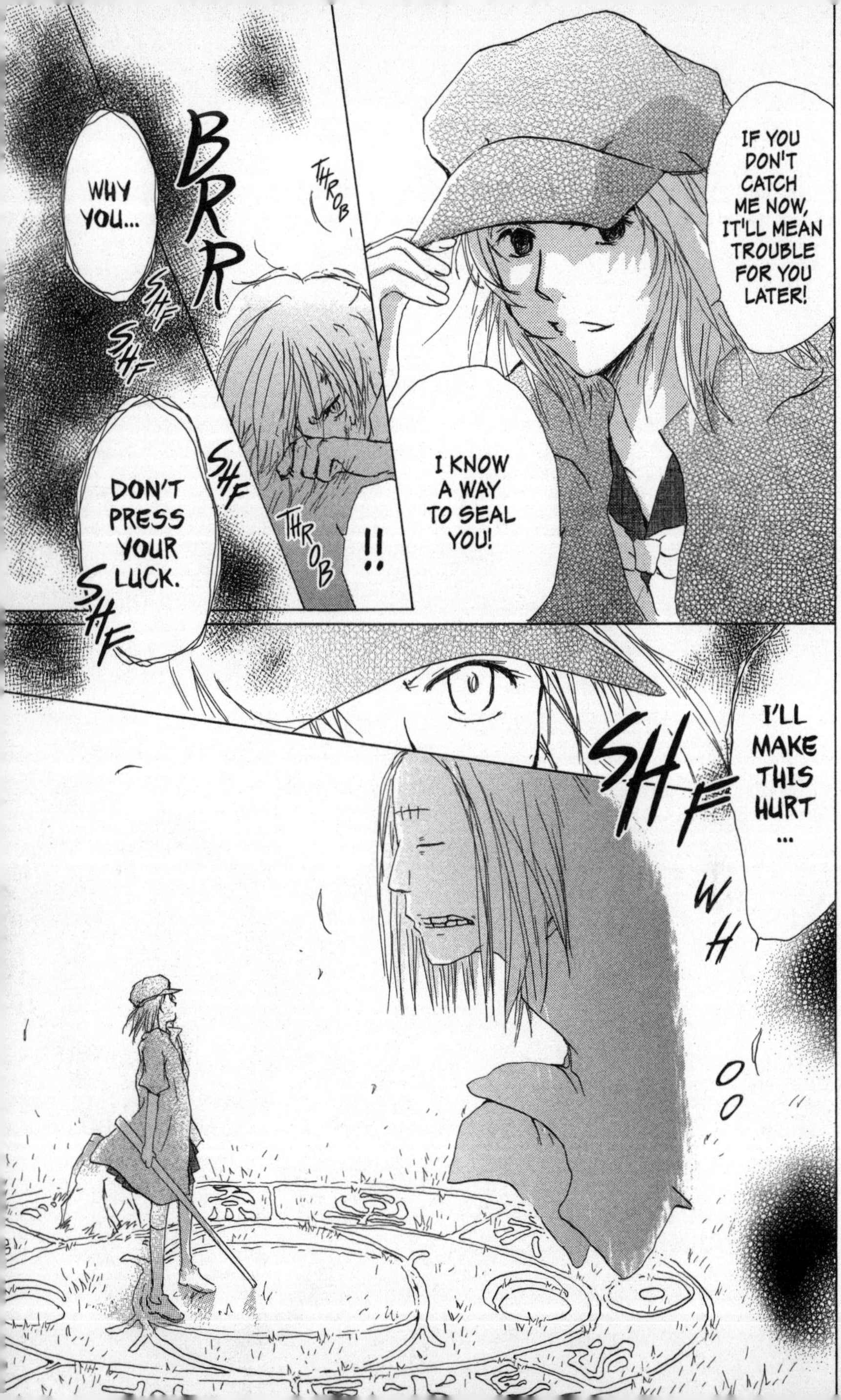
IF YOU DON'T CATCH ME NOW, IT'LL MEAN TROUBLE FOR YOU LATER!
I KNOW A WAY TO SEAL YOU!
THROB
!!
THROB
BRR
WHY YOU...
SHF
SHF
SHF
DON'T PRESS YOUR LUCK.
SHF
I'LL MAKE THIS HURT...
SHF
WHOOO

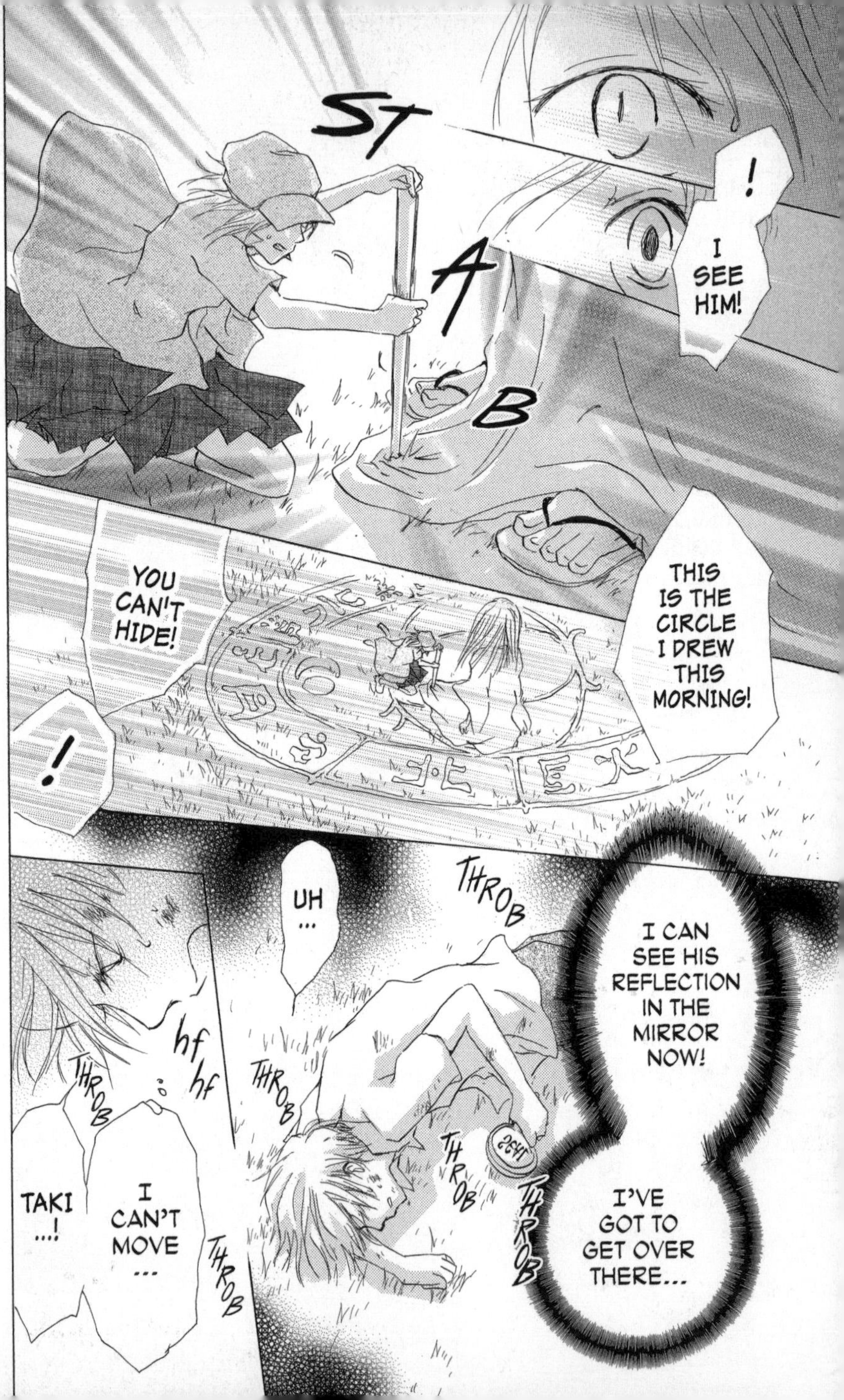
STAB
!
I SEE HIM!
THIS IS THE CIRCLE I DREW THIS MORNING!
YOU CAN'T HIDE!
!
I CAN SEE HIS REFLECTION IN THE MIRROR NOW!
THROB
UH ...
THROB
THROB
THROB
I'VE GOT TO GET OVER THERE...
hf hf
THROB
THROB
I CAN'T MOVE ...
TAKI ...!

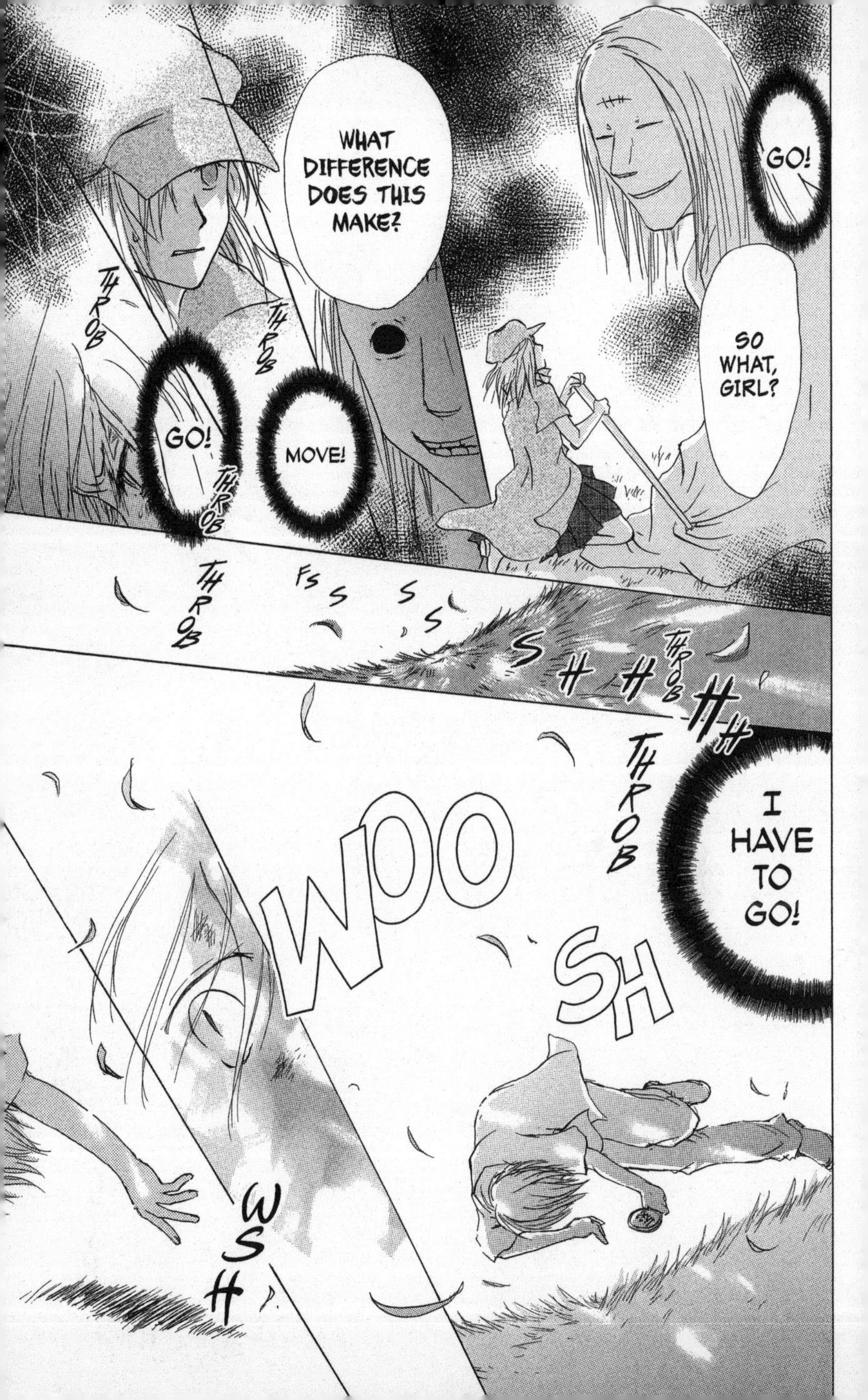
GO!
WHAT DIFFERENCE DOES THIS MAKE?
SO WHAT, GIRL?
THROB
THROB
MOVE!
GO!
THROB
THROB
FSSSS
THROB
SHHHH
THROB
I HAVE TO GO!
WOOOSH
WSH

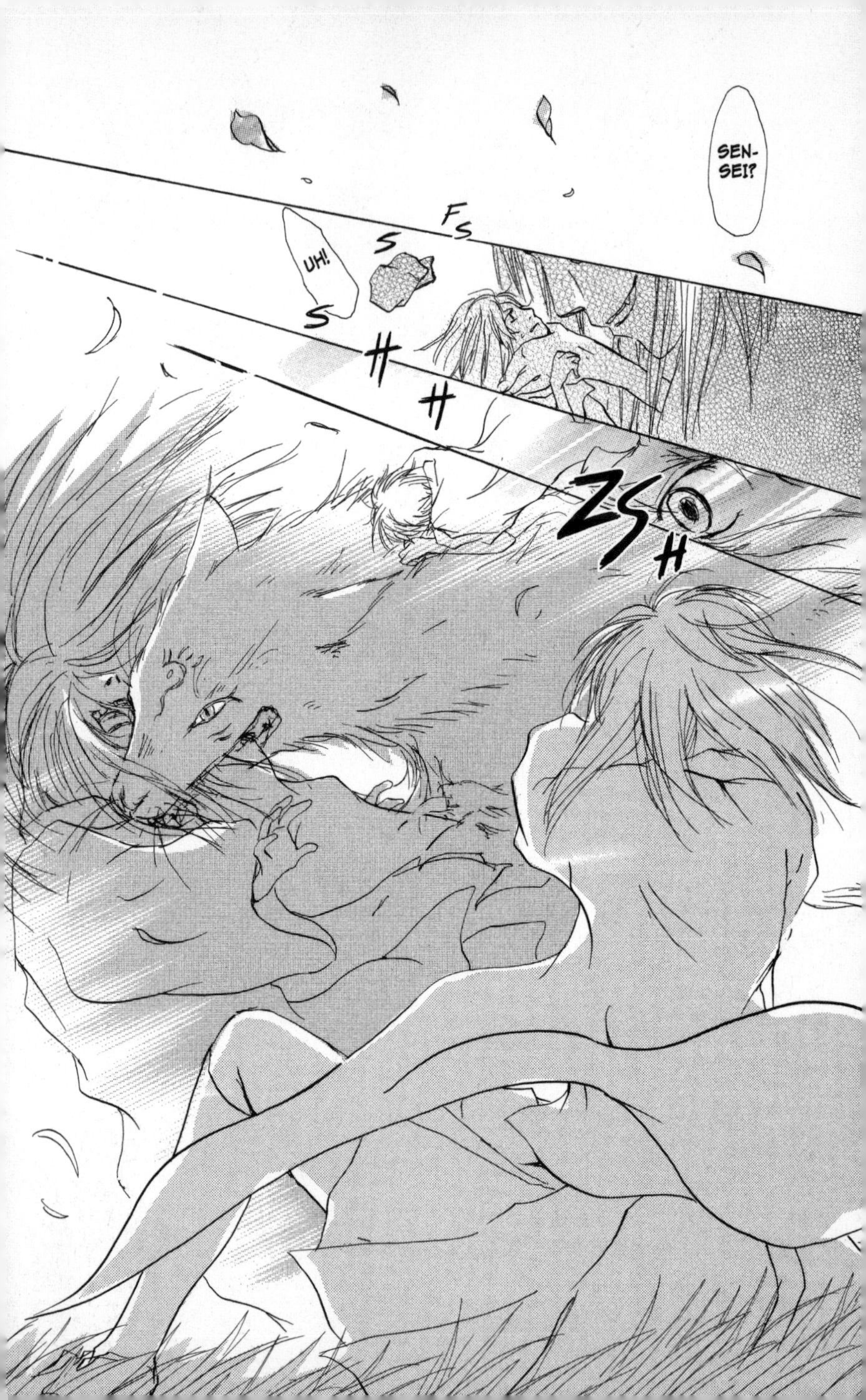
SEN-
SEI?
FS
UH!
S
S
H
H
ZS
H

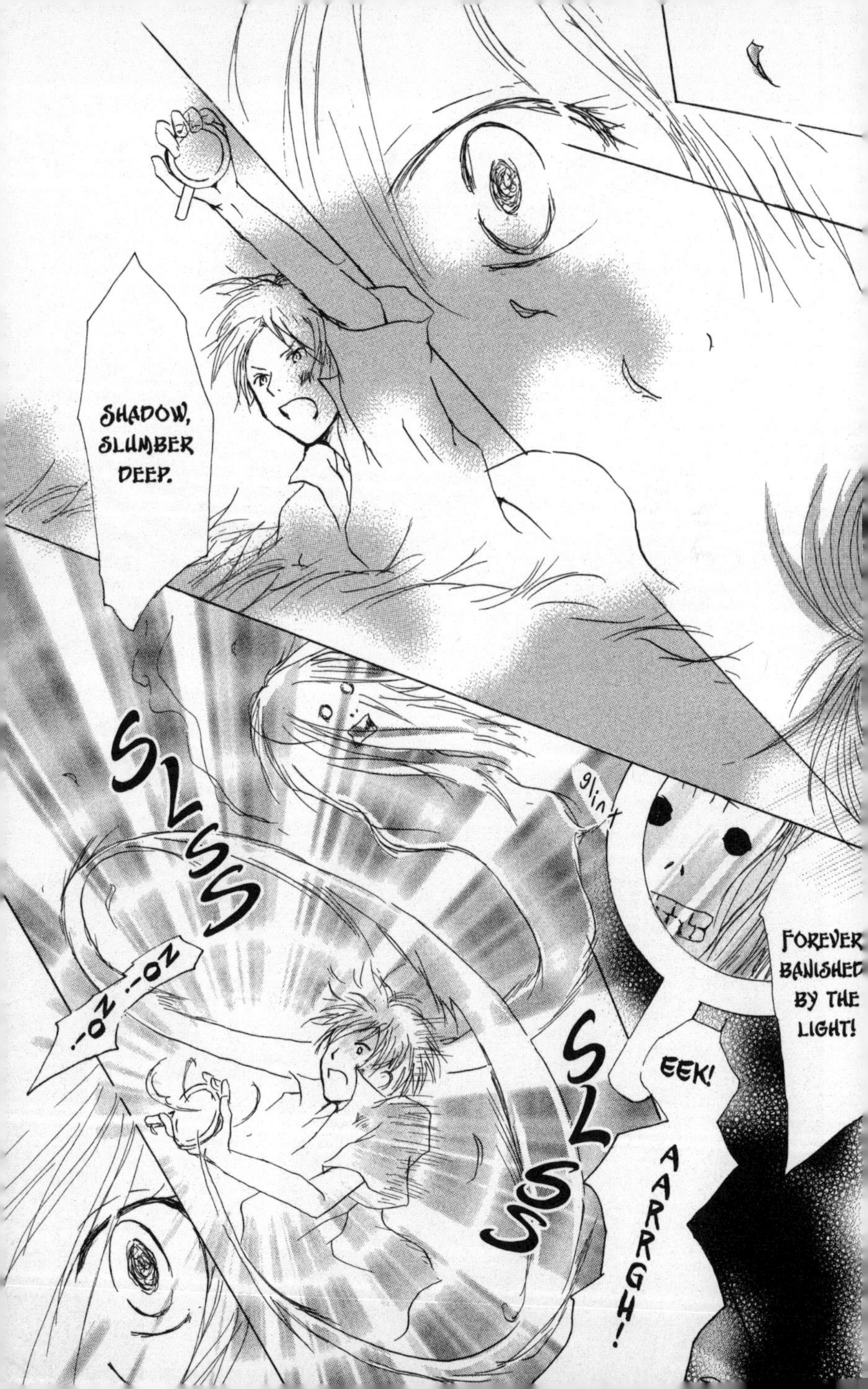
SHADOW, SLUMBER DEEP.
FOREVER BANISHED BY THE LIGHT!
glint
EEK!
AARRGH!

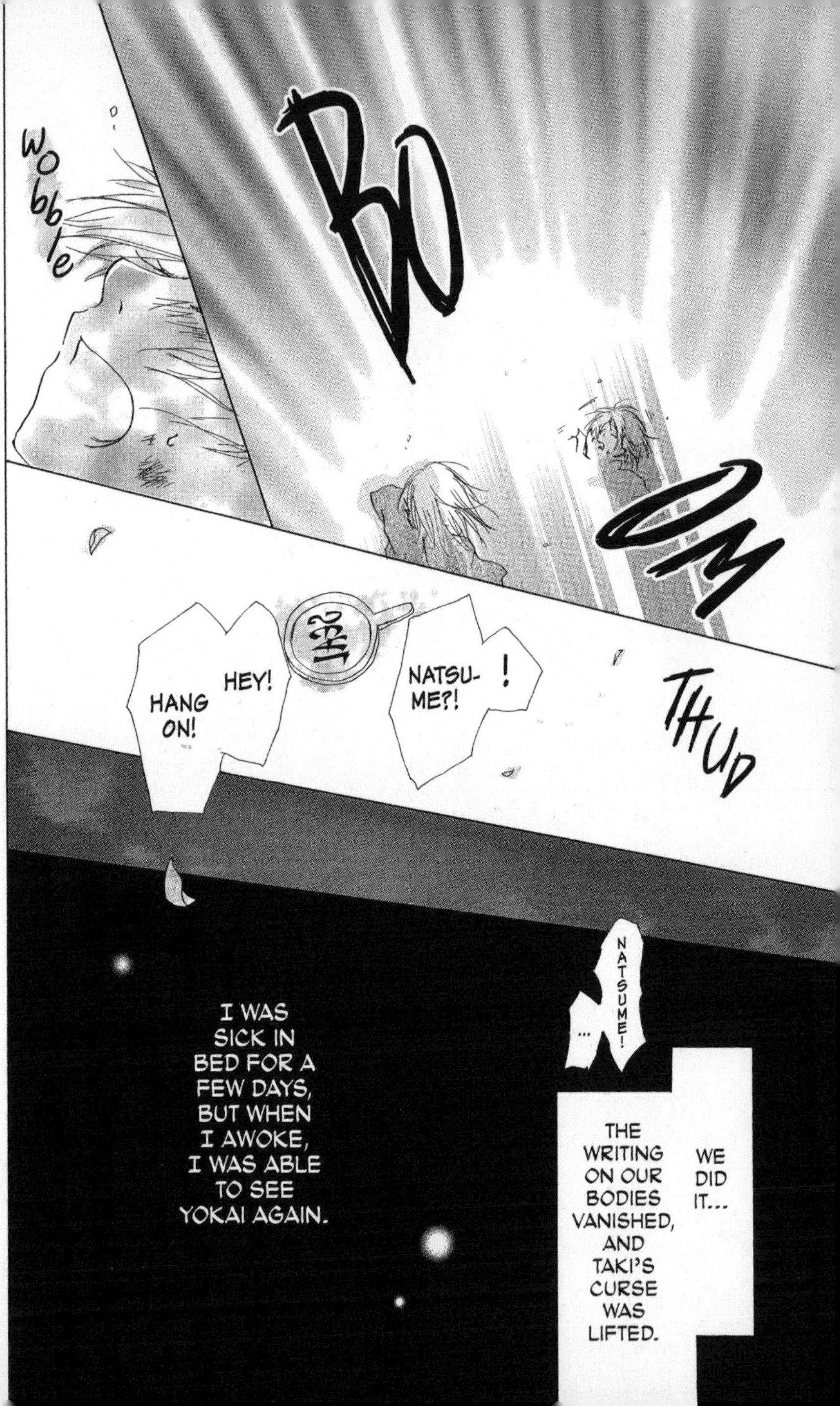
BOOM
wobble
THUD
NATSU-ME?!
!
HEY! HANG ON!
NATSUME!
...
WE DID IT...
THE WRITING ON OUR BODIES VANISHED, AND TAKI'S CURSE WAS LIFTED.
I WAS SICK IN BED FOR A FEW DAYS, BUT WHEN I AWOKE, I WAS ABLE TO SEE YOKAI AGAIN.

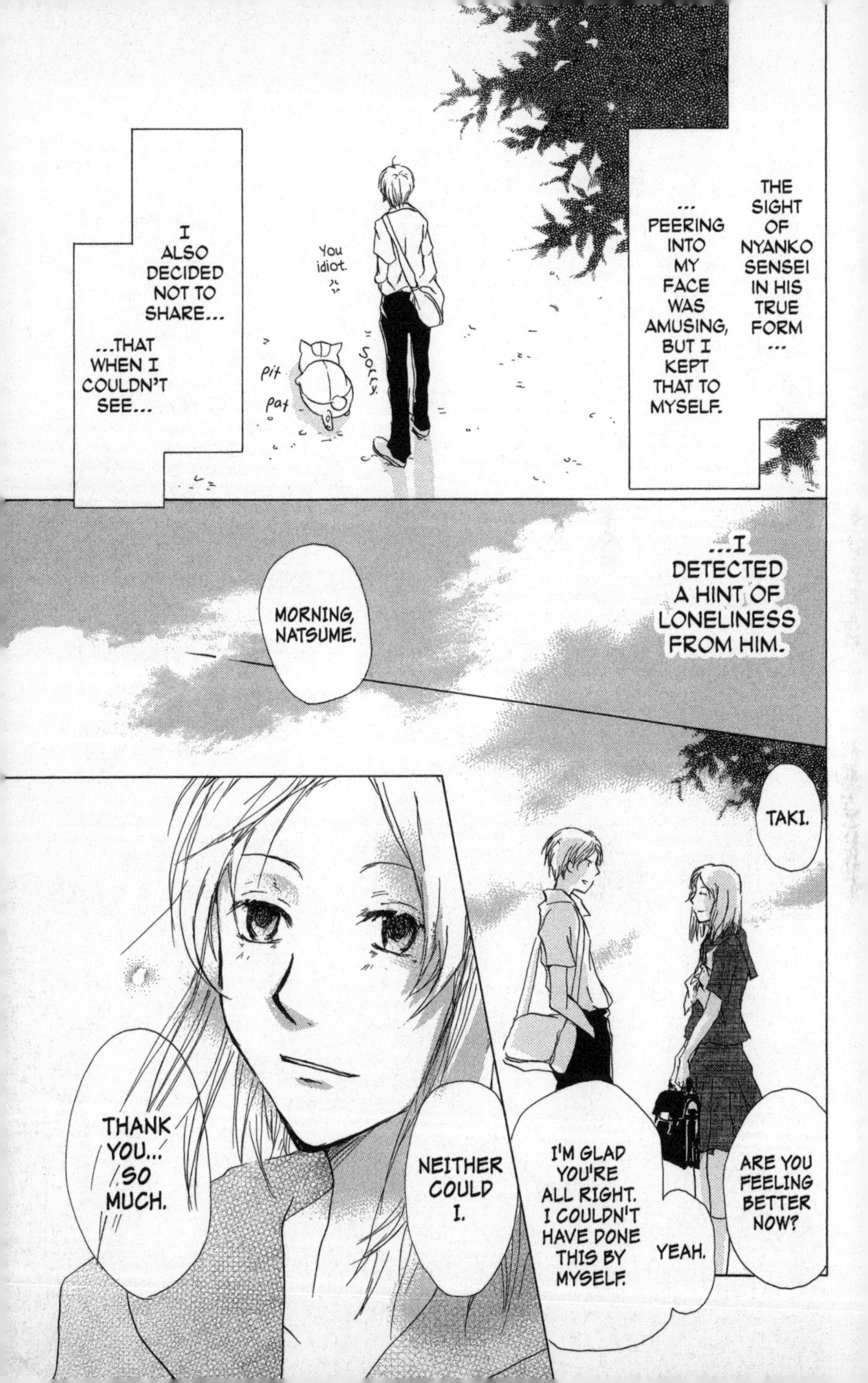
THE SIGHT OF NYANKO SENSEI IN HIS TRUE FORM...
...PEERING INTO MY FACE WAS AMUSING, BUT I KEPT THAT TO MYSELF.
You idiot.
Sorry.
pit pat
I ALSO DECIDED NOT TO SHARE...
...THAT WHEN I COULDN'T SEE...
...I DETECTED A HINT OF LONELINESS FROM HIM.
MORNING, NATSUME.
TAKI.
ARE YOU FEELING BETTER NOW?
YEAH.
I'M GLAD YOU'RE ALL RIGHT. I COULDN'T HAVE DONE THIS BY MYSELF.
NEITHER COULD I.
THANK YOU... SO MUCH.

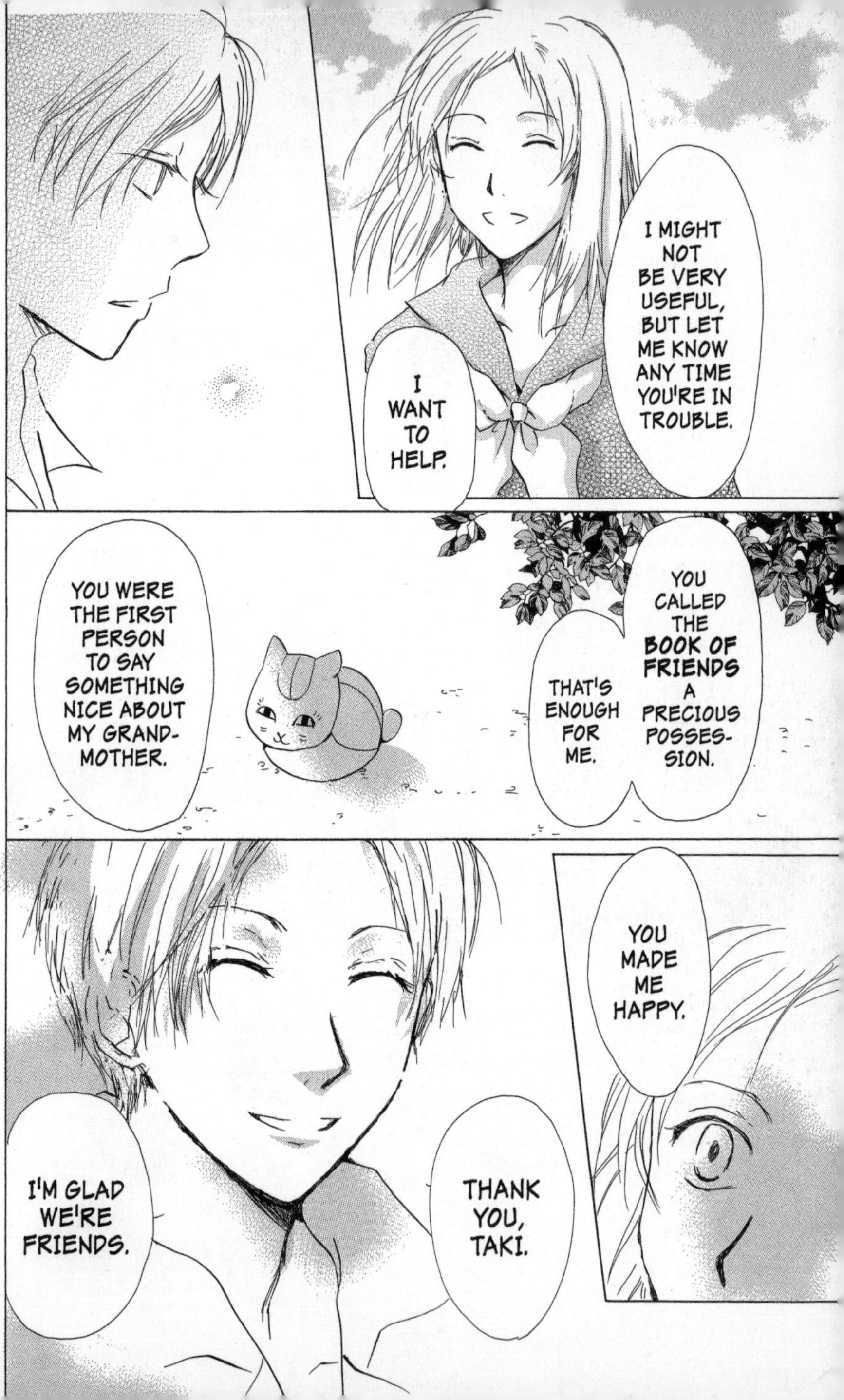
I MIGHT NOT BE VERY USEFUL, BUT LET ME KNOW ANY TIME YOU'RE IN TROUBLE.
I WANT TO HELP.
YOU CALLED THE BOOK OF FRIENDS A PRECIOUS POSSESSION.
THAT'S ENOUGH FOR ME.
YOU WERE THE FIRST PERSON TO SAY SOMETHING NICE ABOUT MY GRANDMOTHER.
YOU MADE ME HAPPY.
THANK YOU, TAKI.
I'M GLAD WE'RE FRIENDS.

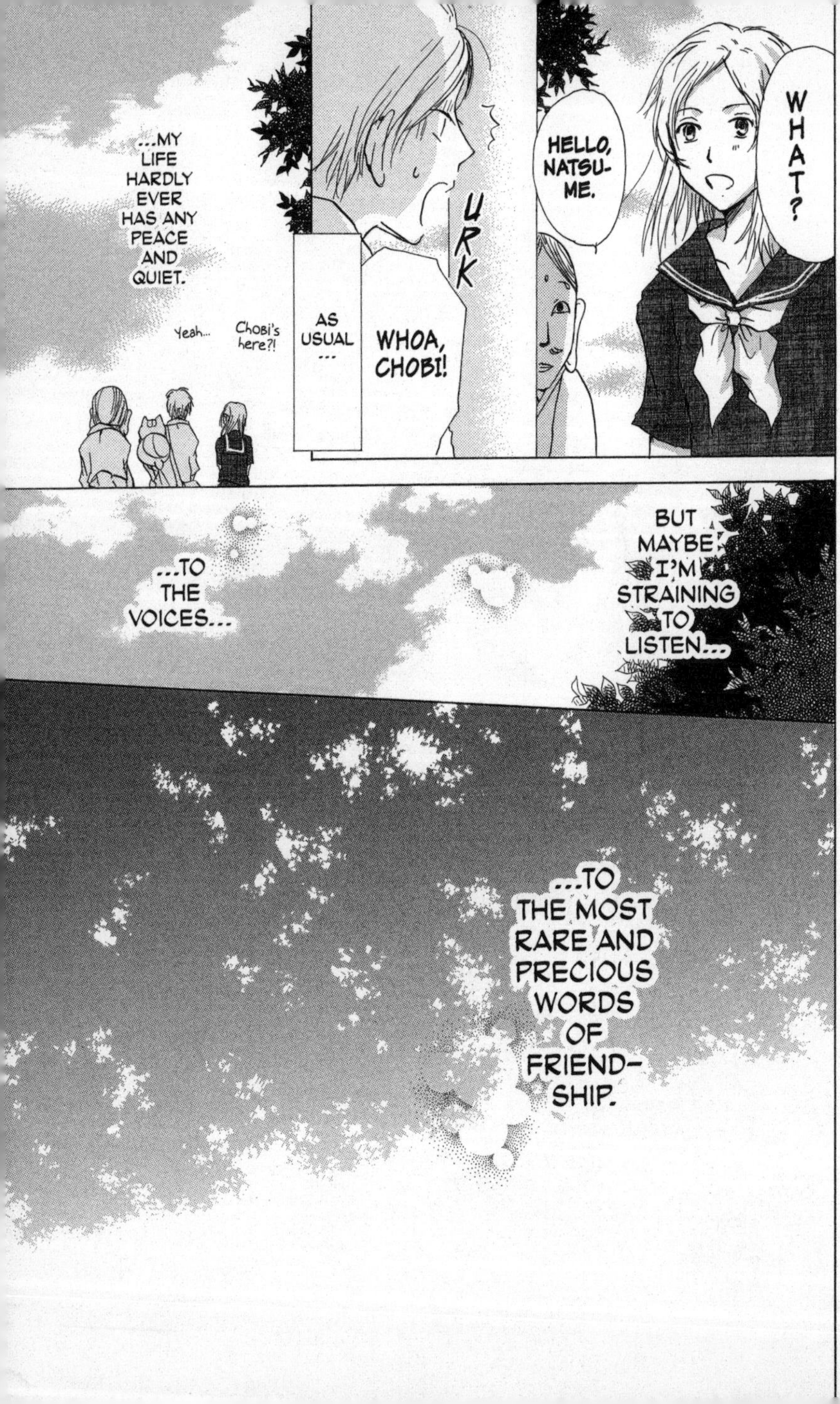
WHAT?
HELLO, NATSUME.
URK
WHOA, CHOBI!
AS USUAL...
...MY LIFE HARDLY EVER HAS ANY PEACE AND QUIET.
Chobi's here?!
Yeah...
BUT MAYBE I'M STRAINING TO LISTEN...
...TO THE VOICES...
...TO THE MOST RARE AND PRECIOUS WORDS OF FRIEND-SHIP.

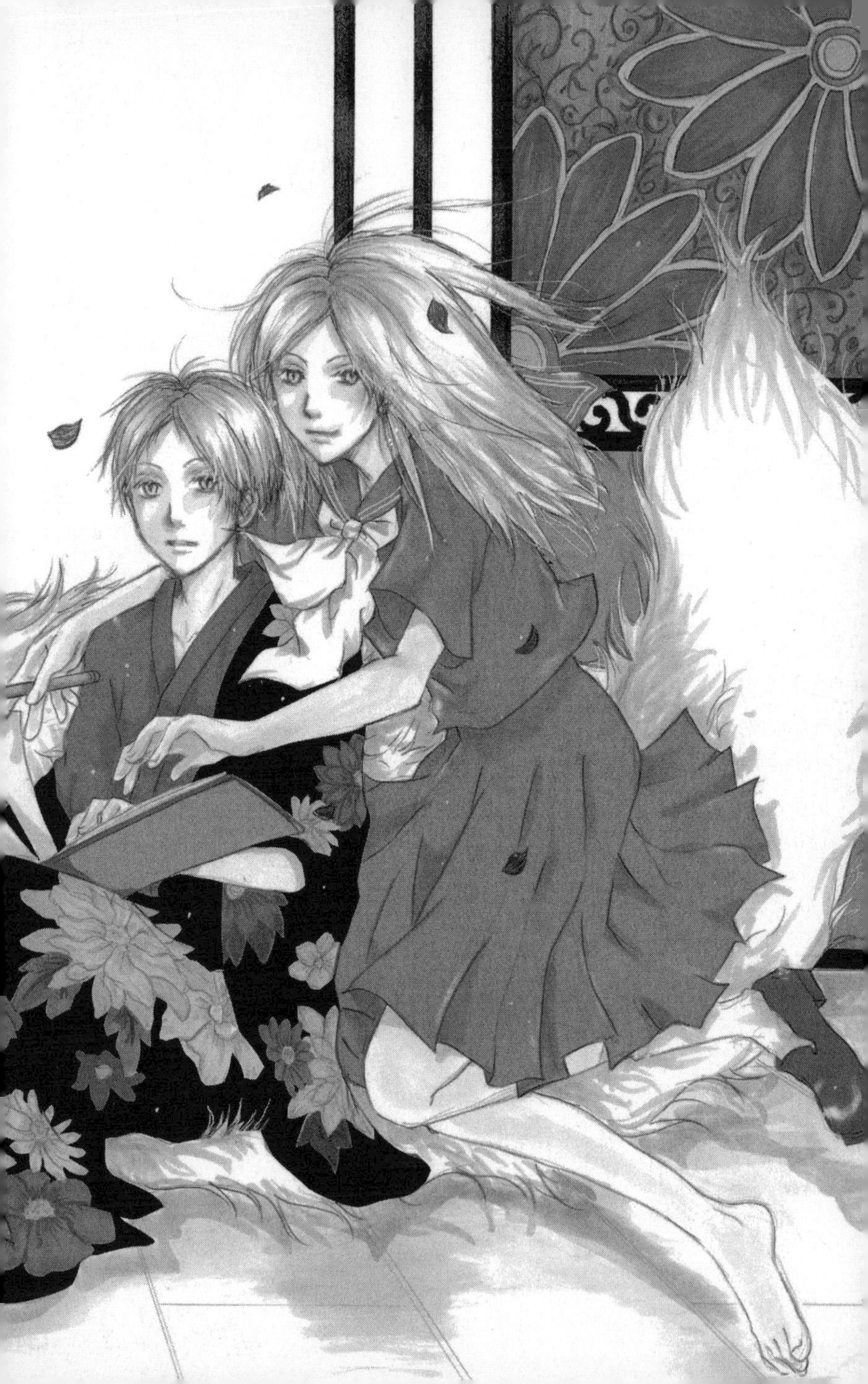

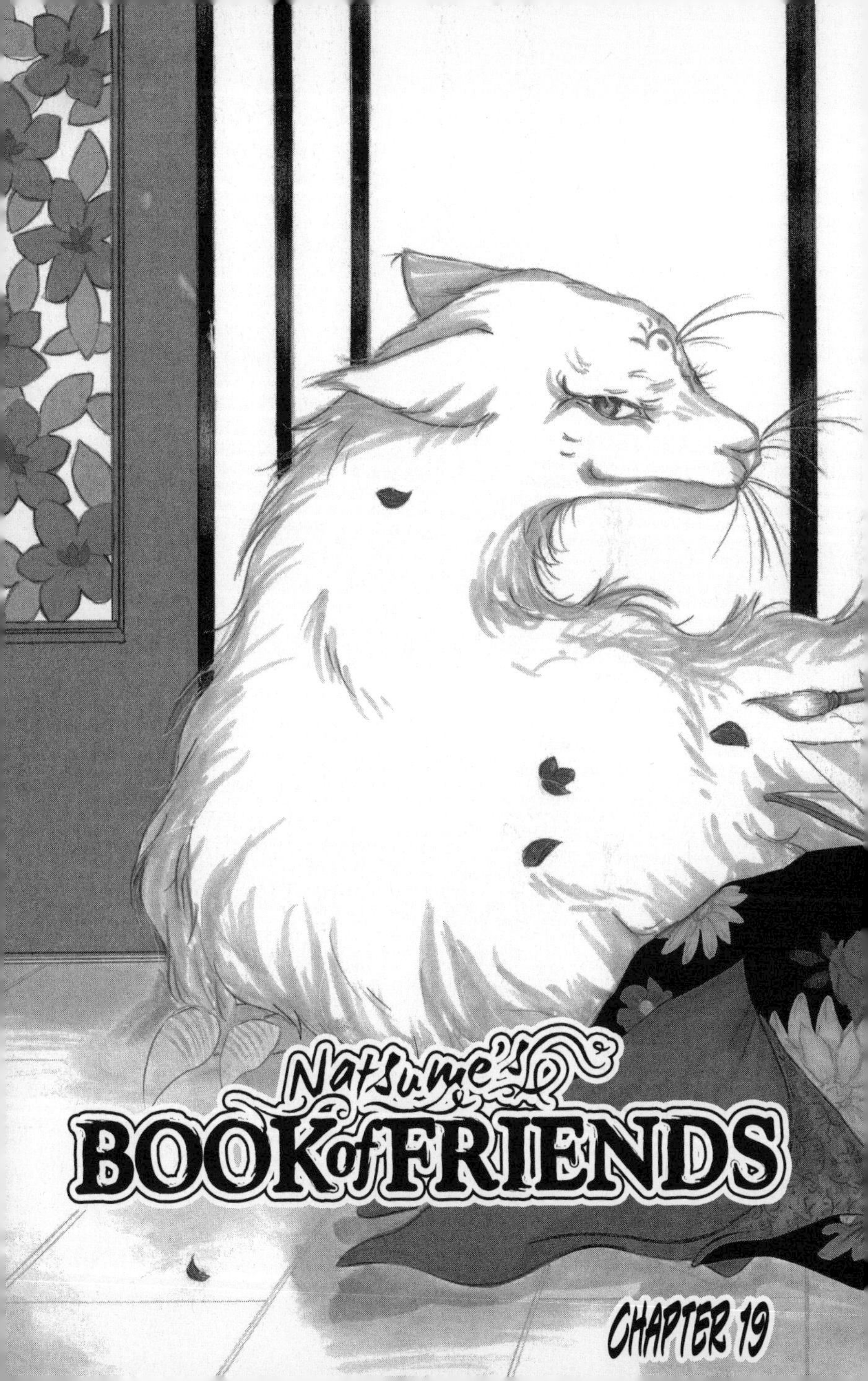
Natsume's
BOOK of FRIENDS
CHAPTER 19

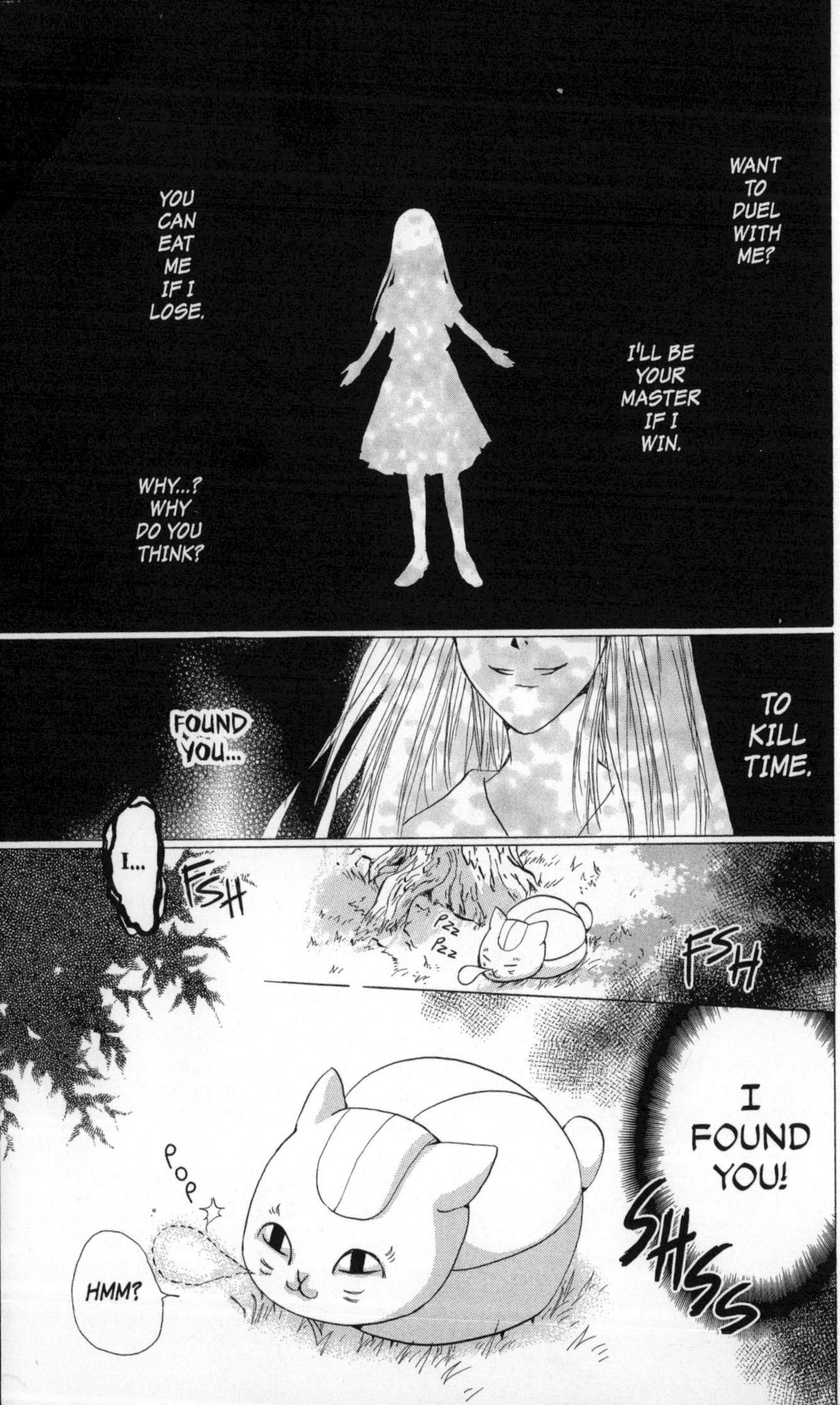
WANT TO DUEL WITH ME?
I'LL BE YOUR MASTER IF I WIN.
YOU CAN EAT ME IF I LOSE.
WHY...? WHY DO YOU THINK?
TO KILL TIME.
FOUND YOU...
I...
FSH
FSH
PZZ PZZ
I FOUND YOU!
SHSS
POP
HMM?

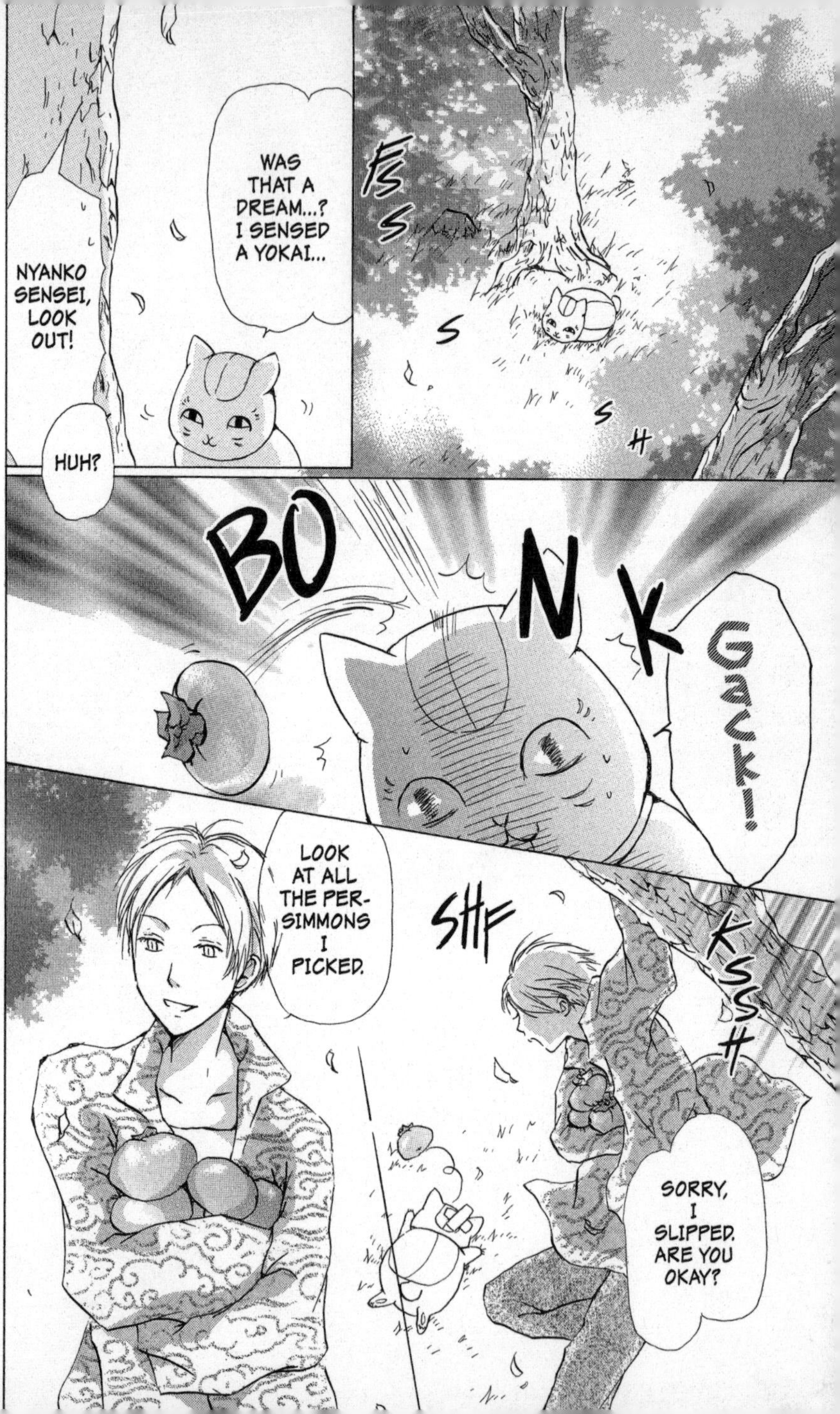
FSS
S
S
SH
WAS THAT A DREAM...? I SENSED A YOKAI...
NYANKO SENSEI, LOOK OUT!
HUH?
BONK
Gack!
KSSSH
SHF
SORRY, I SLIPPED. ARE YOU OKAY?
LOOK AT ALL THE PER-SIMMONS I PICKED.

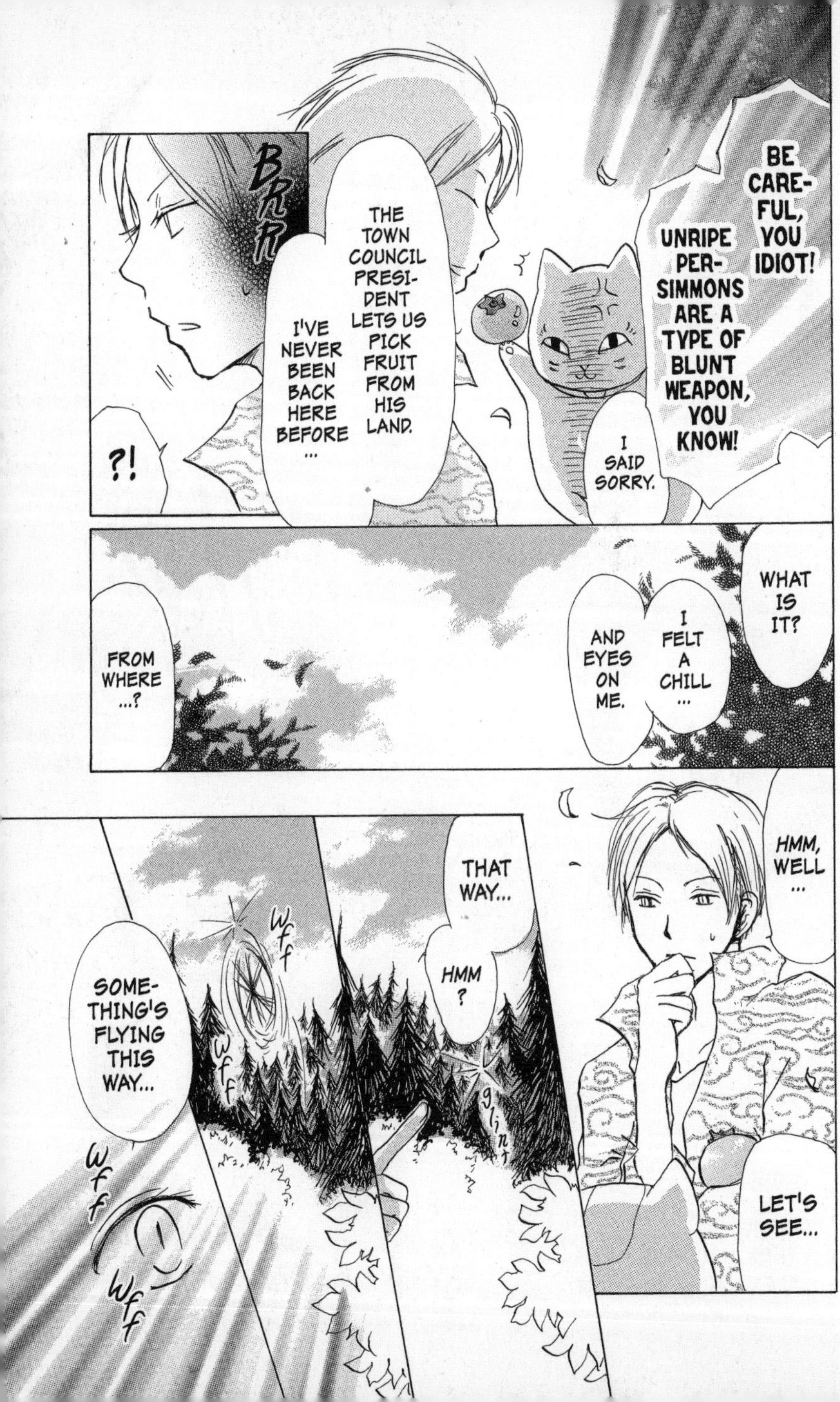

BE CAREFUL, YOU IDIOT!
UNRIPE PERSIMMONS ARE A TYPE OF BLUNT WEAPON, YOU KNOW!
I SAID SORRY.
THE TOWN COUNCIL PRESIDENT LETS US PICK FRUIT FROM HIS LAND.
I'VE NEVER BEEN BACK HERE BEFORE...
BRR
?!
WHAT IS IT?
I FELT A CHILL...
AND EYES ON ME.
FROM WHERE...?
HMM, WELL...
LET'S SEE...
THAT WAY...
HMM?
glint
wff
wff
SOMETHING'S FLYING THIS WAY...
wff
wff

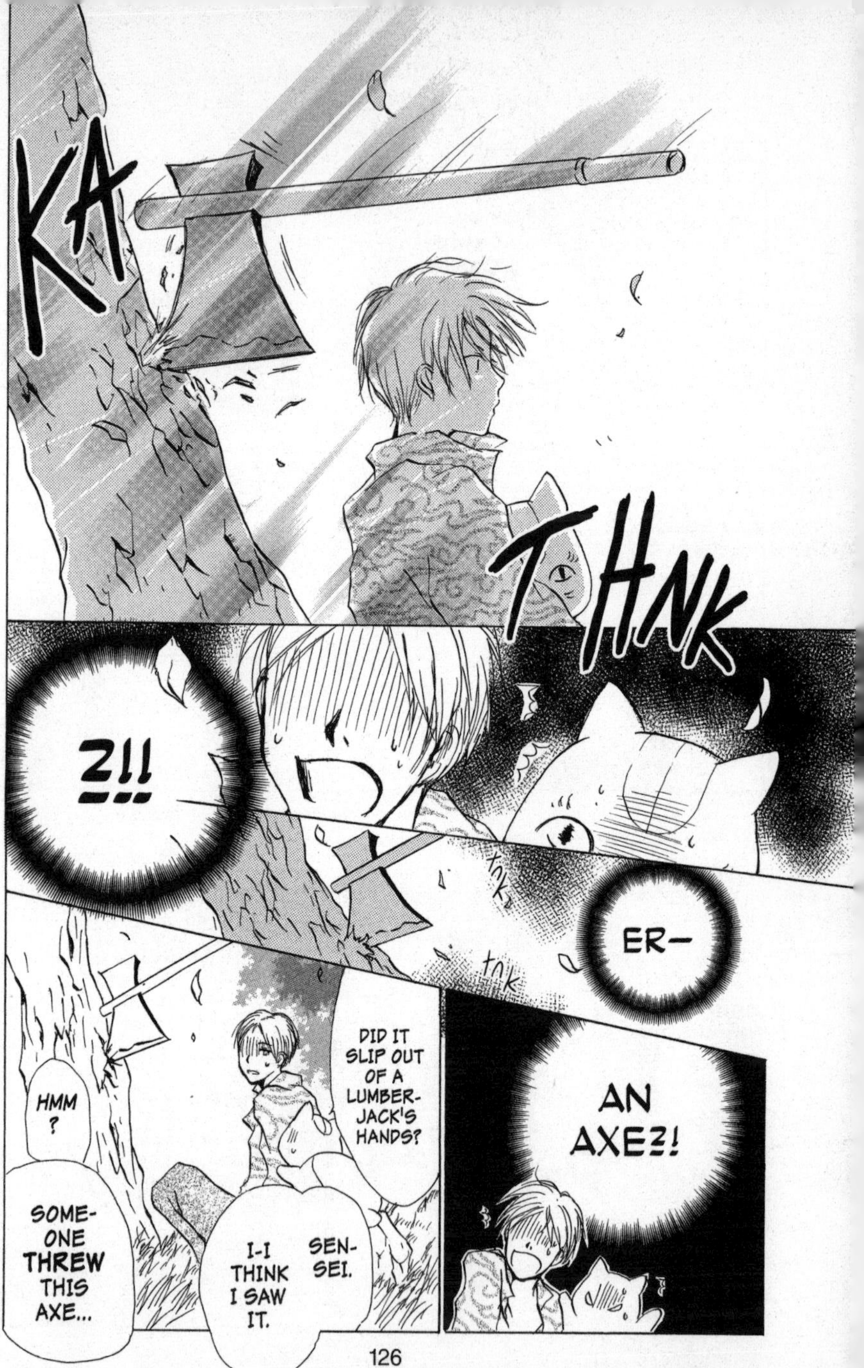
KA
THNK
ER—
tnk
tnk
?!!
AN AXE?!
DID IT SLIP OUT OF A LUMBER-JACK'S HANDS?
HMM?
SEN-SEI.
I-I THINK I SAW IT.
SOME-ONE THREW THIS AXE...

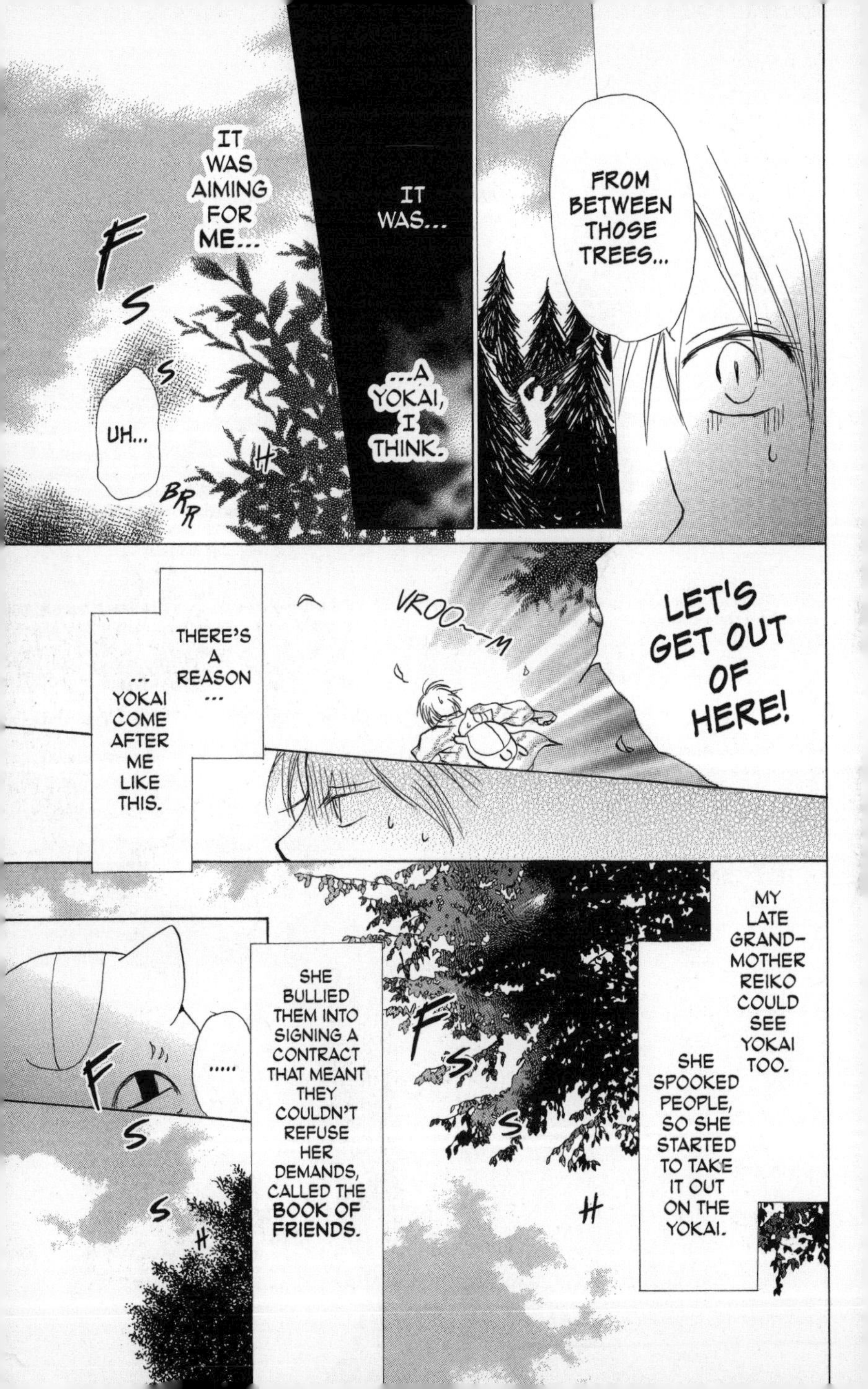
FROM BETWEEN THOSE TREES...
IT WAS...
...A YOKAI, I THINK.
IT WAS AIMING FOR ME...
FSSH
UH...
BRR
LET'S GET OUT OF HERE!
VROO—M
THERE'S A REASON...
...YOKAI COME AFTER ME LIKE THIS.
MY LATE GRAND-MOTHER REIKO COULD SEE YOKAI TOO.
SHE SPOOKED PEOPLE, SO SHE STARTED TO TAKE IT OUT ON THE YOKAI.
FSSH
SHE BULLIED THEM INTO SIGNING A CONTRACT THAT MEANT THEY COULDN'T REFUSE HER DEMANDS, CALLED THE BOOK OF FRIENDS.
.....
FSSH

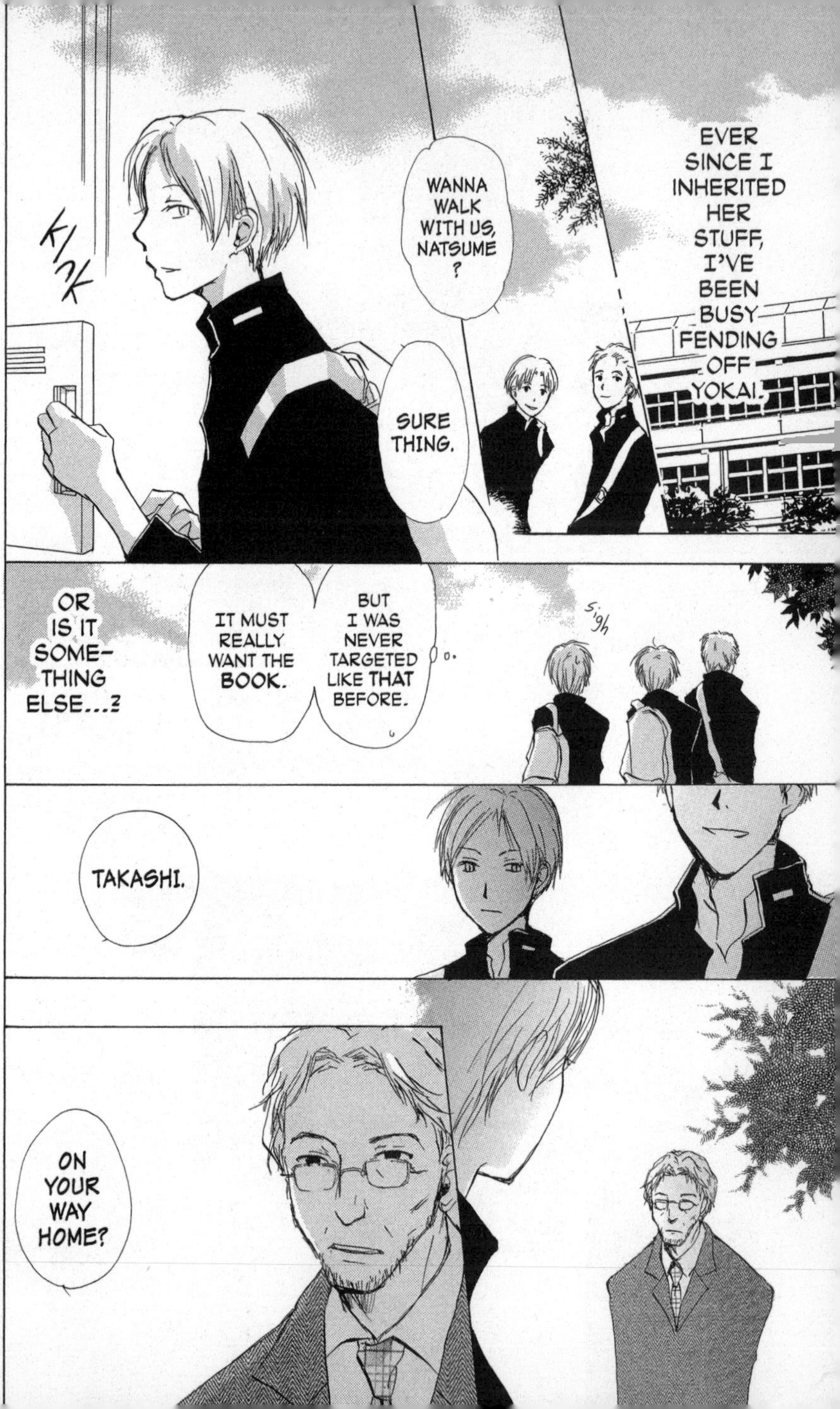
EVER SINCE I INHERITED HER STUFF, I'VE BEEN BUSY FENDING OFF YOKAI.
WANNA WALK WITH US, NATSUME?
SURE THING.
KLIK
sigh
BUT I WAS NEVER TARGETED LIKE THAT BEFORE.
IT MUST REALLY WANT THE BOOK.
OR IS IT SOME-THING ELSE...?
TAKASHI.
ON YOUR WAY HOME?

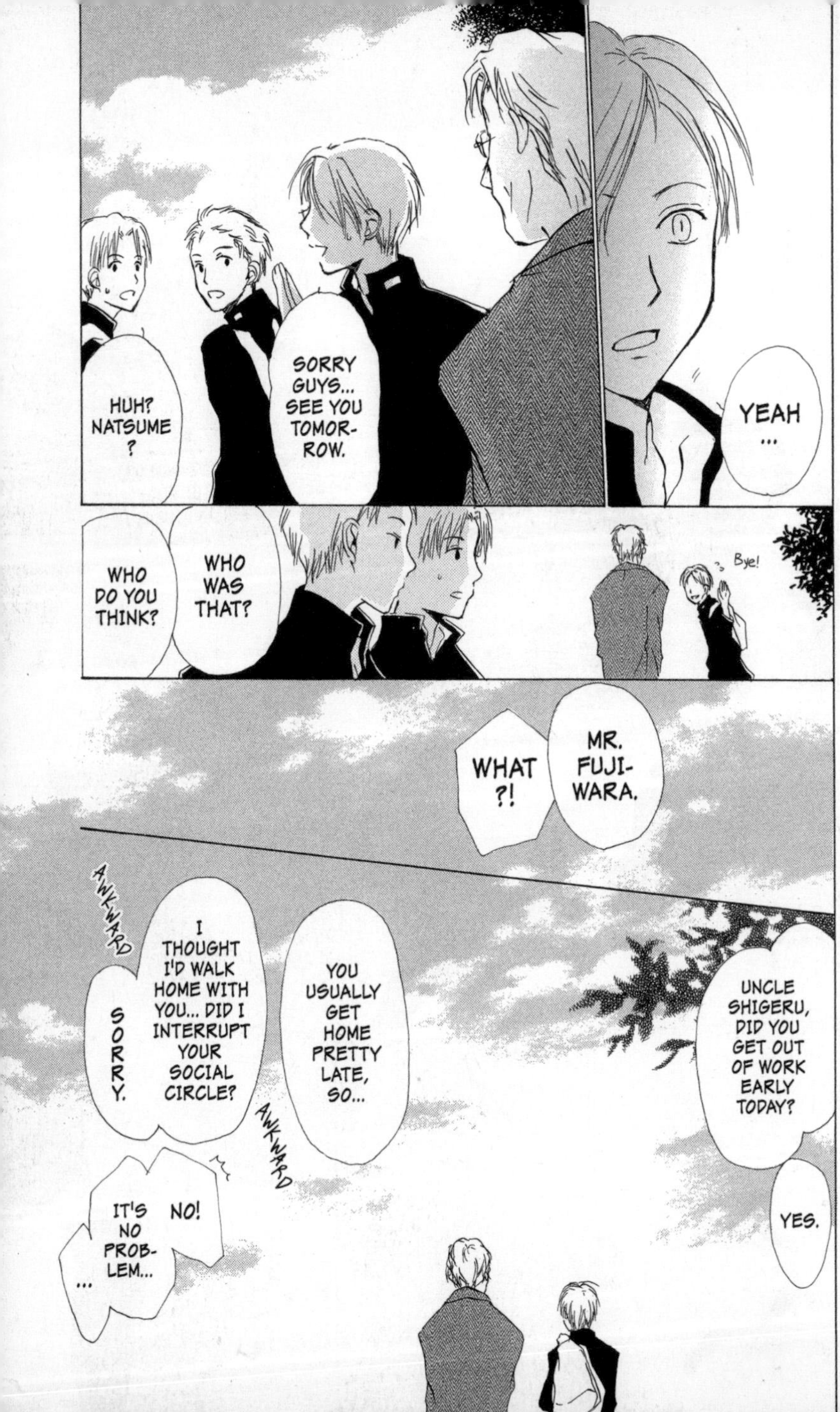
YEAH ...
SORRY GUYS... SEE YOU TOMORROW.
HUH? NATSUME?
Bye!
WHO WAS THAT?
WHO DO YOU THINK?
MR. FUJIWARA.
WHAT?!
UNCLE SHIGERU, DID YOU GET OUT OF WORK EARLY TODAY?
YES.
YOU USUALLY GET HOME PRETTY LATE, SO...
AWKWARD
I THOUGHT I'D WALK HOME WITH YOU... DID I INTERRUPT YOUR SOCIAL CIRCLE?
AWKWARD
SORRY.
NO!
IT'S NO PROBLEM...
...

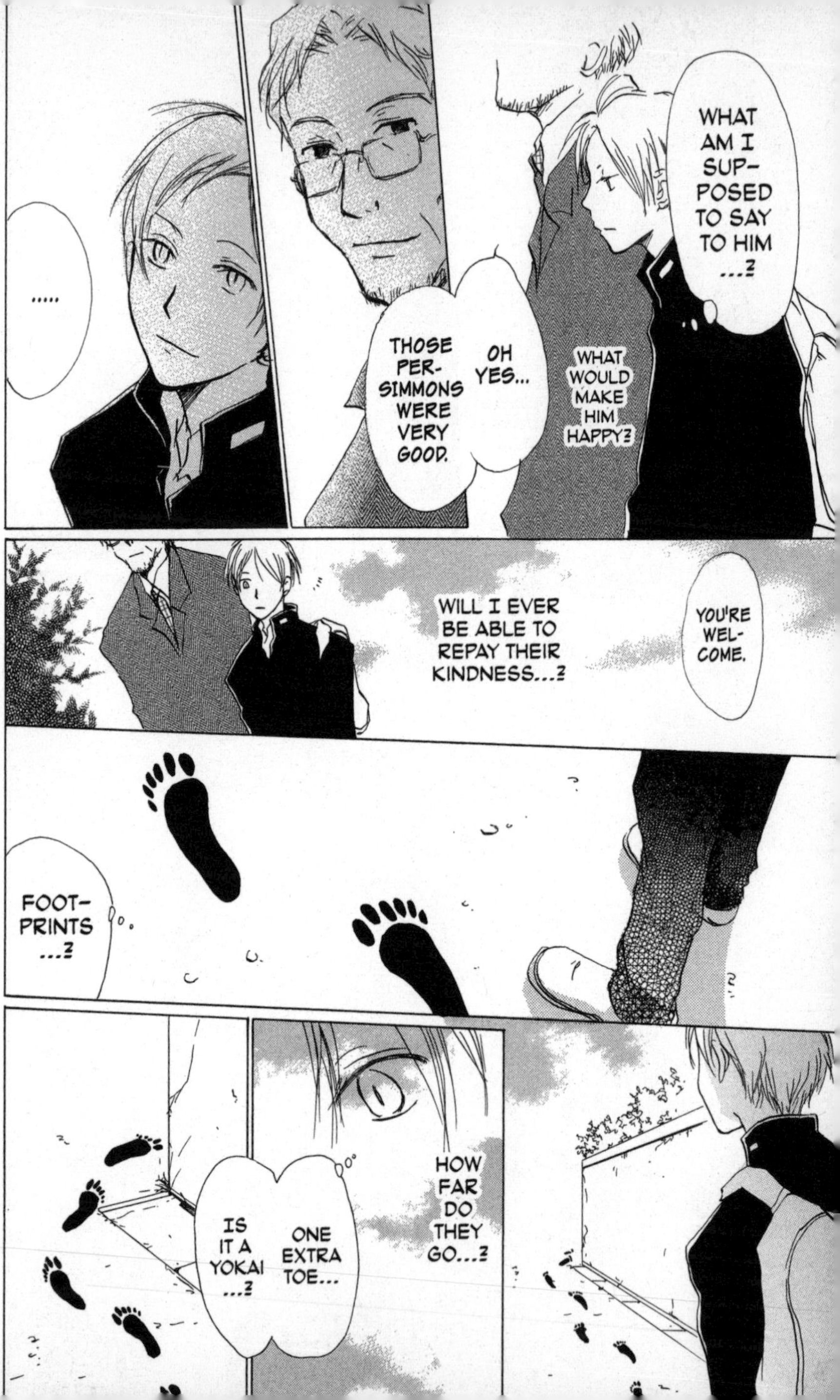
WHAT AM I SUPPOSED TO SAY TO HIM ...?
WHAT WOULD MAKE HIM HAPPY?
OH YES...
THOSE PERSIMMONS WERE VERY GOOD.
.....
YOU'RE WELCOME.
WILL I EVER BE ABLE TO REPAY THEIR KINDNESS...?
FOOTPRINTS ...?
HOW FAR DO THEY GO...?
ONE EXTRA TOE...
IS IT A YOKAI ...?

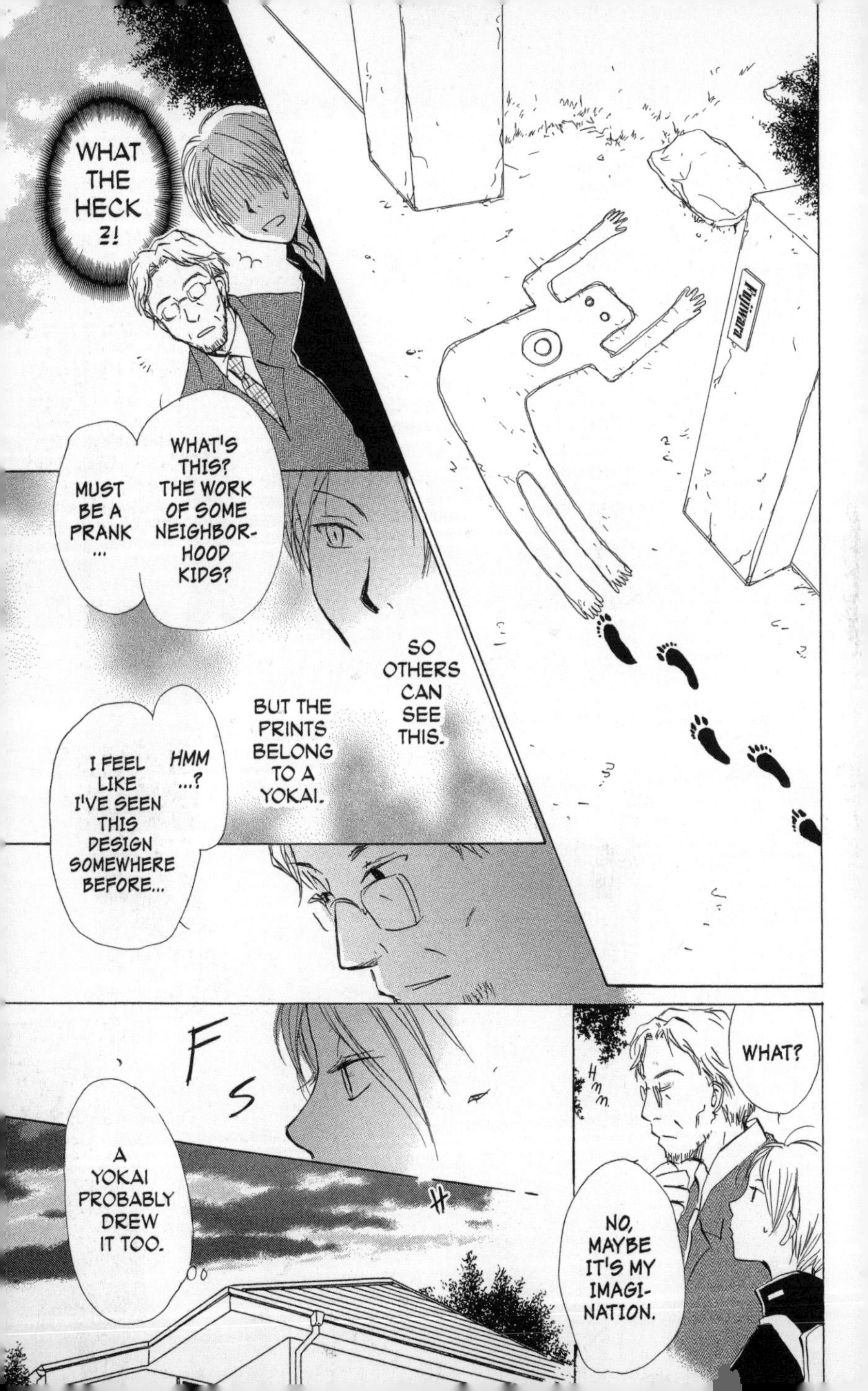
Fujiwara
WHAT THE HECK?!
WHAT'S THIS? THE WORK OF SOME NEIGHBORHOOD KIDS?
MUST BE A PRANK...
SO OTHERS CAN SEE THIS.
BUT THE PRINTS BELONG TO A YOKAI.
HMM ...?
I FEEL LIKE I'VE SEEN THIS DESIGN SOMEWHERE BEFORE...
WHAT?
Hmm
NO, MAYBE IT'S MY IMAGINATION.
FS
A YOKAI PROBABLY DREW IT TOO.

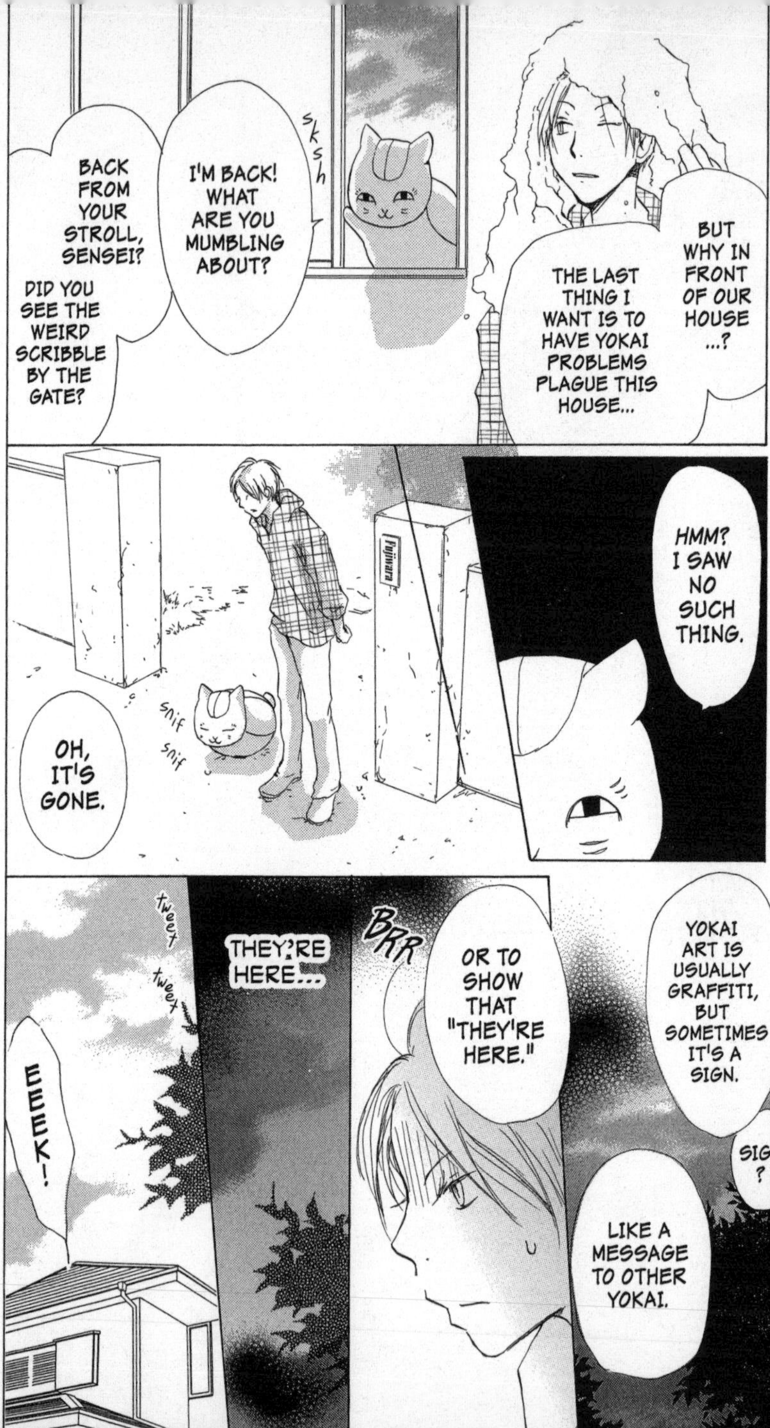
BUT WHY IN FRONT OF OUR HOUSE ...?
THE LAST THING I WANT IS TO HAVE YOKAI PROBLEMS PLAGUE THIS HOUSE...
sksh
I'M BACK! WHAT ARE YOU MUMBLING ABOUT?
BACK FROM YOUR STROLL, SENSEI?
DID YOU SEE THE WEIRD SCRIBBLE BY THE GATE?
HMM? I SAW NO SUCH THING.
Fujiwara
snif
snif
OH, IT'S GONE.
YOKAI ART IS USUALLY GRAFFITI, BUT SOMETIMES IT'S A SIGN.
SIGN?
LIKE A MESSAGE TO OTHER YOKAI.
OR TO SHOW THAT "THEY'RE HERE."
BRR
THEY'RE HERE...
tweet
tweet
EEEEK!

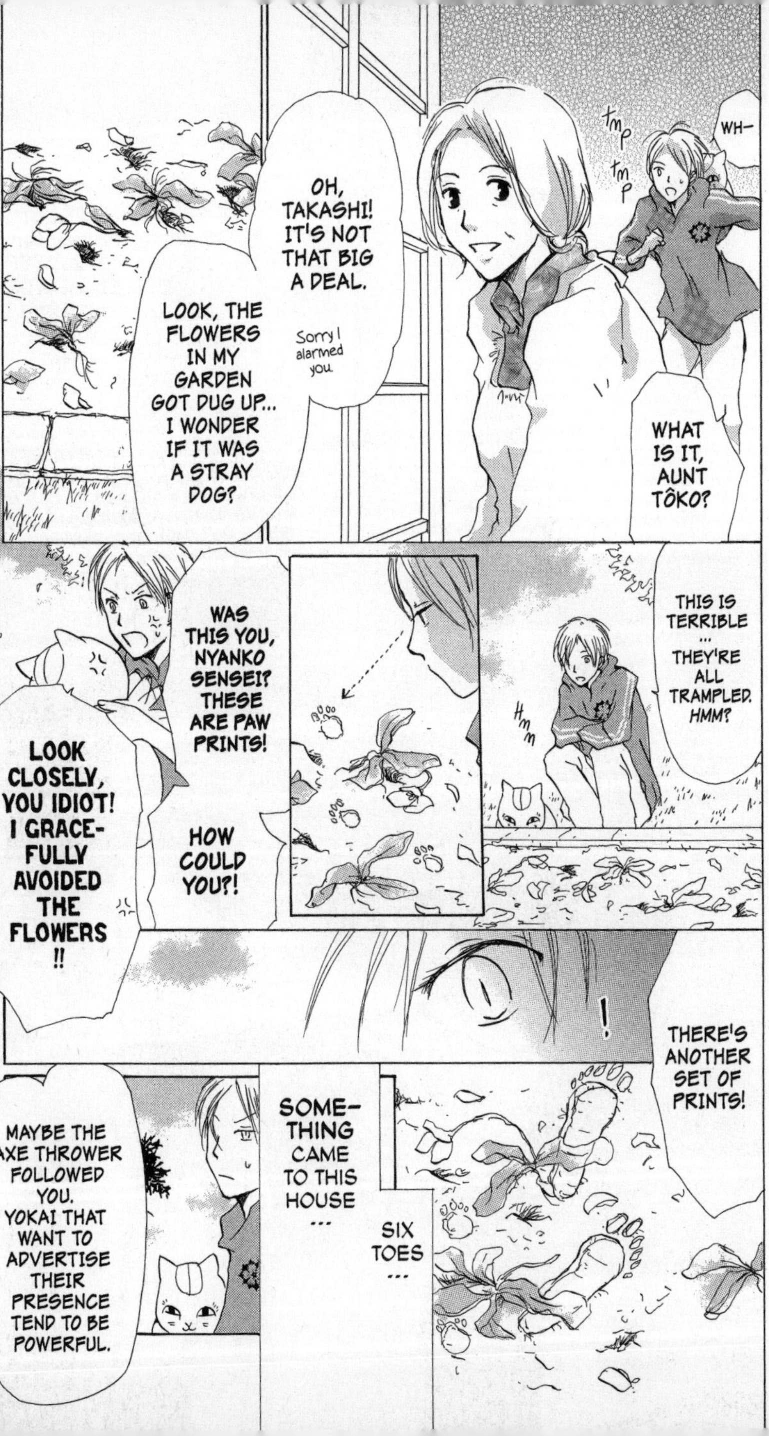
WH-
tmp tmp
WHAT IS IT, AUNT TÔKO?
OH, TAKASHI! IT'S NOT THAT BIG A DEAL.
Sorry I alarmed you.
LOOK, THE FLOWERS IN MY GARDEN GOT DUG UP... I WONDER IF IT WAS A STRAY DOG?
THIS IS TERRIBLE ... THEY'RE ALL TRAMPLED. HMM?
Hmm
WAS THIS YOU, NYANKO SENSEI? THESE ARE PAW PRINTS!
HOW COULD YOU?!
LOOK CLOSELY, YOU IDIOT! I GRACE-FULLY AVOIDED THE FLOWERS !!
!
THERE'S ANOTHER SET OF PRINTS!
SIX TOES ...
SOME-THING CAME TO THIS HOUSE ...
MAYBE THE AXE THROWER FOLLOWED YOU. YOKAI THAT WANT TO ADVERTISE THEIR PRESENCE TEND TO BE POWERFUL.

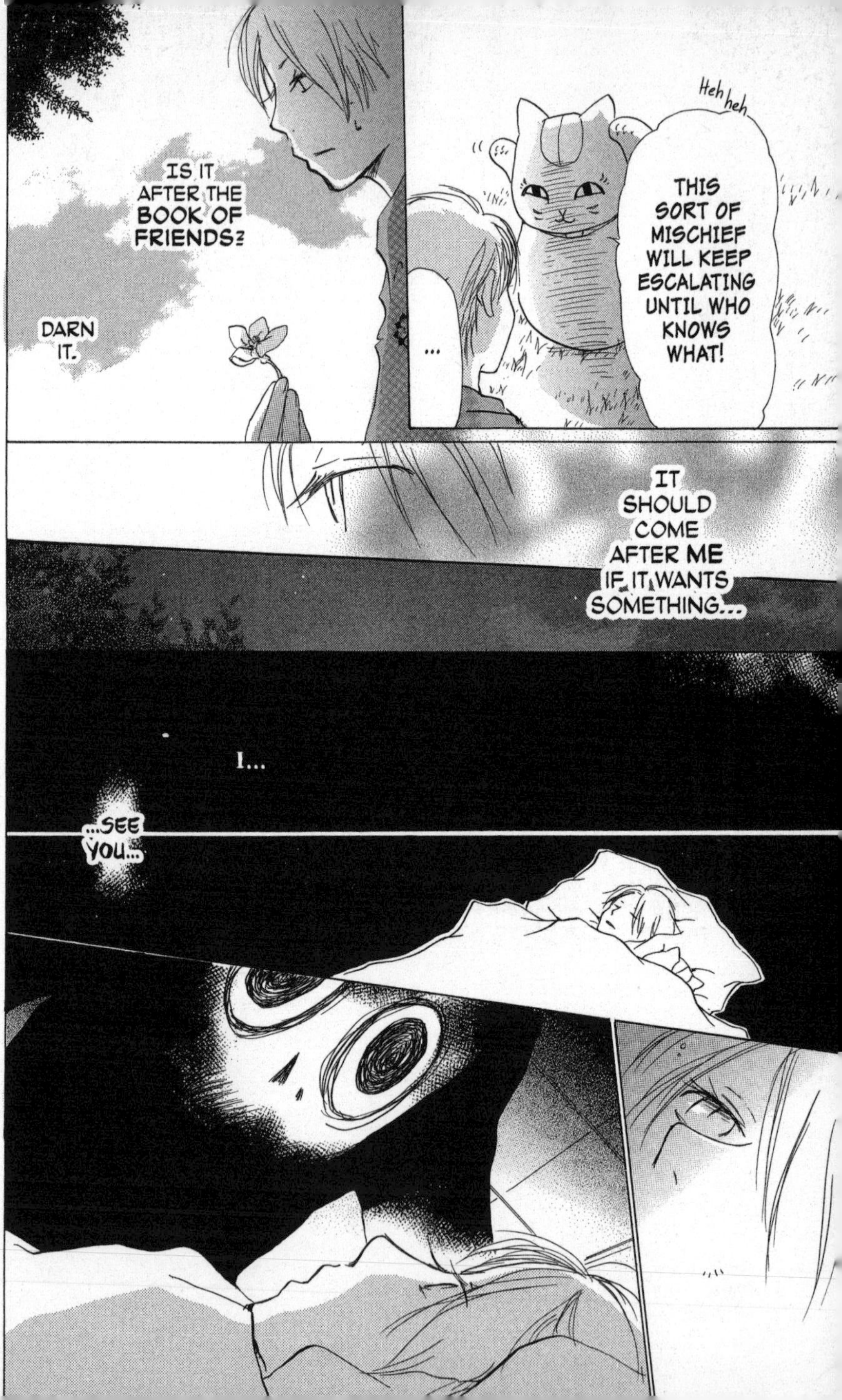
Heh heh
THIS SORT OF MISCHIEF WILL KEEP ESCALATING UNTIL WHO KNOWS WHAT!
...
IS IT AFTER THE BOOK OF FRIENDS?
DARN IT.
IT SHOULD COME AFTER ME IF IT WANTS SOMETHING...
I...
...SEE YOU...

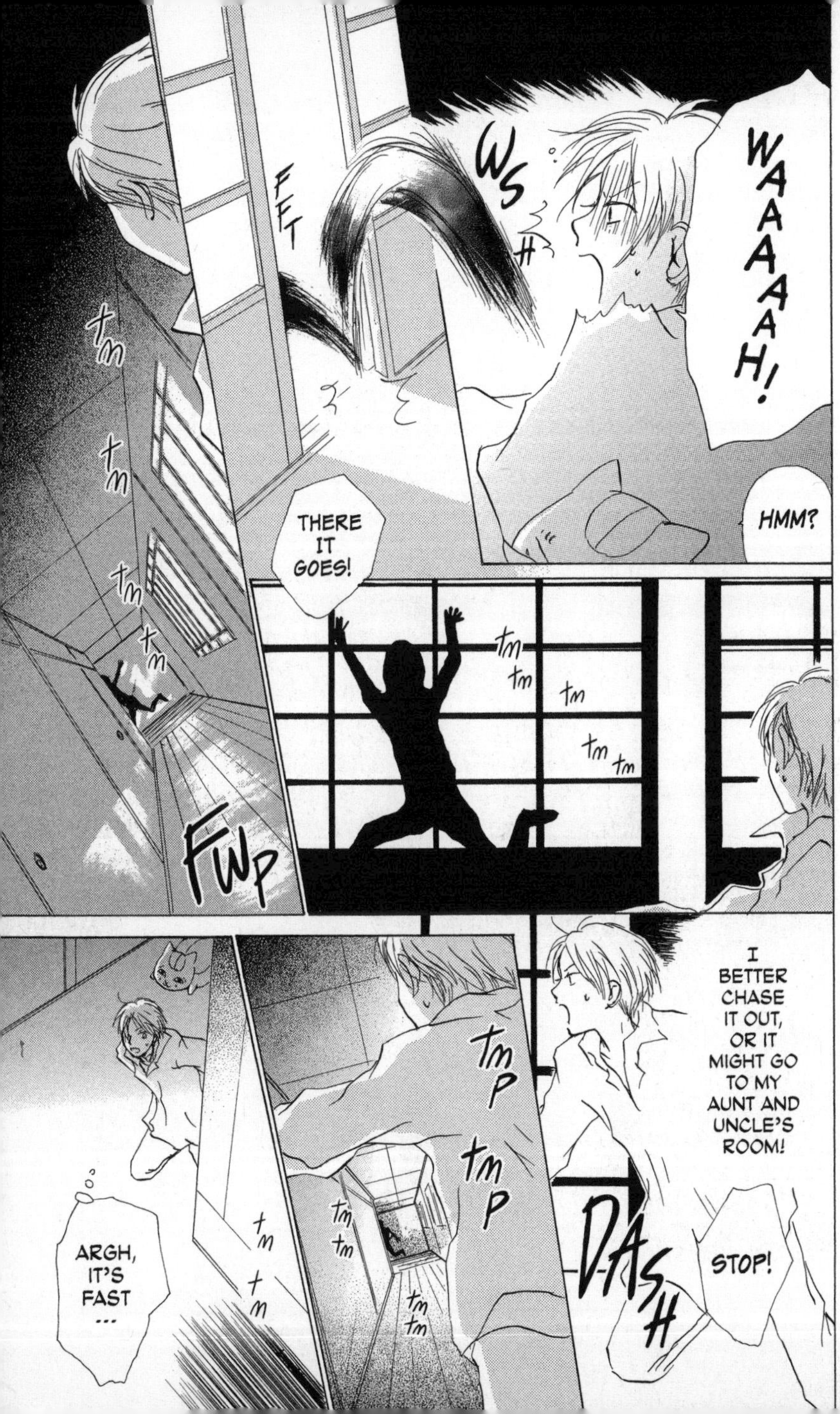
WAAAAAAH!
WSSH
FFT
HMM?
tm tm tm tm tm
THERE IT GOES!
tm tm tm tm
FWP
I BETTER CHASE IT OUT, OR IT MIGHT GO TO MY AUNT AND UNCLE'S ROOM!
STOP!
DASH
tmp tmp
tm tm
tm tm
tm tm
ARGH, IT'S FAST...

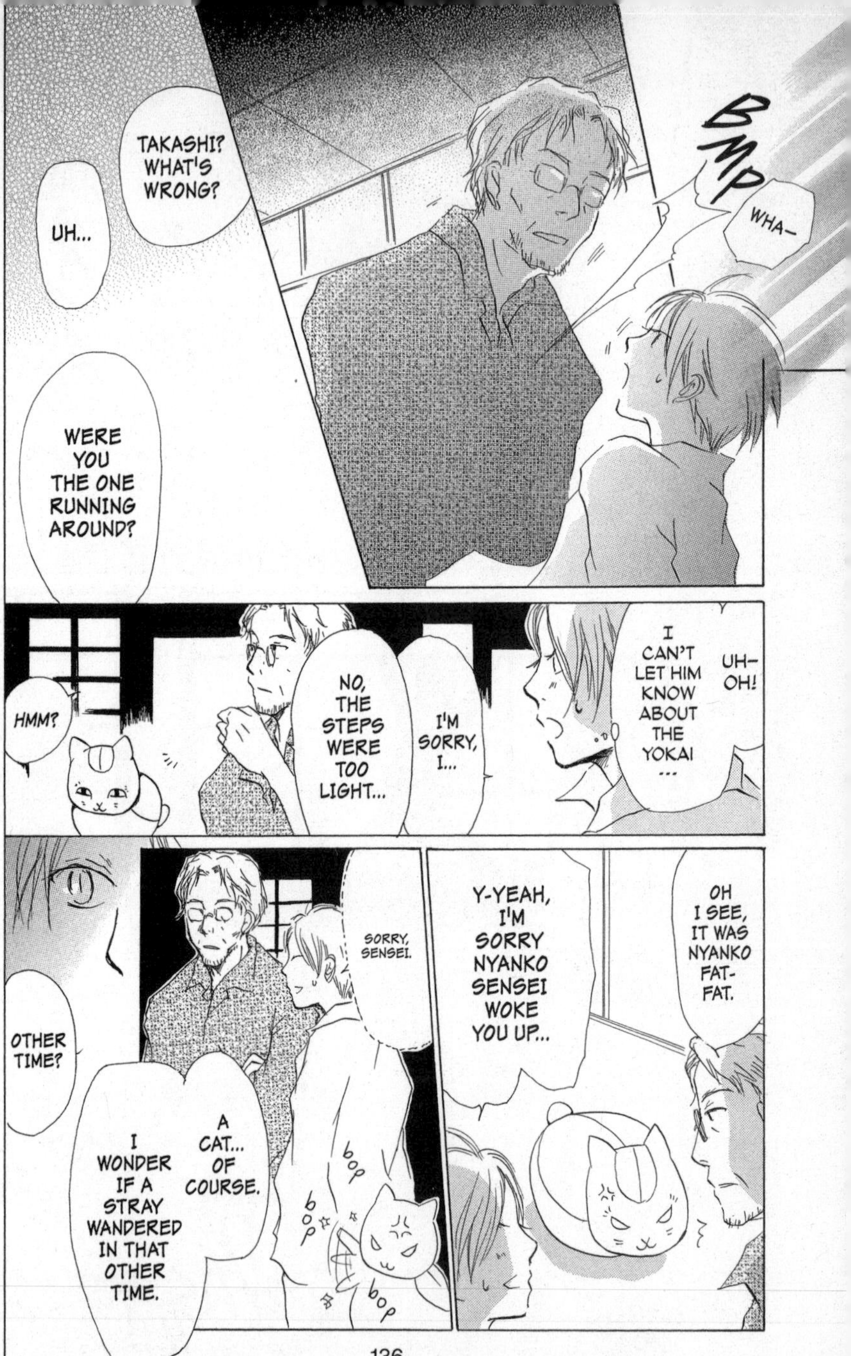
BMP
WHA-
TAKASHI? WHAT'S WRONG?
UH...
WERE YOU THE ONE RUNNING AROUND?
UH-OH!
I CAN'T LET HIM KNOW ABOUT THE YOKAI...
I'M SORRY, I...
NO, THE STEPS WERE TOO LIGHT...
HMM?
OH I SEE, IT WAS NYANKO FAT-FAT.
Y-YEAH, I'M SORRY NYANKO SENSEI WOKE YOU UP...
SORRY, SENSEI.
A CAT... OF COURSE.
bop
bop
bop
OTHER TIME?
I WONDER IF A STRAY WANDERED IN THAT OTHER TIME.

04

❋Dreaming of sheep

I had a dream that I'd have a good year if I got a sheep ornament, so I immediately went out and bought one. I got a sleek, cool-looking sheep, and I brought it back home and sat there gazing at it. Then I noticed a button on its belly, which made the sheep bleat, "meeh meeh" upon pressing it. Suddenly, it occurred to me that this "sheep" looked more like a goat. I remembered that some goats had curved horns too. But then I was confused; don't sheep also go "meeh"? So I decided to believe that this was a sheep. Let it be a sheep!

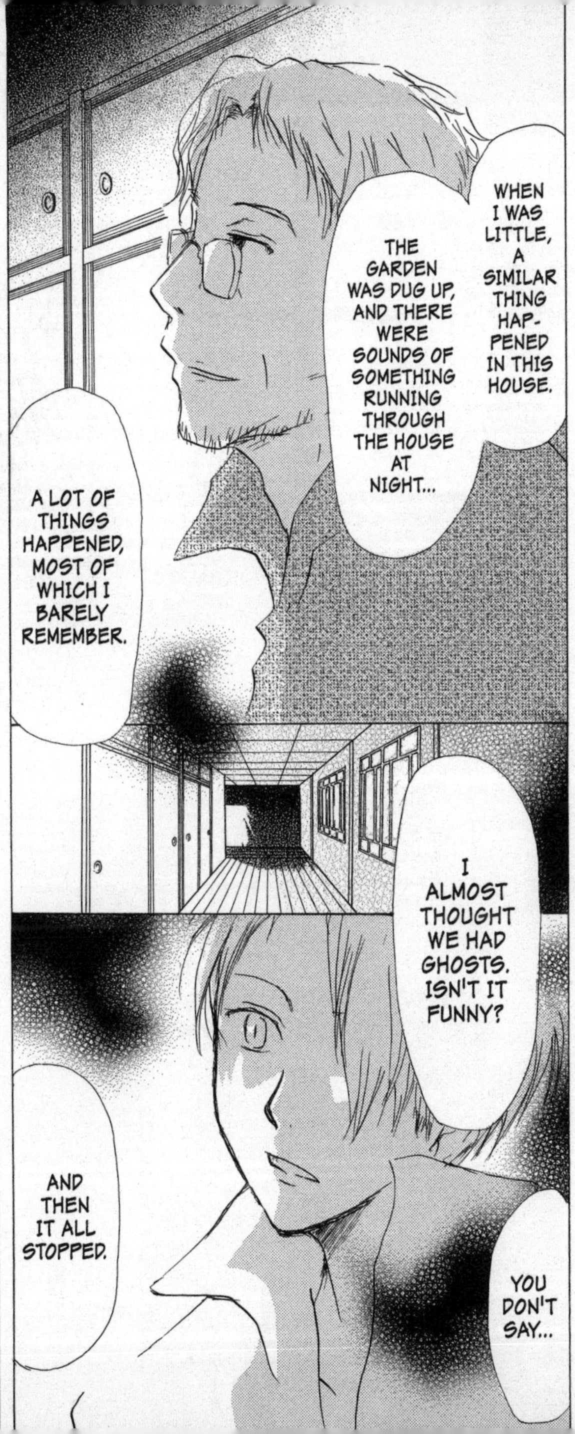
WHEN I WAS LITTLE, A SIMILAR THING HAPPENED IN THIS HOUSE.
THE GARDEN WAS DUG UP, AND THERE WERE SOUNDS OF SOMETHING RUNNING THROUGH THE HOUSE AT NIGHT...
A LOT OF THINGS HAPPENED, MOST OF WHICH I BARELY REMEMBER.
I ALMOST THOUGHT WE HAD GHOSTS. ISN'T IT FUNNY?
AND THEN IT ALL STOPPED.
YOU DON'T SAY...

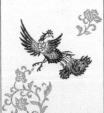

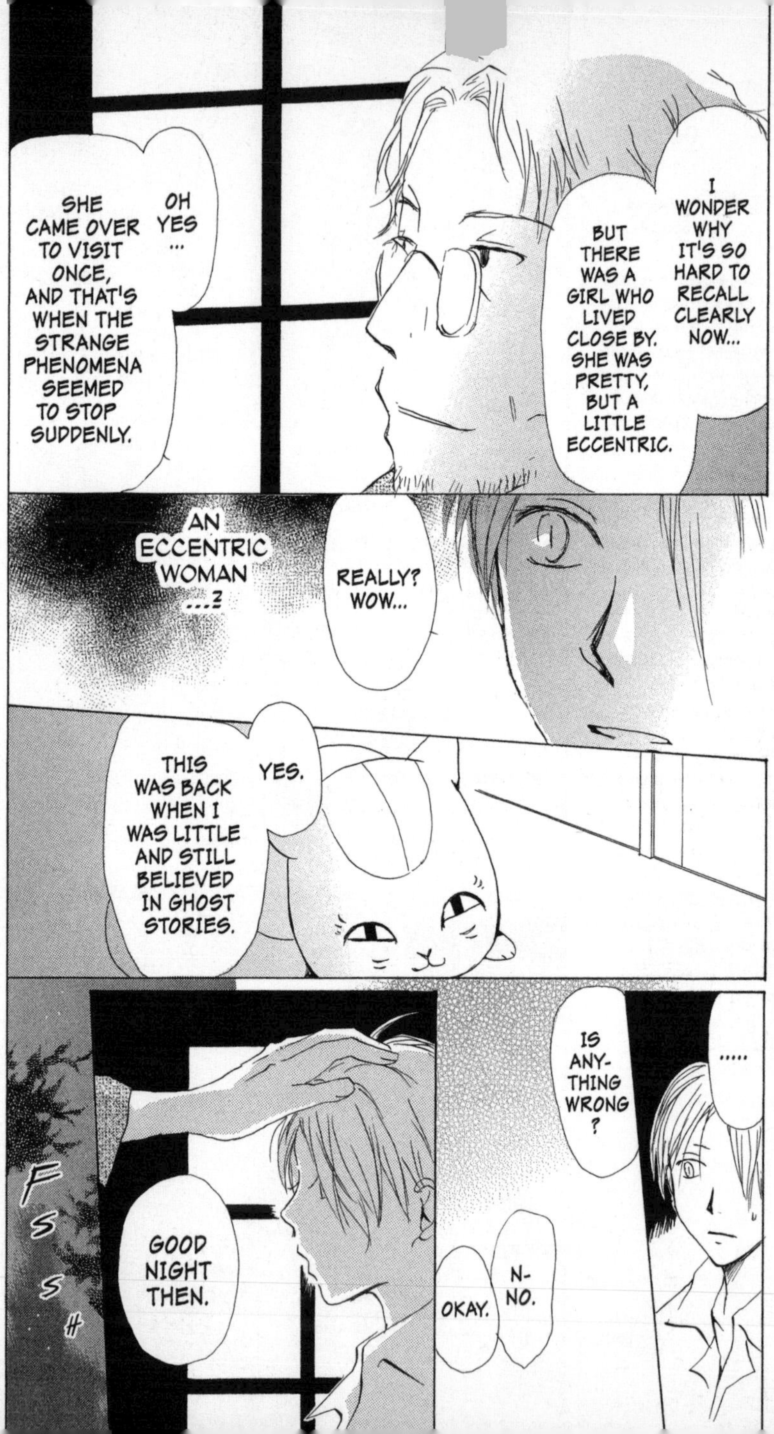
I WONDER WHY IT'S SO HARD TO RECALL CLEARLY NOW...
BUT THERE WAS A GIRL WHO LIVED CLOSE BY. SHE WAS PRETTY, BUT A LITTLE ECCENTRIC.
OH YES...
SHE CAME OVER TO VISIT ONCE, AND THAT'S WHEN THE STRANGE PHENOMENA SEEMED TO STOP SUDDENLY.
REALLY? WOW...
AN ECCENTRIC WOMAN ...?
YES.
THIS WAS BACK WHEN I WAS LITTLE AND STILL BELIEVED IN GHOST STORIES.
.....
IS ANYTHING WRONG?
N-NO.
OKAY.
GOOD NIGHT THEN.
FSSH

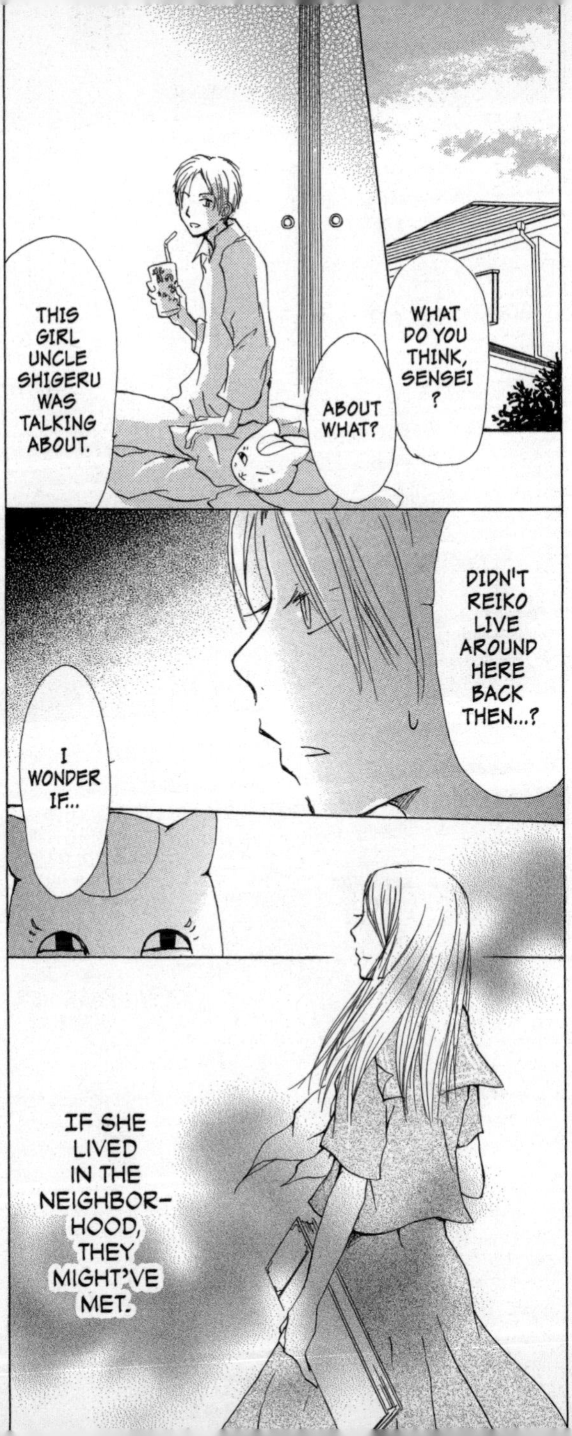
WHAT DO YOU THINK, SENSEI?
ABOUT WHAT?
THIS GIRL UNCLE SHIGERU WAS TALKING ABOUT.
DIDN'T REIKO LIVE AROUND HERE BACK THEN...?
I WONDER IF...
IF SHE LIVED IN THE NEIGHBOR-HOOD, THEY MIGHT'VE MET.

05

❋Electronics Stores

Wandering around an electronics store is fun. I'm not the science-y type at all, but I get so excited looking at electric appliances for some reason. I wish I could be more of an expert, but I still have a lot to learn. It's so fun to watch the repair man take apart the TV or the VCR. I couldn't ever take things apart and put them back together myself, but after a period of imagining how things are built, I can often come up with ideas for my manga, or figure out the solution to a problem. It seems that looking at electronics influences my brain into processing information more smoothly.

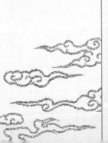

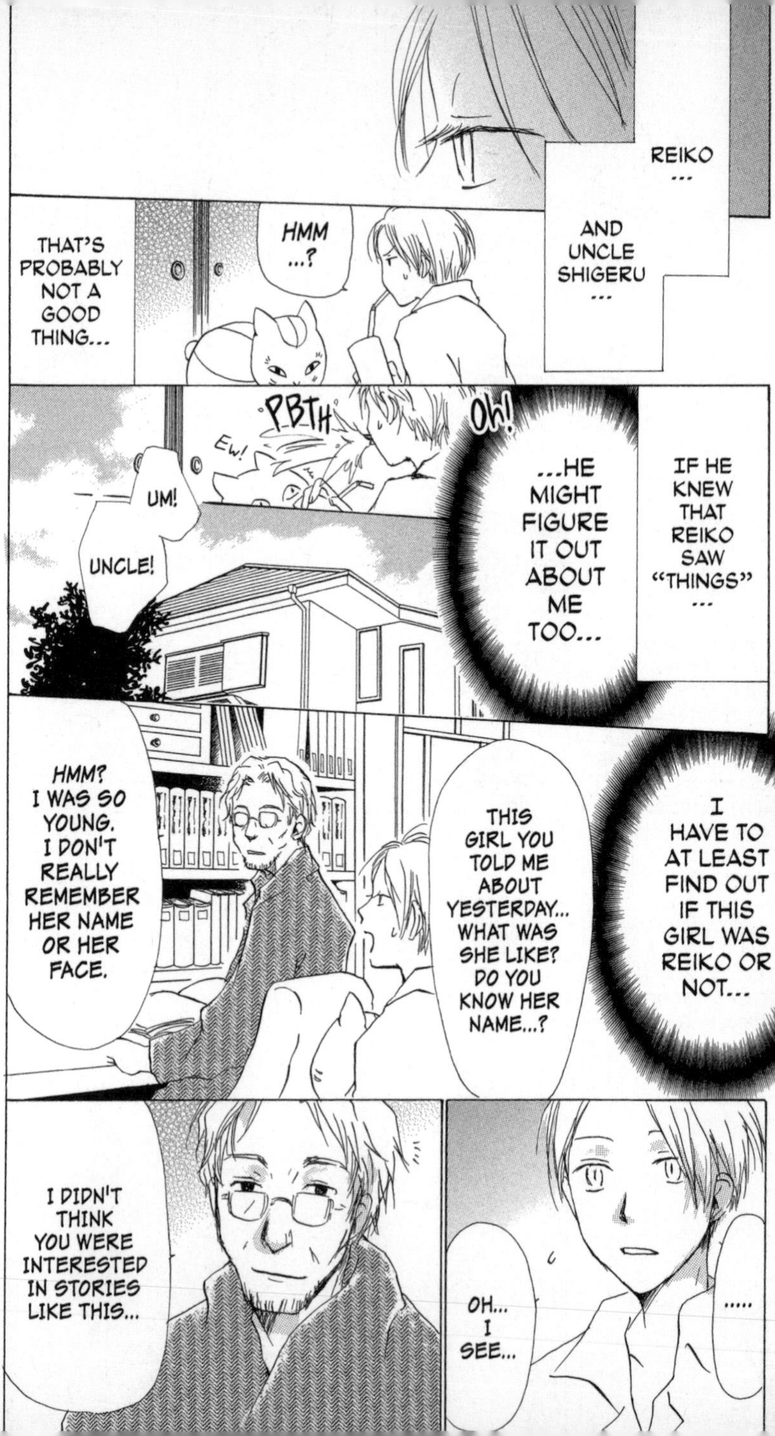
REIKO ...
AND UNCLE SHIGERU ...
HMM ...?
THAT'S PROBABLY NOT A GOOD THING...
IF HE KNEW THAT REIKO SAW "THINGS" ...
...HE MIGHT FIGURE IT OUT ABOUT ME TOO...
Oh!
PBTH
Ew!
UM!
UNCLE!
I HAVE TO AT LEAST FIND OUT IF THIS GIRL WAS REIKO OR NOT...
THIS GIRL YOU TOLD ME ABOUT YESTERDAY... WHAT WAS SHE LIKE? DO YOU KNOW HER NAME...?
HMM? I WAS SO YOUNG. I DON'T REALLY REMEMBER HER NAME OR HER FACE.
.....
OH... I SEE...
I DIDN'T THINK YOU WERE INTERESTED IN STORIES LIKE THIS...

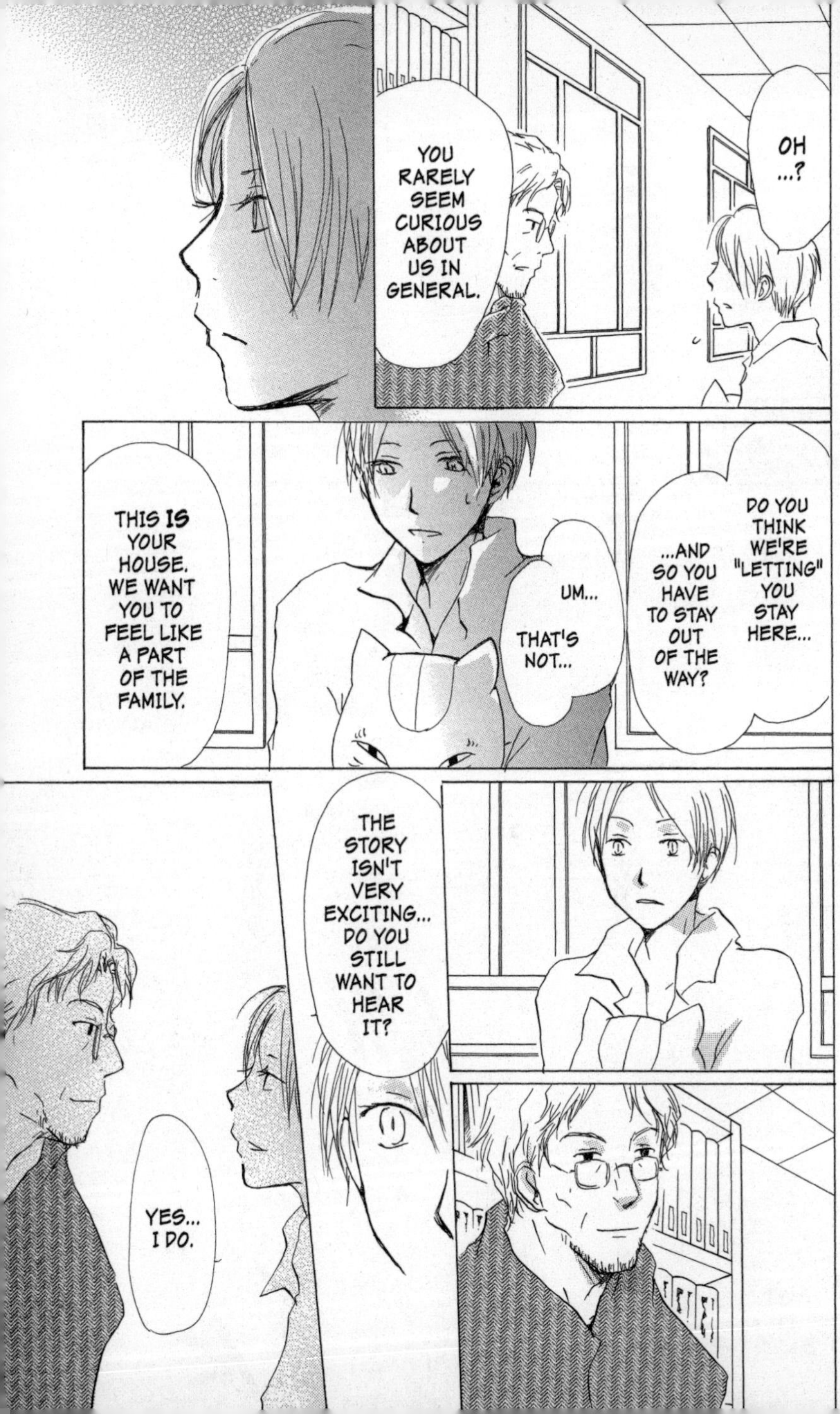
OH ...?
YOU RARELY SEEM CURIOUS ABOUT US IN GENERAL.
DO YOU THINK WE'RE "LETTING" YOU STAY HERE...
...AND SO YOU HAVE TO STAY OUT OF THE WAY?
UM... THAT'S NOT...
THIS **IS** YOUR HOUSE. WE WANT YOU TO FEEL LIKE A PART OF THE FAMILY.
THE STORY ISN'T VERY EXCITING... DO YOU STILL WANT TO HEAR IT?
YES... I DO.

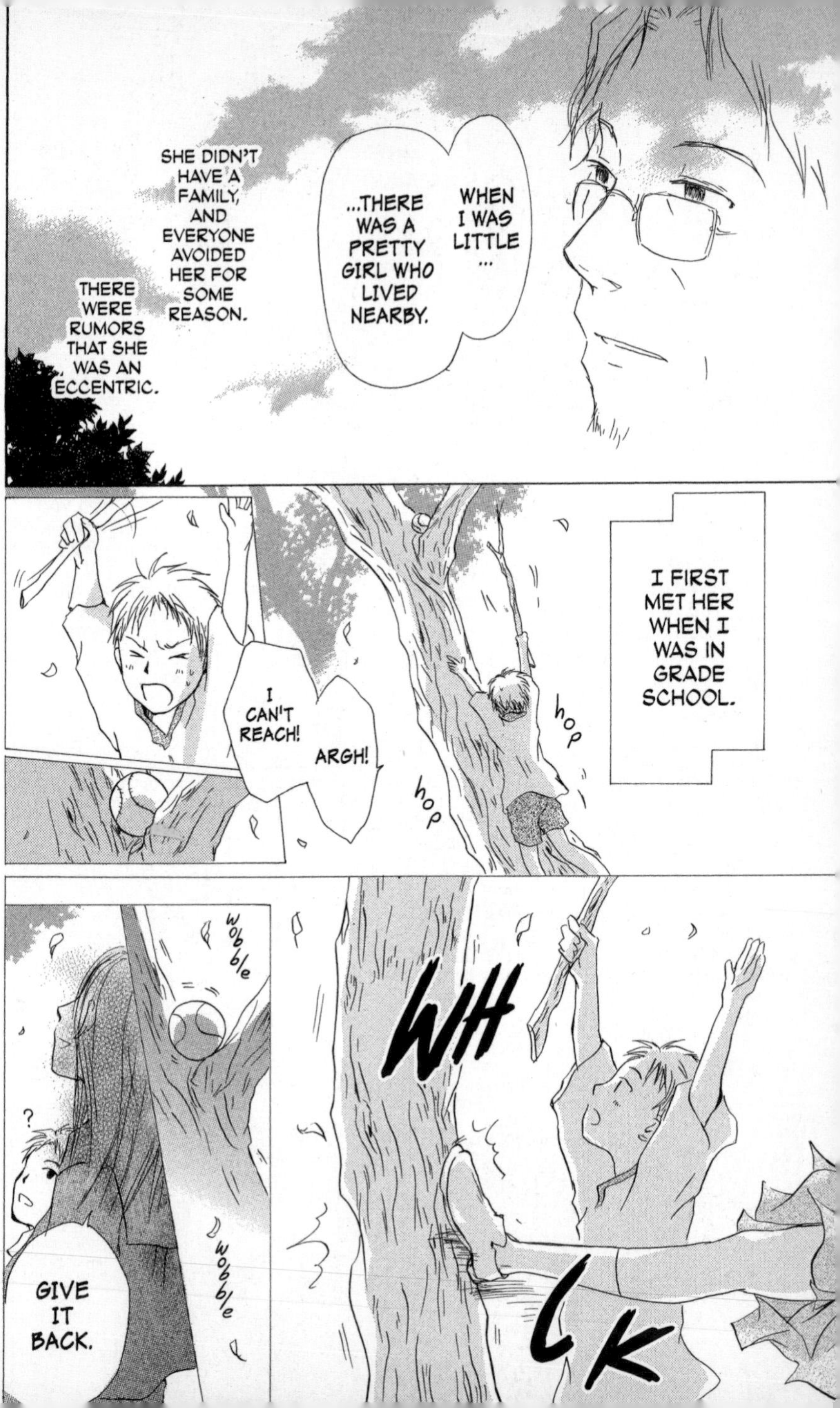
WHEN I WAS LITTLE ...
...THERE WAS A PRETTY GIRL WHO LIVED NEARBY.
SHE DIDN'T HAVE A FAMILY, AND EVERYONE AVOIDED HER FOR SOME REASON.
THERE WERE RUMORS THAT SHE WAS AN ECCENTRIC.
I FIRST MET HER WHEN I WAS IN GRADE SCHOOL.
hop
hop
I CAN'T REACH!
ARGH!
WH
CK
wobble
wobble
?
GIVE IT BACK.

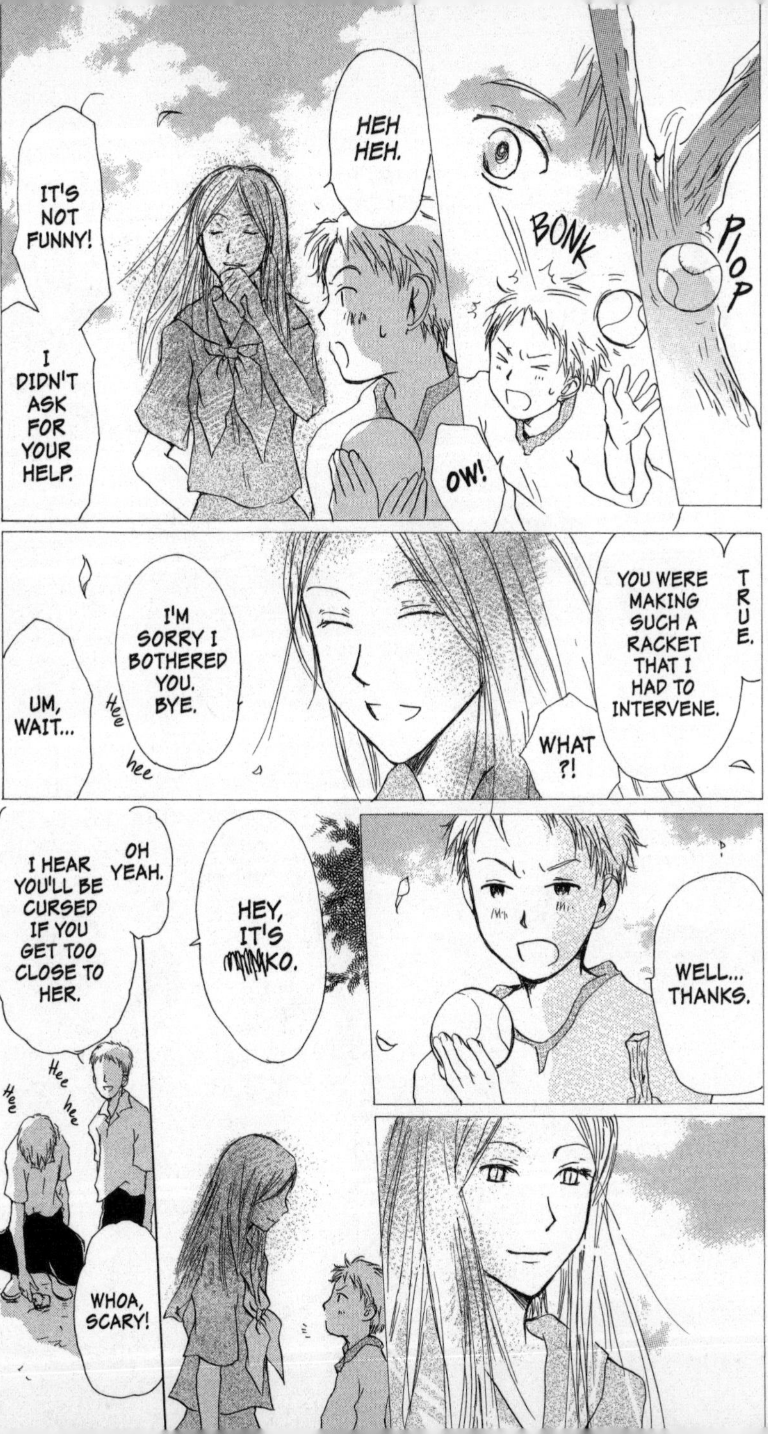
PLOP
BONK
OW!
HEH HEH.
IT'S NOT FUNNY!
I DIDN'T ASK FOR YOUR HELP.
TRUE.
YOU WERE MAKING SUCH A RACKET THAT I HAD TO INTERVENE.
WHAT?!
I'M SORRY I BOTHERED YOU. BYE.
Hee hee
UM, WAIT...
WELL... THANKS.
HEY, IT'S [redacted]KO.
OH YEAH.
I HEAR YOU'LL BE CURSED IF YOU GET TOO CLOSE TO HER.
Hee hee
Hee hee
WHOA, SCARY!

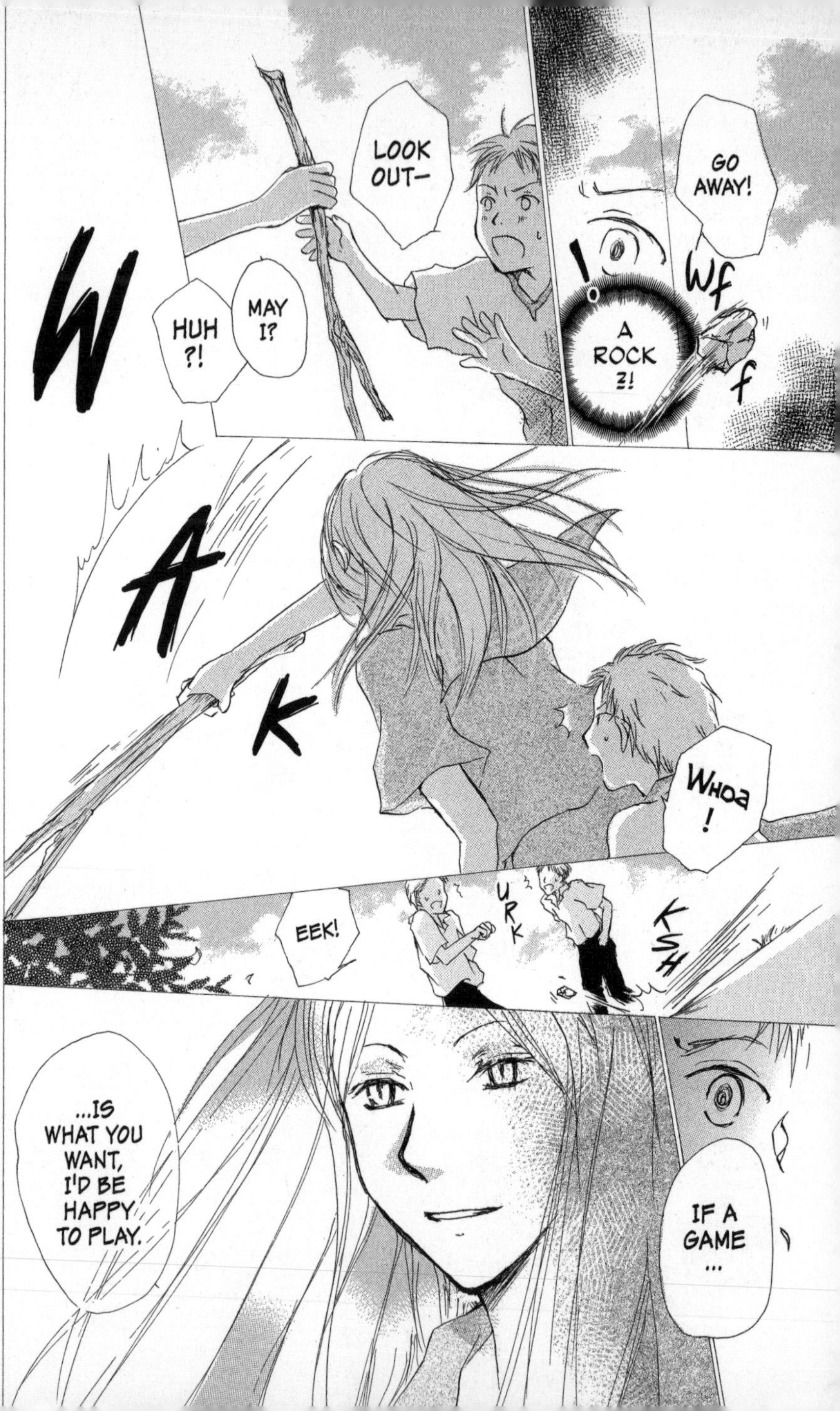
GO AWAY!
Wf
A ROCK ?!
f
LOOK OUT–
MAY I?
HUH ?!
W
A
K
Whoa !
KSH
URK
EEK!
IF A GAME ...
...IS WHAT YOU WANT, I'D BE HAPPY TO PLAY.

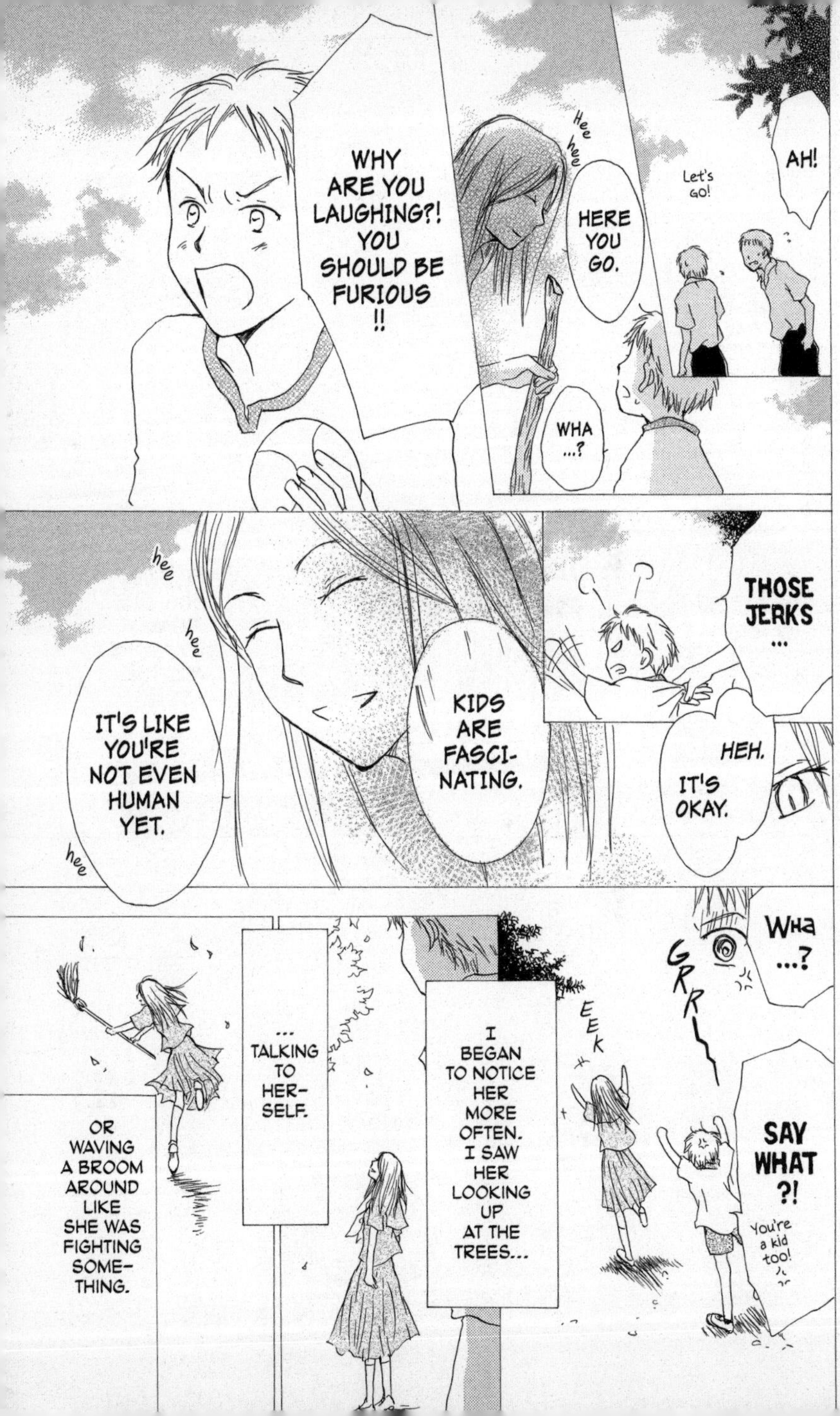
AH!
Let's GO!
Hee hee
HERE YOU GO.
WHA ...?
WHY ARE YOU LAUGHING?! YOU SHOULD BE FURIOUS!!
THOSE JERKS ...
HEH. IT'S OKAY.
KIDS ARE FASCI-NATING.
hee
hee
IT'S LIKE YOU'RE NOT EVEN HUMAN YET.
hee
Wha ...?
GRR
SAY WHAT?!
You're a kid too!
EEK
I BEGAN TO NOTICE HER MORE OFTEN. I SAW HER LOOKING UP AT THE TREES...
... TALKING TO HER-SELF.
OR WAVING A BROOM AROUND LIKE SHE WAS FIGHTING SOME-THING.

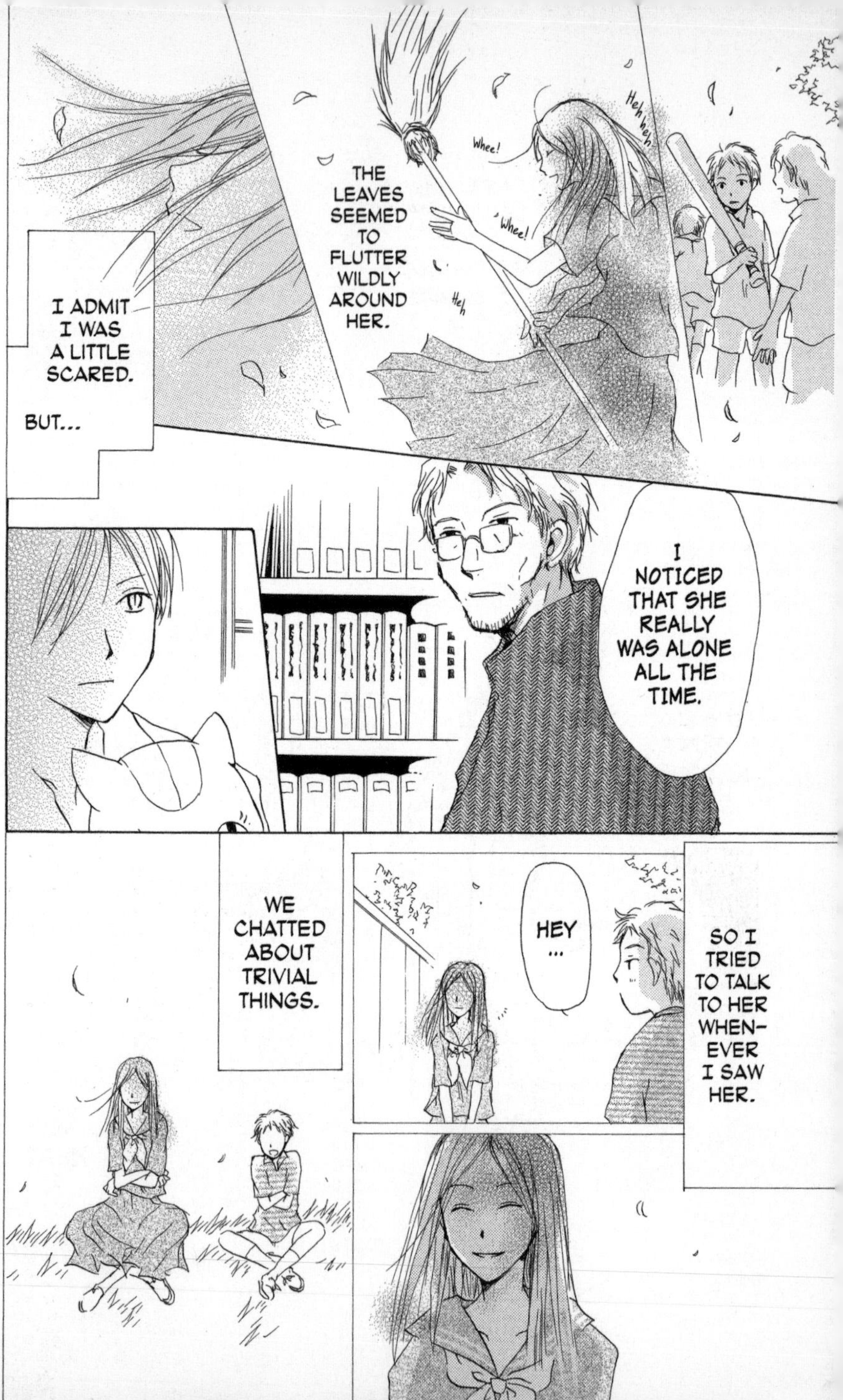

Heh heh
Whee!
Whee!
Heh
THE LEAVES SEEMED TO FLUTTER WILDLY AROUND HER.
I ADMIT I WAS A LITTLE SCARED.
BUT...
I NOTICED THAT SHE REALLY WAS ALONE ALL THE TIME.
SO I TRIED TO TALK TO HER WHEN-EVER I SAW HER.
HEY ...
WE CHATTED ABOUT TRIVIAL THINGS.

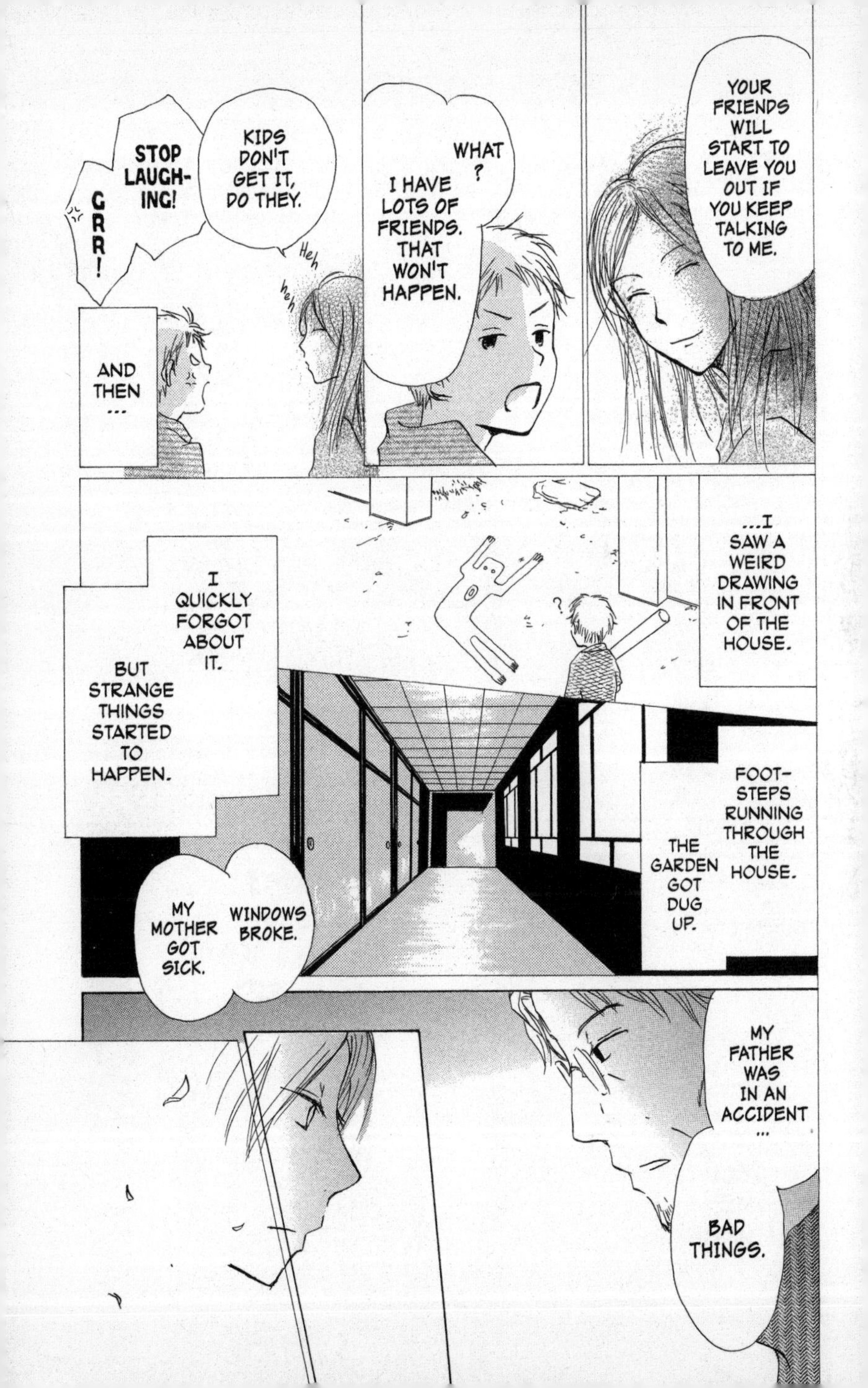
YOUR FRIENDS WILL START TO LEAVE YOU OUT IF YOU KEEP TALKING TO ME.
WHAT?
I HAVE LOTS OF FRIENDS. THAT WON'T HAPPEN.
KIDS DON'T GET IT, DO THEY.
Heh heh
STOP LAUGHING!
GRR!
AND THEN...
...I SAW A WEIRD DRAWING IN FRONT OF THE HOUSE.
I QUICKLY FORGOT ABOUT IT.
BUT STRANGE THINGS STARTED TO HAPPEN.
FOOT-STEPS RUNNING THROUGH THE HOUSE.
THE GARDEN GOT DUG UP.
WINDOWS BROKE.
MY MOTHER GOT SICK.
MY FATHER WAS IN AN ACCIDENT...
BAD THINGS.

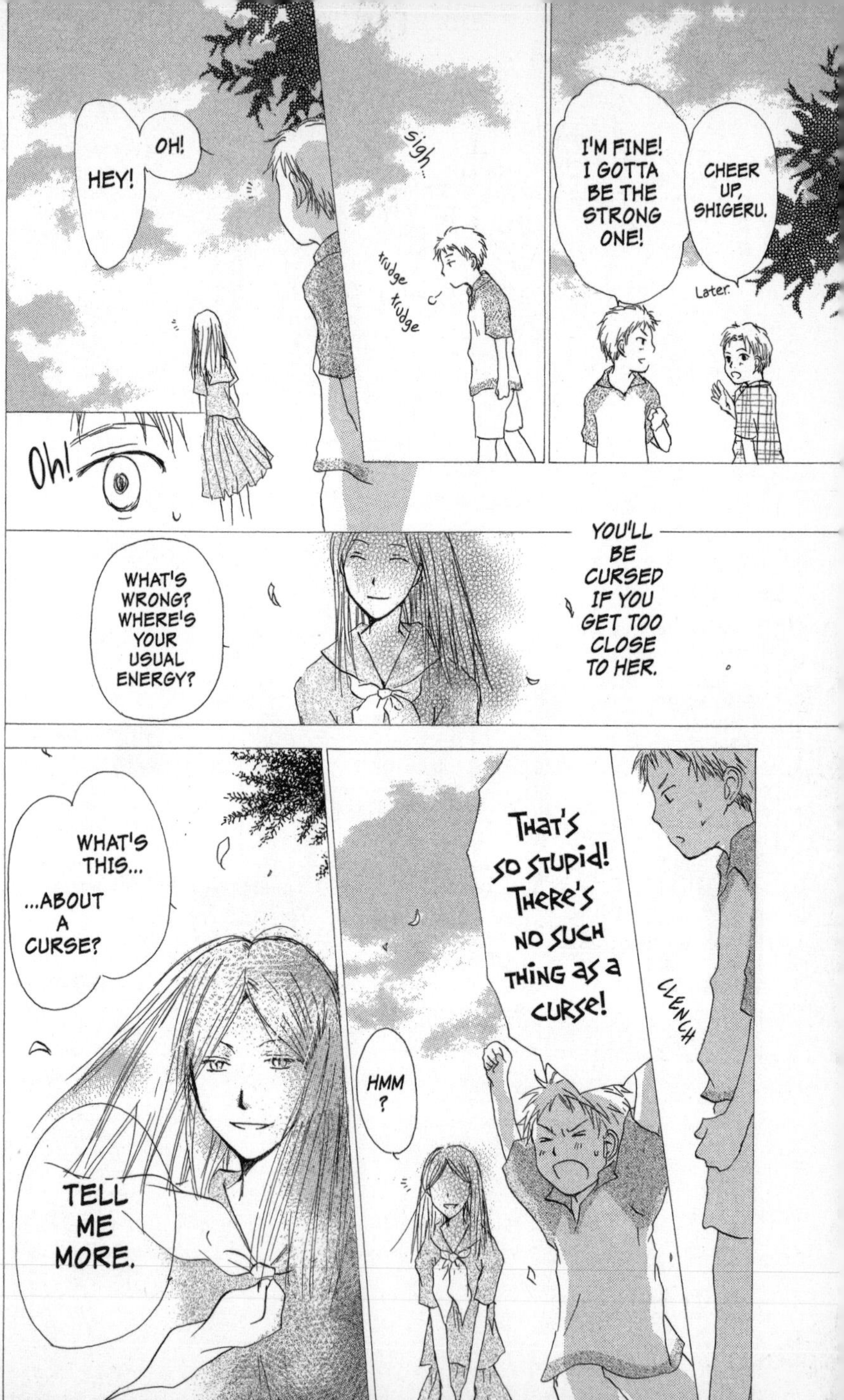
CHEER UP, SHIGERU.
I'M FINE! I GOTTA BE THE STRONG ONE!
Later.
sigh...
trudge trudge
OH!
HEY!
Oh!
YOU'LL BE CURSED IF YOU GET TOO CLOSE TO HER.
WHAT'S WRONG? WHERE'S YOUR USUAL ENERGY?
CLENCH
THAT'S SO STUPID! THERE'S NO SUCH THING AS A CURSE!
HMM?
WHAT'S THIS...
...ABOUT A CURSE?
TELL ME MORE.

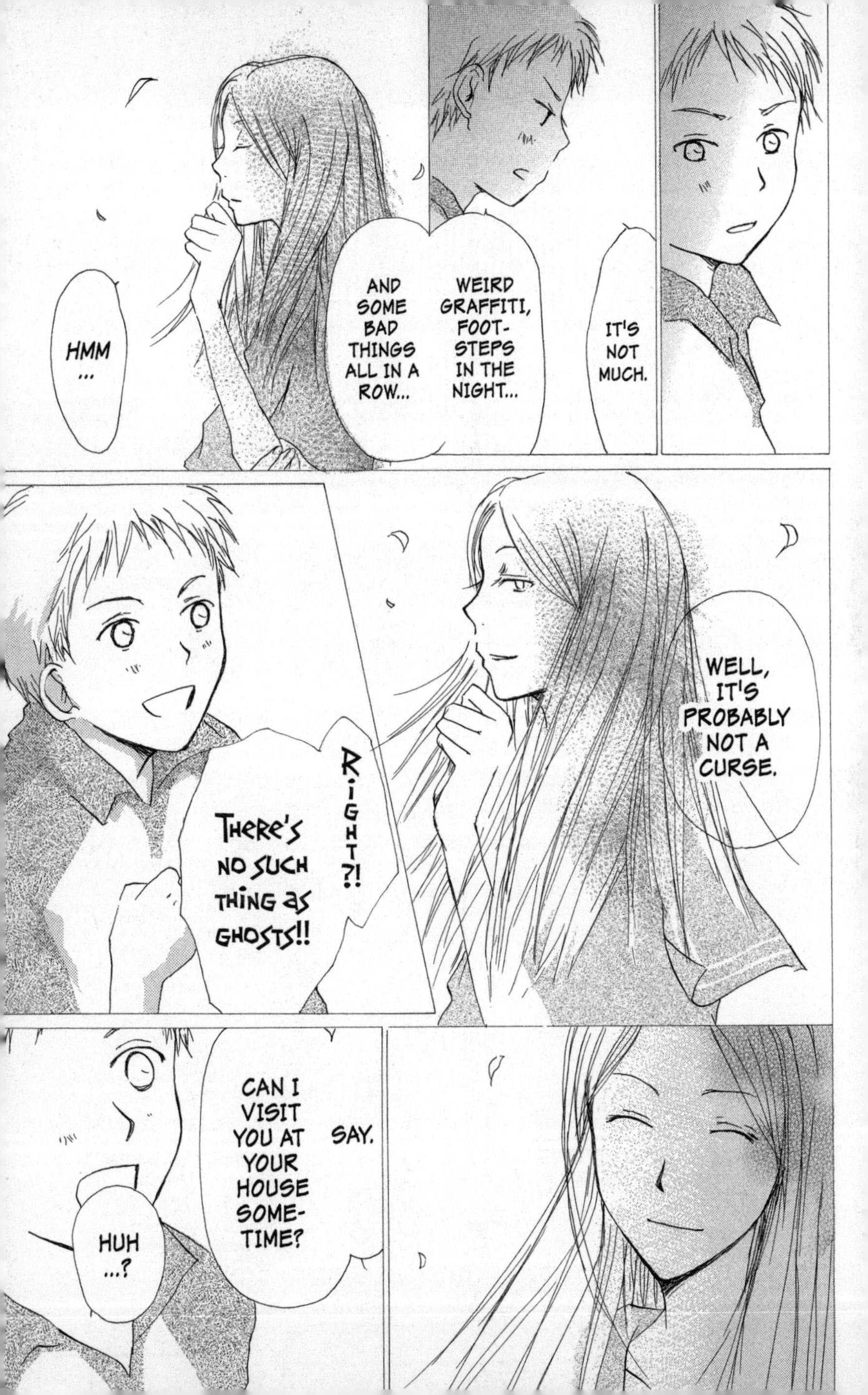
IT'S NOT MUCH.
WEIRD GRAFFITI, FOOT-STEPS IN THE NIGHT...
AND SOME BAD THINGS ALL IN A ROW...
HMM ...
WELL, IT'S PROBABLY NOT A CURSE.
There's no such thing as GHOSTS!!
RIGHT?!
SAY.
CAN I VISIT YOU AT YOUR HOUSE SOME-TIME?
HUH ...?

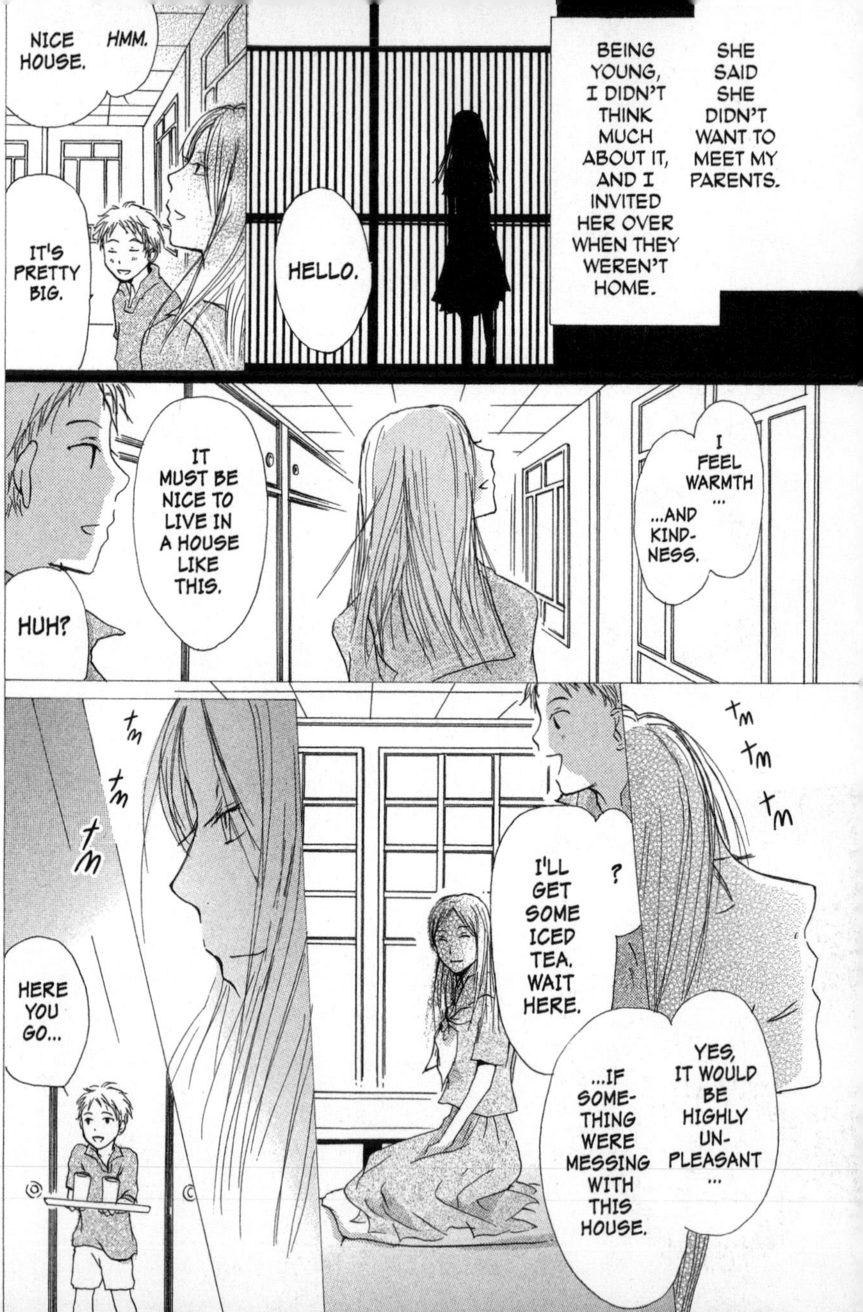
SHE SAID SHE DIDN'T WANT TO MEET MY PARENTS.
BEING YOUNG, I DIDN'T THINK MUCH ABOUT IT, AND I INVITED HER OVER WHEN THEY WEREN'T HOME.
HELLO.
HMM.
NICE HOUSE.
IT'S PRETTY BIG.
I FEEL WARMTH...
...AND KINDNESS.
IT MUST BE NICE TO LIVE IN A HOUSE LIKE THIS.
HUH?
tm tm tm
?
I'LL GET SOME ICED TEA. WAIT HERE.
YES, IT WOULD BE HIGHLY UN-PLEASANT...
...IF SOME-THING WERE MESSING WITH THIS HOUSE.
tm tm tm
HERE YOU GO...

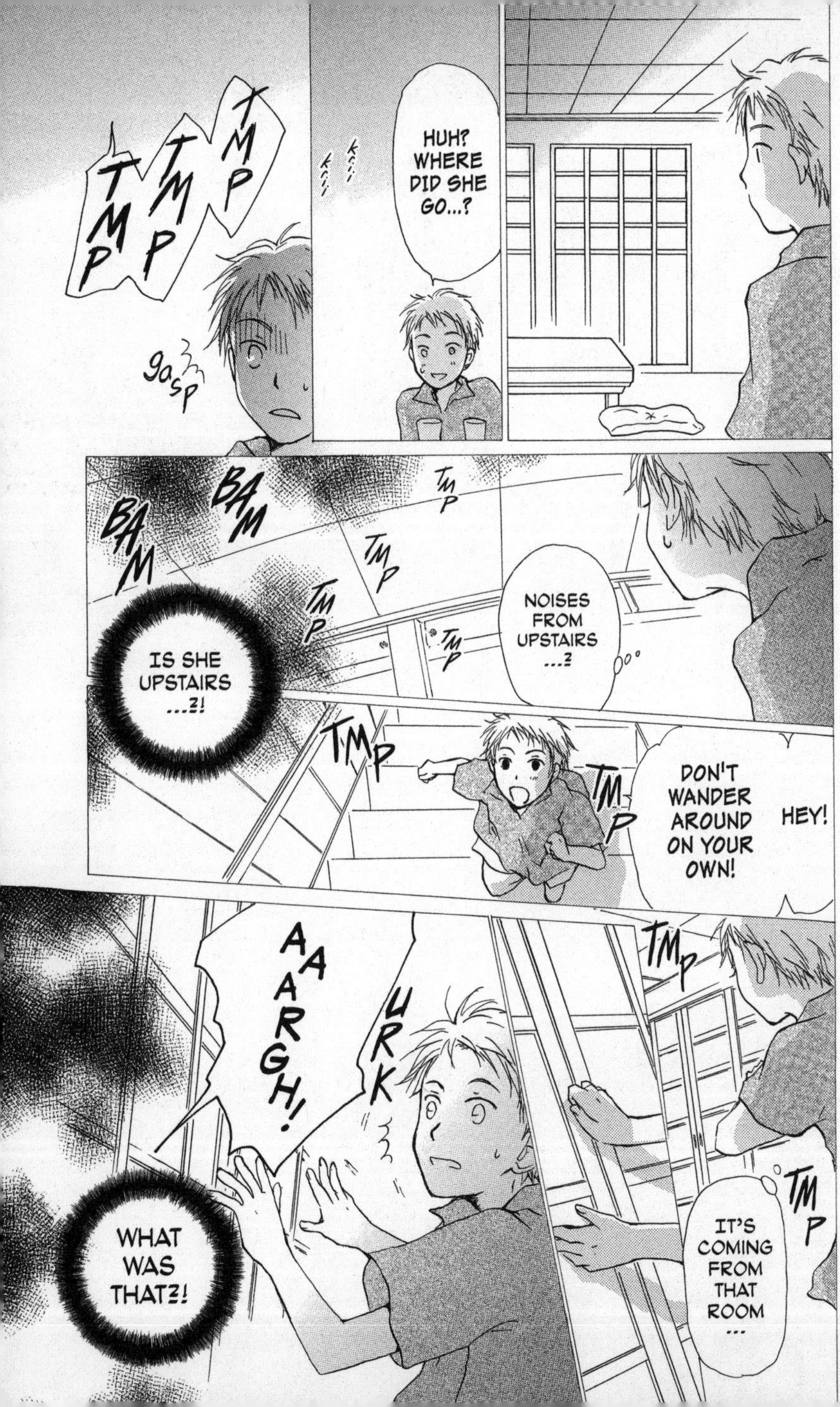
HUH? WHERE DID SHE GO...?
TMP TMP TMP
gasp
TMP
TMP
TMP
TMP
NOISES FROM UPSTAIRS...?
BAM BAM
IS SHE UPSTAIRS...?!
HEY!
DON'T WANDER AROUND ON YOUR OWN!
TMP
TMP
TMP
TMP
IT'S COMING FROM THAT ROOM...
URK
AAARGH!
WHAT WAS THAT?!

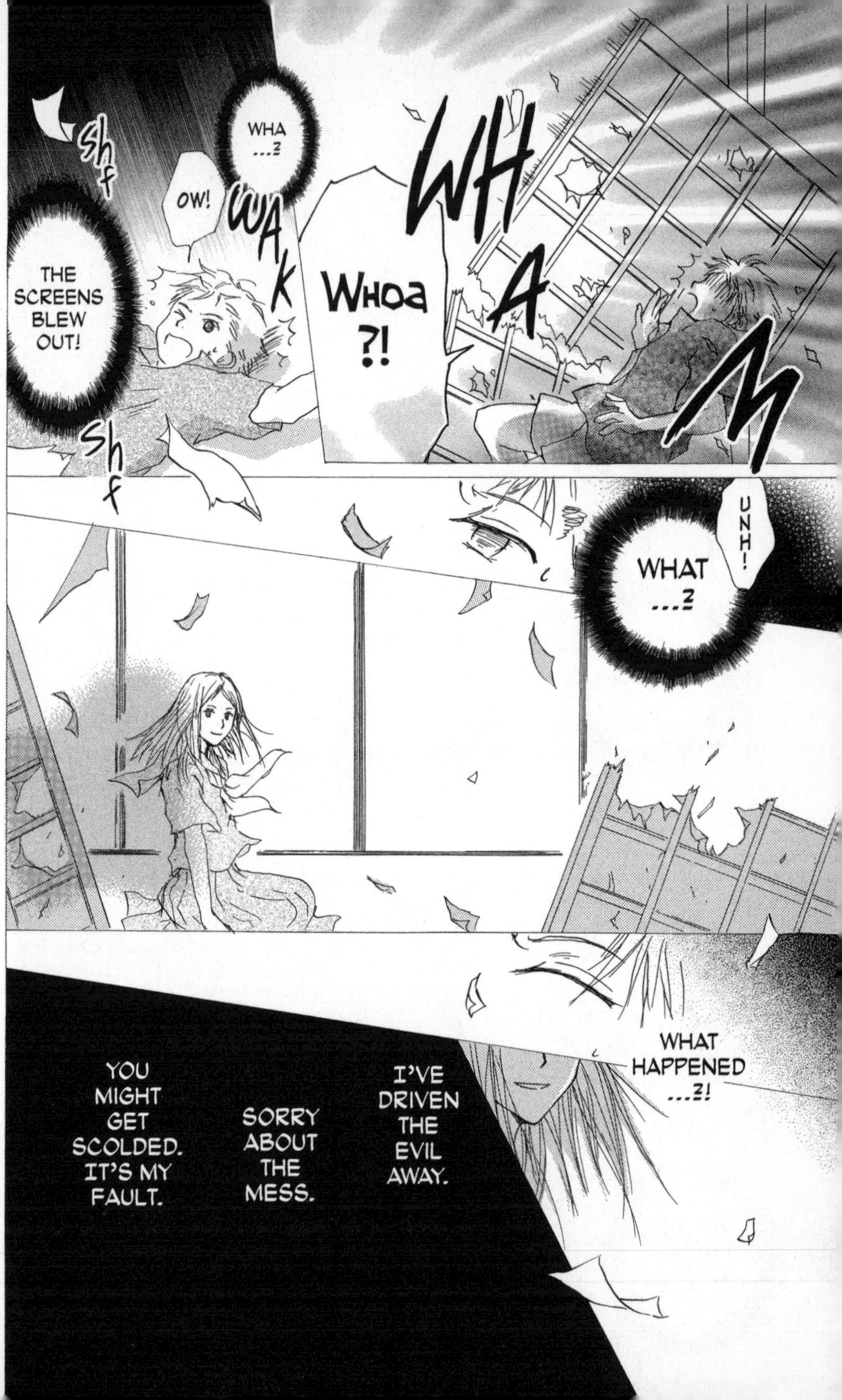
WHAM
Whoa ?!
WHA ...?
OW!
WAK
THE SCREENS BLEW OUT!
Shf
Shf
UNH!
WHAT ...?
WHAT HAPPENED ...?!
I'VE DRIVEN THE EVIL AWAY.
SORRY ABOUT THE MESS.
YOU MIGHT GET SCOLDED. IT'S MY FAULT.

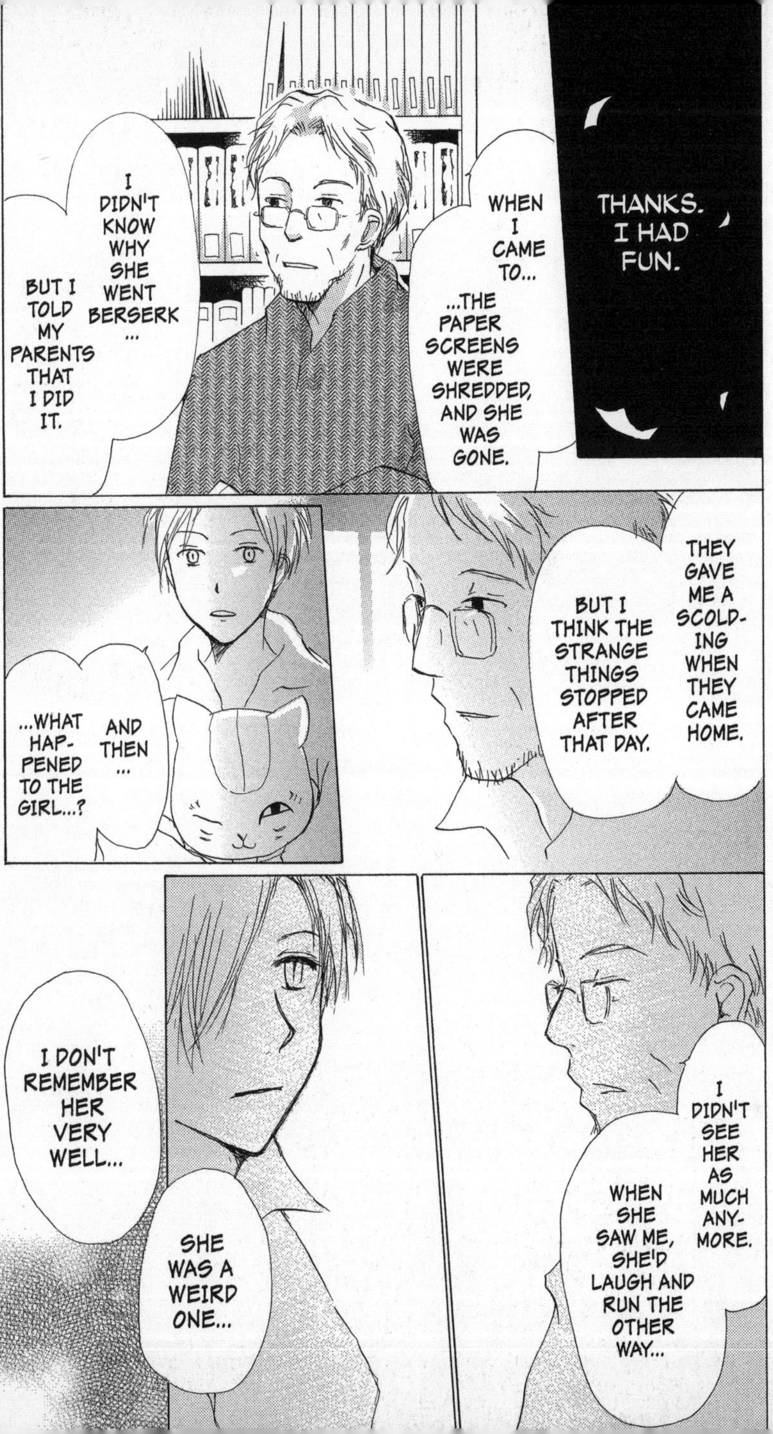
THANKS. I HAD FUN.
WHEN I CAME TO... ...THE PAPER SCREENS WERE SHREDDED, AND SHE WAS GONE.
I DIDN'T KNOW WHY SHE WENT BERSERK...
BUT I TOLD MY PARENTS THAT I DID IT.
THEY GAVE ME A SCOLD-ING WHEN THEY CAME HOME.
BUT I THINK THE STRANGE THINGS STOPPED AFTER THAT DAY.
AND THEN...
...WHAT HAP-PENED TO THE GIRL...?
I DIDN'T SEE HER AS MUCH ANY-MORE.
WHEN SHE SAW ME, SHE'D LAUGH AND RUN THE OTHER WAY...
I DON'T REMEMBER HER VERY WELL...
SHE WAS A WEIRD ONE...

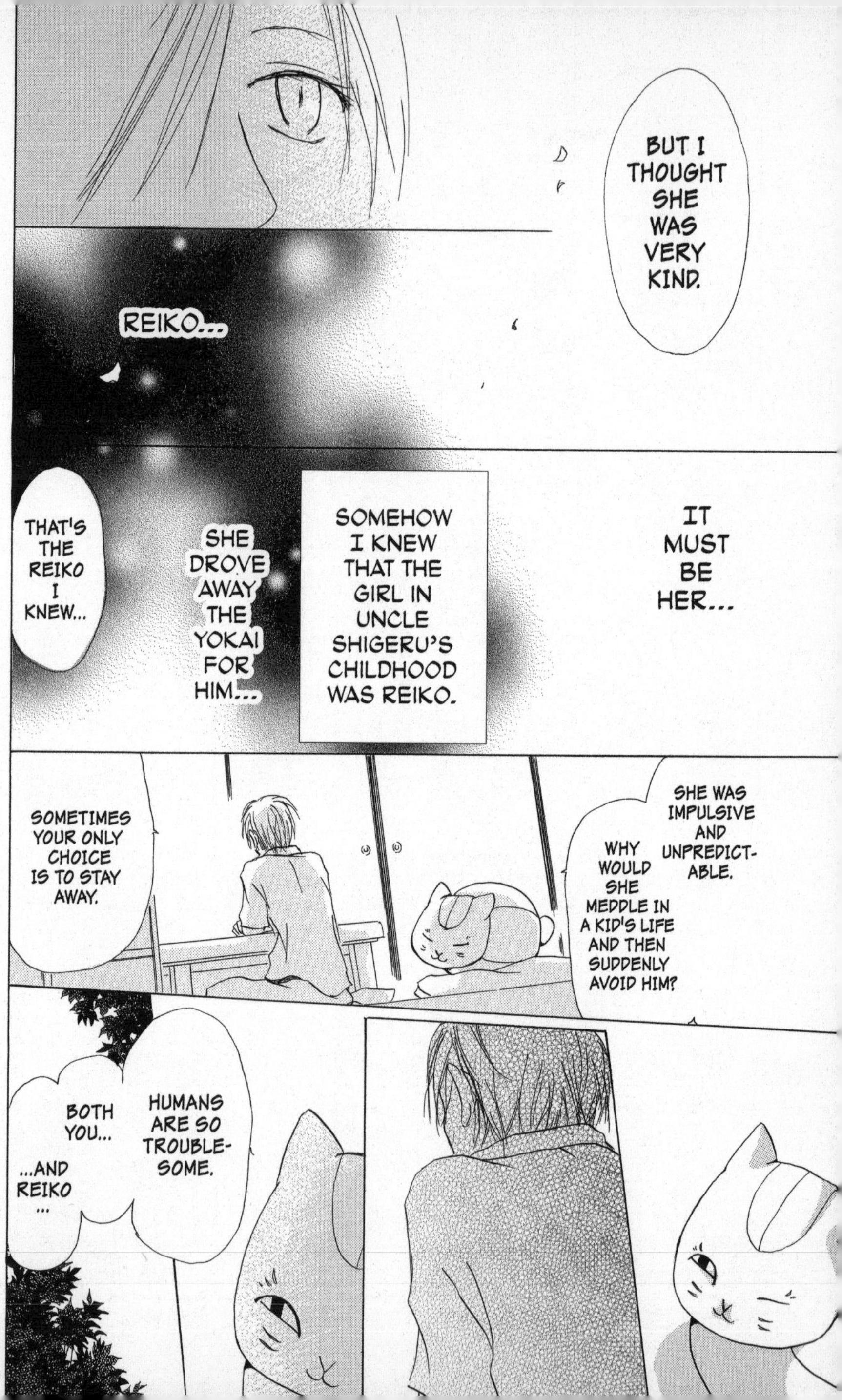
BUT I THOUGHT SHE WAS VERY KIND.
REIKO...
IT MUST BE HER...
SOMEHOW I KNEW THAT THE GIRL IN UNCLE SHIGERU'S CHILDHOOD WAS REIKO.
SHE DROVE AWAY THE YOKAI FOR HIM...
THAT'S THE REIKO I KNEW...
SHE WAS IMPULSIVE AND UNPREDICT-ABLE.
WHY WOULD SHE MEDDLE IN A KID'S LIFE AND THEN SUDDENLY AVOID HIM?
SOMETIMES YOUR ONLY CHOICE IS TO STAY AWAY.
HUMANS ARE SO TROUBLE-SOME.
BOTH YOU...
...AND REIKO...

06

❋Music

It's an important part of my creative process to listen to music while thinking, but I haven't been able to do that as much since working on Natsume. I don't have many opportunities to discover new music or songs, so please let me know if you have any recommendations.

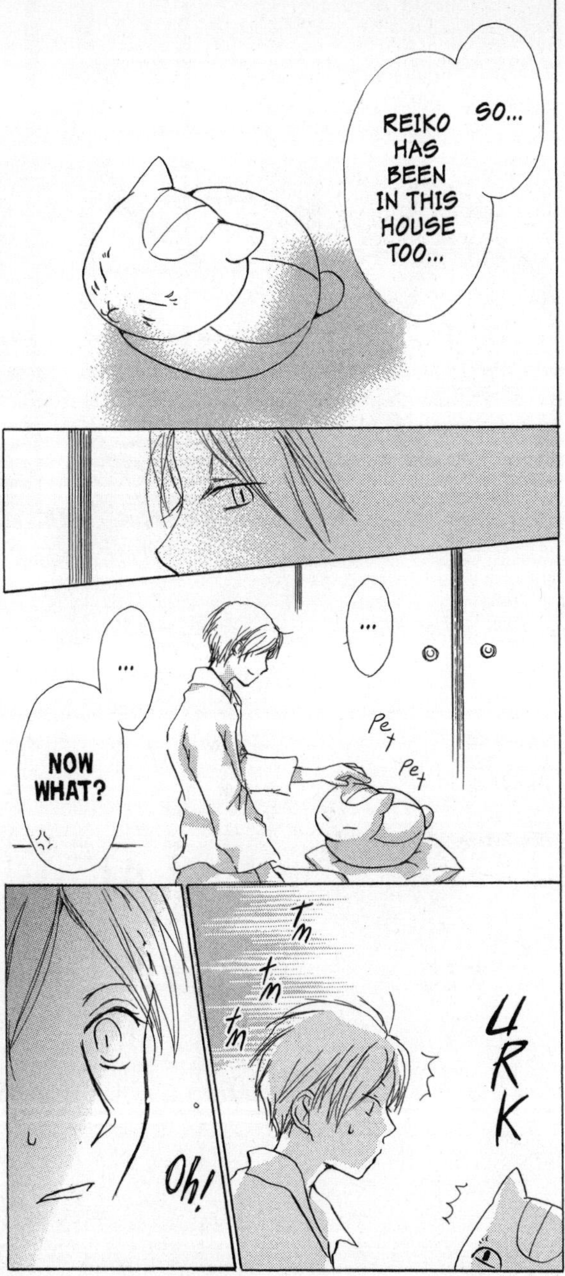
SO...
REIKO HAS BEEN IN THIS HOUSE TOO...
...
...
NOW WHAT?
Pet
Pet
tm
tm
tm
tm
URK
Oh!

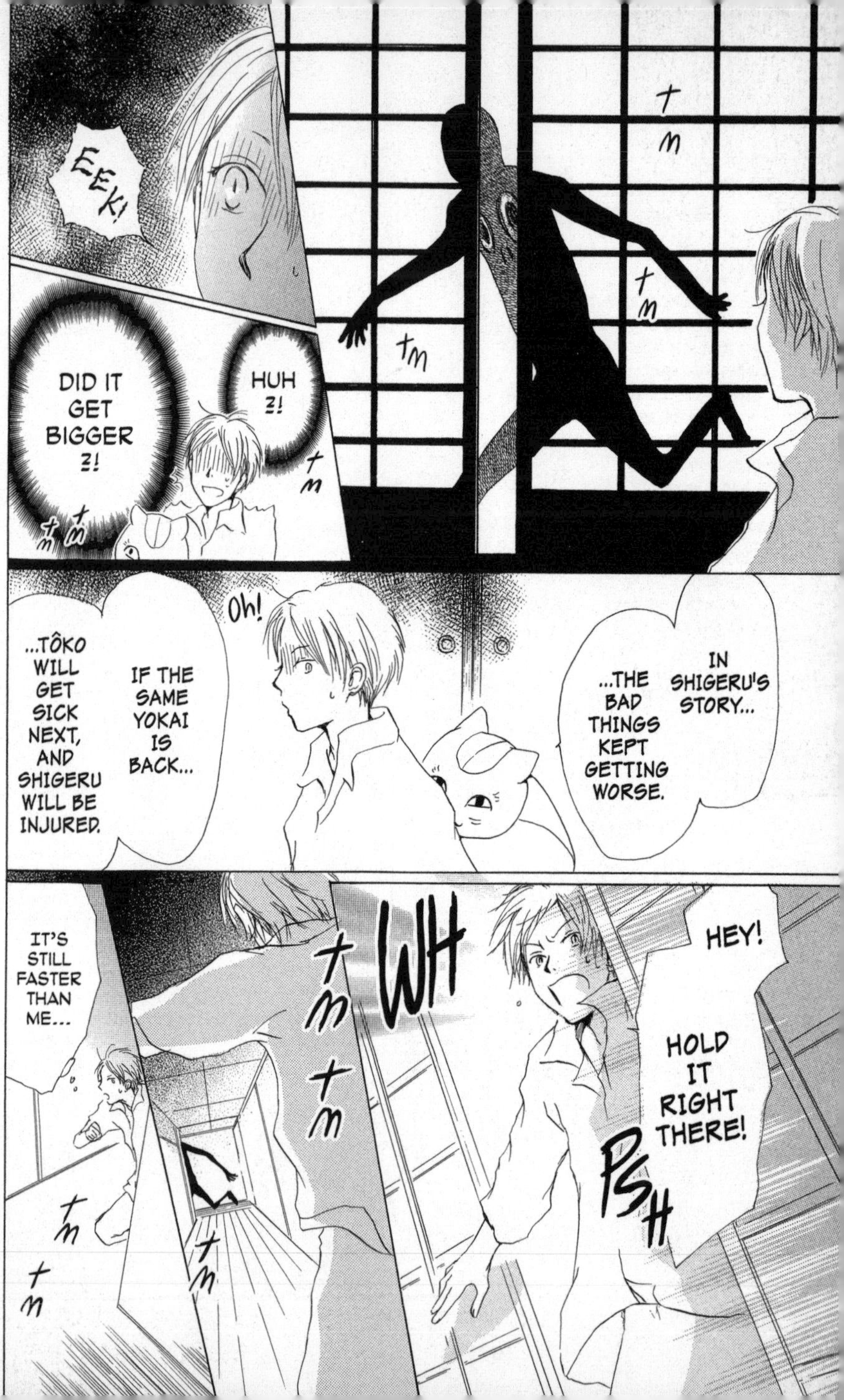
tm
tm
tm
EEK!
HUH?!
DID IT GET BIGGER?!
tm
tm
IN SHIGERU'S STORY...
...THE BAD THINGS KEPT GETTING WORSE.
Oh!
IF THE SAME YOKAI IS BACK...
...TÔKO WILL GET SICK NEXT, AND SHIGERU WILL BE INJURED.
HEY!
HOLD IT RIGHT THERE!
PSH
WH
tm
tm
IT'S STILL FASTER THAN ME...
tm
tm
tm

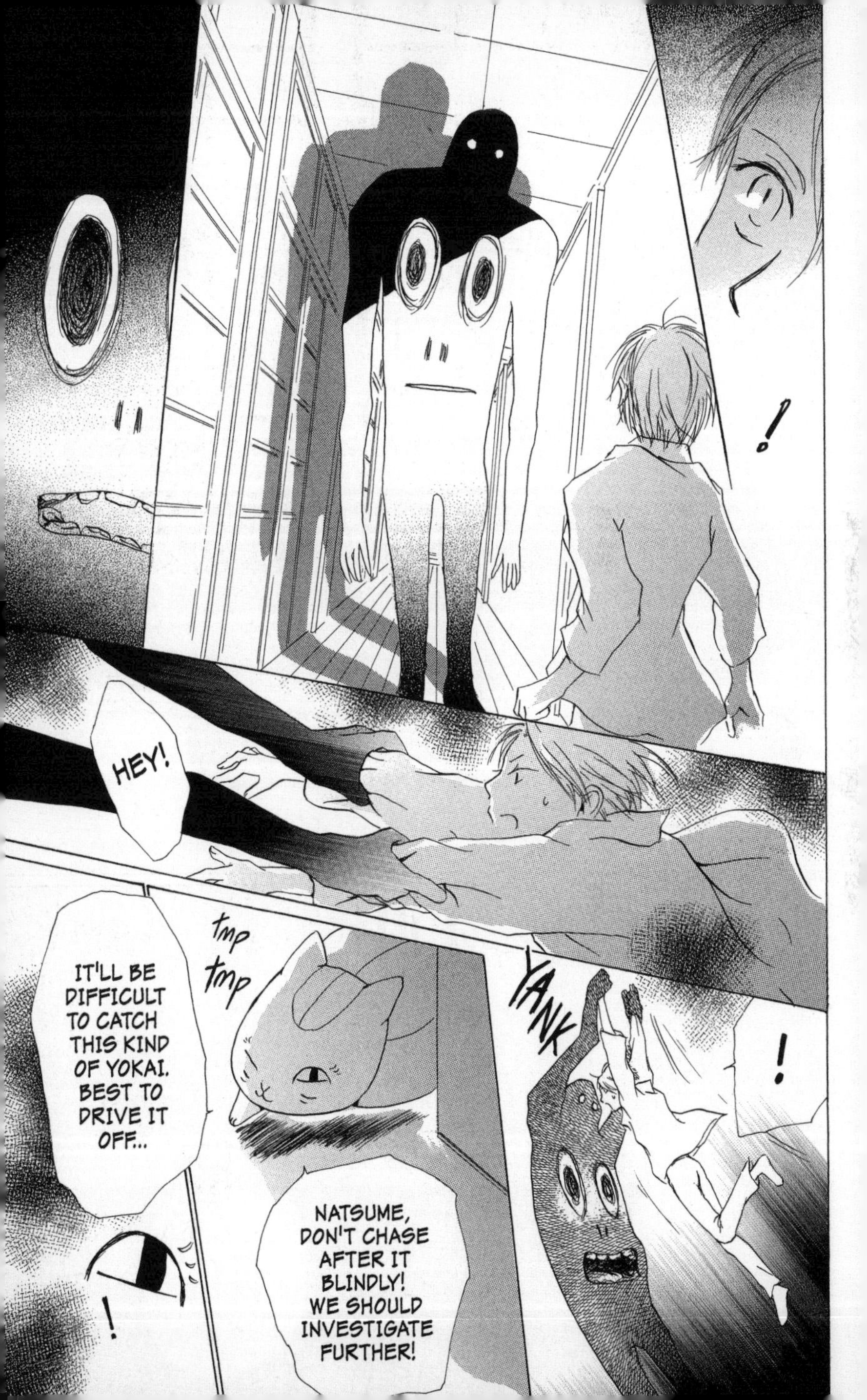
!
HEY!
YANK
!
tmp tmp
IT'LL BE DIFFICULT TO CATCH THIS KIND OF YOKAI. BEST TO DRIVE IT OFF...
NATSUME, DON'T CHASE AFTER IT BLINDLY! WE SHOULD INVESTIGATE FURTHER!
!

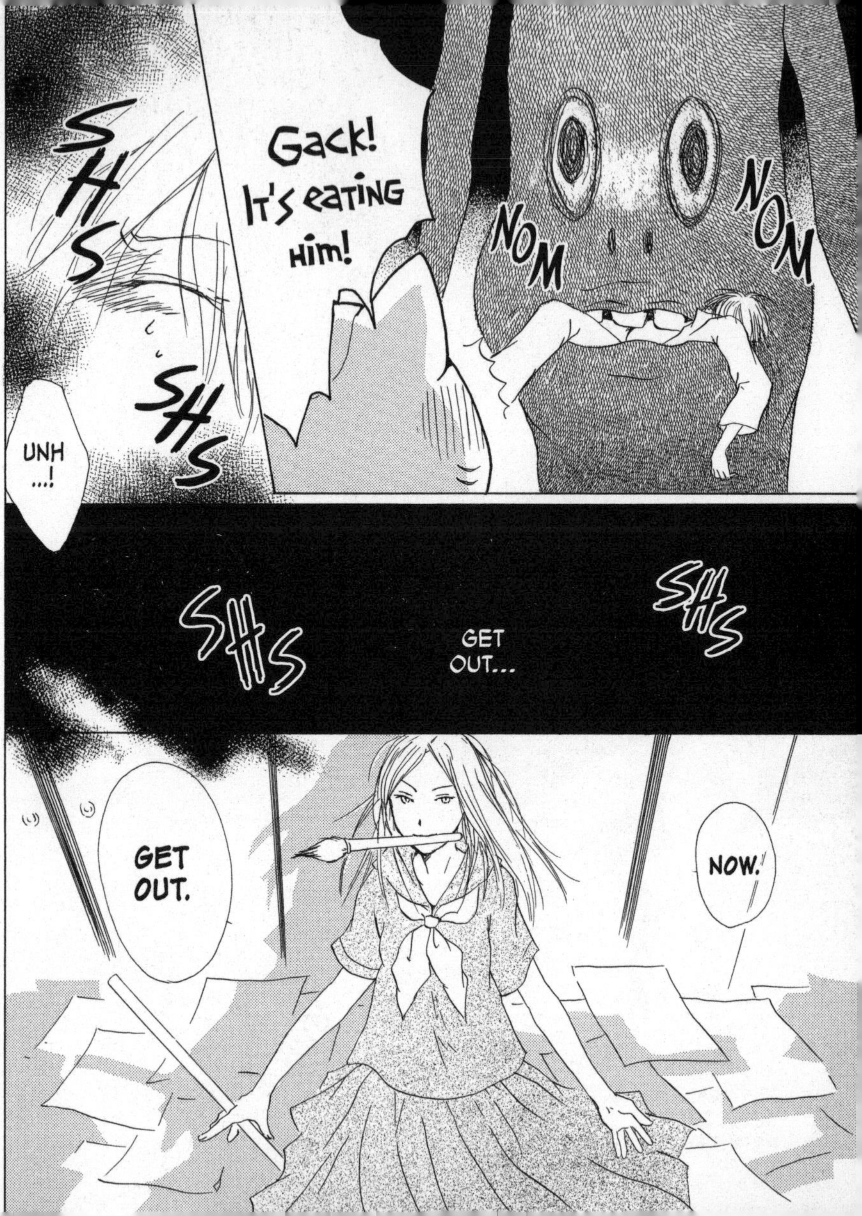
NOM
Gack! It's eating him!
NOM
SHS
SHS
UNH ...!
SHS
GET OUT...
SHS
NOW.
GET OUT.

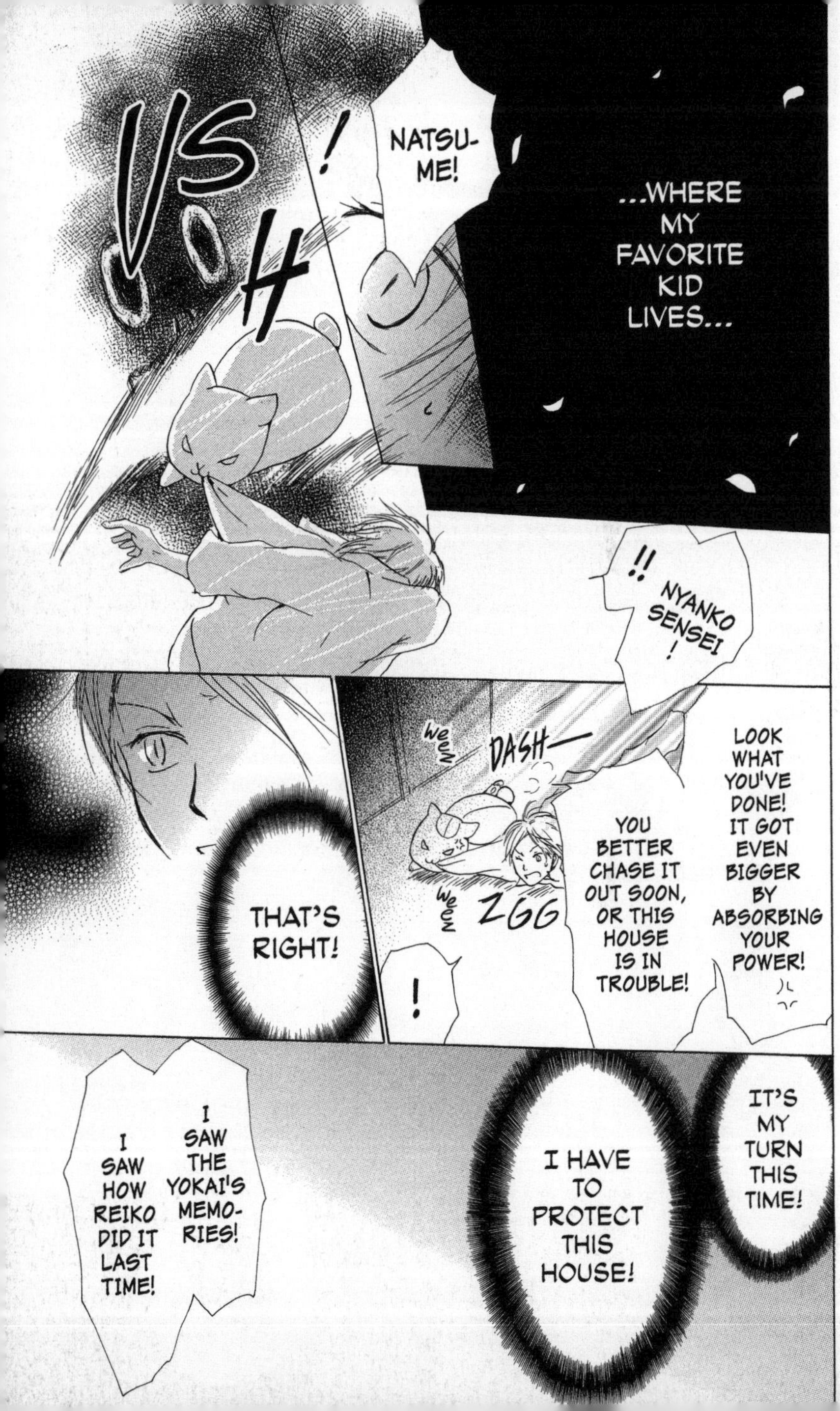
...WHERE MY FAVORITE KID LIVES...
NATSU-ME!
!
VOOSH
!! NYANKO SENSEI!
LOOK WHAT YOU'VE DONE! IT GOT EVEN BIGGER BY ABSORBING YOUR POWER!
YOU BETTER CHASE IT OUT SOON, OR THIS HOUSE IS IN TROUBLE!
DASH—
ween
ween
ZGG
!
THAT'S RIGHT!
IT'S MY TURN THIS TIME!
I HAVE TO PROTECT THIS HOUSE!
I SAW THE YOKAI'S MEMO-RIES!
I SAW HOW REIKO DID IT LAST TIME!

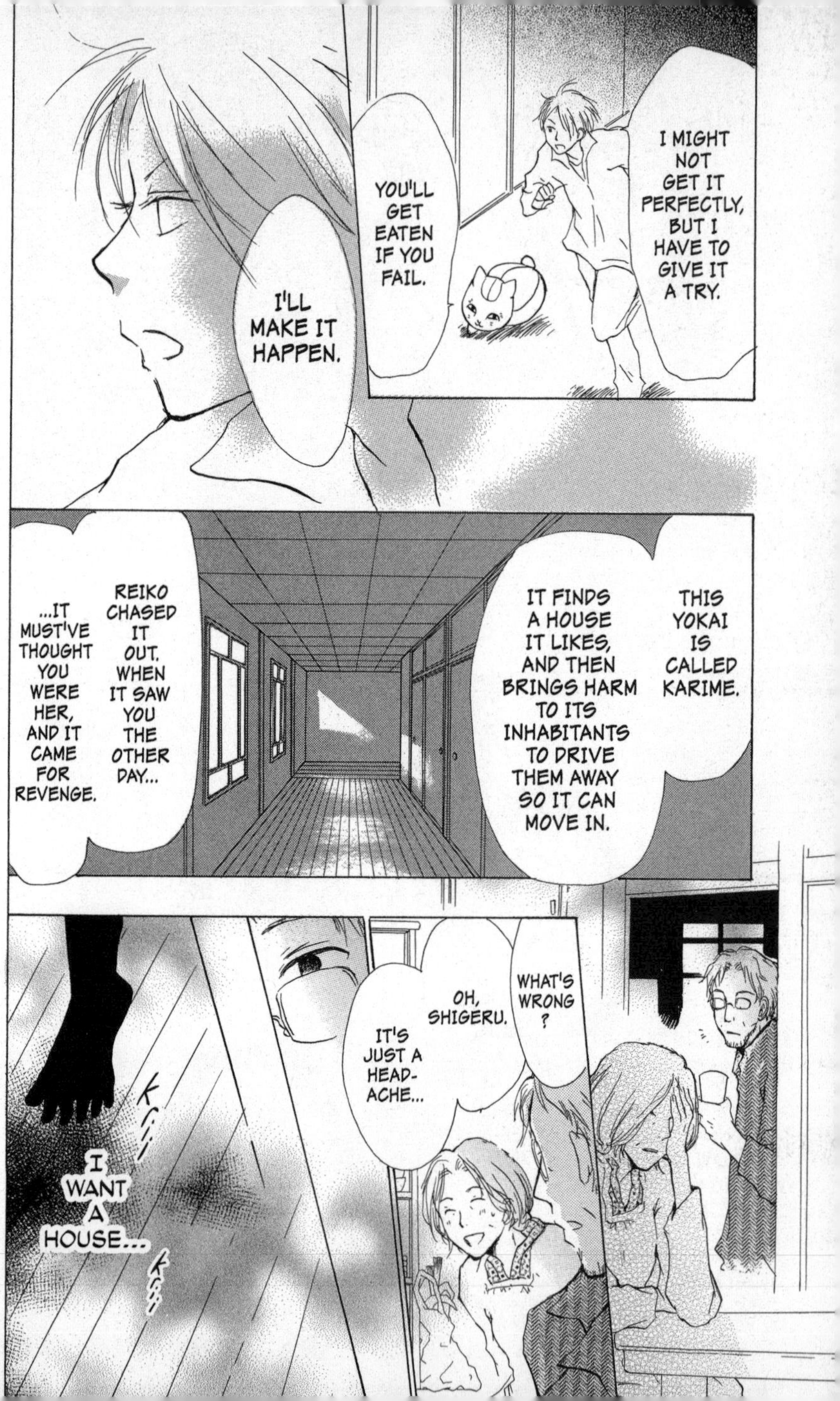
I MIGHT NOT GET IT PERFECTLY, BUT I HAVE TO GIVE IT A TRY.
YOU'LL GET EATEN IF YOU FAIL.
I'LL MAKE IT HAPPEN.
THIS YOKAI IS CALLED KARIME.
IT FINDS A HOUSE IT LIKES, AND THEN BRINGS HARM TO ITS INHABITANTS TO DRIVE THEM AWAY SO IT CAN MOVE IN.
REIKO CHASED IT OUT. WHEN IT SAW YOU THE OTHER DAY...
...IT MUST'VE THOUGHT YOU WERE HER, AND IT CAME FOR REVENGE.
WHAT'S WRONG?
OH, SHIGERU.
IT'S JUST A HEADACHE...
KRII
I WANT A HOUSE...
KRII

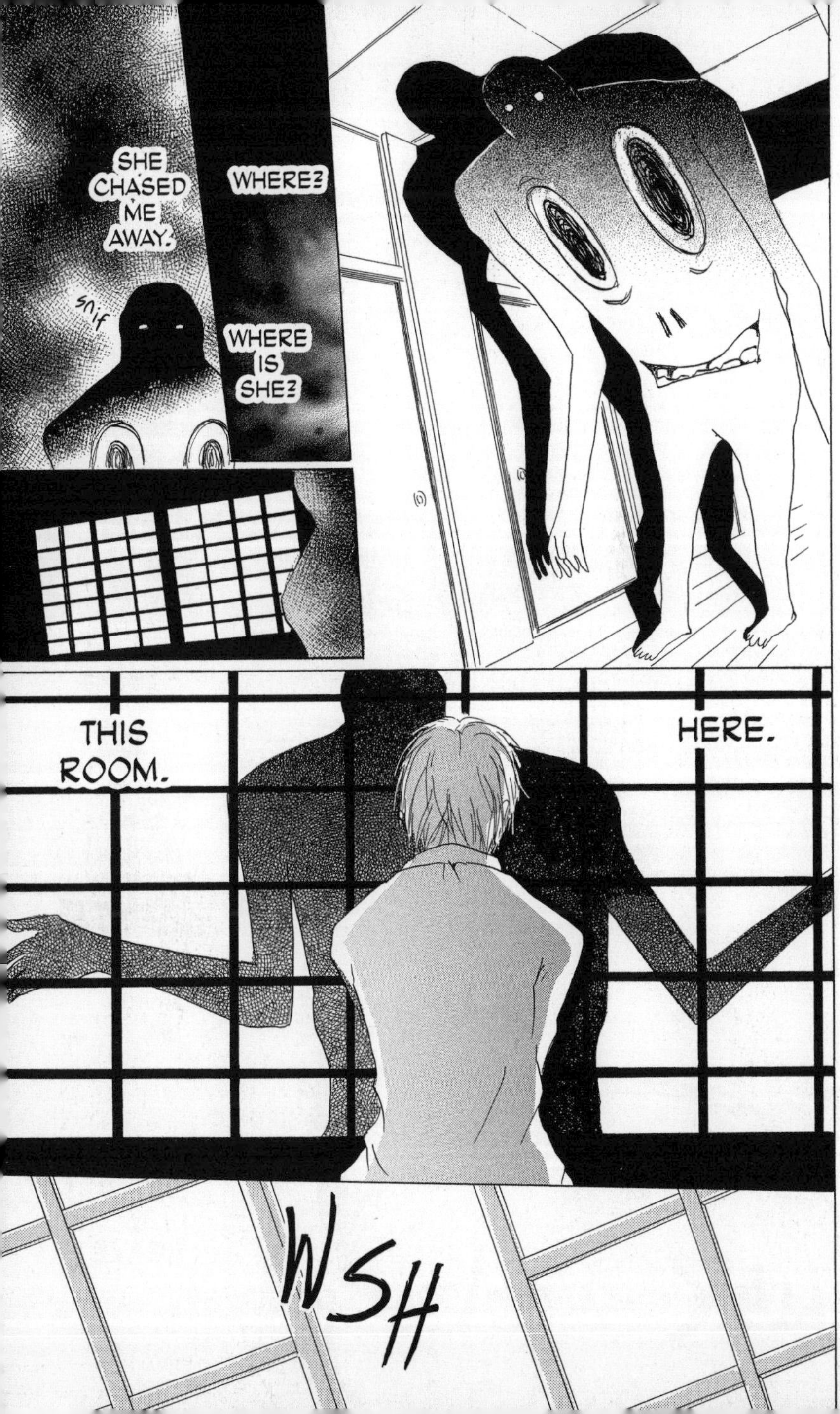
WHERE?
WHERE IS SHE?
SHE CHASED ME AWAY.
snif
HERE.
THIS ROOM.
WSH

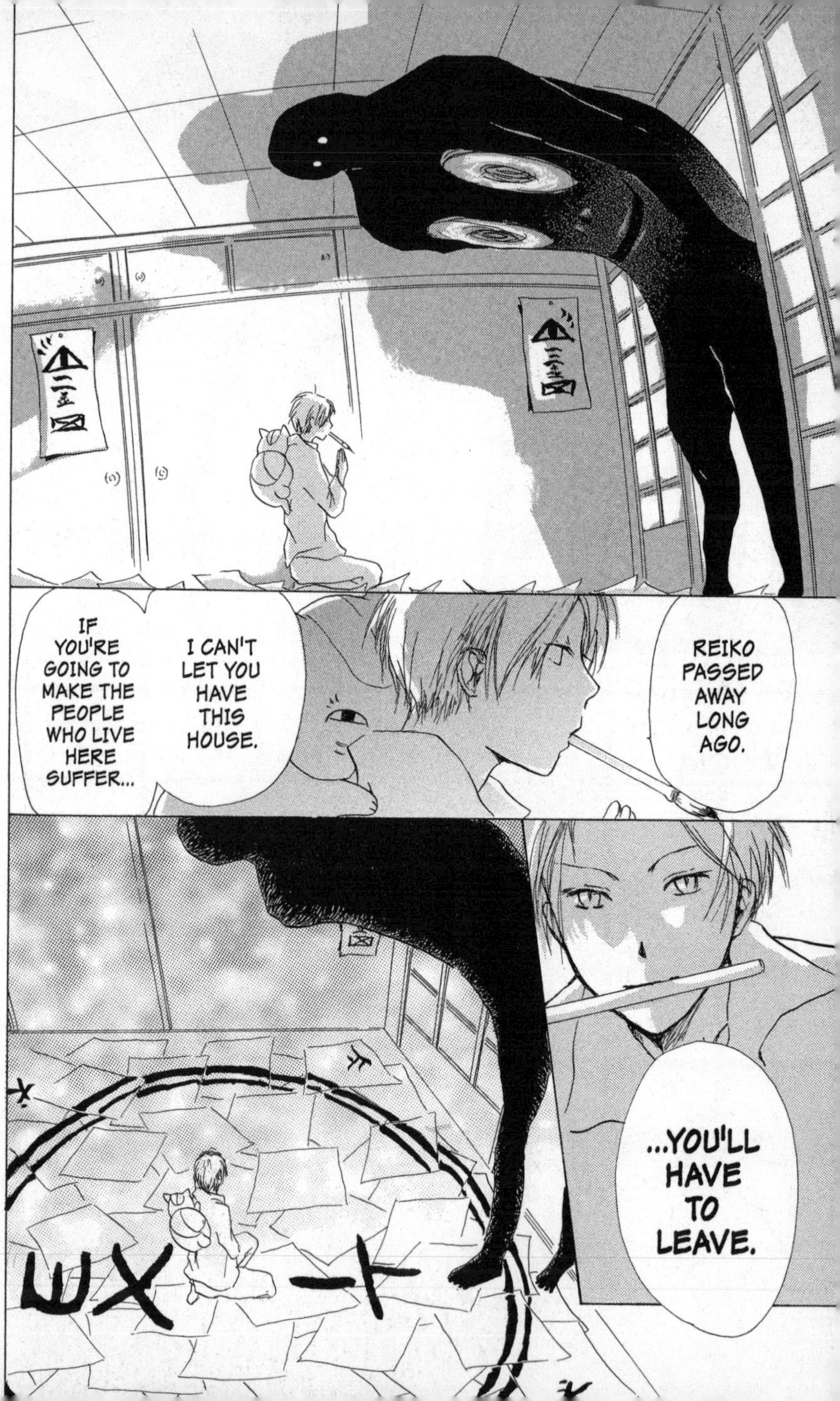
REIKO PASSED AWAY LONG AGO.
I CAN'T LET YOU HAVE THIS HOUSE.
IF YOU'RE GOING TO MAKE THE PEOPLE WHO LIVE HERE SUFFER...
...YOU'LL HAVE TO LEAVE.

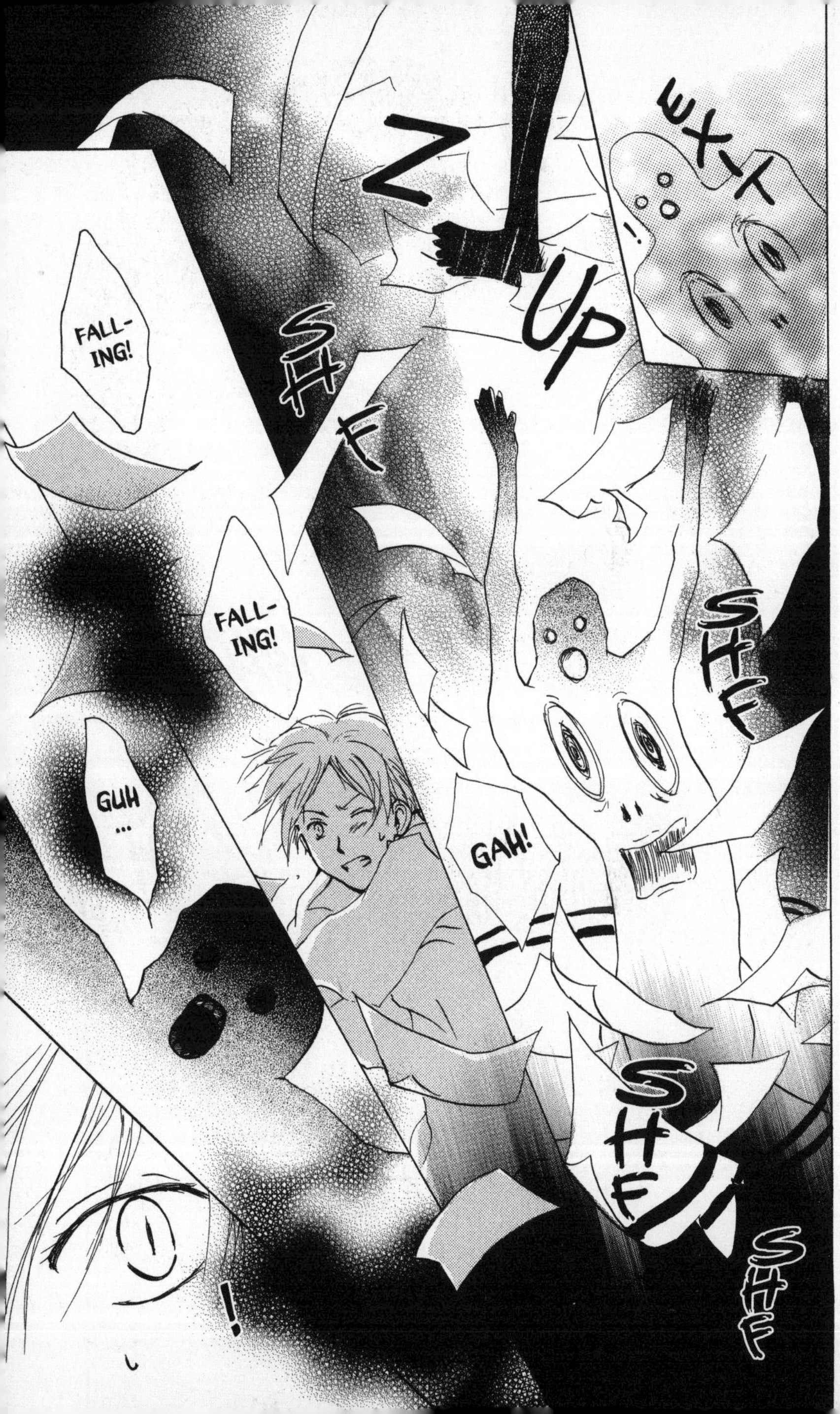

!
ZUP
SHF
FALL-ING!
SHF
SHF
FALL-ING!
GAH!
GUH ...
SHF
SHF
!

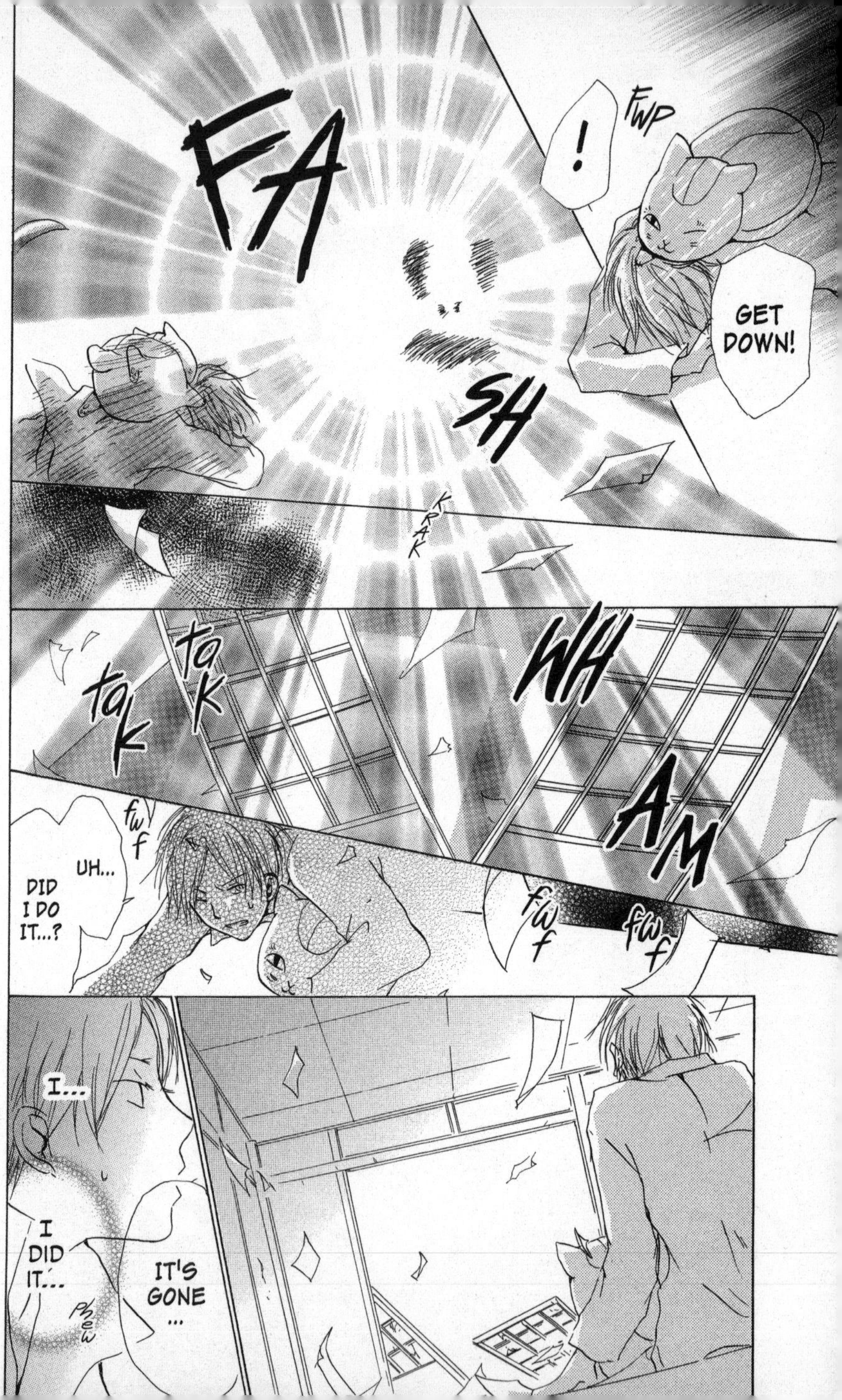
!
FWP
GET DOWN!
FA
SH
KRAK
WH
AM
tak
tak
fwf
fwf
fwf
UH...
DID I DO IT...?
I...
IT'S GONE ...
I DID IT...
Phew

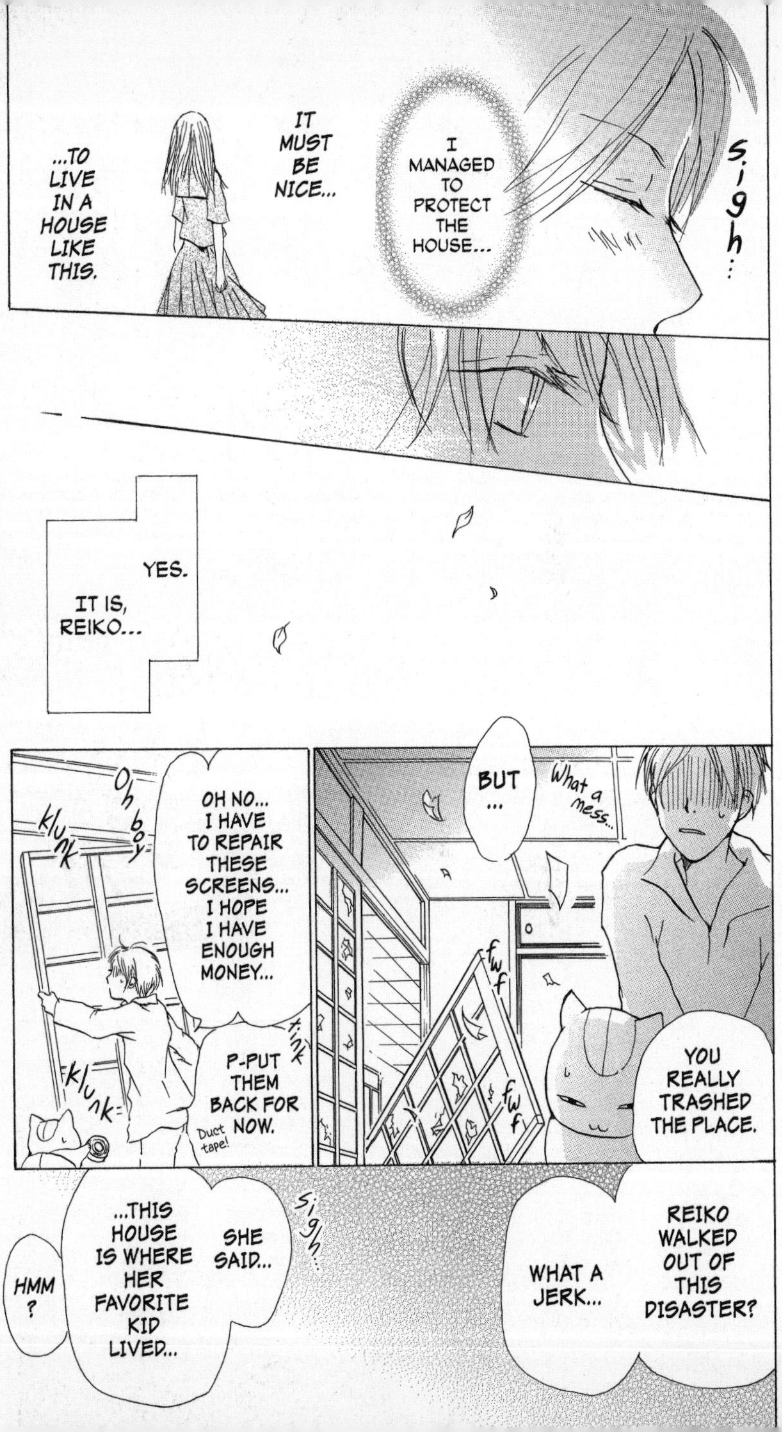
Sigh...
I MANAGED TO PROTECT THE HOUSE...
IT MUST BE NICE...
...TO LIVE IN A HOUSE LIKE THIS.
YES.
IT IS, REIKO...
BUT ...
What a mess...
fwf
fwf
YOU REALLY TRASHED THE PLACE.
Oh boy
klunk
OH NO... I HAVE TO REPAIR THESE SCREENS... I HOPE I HAVE ENOUGH MONEY...
tink
P-PUT THEM BACK FOR NOW.
Duct tape!
klunk
REIKO WALKED OUT OF THIS DISASTER?
WHAT A JERK...
Sigh...
SHE SAID...
...THIS HOUSE IS WHERE HER FAVORITE KID LIVED...
HMM?

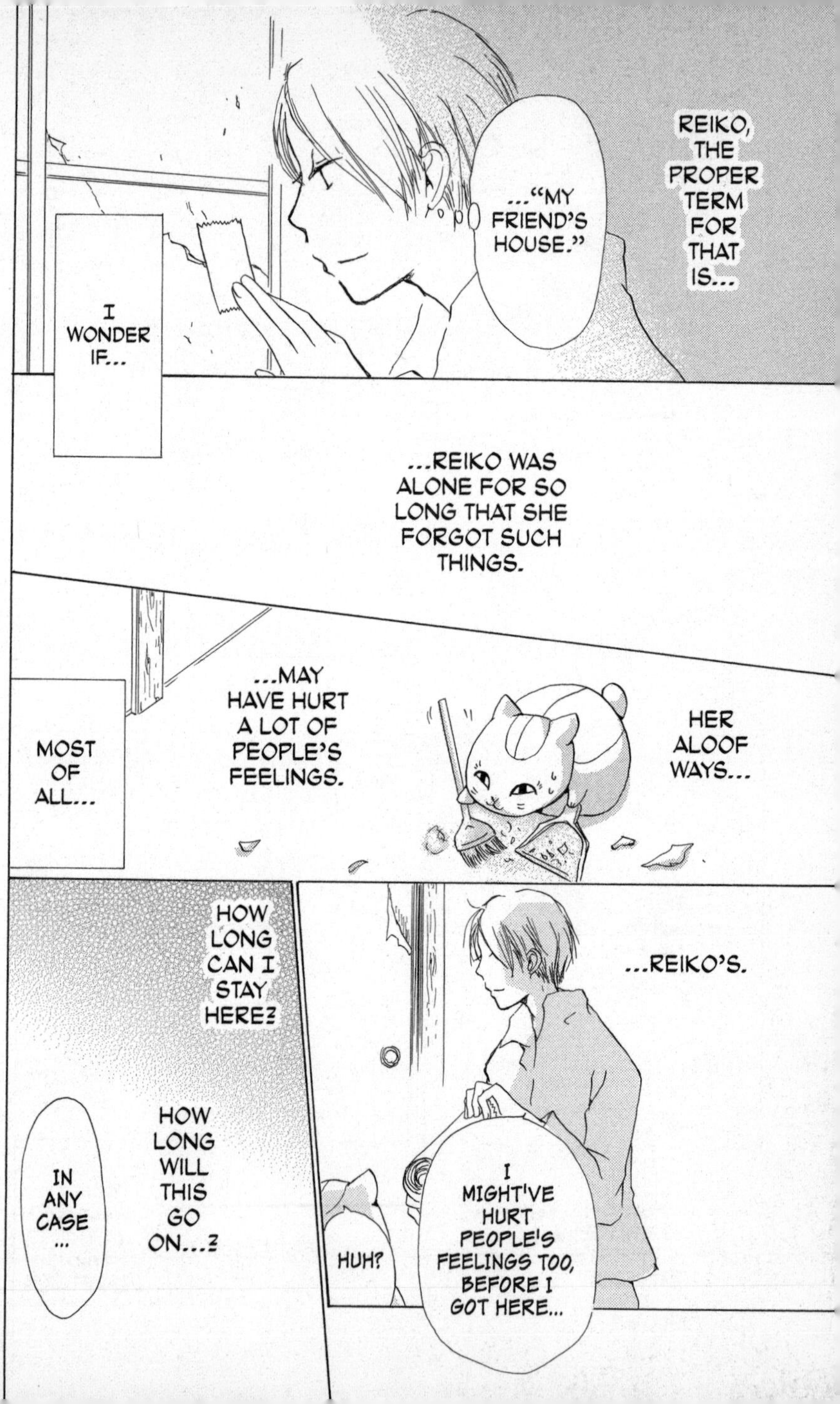
REIKO, THE PROPER TERM FOR THAT IS...
..."MY FRIEND'S HOUSE."
I WONDER IF...
...REIKO WAS ALONE FOR SO LONG THAT SHE FORGOT SUCH THINGS.
HER ALOOF WAYS...
...MAY HAVE HURT A LOT OF PEOPLE'S FEELINGS.
MOST OF ALL...
...REIKO'S.
I MIGHT'VE HURT PEOPLE'S FEELINGS TOO, BEFORE I GOT HERE...
HUH?
HOW LONG CAN I STAY HERE?
HOW LONG WILL THIS GO ON...?
IN ANY CASE...

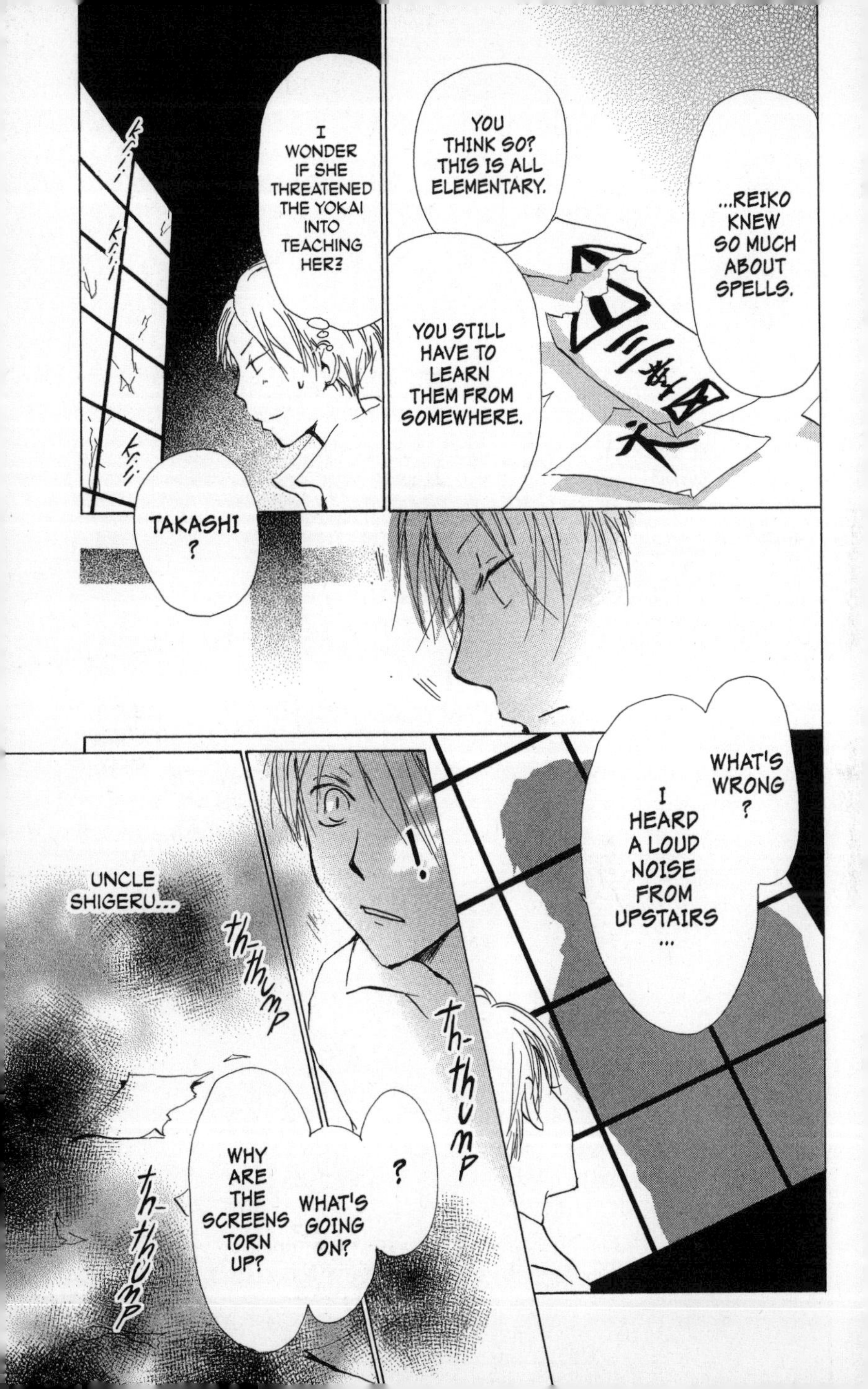
...REIKO KNEW SO MUCH ABOUT SPELLS.
YOU THINK SO? THIS IS ALL ELEMENTARY.
YOU STILL HAVE TO LEARN THEM FROM SOMEWHERE.
I WONDER IF SHE THREATENED THE YOKAI INTO TEACHING HER?
TAKASHI?
WHAT'S WRONG?
I HEARD A LOUD NOISE FROM UPSTAIRS...
!
UNCLE SHIGERU...
th-thump
th-thump
?
WHAT'S GOING ON?
WHY ARE THE SCREENS TORN UP?
th-thump

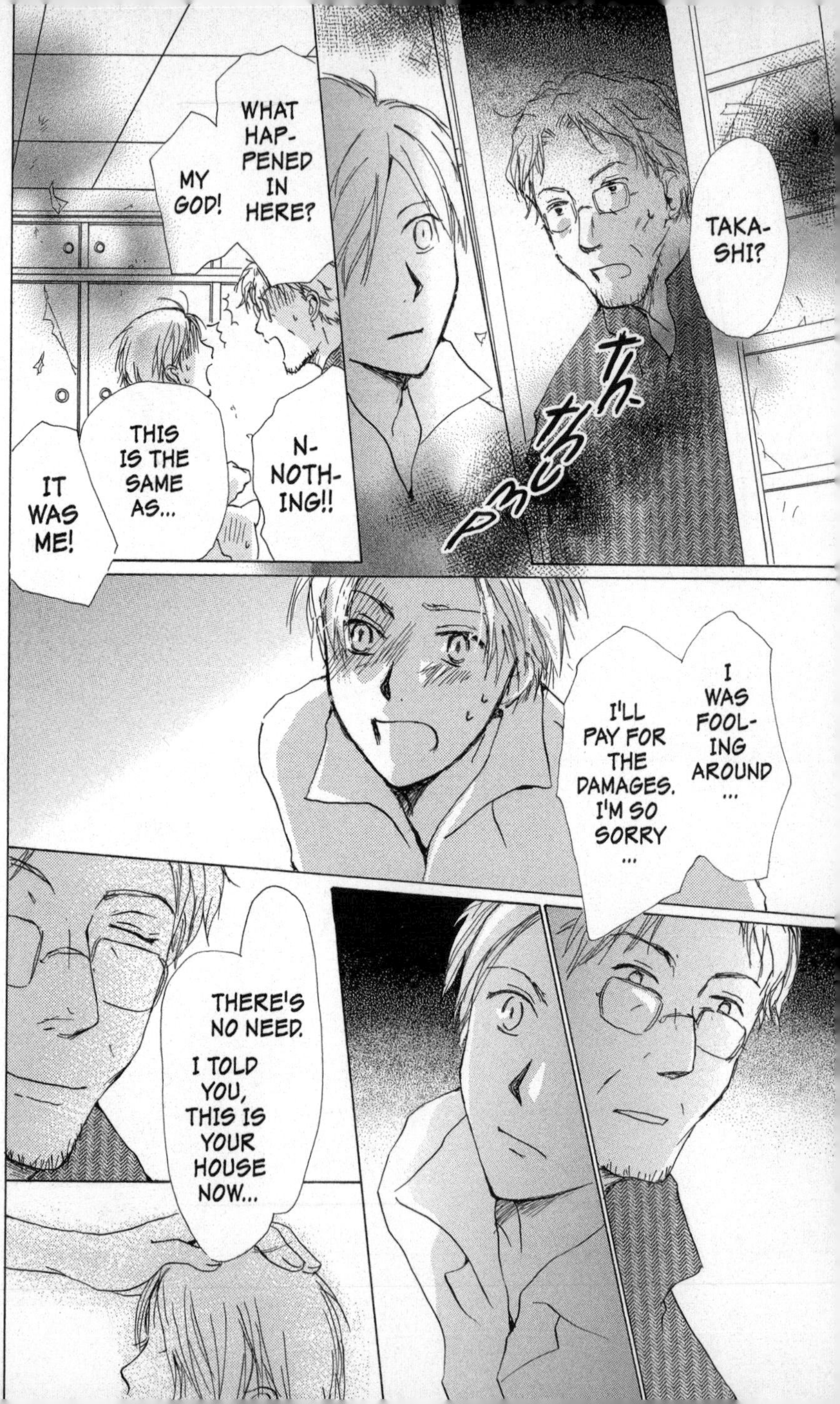
TAKA-SHI?
WHAT HAP-PENED IN HERE?
MY GOD!
N-NOTH-ING!!
THIS IS THE SAME AS...
IT WAS ME!
I WAS FOOL-ING AROUND...
I'LL PAY FOR THE DAMAGES. I'M SO SORRY...
THERE'S NO NEED.
I TOLD YOU, THIS IS YOUR HOUSE NOW...

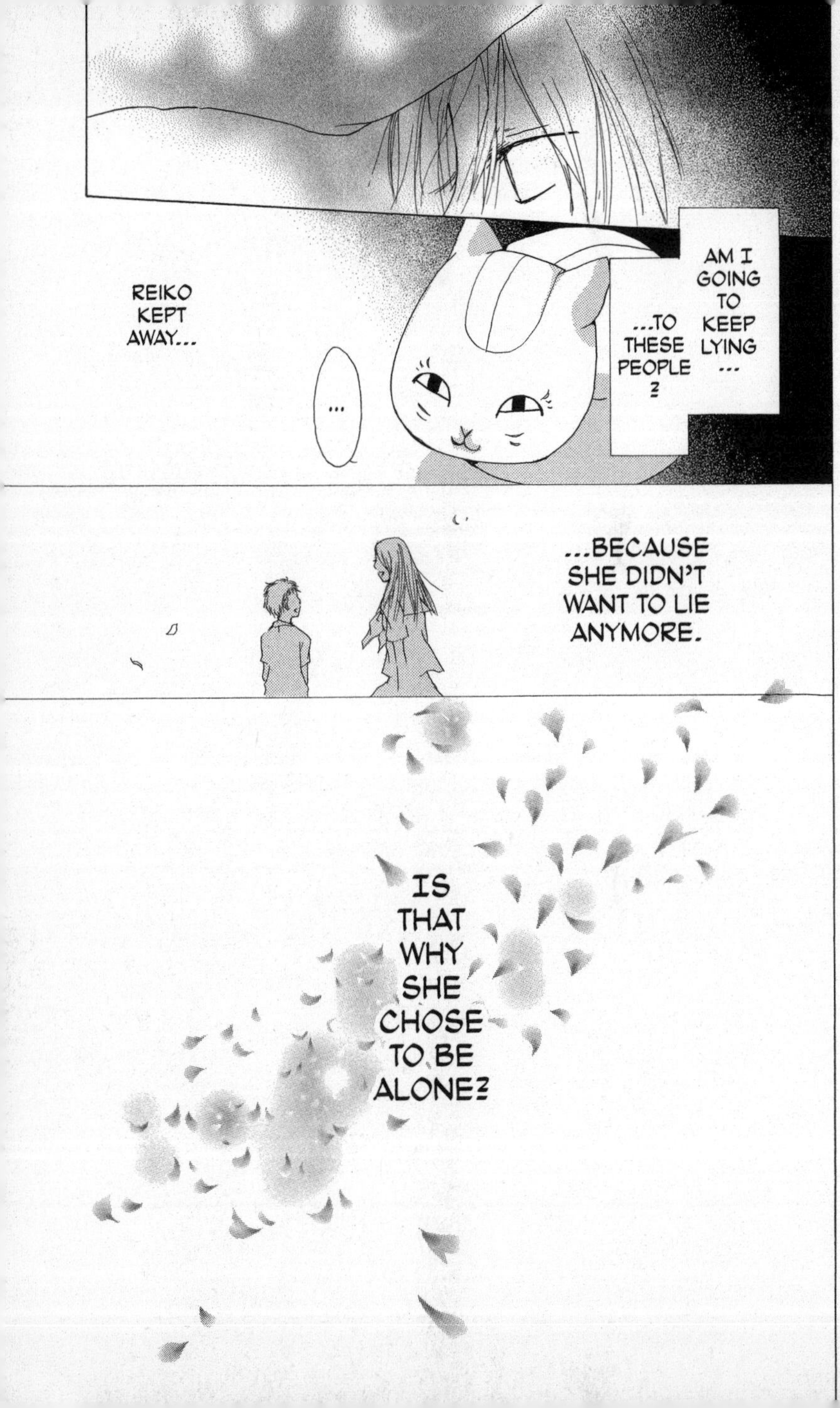
AM I GOING TO KEEP LYING...
...TO THESE PEOPLE?
...
REIKO KEPT AWAY...
...BECAUSE SHE DIDN'T WANT TO LIE ANYMORE.
IS THAT WHY SHE CHOSE TO BE ALONE?

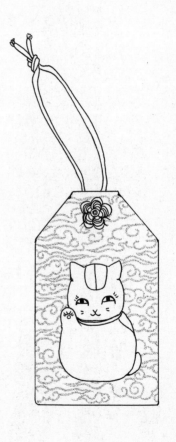

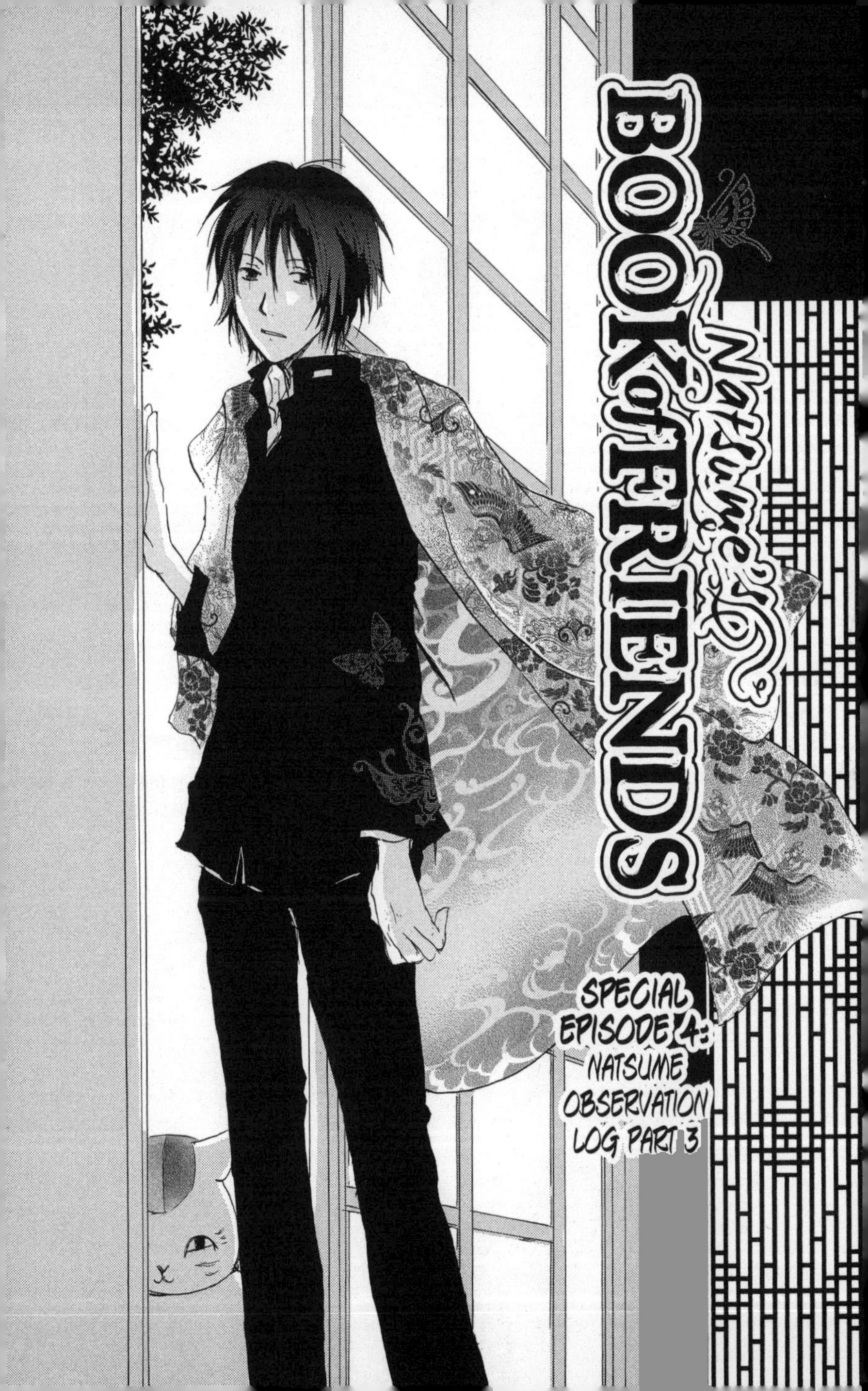
Natsume's
BOOK of FRIENDS
SPECIAL EPISODE 4: NATSUME OBSERVATION LOG PART 3

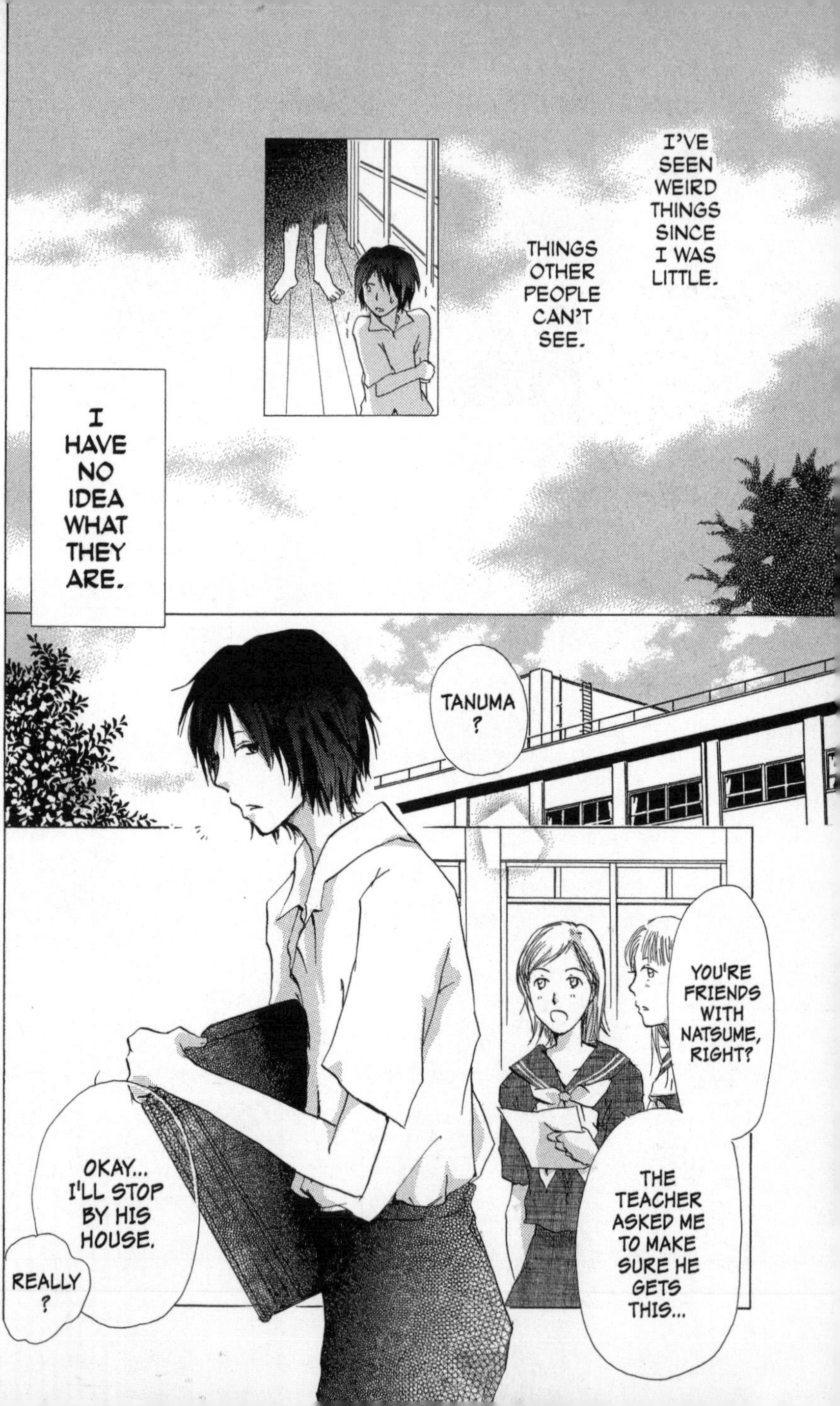
I'VE SEEN WEIRD THINGS SINCE I WAS LITTLE.
THINGS OTHER PEOPLE CAN'T SEE.
I HAVE NO IDEA WHAT THEY ARE.
TANUMA?
YOU'RE FRIENDS WITH NATSUME, RIGHT?
THE TEACHER ASKED ME TO MAKE SURE HE GETS THIS...
OKAY... I'LL STOP BY HIS HOUSE.
REALLY?

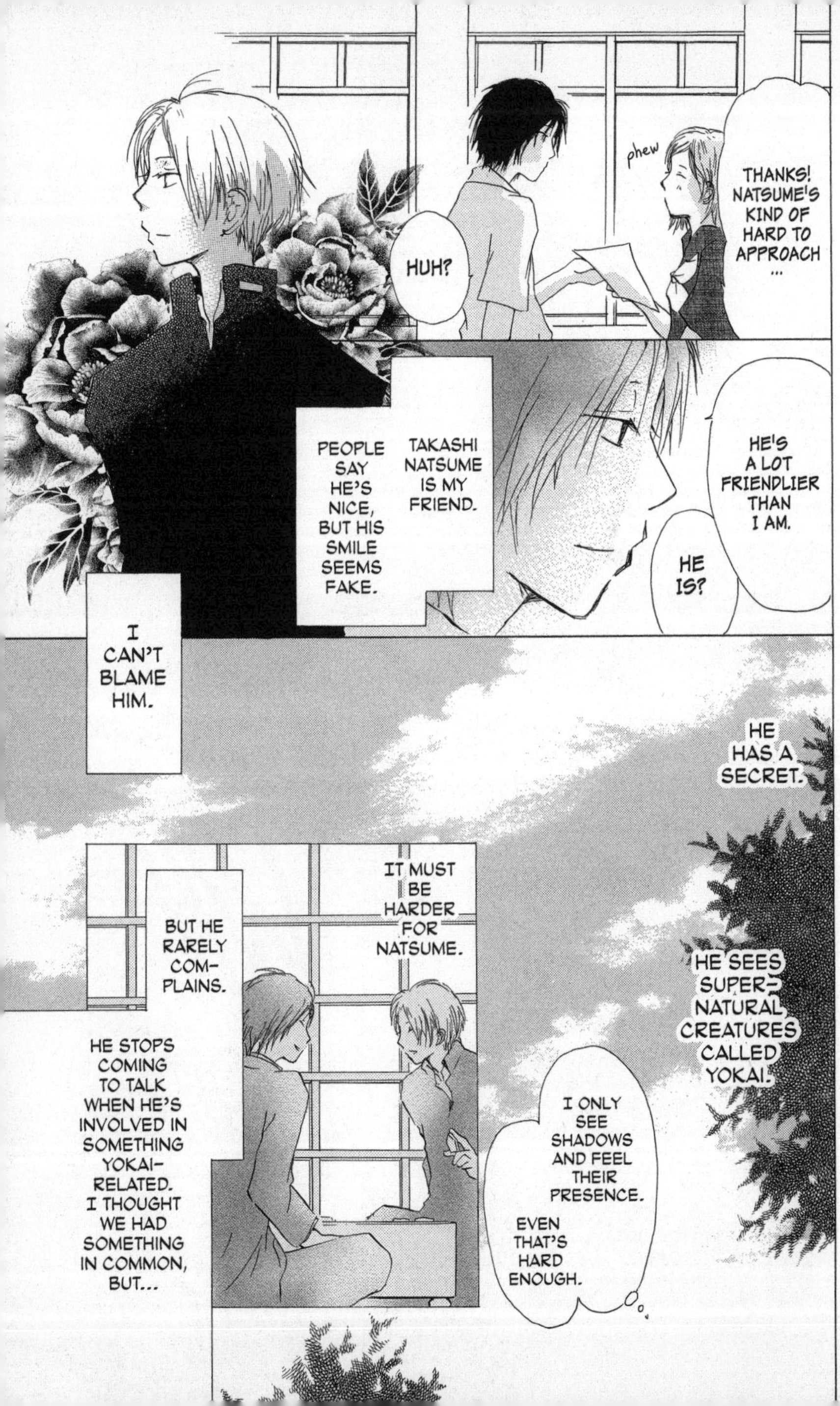
phew
THANKS! NATSUME'S KIND OF HARD TO APPROACH ...
HUH?
HE'S A LOT FRIENDLIER THAN I AM.
HE IS?
TAKASHI NATSUME IS MY FRIEND.
PEOPLE SAY HE'S NICE, BUT HIS SMILE SEEMS FAKE.
I CAN'T BLAME HIM.
HE HAS A SECRET.
HE SEES SUPER-NATURAL CREATURES CALLED YOKAI.
I ONLY SEE SHADOWS AND FEEL THEIR PRESENCE.
EVEN THAT'S HARD ENOUGH.
IT MUST BE HARDER FOR NATSUME.
BUT HE RARELY COM-PLAINS.
HE STOPS COMING TO TALK WHEN HE'S INVOLVED IN SOMETHING YOKAI-RELATED. I THOUGHT WE HAD SOMETHING IN COMMON, BUT...

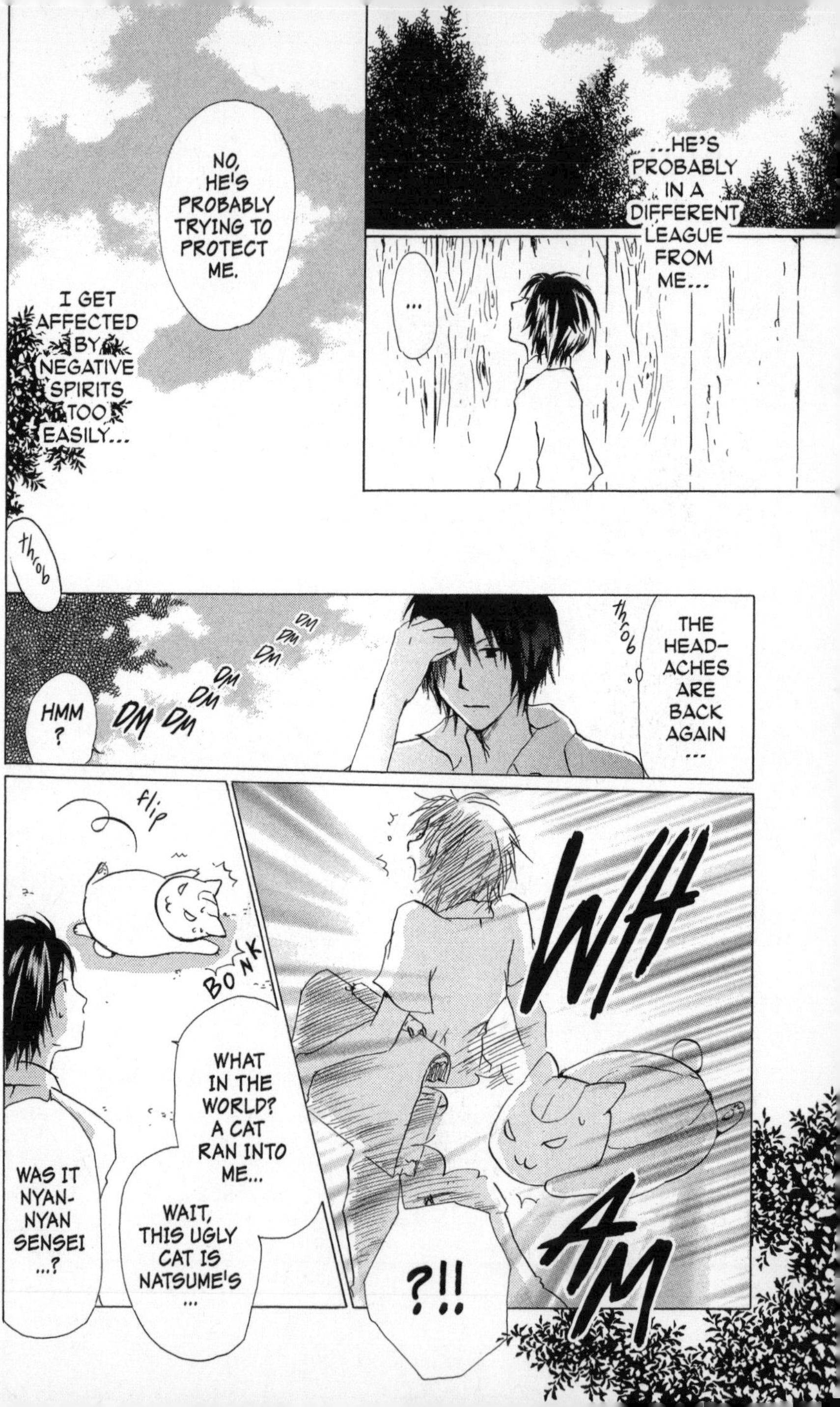
...HE'S PROBABLY IN A DIFFERENT LEAGUE FROM ME...
...
NO, HE'S PROBABLY TRYING TO PROTECT ME.
I GET AFFECTED BY NEGATIVE SPIRITS TOO EASILY...
throb
throb
THE HEADACHES ARE BACK AGAIN...
DM DM DM DM DM DM DM
HMM?
WHAM
?!!
WHAT IN THE WORLD? A CAT RAN INTO ME...
WAIT, THIS UGLY CAT IS NATSUME'S...
flip
BONK
WAS IT NYAN-NYAN SENSEI...?

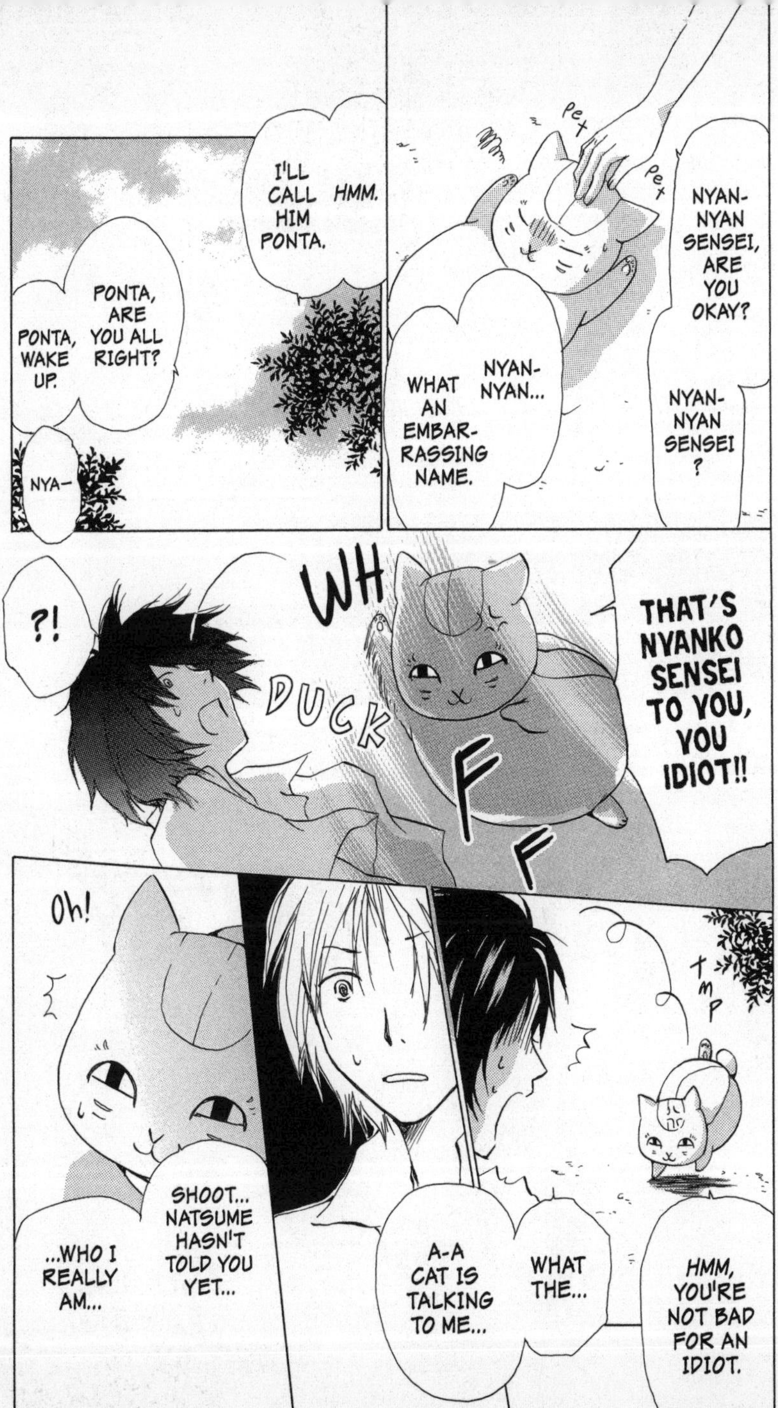

Pet
Pet
NYAN-NYAN SENSEI, ARE YOU OKAY?
NYAN-NYAN SENSEI?
NYAN-NYAN...
WHAT AN EMBARRASSING NAME.
HMM.
I'LL CALL HIM PONTA.
PONTA, ARE YOU ALL RIGHT?
PONTA, WAKE UP.
NYA—
THAT'S NYANKO SENSEI TO YOU, YOU IDIOT!!
WH
?!
DUCK
FF
TMP
HMM, YOU'RE NOT BAD FOR AN IDIOT.
WHAT THE...
A-A CAT IS TALKING TO ME...
Oh!
SHOOT... NATSUME HASN'T TOLD YOU YET...
...WHO I REALLY AM...

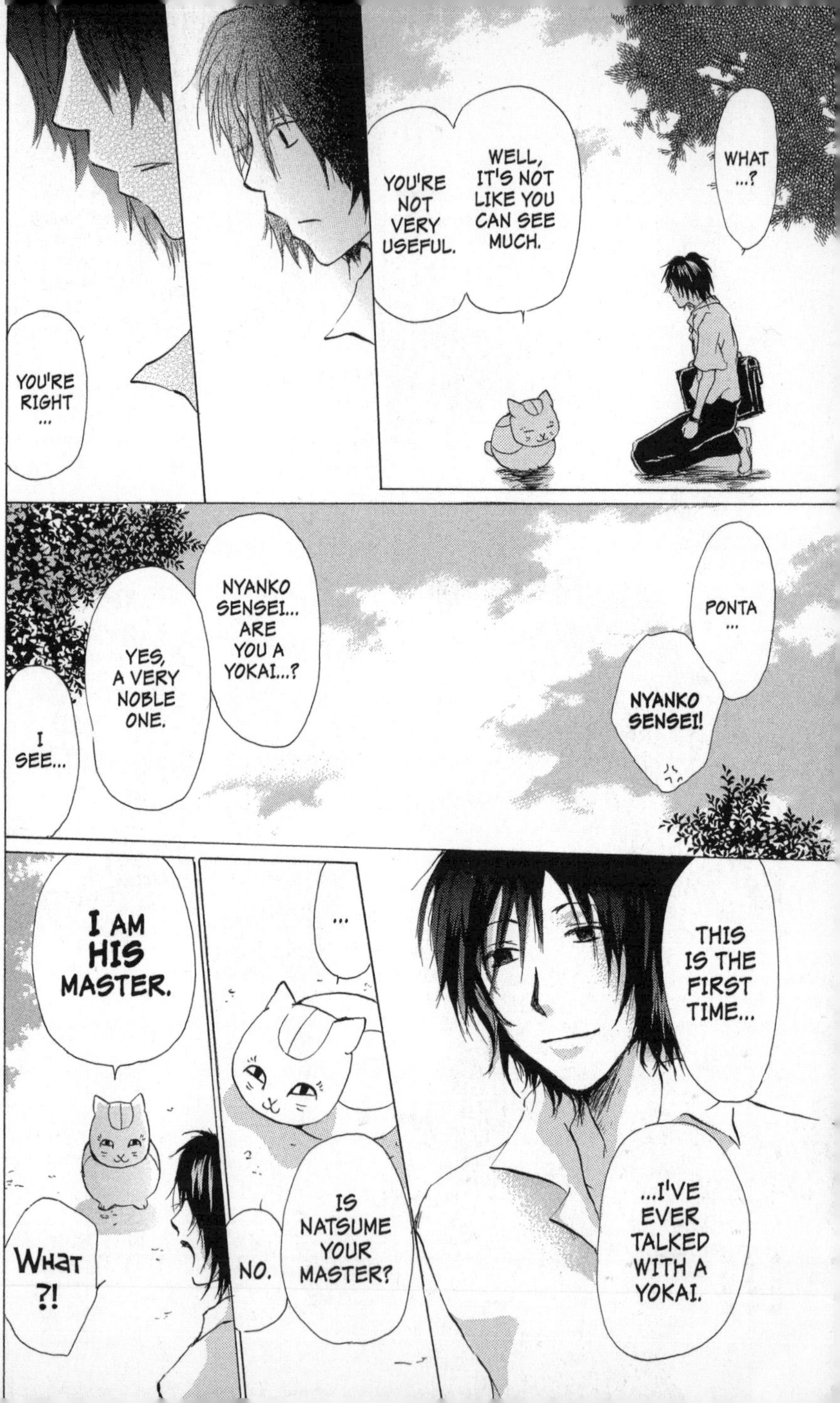
WHAT ...?
WELL, IT'S NOT LIKE YOU CAN SEE MUCH.
YOU'RE NOT VERY USEFUL.
YOU'RE RIGHT ...
PONTA ...
NYANKO SENSEI!
NYANKO SENSEI... ARE YOU A YOKAI...?
YES, A VERY NOBLE ONE.
I SEE...
THIS IS THE FIRST TIME...
...I'VE EVER TALKED WITH A YOKAI.
...
IS NATSUME YOUR MASTER?
NO.
I AM HIS MASTER.
WHAT ?!

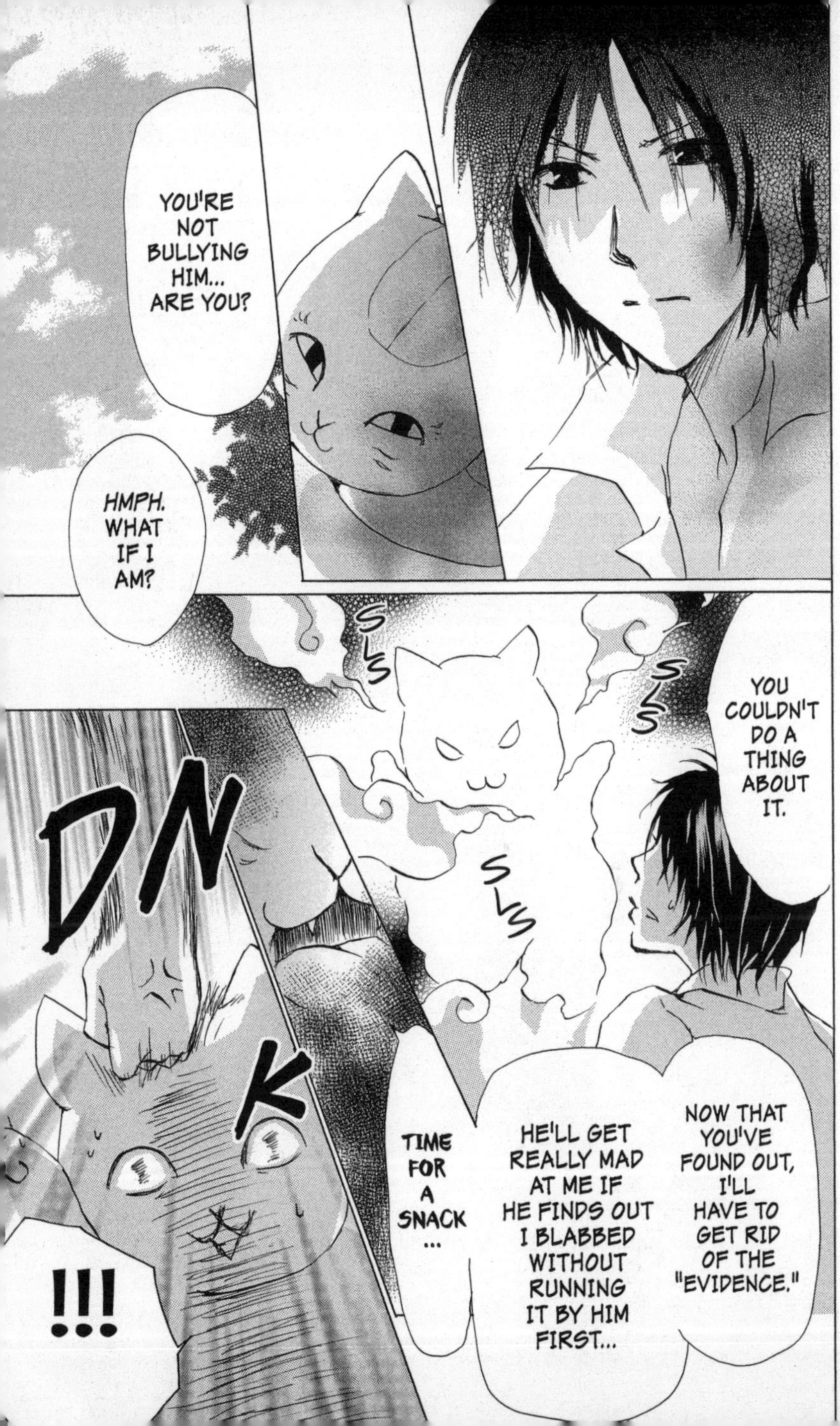
YOU'RE NOT BULLYING HIM... ARE YOU?
HMPH. WHAT IF I AM?
SLS
SLS
YOU COULDN'T DO A THING ABOUT IT.
SLS
NOW THAT YOU'VE FOUND OUT, I'LL HAVE TO GET RID OF THE "EVIDENCE."
HE'LL GET REALLY MAD AT ME IF HE FINDS OUT I BLABBED WITHOUT RUNNING IT BY HIM FIRST...
TIME FOR A SNACK...
DNK
!!!

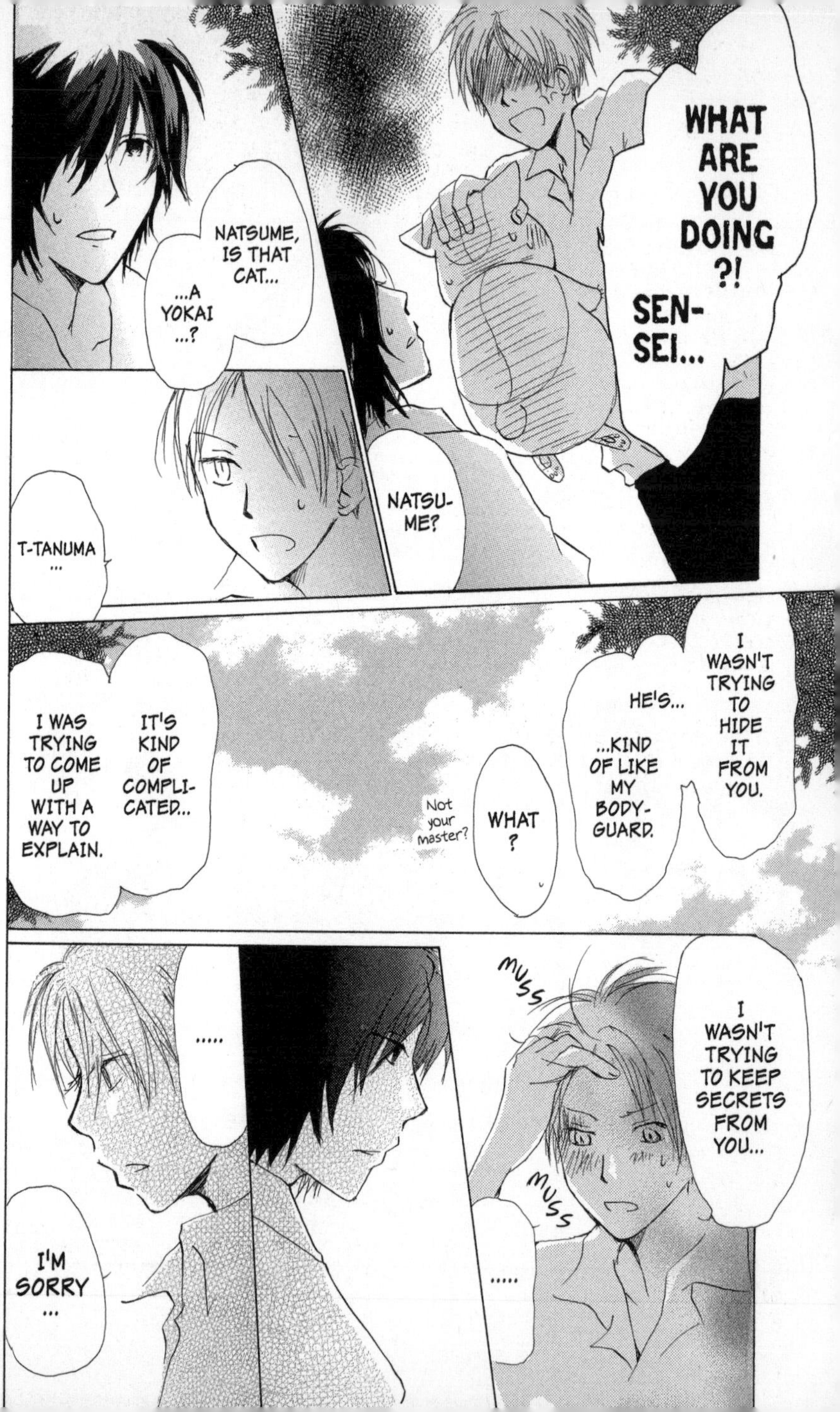
WHAT ARE YOU DOING?!
SEN-SEI...
NATSUME, IS THAT CAT...
...A YOKAI...?
NATSU-ME?
T-TANUMA...
I WASN'T TRYING TO HIDE IT FROM YOU.
HE'S...
...KIND OF LIKE MY BODY-GUARD.
WHAT?
Not your master?
IT'S KIND OF COMPLI-CATED...
I WAS TRYING TO COME UP WITH A WAY TO EXPLAIN.
MUSS
I WASN'T TRYING TO KEEP SECRETS FROM YOU...
MUSS
.....
.....
I'M SORRY...

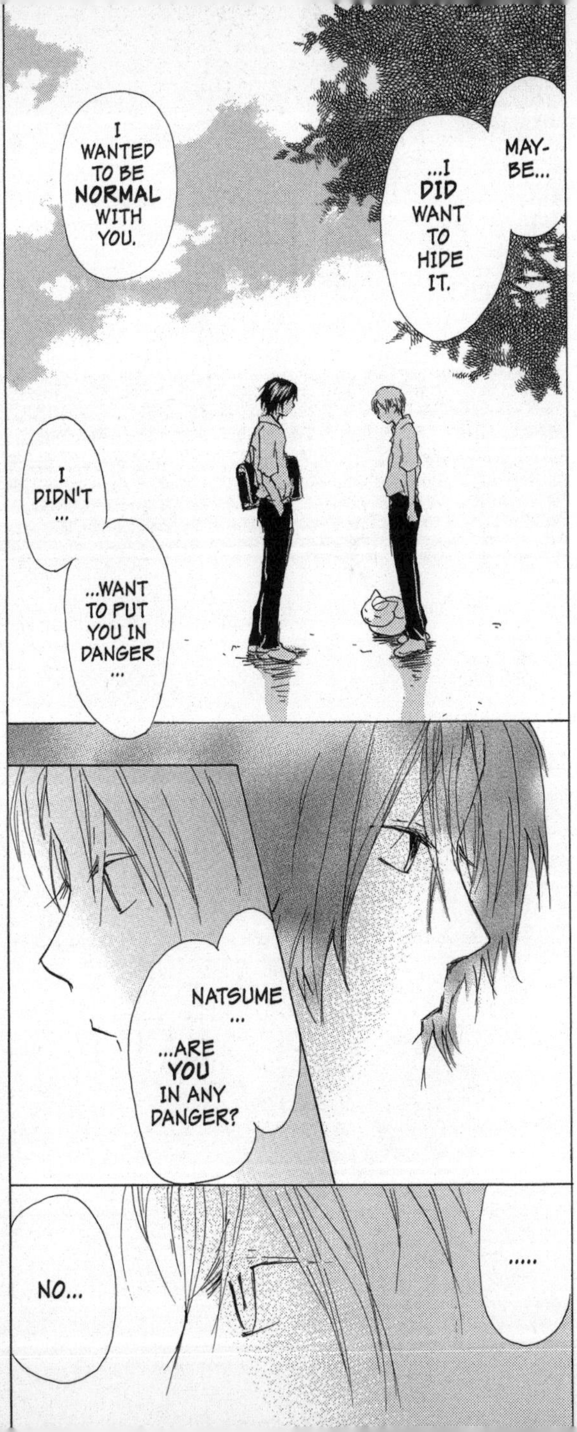
MAY-BE...
...I DID WANT TO HIDE IT.
I WANTED TO BE NORMAL WITH YOU.
I DIDN'T...
...WANT TO PUT YOU IN DANGER...
NATSUME...
...ARE YOU IN ANY DANGER?
.....
NO...

07

I'm not able to respond to all the fan letters I get, but I take great care to read each and every one. I'll keep working hard to create something worth reading. I'll always cherish the presents and pretty pictures I receive. Thank you so much.

I'm such a slow writer as usual, but I'm passionate about creating more manga.

Thanks to everyone for their support.

End of 1/4 columns.

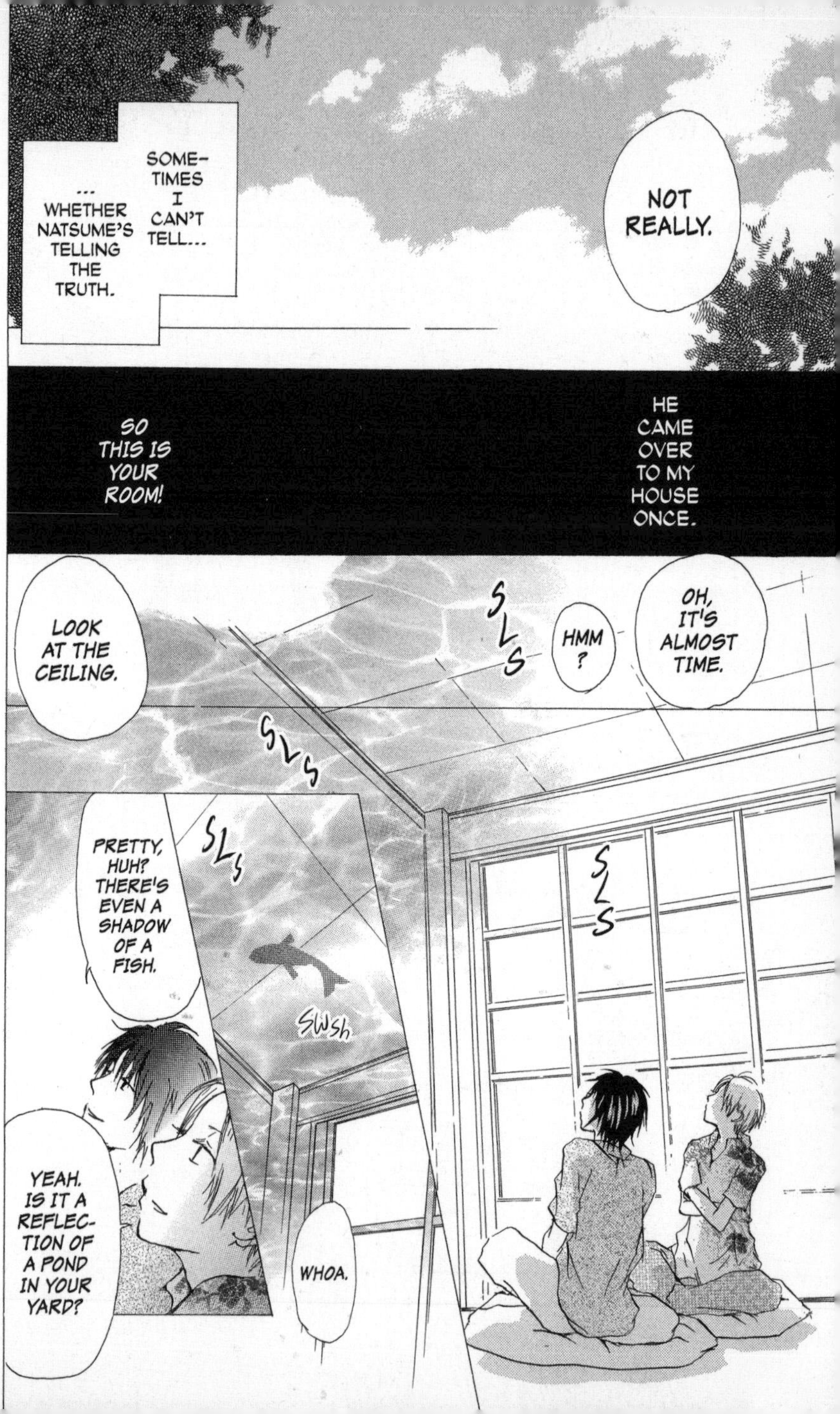
NOT REALLY.
SOME-TIMES I CAN'T TELL...
...WHETHER NATSUME'S TELLING THE TRUTH.
HE CAME OVER TO MY HOUSE ONCE.
SO THIS IS YOUR ROOM!
OH, IT'S ALMOST TIME.
HMM?
SLS
LOOK AT THE CEILING.
SLS
SLS
PRETTY, HUH? THERE'S EVEN A SHADOW OF A FISH.
SLS
SWSH
WHOA.
YEAH. IS IT A REFLEC-TION OF A POND IN YOUR YARD?

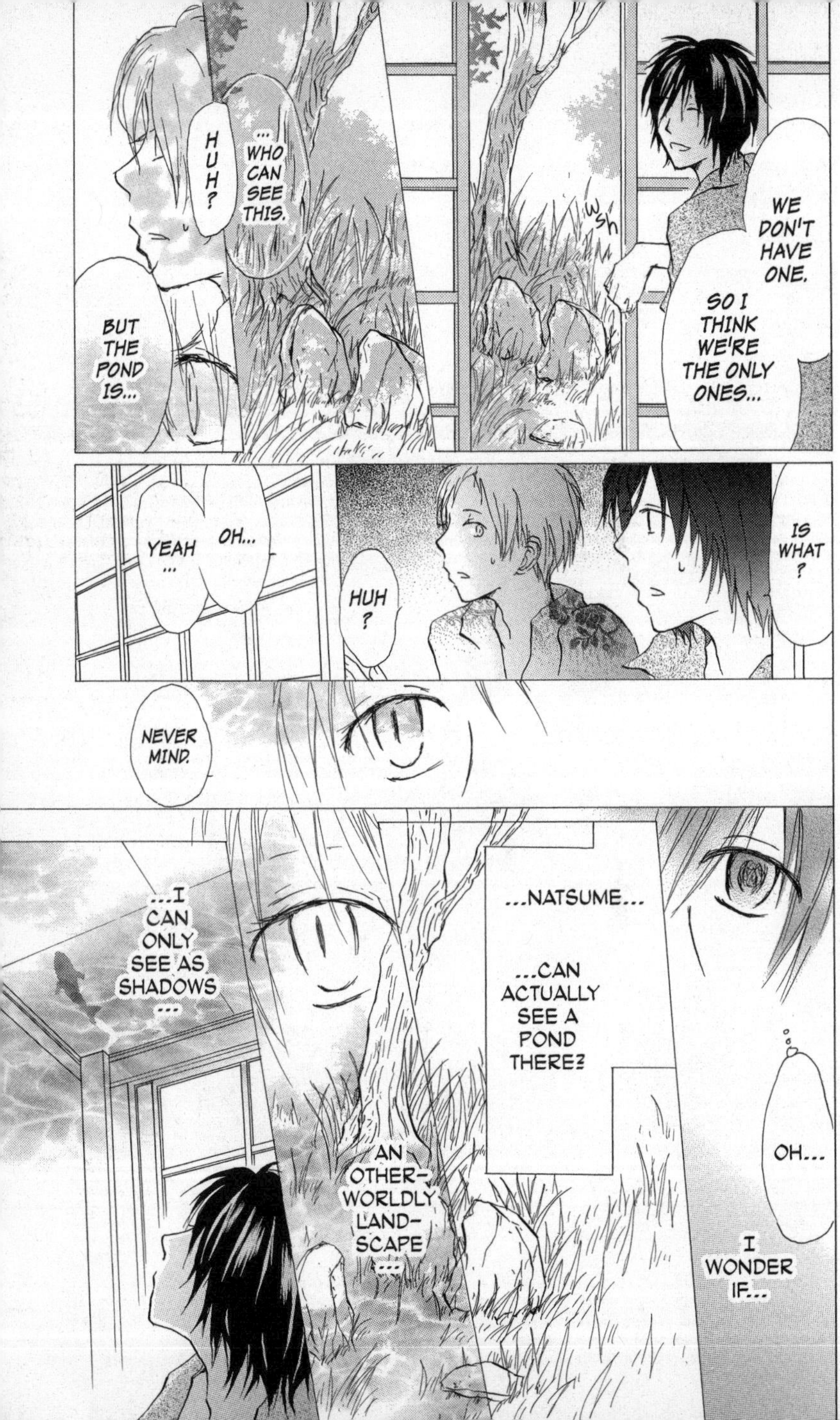
WE DON'T HAVE ONE.
SO I THINK WE'RE THE ONLY ONES...
WSH
...WHO CAN SEE THIS.
HUH?
BUT THE POND IS...
IS WHAT?
HUH?
OH...
YEAH...
NEVER MIND.
...NATSUME...
...CAN ACTUALLY SEE A POND THERE?
OH...
I WONDER IF...
AN OTHER-WORLDLY LAND-SCAPE...
...I CAN ONLY SEE AS SHADOWS...

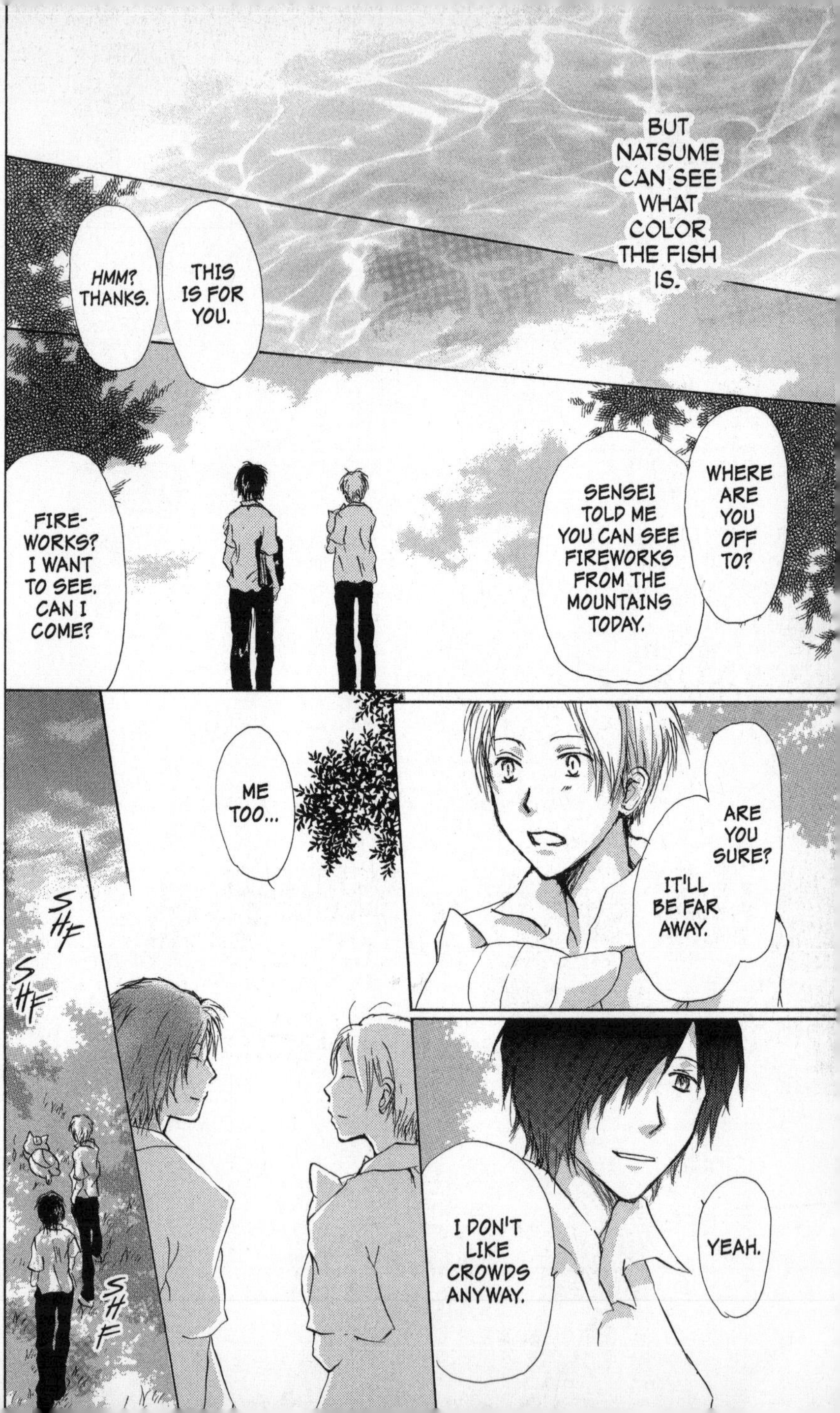
BUT NATSUME CAN SEE WHAT COLOR THE FISH IS.
THIS IS FOR YOU.
HMM? THANKS.
WHERE ARE YOU OFF TO?
SENSEI TOLD ME YOU CAN SEE FIREWORKS FROM THE MOUNTAINS TODAY.
FIRE-WORKS? I WANT TO SEE. CAN I COME?
ARE YOU SURE?
IT'LL BE FAR AWAY.
YEAH.
I DON'T LIKE CROWDS ANYWAY.
ME TOO...
SHF
SHF
SHF

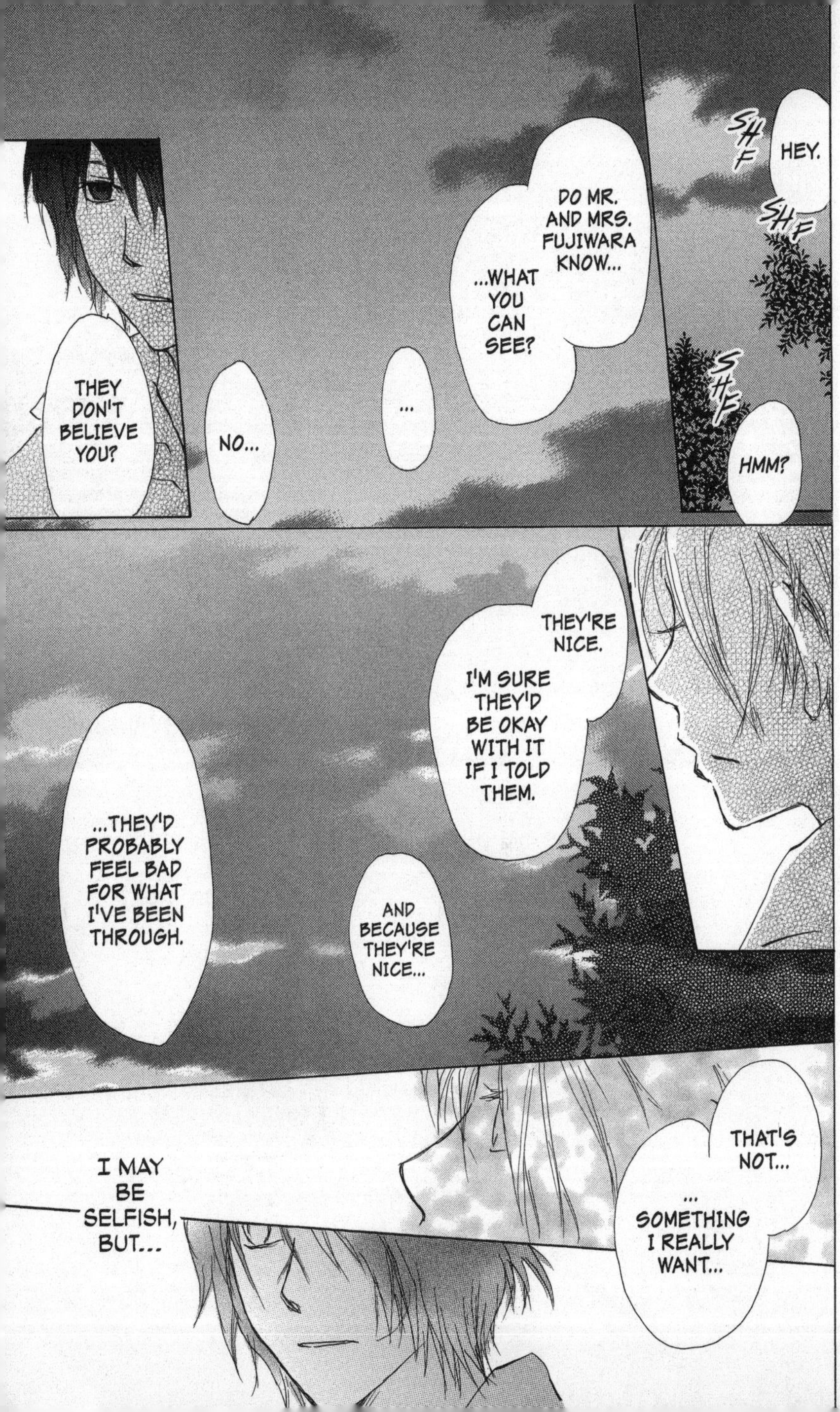

SHF
HEY.
SHF
SHF
HMM?
DO MR. AND MRS. FUJIWARA KNOW...
...WHAT YOU CAN SEE?
...
NO...
THEY DON'T BELIEVE YOU?
THEY'RE NICE.
I'M SURE THEY'D BE OKAY WITH IT IF I TOLD THEM.
AND BECAUSE THEY'RE NICE...
...THEY'D PROBABLY FEEL BAD FOR WHAT I'VE BEEN THROUGH.
THAT'S NOT...
...SOMETHING I REALLY WANT...
I MAY BE SELFISH, BUT...

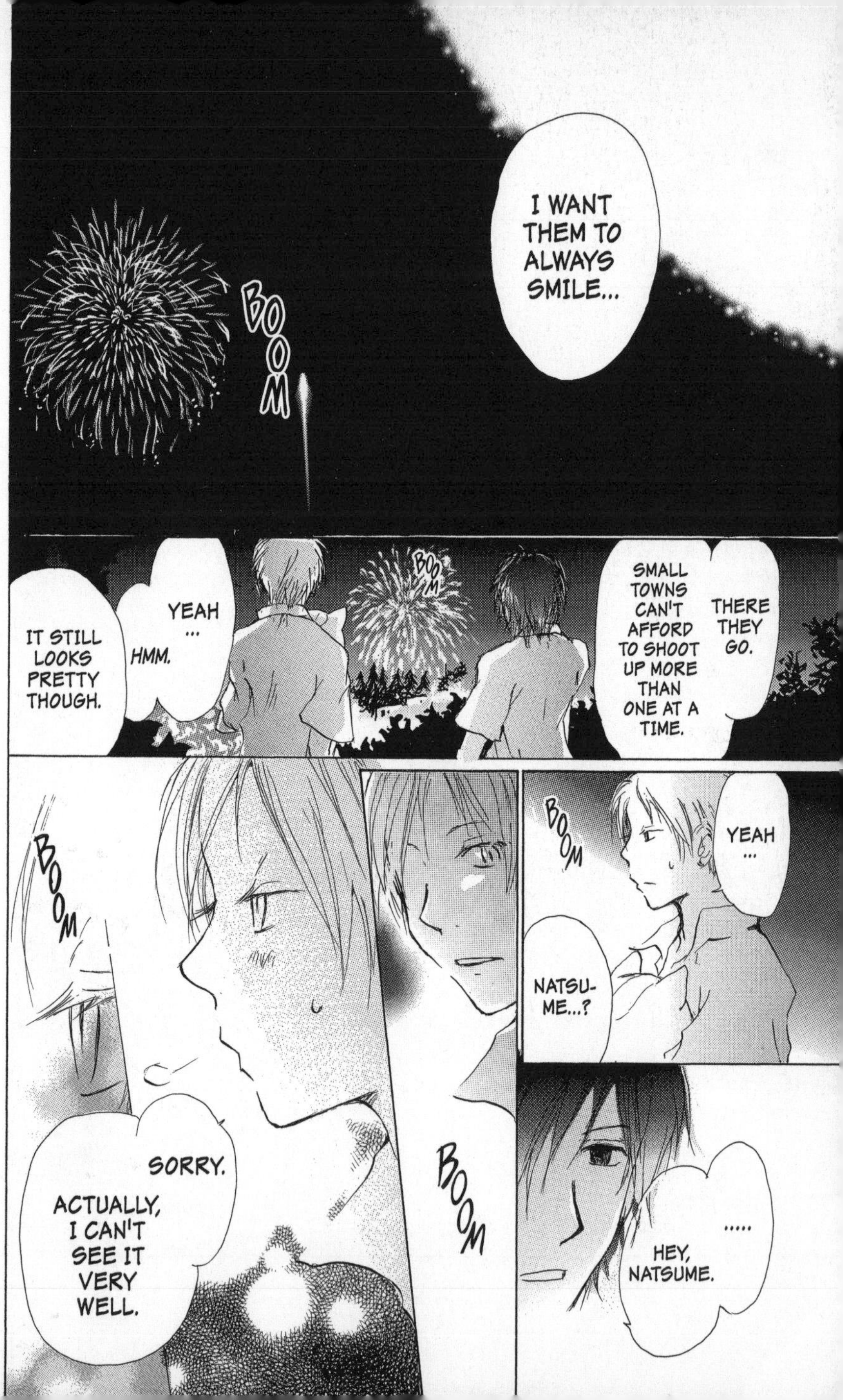
I WANT THEM TO ALWAYS SMILE...
BOOM
THERE THEY GO.
SMALL TOWNS CAN'T AFFORD TO SHOOT UP MORE THAN ONE AT A TIME.
BOOM
YEAH ...
HMM.
IT STILL LOOKS PRETTY THOUGH.
YEAH ...
BOOM
NATSU-ME...?
.....
HEY, NATSUME.
BOOM
SORRY.
ACTUALLY, I CAN'T SEE IT VERY WELL.
BOOM

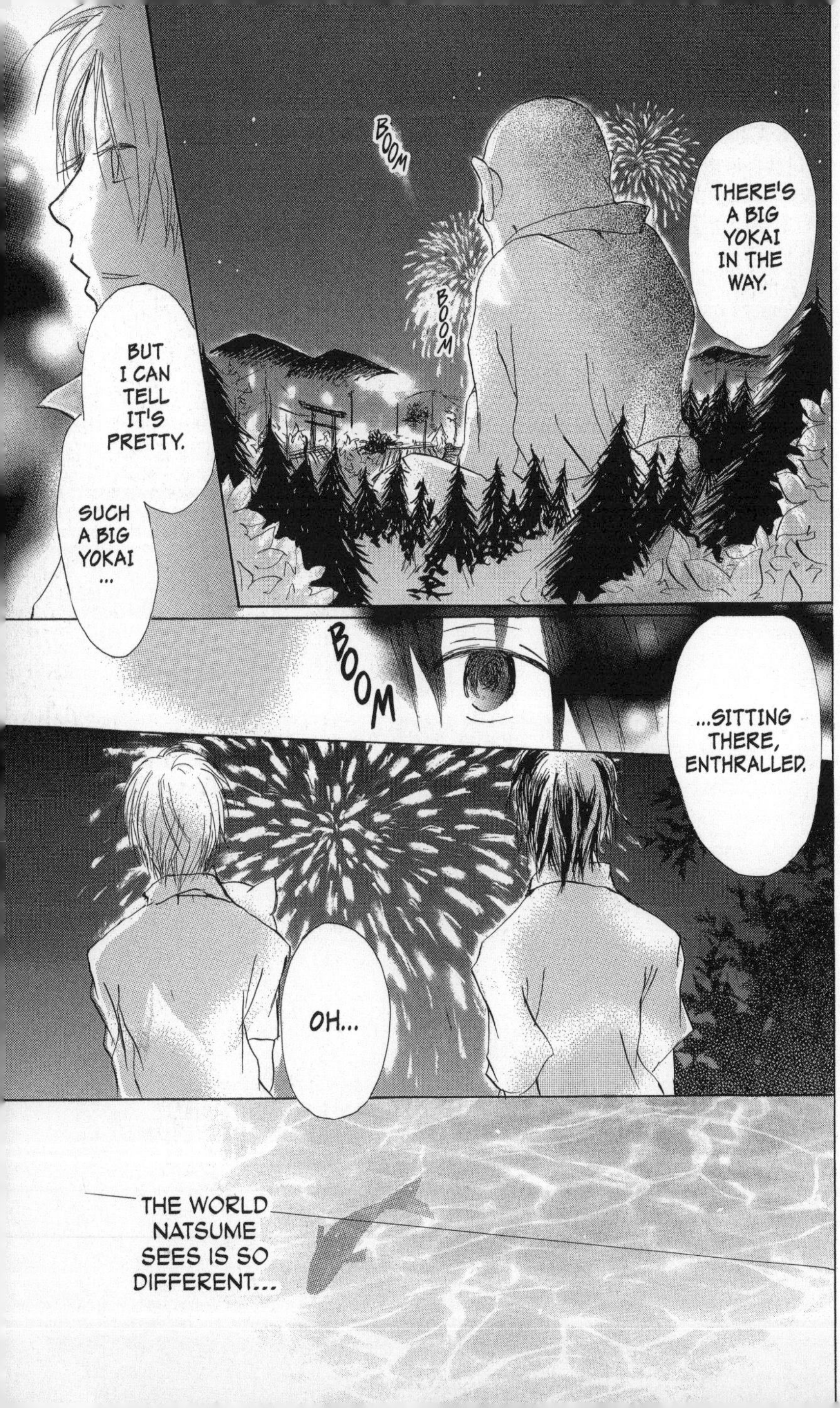
THERE'S A BIG YOKAI IN THE WAY.
BOOM
BOOM
BUT I CAN TELL IT'S PRETTY.
SUCH A BIG YOKAI ...
...SITTING THERE, ENTHRALLED.
BOOM
OH...
THE WORLD NATSUME SEES IS SO DIFFERENT...

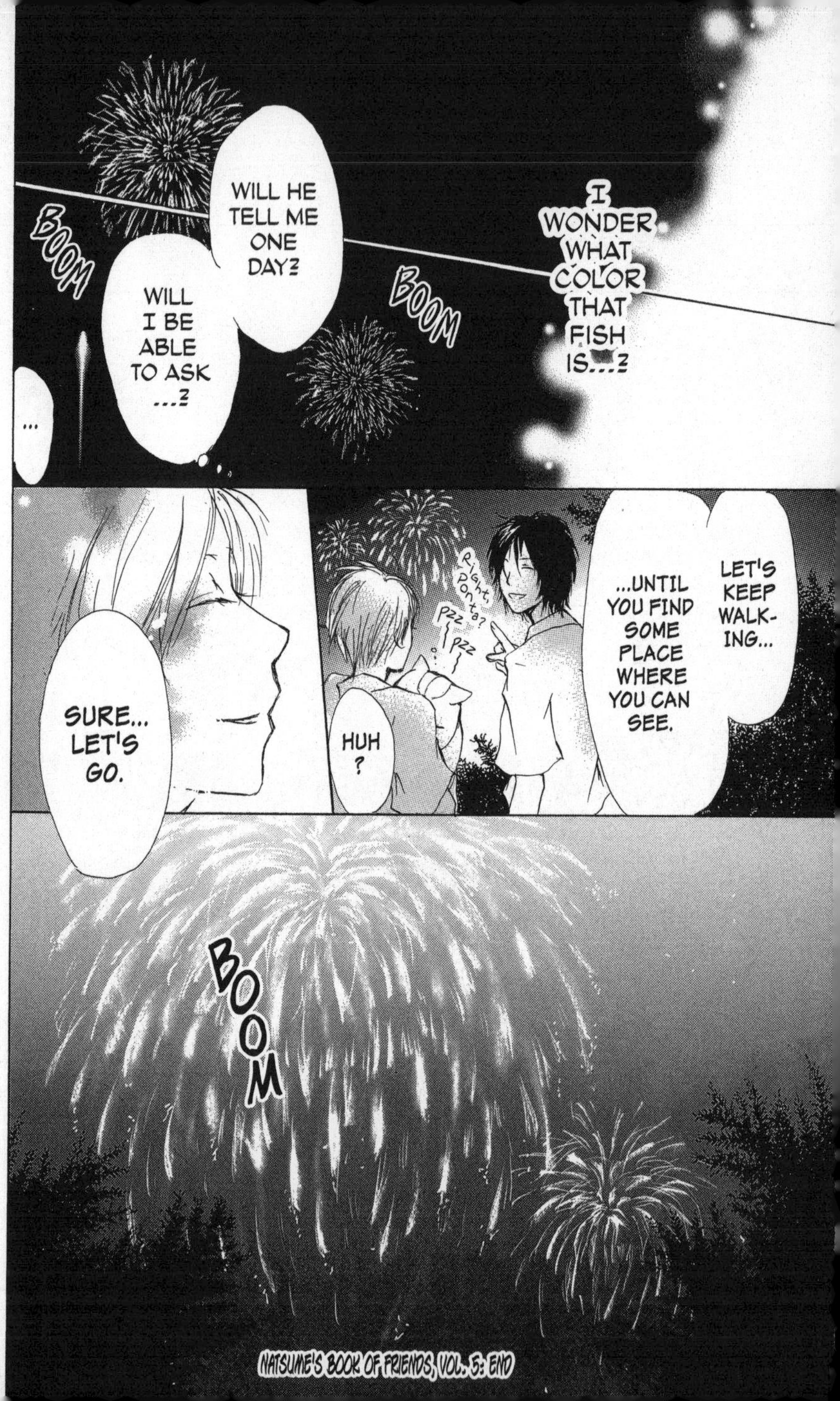
I WONDER WHAT COLOR THAT FISH IS...?
BOOM
WILL HE TELL ME ONE DAY?
WILL I BE ABLE TO ASK ...?
BOOM
...
LET'S KEEP WALKING...
...UNTIL YOU FIND SOME PLACE WHERE YOU CAN SEE.
Right, Ponta?
pzz
pzz
HUH?
SURE... LET'S GO.
BOOM
NATSUME'S BOOK OF FRIENDS, VOL. 5: END

AFTER-WORD

Thanks for reading. The episodes in this volume became rather frantic. There weren't as many quiet moments, but I hope you enjoyed them. Now that Natsume has a stable life, I figure he'd start to want more out of it, which is a very human tendency. Since he used to be more passive, time will tell if this will work out for the best.

There will be spoilers, so please read this only after you've read the rest of the book.

CHAPTER 16 Ageless Feelings

This is the first episode that was published in monthly *LaLa* (as opposed to *LaLa DX*). They gave me space in three issues to work with, so I considered coming up with a new character. But I figured the first episode should stand alone, and had to quickly come up with another idea. I remembered that when I drew the kappa a couple years ago, my editor commented that it was the first "mainstream" yokai in the series. So I decided on a mermaid this time. I wanted to try a melancholic Japanese mermaid with black, straight hair looking like a wet snake, but everything else looked rather plain, so I made her look cute, with flowing hair. I had so much trouble with the story that I had to rewrite the whole thing multiple times, but my editor encouraged me to work through it.

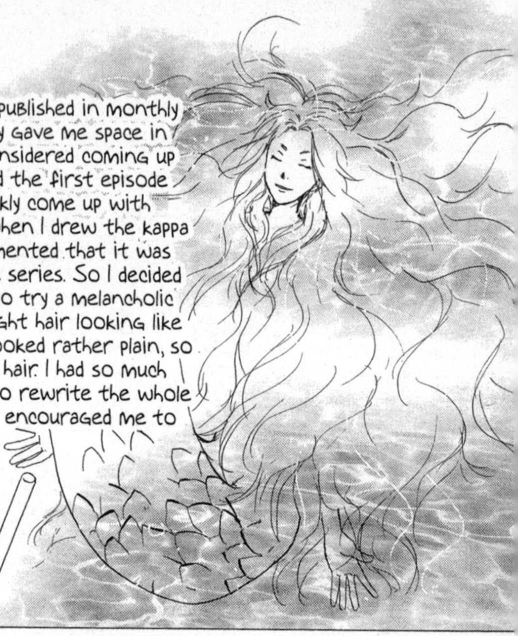

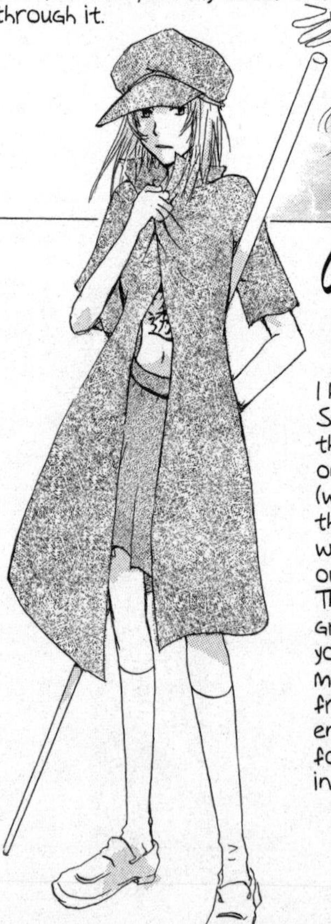

CHAPTER 17, 18 Do Not Call

I had a lot of fun working on this one. Strange how having a girl in the story makes things go so smoothly for me. I was working on this story at the same time as Chapter 19 (which I was submitting for *LaLa DX*) so I had the most work I've ever had at one time. I wished I had had more pages to work things out, but overall, it was a positive experience. The story evolved from the ideas I had of big graffiti, and the concept of being able to see yokai conditionally. Natsume was never able to meet his grandmother, but Taki was good friends with her grandfather. They had different relationships, but sometimes that allows for better perspectives. I also had fun drawing a frightened Nyanko Sensei.

CHAPTER 19
Temporary House

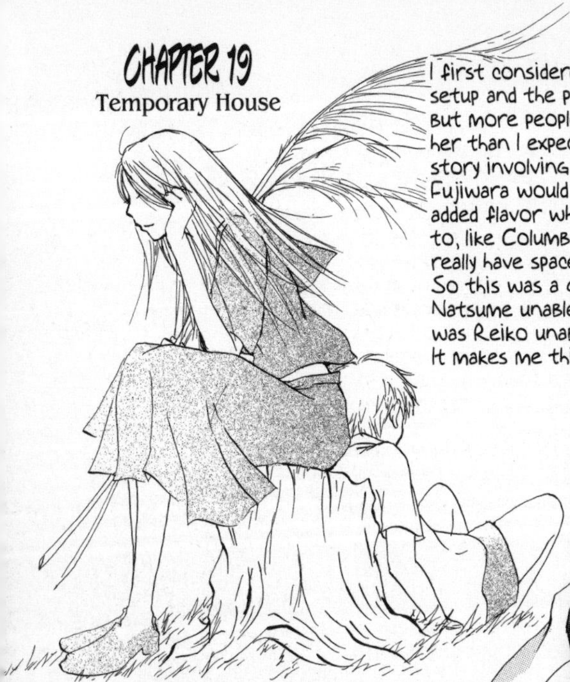

I first considered Reiko to only be the setup and the punch line to the story, but more people were interested in her than I expected, so I did a proper story involving her. I knew what Mr. Fujiwara would be like, but I thought it added flavor when he was only alluded to, like Columbo's wife. And I didn't really have space to fit him in before. So this was a good opportunity. Is Natsume unable to be like Reiko, or was Reiko unable to be like Natsume? It makes me think.

SPECIAL EPISODE
The Same View

Tanuma hadn't shown up in a while, and I had thought that he and Natsume would have a good relationship by now. But when I started on the episode, I discovered that they were still pretty awkward with each other. I'm used to Natsume smiling and talking about neutral topics, but it was fun drawing Natsume getting flustered and making the wrong decision in a conversation. It's hard to work Tanuma into the plot since Natsume never goes to him when he's involved in yokai business. I cut his bangs to "expand his world view," but people said he looked better with longer hair (I rarely get requests from readers on how the characters look), so I grew them out again.

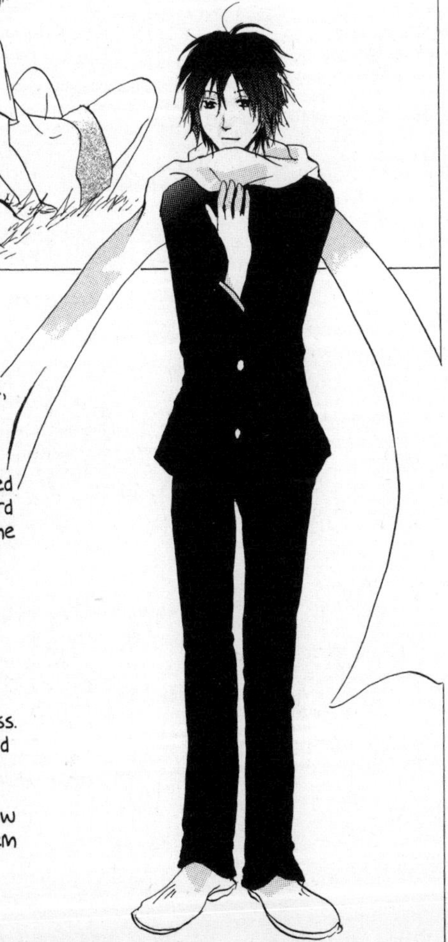

I enjoy working on each episode so much. I'm fortunate that I get to have a relationship with these characters for so long. I'll take great care in developing them.

Finally, I'd like to report some great news. Natsume's Book of Friends is going to be an anime. I hope to have more details for the next volume. It's possible some readers may worry about how it'll look. But I consider myself lucky that another incarnation of my work will be created with the help of all these people. I hope you'll wait and see.

Thank you to all my readers and my editors.

Let me know what you thought, if possible.

Yuki Midorikawa
c/o Shojo Beat
Published by VIZ Media, LLC.
P.O. Boz 77010
San Francicso, CA 94107

Special thanks to:
Tamao Ohki
Chika
Mr. Sato
My sister

Thank you so much for reading.

Yuki Midorikawa
緑川 ゆき Jan. 2008

AFTERWORD: END

Natsume's BOOK of FRIENDS

VOLUME 5 END NOTES

PAGE 68, PANEL 1: *chobi*
Something small, most commonly used to describe a micro moustache (*chobi hige*).

PAGE 75, PANEL 1: *Tengu*
A yokai commonly shown with a long nose and crow wings.

PAGE 125, PANEL 1: *Blunt weapon*
This alludes to the folktale *The Battle of the Monkey and Crab*.

PAGE 152, PANEL 1: *Shoji screens*
Traditional sliding partitions made of a wood frame that is covered on one side with a sheet of paper. If the paper rips, the whole screen must be recovered.

Yuki Midorikawa
is the creator of *Natsume's Book of Friends*, which was nominated for the Manga Taisho (Cartoon Grand Prize). Her other titles published in Japan include *Hotarubi no Mori e* (Into the Forest of Fireflies), *Hiiro no Isu* (The Scarlet Chair) and *Akaku Saku Koe* (The Voice That Blooms Red).

NATSUME'S BOOK OF FRIENDS

Vol. 5
Shojo Beat Edition

STORY AND ART BY **Yuki Midorikawa**

Translation & Adaptation **Lillian Olsen**
Touch-up Art & Lettering **Sabrina Heep**
Design **Fawn Lau**
Editor **Pancha Diaz**

Natsume Yujincho by Yuki Midorikawa
© Yuki Midorikawa 2008
All rights reserved.
First published in Japan in 2008 by HAKUSENSHA, Inc., Tokyo.
English language translation rights arranged with HAKUSENSHA, Inc., Tokyo.

The stories, characters and incidents mentioned in this publication are entirely fictional.

Printed in the U.S.A.

Published by VIZ Media, LLC
P.O. Box 77010
San Francisco, CA 94107

10 9 8 7 6 5 4 3 2
First printing, January 2011
Second printing, June 2013

PARENTAL ADVISORY
NATSUME'S BOOK OF FRIENDS is rated T for Teen and is recommended for ages 16 and up. This volume contains fantasy violence.
ratings.viz.com

www.viz.com

www.shojobeat.com

SURPRISE!

You may be reading the wrong way!

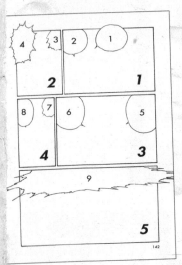

It's true: In keeping with the original Japanese comic format, this book reads from right to left— so action, sound effects, and word balloons are completely reversed. This preserves the orientation of the original artwork—plus, it's fun! Check out the diagram shown here to get the hang of things, and then turn to the other side of the book to get started!

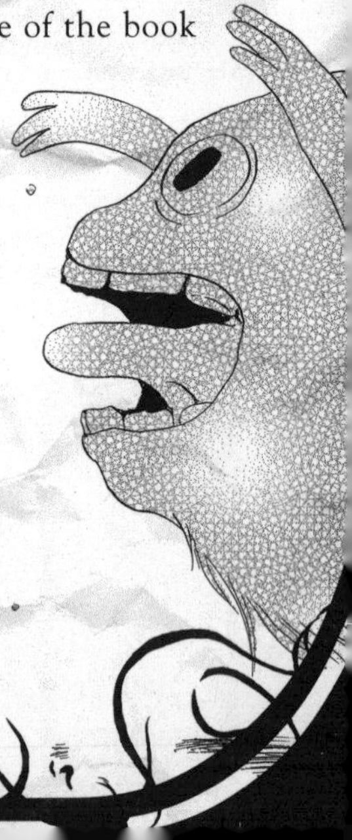